Praise for
TO END ALL WARS

"Adam Hochschild has contributed a riveting narrative history that broadens the focus beyond generals and heads of state. . . . In *To End All Wars*, he has assembled an irresistible, unforgettable cast of characters."
— *Boston Globe*

"This is a book to make one feel deeply and painfully, and also to think hard."   —Christopher Hitchens, *New York Times Book Review*

"Hochschild's *To End All Wars* may not be family history, but no one could say that it is impersonal. Not only is it imbued with the author's passionate admiration for the conscientious objectors and other resistant figures who suffered so nobly, but it fairly crackles with his indignation that such a war should have been fought at all."
— *San Francisco Chronicle*

"In this deeply moving history of the so-called Great War, those opposing its mindless folly receive equal billing with the politicians, generals, and propagandists obdurately insisting on its perpetuation. Implicit in Adam Hochschild's account is this chilling warning: once governments become captive of wars they purport to control, they turn next on their own people."
—Andrew J. Bacevich, author of *Washington Rules: America's Path to Permanent War*

"[Hochschild's] writing is as clear and stirring as a church bell."
— *Cleveland Plain Dealer*

"Hochschild has once again produced a moving account of one of the most terrible events of the recent past, bringing this story to life like few historians writing today."
— *Seattle Times*

"An absorbing, well-researched account."
— *Newsday*

"Adam Hochschild is the rare historian who fuses deep scholarship with novelistic flair. In his hands, World War I becomes a clash not only of empires and armies, but of individuals: king and Kaiser, warriors and pacifists, coal miners and aristocrats. Epic yet human-scaled, this is history for buffs and novices alike, a stirring and provocative exploration of the Great War and the nature of war itself."
— Tony Horwitz, author of *A Voyage Long and Strange*

"Compelling. . . . A gifted storyteller, with an eye for the telling detail, Hochschild effectively and eloquently brings to life the senselessness of the war."
— *Oregonian*

"Hochschild gives as stirring an account as anyone. . . . More important, he shows how the working of conscience can bring about, or begin to bring about, a systemic change."
— *Huffington Post*

"Hochschild writes with a novelist's flair, bringing the people in this book alive."
— *Washington Independent Review of Books*

TO END ALL WARS

BOOKS BY ADAM HOCHSCHILD

Half the Way Home:
A Memoir of Father and Son

The Mirror at Midnight:
A South African Journey

The Unquiet Ghost:
Russians Remember Stalin

Finding the Trapdoor:
Essays, Portraits, Travels

King Leopold's Ghost:
A Story of Greed, Terror, and
Heroism in Colonial Africa

Bury the Chains:
Prophets and Rebels in the Fight
to Free an Empire's Slaves

To End All Wars: A Story of
Loyalty and Rebellion, 1914–1918

TO END
ALL WARS

A Story of
Loyalty and Rebellion,
1914–1918

Adam Hochschild

MARINER BOOKS
HOUGHTON MIFFLIN HARCOURT
BOSTON   NEW YORK

For Tom Engelhardt,
analyst of empire, emperor among editors

First Mariner Books edition 2012

Copyright © 2011 by Adam Hochschild

For information about permission to reproduce selections from this book,
write to Permissions, Houghton Mifflin Harcourt Publishing Company,
215 Park Avenue South, New York, New York 10003.

www.hmhbooks.com

Library of Congress Cataloging-in-Publication Data
Hochschild, Adam.
To end all wars : a story of loyalty and rebellion, 1914–1918 /
Adam Hochschild.
p. cm.
Includes bibliographical references and index.
ISBN 978-0-618-75828-9   ISBN 978-0-547-75031-6 (pbk.)
1. World War, 1914–1918 — Great Britain. 2. World War, 1914–1918 —
Social aspects — Great Britain. 3. Soldiers — Great Britain — Biography.
4. Conscientious objectors — Great Britain — Biography. 5. Loyalty —
Case studies. 6. World War, 1914–1918 — Psychological aspects. 7. World
War, 1914–1918 — Moral and ethical aspects. 8. Militarism — Great
Britain — History — 20th century. 9. Pacifism — Great Britain — History — 20th century. I. Title.
D546.H63 2011
940.3'41 — dc22   2010025836

Book design by Melissa Lotfy
Maps by Mapping Specialists, Ltd.

Printed in the United States of America
DOC 10 9 8 7 6 5 4 3

CONTENTS

MAPS

INTRODUCTION:
CLASH OF DREAMS

AN EARLY AUTUMN BITE is in the air as a gold-tinged late afternoon falls over the rolling countryside of northern France. Where the land dips between gentle rises, it is already in shadow. Dotting the fields are machine-packed rolls, high as a person's head, of the year's final hay crop. Massive tractors pull boxcar-sized cartloads of potatoes, or corn chopped up for cattle feed. Up a low hill, a grove of trees screens the evidence of another kind of harvest, reaped on this spot nearly a century ago. Each gravestone in the small cemetery has a name, rank, and serial number; 162 have crosses, and one has a Star of David. When known, a man's age is engraved on the stone as well: 19, 22, 23, 26, 34, 21, 20. Ten of the graves simply say, "A Soldier of the Great War, Known unto God." Almost all the dead are from Britain's Devonshire Regiment, the date on their gravestones July 1, 1916, the first day of the Battle of the Somme. Most were casualties of a single German machine gun several hundred yards from this spot, and were buried here in a section of the front-line trench they had climbed out of that morning. Captain Duncan Martin, 30, a company commander and an artist in civilian life, had made a clay model of the battlefield across which the British planned to attack. He predicted to his fellow officers the exact place at which he and his men would come under fire from the nearby German machine gun as they emerged onto an exposed hillside. He, too, is buried here, one of some 21,000 British soldiers killed or fatally wounded on the day of greatest bloodshed in the history of their country's military, before or since.

On a stone plaque next to the graves are the words this regiment's survivors carved on a wooden sign when they buried their dead:

THE DEVONSHIRES HELD THIS TRENCH
THE DEVONSHIRES HOLD IT STILL

The comments in the cemetery's visitors' book are almost all from England: Bournemouth, London, Hampshire, Devon. "Paid our respects to 3 of our townsfolk." "Sleep on, boys." "Lest we forget." "Thanks, lads." "Gt. Uncle thanks, rest in peace." Why does it bring a lump to the throat to see words like *sleep, rest, sacrifice,* when my reason for being here is the belief that this war was needless folly and madness? Only one visitor strikes a different note: "Never again." On a few pages the ink of the names and remarks has been smeared by raindrops—or, was it tears?

The bodies of soldiers of the British Empire lie in 400 cemeteries in the Somme battlefield region alone, a rough crescent of territory less than 20 miles long, but graves are not the only mark the war has made on the land. Here and there, a patch of ground gouged by thousands of shell craters has been left alone; decades of erosion have softened the scarring, but what was once a flat field now looks like rugged, grassed-over sand dunes. On the fields that have been smoothed out again, like those surrounding the Devonshires' cemetery, some of the tractors have armor plating beneath the driver's seat, because harvesting machinery cannot distinguish between potatoes, sugar beets, and live shells. More than 700 million artillery and mortar rounds were fired on the Western Front between 1914 and 1918, of which an estimated 15 percent failed to explode. Every year these leftover shells kill people—36 in 1991 alone, for instance, when France excavated the track bed for a new high-speed rail line. Dotted throughout the region are patches of uncleared forest or scrub surrounded by yellow danger signs in French and English warning hikers away. The French government employs teams of *démineurs,* roving bomb-disposal specialists, who respond to calls when villagers discover shells; they collect and destroy 900 tons of unexploded munitions each year. More than 630 French *démineurs* have died in the line of duty since 1946. Like those shells, the First World War itself has remained in our lives, below the surface, because we live in a world that was so much formed by it and by the industrialized total warfare it inaugurated.

Even though I was born long after it ended, the war always seemed a presence in our family. My mother would tell me about the wild enthusiasm of crowds at military parades when—at last!—the United States joined the Allies. A beloved first cousin of hers marched off to the sound of those cheers, to be killed in the final weeks of fighting; she never forgot the shock and disillusionment. And no one in my father's family thought it absurd that two of his relatives had fought on opposite sides of the First World War, one in the French army, one in the German. If your country called, you went.

My father's sister married a man who fought for Russia in that war, and we owed his presence in our lives to events triggered by it: the Russian Revolution and the bitter civil war that followed—after which, finding himself on the losing side, he came to America. We shared a summer household with this aunt and uncle, and friends of his who were also veterans of 1914–1918 were regular visitors. As a boy, I vividly remember standing next to one of them, all of us in bathing suits and about to go swimming, and then looking down and seeing the man's foot: all his toes had been sheared off by a German machine-gun bullet somewhere on the Eastern Front.

The war also lived on in the illustrated adventure tales that British cousins sent me for Christmas. Young Tim or Tom or Trevor, though a mere teenager whom the colonel had declared too young for combat, would bravely dodge flying shrapnel to carry that same wounded colonel to safety after the regiment, bagpipes playing, had gone "over the top" into no man's land. In later episodes, he always managed to find some way—as a spy or an aviator or through sheer boldness—around the deadlock of trench warfare.

As I grew older and learned more history, I found that this very deadlock had its own fascination. For more than three years the armies on the Western Front were virtually locked in place, burrowed into trenches with dugouts sometimes 40 feet below ground, periodically emerging for terrible battles that gained at best a few miles of muddy, shell-blasted wasteland. The destructiveness of those battles still seems beyond belief. In addition to the dead, on the first day of the Somme offensive another 36,000 British troops were wounded. The magnitude of slaughter in the war's entire span was beyond anything in European experience: more than 35 percent of all German men who were be-tween the ages of 19 and 22 when the fighting broke out, for example, were killed in the next four and a half years, and many of the remain-der grievously wounded. For France, the toll was proportionately even higher: one *half* of all Frenchmen aged 20 to 32 at the war's outbreak were dead when it was over. "The Great War of 1914–18 lies like a band of scorched earth dividing that time from ours," wrote the historian Barbara Tuchman. British stonemasons in Belgium were still at work carving the names of their nation's missing onto memorials when the Germans invaded for the next war, more than 20 years later. Cities and towns in the armies' path were reduced to jagged rubble, forests and farms to charred ruins. "This is not war," a wounded soldier among Britain's Indian troops wrote home from Europe. "It is the ending of the world."

In today's conflicts, whether the casualties are child soldiers in Af-rica or working-class, small-town Americans in Iraq or Afghanistan, we are accustomed to the poor doing a disproportionate share of the dying. But from 1914 to 1918, by contrast, in all the participating coun-tries the war was astonishingly lethal for their ruling classes. On both sides, officers were far more likely to be killed than the men whom they led over the parapets of trenches and into machine-gun fire, and they themselves were often from society's highest reaches. Roughly 12 per-cent of all British soldiers who took part in the war were killed, for in-stance, but for peers or sons of peers in uniform the figure was 19 per-cent. Of all men who graduated from Oxford in 1913, 31 percent were killed. The German chancellor, Theobald von Bethmann-Hollweg, lost his eldest son; so did British Prime Minister Herbert Asquith. A future British prime minister, Andrew Bonar Law, lost two sons, as did Vis-count Rothermere, newspaper mogul and wartime air minister. Gen-eral Erich Ludendorff, the war's key German commander, lost two stepsons and had to personally identify the decomposing body of one, exhumed from a battlefield grave. Herbert Lawrence, chief of the Brit-ish general staff on the Western Front, lost two sons; his counterpart in the French army, Noël de Castelnau, lost three. The grandson of one of England's richest men, the Duke of Westminster, received a fatal bullet through the head three days after writing his mother, "Supply me with socks and chocolates which are the two absolute necessities of life."

Part of what draws us to this war, then, is the way it forever shattered the self-assured, sunlit Europe of hussars and dragoons in plumed helmets and emperors waving from open, horse-drawn carriages. As the poet and soldier Edmund Blunden put it in describing that deadly first day of the Battle of the Somme, neither side "had won, nor could win, the War. The War had won." Under the pressure of the unending carnage two empires, the Austro-Hungarian and the Ottoman, dissolved completely, the German Kaiser lost his throne, and the Tsar of Russia and his entire photogenic family—his son in a sailor suit, his daughters in white dresses—lost their lives. Even the victors were losers: Britain and France together suffered more than two million dead and ended the war deep in debt; protests sparked by returning colonial veterans began the long unraveling of the British Empire, and a swath of northern France was reduced to ashes. The four-and-a-half-year tsunami of destruction permanently darkened our worldview. "Humanity? Can anyone really believe in the reasonableness of humanity after the last war," asked the Russian poet Alexander Blok a few years later, "with new, inevitable, and crueler wars in the offing?"

And in the offing they were. "It cannot be that two million Germans should have fallen in vain," Adolf Hitler fulminated less than four years after the war ended. ". . . No, we do not pardon, we demand —vengeance!" Germany's defeat, and the vindictiveness of the Allies in the peace settlement that followed, irrevocably sped the rise of Nazism and the coming of an even more destructive war 20 years later—and of the Holocaust as well. The First World War, of course, also helped bring to power in Russia a regime whose firing squads and gulag of Arctic and Siberian prison camps would sow death and terror in peacetime on a scale that surpassed many wars.

Like my uncle's friend with no toes on one foot, many of the war's more than 21 million wounded survived for long years after. Once in the 1960s I visited a stone, fortress-like state mental hospital in northern France, and some of the aged men I saw sitting like statues on benches in the courtyard there, faces blank, were shell-shock victims from the trenches. Millions of veterans, crippled in body or in spirit, filled such institutions for decades. The war's shadow stretched also onto tens of millions of people born after it ended, the children of survivors. I once interviewed the British writer John Berger, born in London in 1926, but who sometimes felt, he told me, as if "I was born near Ypres on the Western Front in 1917. The first thing I really remember about [my father] was him waking up screaming in the middle of the night, having one of his recurring nightmares about the war."

Why does this long-ago war intrigue us still? One reason, surely, is the stark contrast between what people believed they were fighting for and the shattered, embittered world the war actually created. On both sides participants felt they had good reasons for going to war, and on the Allied side they *were* good reasons. German troops, after all, with no justification, invaded France and, violating a treaty guaranteeing its neutrality, marched into Belgium as well. People in other countries, like Britain, understandably saw coming to the aid of the invasion's victims as a noble cause. And didn't France and Belgium have the right to defend themselves? Even those of us today who opposed the American wars in Vietnam or Iraq often hasten to add that we'd defend our country if it were attacked. And yet, if the leaders of any one of the major European powers had been able to look forward in time and see the full consequences, would they still have so quickly sent their soldiers marching off to battle in 1914?

What kings and prime ministers did not foresee, many more far-sighted citizens did. From the beginning, tens of thousands of people on both sides recognized the war for the catastrophe it was. They believed it was not worth the inevitable cost in blood, some of them anticipated with tragic clarity at least part of the nightmare that would engulf Europe as a result, and they spoke out. Moreover, they spoke out at a time when it took great courage to do so, for the air was filled with fervent nationalism and a scorn for dissenters that often turned violent. A handful of German parliamentarians bravely opposed war credits, and radicals like Rosa Luxemburg and Karl Liebknecht later went to prison—as did the American socialist leader Eugene V. Debs. But it was in Britain, more than anywhere else, that significant numbers of intrepid war opponents acted on their beliefs and paid the price. By the conflict's end, more than 20,000 British men of military age had refused the draft. Many refused noncombatant alternative service too, and more than 6,000 served prison terms under harsh conditions: hard labor, a bare-bones diet, and a strict "rule of silence" that forbade them from talking to one another.

Before it became clear just how many Britons would refuse to fight, some 50 early resisters were forcibly inducted into the army and transported, some in handcuffs, across the English Channel to France. A few weeks before that famous first day on the Somme, a less known scene unfolded at a British army camp not far away, within the sound of artillery fire from the front. The group of war opponents was told that if they continued to disobey orders, they would be sentenced to death. In an act of great collective courage that echoes down the years, not a single man wavered. Only at the last minute, thanks to frantic lobbying in London, were their lives saved. These resisters and their comrades did not come close to stopping the war, and have won no place in the standard history books, but their strength of conviction remains one of the glories of a dark time.

Those sent to jail for opposing the war included not just young men who defied the draft, but older men—and a few women. If we could time-travel our way into British prisons in late 1917 and early 1918 we would meet some extraordinary people, including the nation's leading investigative journalist, a future winner of the Nobel Prize, more than half a dozen future members of Parliament, one future cabinet minister, and a former newspaper editor who was publishing a clandestine journal for his fellow inmates on toilet paper. It would be hard to find a more distinguished array of people ever behind bars in a Western country.

In part, this book is the story of some of these war resisters and of the example they set, if not for their own time, then perhaps for the future. I wish theirs was a victorious story, but it is not. Unlike, say, witch-burning, slavery, and apartheid, which were once taken for granted and are now officially outlawed, war is still with us. Uniforms, parades, and martial music continue to cast their allure, and the appeal of high technology has been added to that; throughout the world boys and men still dream of military glory as much as they did a century ago. And so, in much greater part, this is a book about those who actually fought the war of 1914–1918, for whom the magnetic attraction of combat, or at least the belief that it was patriotic and necessary, proved so much stronger than human revulsion at mass death or any perception that, win or lose, this was a war that would change the world for the worse.

Where today we might see mindless killing, many of those who presided over the war's battles saw only nobility and heroism. "They advanced in line after line," recorded one British general of his men in action on that fateful July 1, 1916, at the Somme, writing in the stilted third-person usage of official reports, ". . . and not a man shirked going through the extremely heavy barrage, or facing the machine-gun and rifle fire that finally wiped them out. . . . He saw the lines which advanced in such admirable order melting away under the fire. Yet not a man wavered, broke the ranks, or attempted to come back. He has never seen, indeed could never have imagined, such a magnificent display of gallantry, discipline and determination. The reports that he had had from the very few survivors of this marvellous advance bear out what he saw with his own eyes, viz, that hardly a man of ours got to the German front line."

What was in the minds of such generals? How could they feel such a slaughter to be admirable or magnificent, worth more than the lives of their own sons? We can ask the same question of those who are quick to advocate military confrontation today, when, as in 1914, wars so often have unintended consequences.

A war is usually written about as a duel between sides. I have tried instead to evoke this war through the stories within one country, Britain, of some men and women from the great majority who passionately believed it was worth fighting and some of those who were equally convinced it should not be fought at all. In a sense, then, this is a story about loyalties. What should any human being be most loyal to? Country? Military duty? Or the ideal of international brotherhood? And what happens to loyalty within a family if, as happened in several of the families in these pages, some members join in the fight while a brother, a sister, a son, takes a stance of opposition that the public sees as cowardly or criminal?

This is also a story about clashing sets of dreams. For some of the people I follow here, the dream was that the war would rejuvenate the national spirit and the bonds of empire; that it would be short; that Britain would win by the time-honored means that had always won wars: pluck, discipline, and the cavalry charge. For war opponents, the dream was that the workingmen of Europe would never fight each other in battle; or, once the war began, that soldiers on both sides would see its madness and refuse to fight on; or, finally, that the Russian Revolution, in claiming to reject war and exploitation forever, was a shining example that other nations would soon follow.

As I tried to make sense of why these two very different sets of people acted as they did in the crucible of wartime, I realized that I needed to understand their lives in the years leading up to the war—when they often faced earlier choices about loyalties. And so this book about the first great war of the modern age begins not in August 1914 but several decades earlier, in an England that was quite different from the peaceful, bucolic land of country estates and weekend house parties so familiar to us from countless film and TV dramas. Part of this prewar era, in fact, Britain was fighting another war—which produced its own vigorous opposition movement. And, at home, it was in the grips of a prolonged, angry struggle over who should have the vote, a conflict that saw huge demonstrations, several deaths, mass imprisonments, and more deliberate destruction of property than the country had known for the better part of a century.

The story that follows is in no way a comprehensive history of the First World War and the period before it, for I've left out many well-known battles, episodes, and leaders. Nor is it about people usually thought of as a group, like the war poets or the Bloomsbury set; generally I've avoided such familiar figures. Some of those whose lives I trace here, close as they had once been, fell out so bitterly over the war that they broke off all contact with each other, and were they alive today would be dismayed to find themselves side by side in the same book. But each of them started by being bound to one or more of the others by ties of family or friendship, by shared beliefs, or, in several cases, by forbidden love. And all of them were citizens of a country undergoing a cataclysm where, in the end, the trauma of the war overwhelmed everything else.

The men and women in the following pages are a cast of characters I have collected slowly over the years, as I found people whose lives embodied very different answers to the choices faced by those who lived at a time when the world was aflame. Among them are generals, labor activists, feminists, *agents provocateurs,* a writer turned propagandist, a lion tamer turned revolutionary, a cabinet minister, a crusading working-class journalist, three soldiers brought before a firing squad at dawn, and a young idealist from the English Midlands who, long after his struggle against the war was over, would be murdered by the Soviet secret police. In following a collection of people through a tumultuous time, this book may seem in form more akin to fiction than to a traditional work of history. (Indeed, the life story of one woman here inspired one of the best recent novels about the war.) But everything in it actually happened. For history, when examined closely, always yields up people, events, and moral testing grounds more revealing than any but the greatest of novelists could invent.

I

Dramatis Personae

1

BROTHER AND SISTER

THE CITY HAD NEVER seen such a parade. Nearly 50,000 brilliantly uniformed troops converged on St. Paul's Cathedral in two great columns. One was led by the country's most beloved military hero, the mild-mannered Field Marshal Lord Roberts of Kandahar, a mere five feet two inches in height, astride a white Arabian horse like those he had ridden during more than 40 years of routing assorted Afghans, Indians, and Burmese who had the temerity to rebel against British rule. Mounted at the head of the other column, at six feet eight inches, was the tallest man in the army, Captain Oswald Ames of the Life Guards, wearing his regiment's traditional breastplate, which, with the sunlight glinting off it, seemed as if it might deflect an enemy's lance by its dazzling gleam alone. His silver helmet topped with a long horsehair panache made him appear taller still.

It was June 22, 1897, and London had spent £250,000 — the equivalent of more than $30 million today — on street decorations alone. Above the marching troops, Union Jacks flew from every building; blue, red, and white bunting and garlands adorned balconies; and lampposts were bedecked with baskets of flowers. From throughout the British Empire came foot soldiers and the elite troops of the cavalry: New South Wales Lancers from Australia, the Trinidad Light Horse, South Africa's Cape Mounted Rifles, Canadian Hussars, Zaptich horsemen from Cyprus in tasseled fezzes, and bearded lancers from the Punjab. Rooftops, balconies, and special bleachers built for this day were packed. A triumphal archway near Paddington station was emblazoned "Our Hearts Her Throne." On the Bank of England appeared "She Wrought Her People Lasting Good." Dignitaries filled the carriages that rolled along the parade route—the papal nuncio shared one with the envoy of the Chinese Emperor—but the most thunderous cheers were reserved for the royal carriage, drawn by eight cream-colored horses. Queen Victoria, holding a black lace parasol and nodding to the crowds, was marking the 60th anniversary of her ascent to the throne. Her black moiré dress was embroidered with silver roses, thistles, and shamrocks, symbols of the united lands at the pinnacle of the British Empire: England, Scotland, and Ireland.

The sun emerged patriotically from an overcast sky just after the Queen's carriage left Buckingham Palace. The dumpy monarch, whose round, no-nonsense face no portrait painter or photographer ever seems to have caught in a smile, presided over the largest empire the world had ever seen. For this great day a clothier advertised a "Diamond Jubilee Lace Shirt," poets wrote Jubilee odes, and Sir Arthur Sullivan, of Gilbert and Sullivan, composed a Jubilee hymn. "How many millions of years has the sun stood in heaven?" said the *Daily Mail*. "But the sun never looked down until yesterday upon the embodiment of so much energy and power."

Victoria's empire was not known for its modesty. "I contend that we are the first race in the world," the future diamond mogul Cecil Rhodes declared when still an Oxford undergraduate, "and that the more of the world we inhabit the better it is for the human race." Later, he went on to say, "I would annex the planets if I could." No other celestial body yet sported the Union Jack, but British territory did cover nearly a quarter of the earth. To be sure, some of that land was barren Arctic tundra belonging to Canada, which was in effect an independent country. But most Canadians—French-speakers and native Indians largely excepted—were happy to think of themselves as subjects of the Queen this splendid day, and the nation's prime minister, although a Francophone, had made a voyage to England to attend the Diamond Jubilee and accept a knighthood. True, a few of the territories optimistically colored pink on the map, such as the Transvaal republic in South Africa, did not think of themselves as British at all. Nonetheless, Trans-

vaal President Paul Kruger released two Englishmen from jail in honor
of the Jubilee. In India, the Nizam of Hyderabad, who also did not
consider himself subservient to the British, marked the occasion by setting free every tenth convict in his prisons. Gunboats in Cape Town
harbor fired a salute, Rangoon staged a ball, Australia issued extra food
and clothing to the Aborigines, and in Zanzibar the sultan held a Jubilee banquet.

At this moment of celebration, even foreigners forgave the British
their sins. In Paris, *Le Figaro* declared that imperial Rome was "equaled,
if not surpassed," by Victoria's realm; across the Atlantic, the *New York
Times* virtually claimed membership in the empire: "We are a part, and
a great part, of the Greater Britain which seems so plainly destined to
dominate this planet." In the Queen's honor, Santa Monica, California,
held a sports festival, and a contingent of the Vermont National Guard
crossed the border to join a Jubilee parade in Montreal.

Victoria was overwhelmed by the outpouring of affection and loyalty, and at times during the day her usually impassive face was streaked
with tears. The overseas cables had been kept clear of traffic until, at
Buckingham Palace, the Queen pressed an electric button linked to
the Central Telegraph Office. From there, as the assorted lancers, hussars, camel troopers, turbaned Sikhs, Borneo Dayak police, and Royal
Niger Constabulary marched through the city, her greeting flashed in
Morse code to every part of the empire, Barbados to Ceylon, Nairobi
to Hong Kong: "From my heart I thank my beloved people. May God
bless them."

The troops who drew the loudest cheers at the Diamond Jubilee parade
were those who, everyone knew, were certain to lead the way to victory
in Britain's wars to come: the cavalry. In peacetime as well, Britain's ruling class knew it belonged on horseback. It was, as a radical journalist
of the day put it, "a small select aristocracy born booted and spurred
to ride," who thought of everyone else as "a large dim mass born sad-
dled and bridled to be ridden." The wealthy bred racehorses, high society flocked to horse sales, and several cabinet members were stew-
ards of the Jockey Club. When a horse belonging to Lord Rosebery,
the prime minister, won the prestigious, high-stakes Epsom Derby, in
1894, a friend sent him a telegram: "Only heaven left." Devoted fox
hunters donned their red coats and black hats to gallop across fields

and leap stone walls in pursuit of baying hounds as often as five or six days a week. The Duke of Rutland's private chaplain was rumored to wear boots and spurs under his cassock. Horses and hunts were admired even by sailors, and for those who could afford it, a favorite tattoo showed riders and hounds covering a man's entire back, in pursuit of a fox heading for the crack between his buttocks. Hunting, after all, was as close as one could come in civilian life to the glory of a cavalry charge.

For any wellborn young Englishman making a military career, it was only natural to prefer the cavalry. Joining it was not the privilege of all, however, for this was the army's most expensive branch. Until 1871, British officers had to purchase their commissions, as one might buy membership in an exclusive club. ("Good God," one new subaltern is said to have remarked when a deposit from the War Office appeared on his bank statement. "I didn't know we were *paid*.") After reforms abolished the sale of commissions, an infantry or artillery lieutenant might belong to a regiment so lacking in elegance that he could live on his own salary, but not a cavalry officer. There were the necessary club memberships, a personal servant and a groom, uniforms, saddles, and above all else buying and maintaining one's horses: a charger or two for battles, two hunters for pursuing foxes, and of course a couple of polo ponies. A private income of at least £500 a year—some $60,000 today—was essential. And so the ranks of cavalry officers were filled with men from large country houses.

The late-nineteenth-century horseman's sword and lance were not so different from those wielded at Agincourt in 1415, and so cavalry warfare embodied the idea that in battle it was not modern weaponry that mattered but the courage and skill of the warrior. Although the cavalry made up only a small percentage of British forces, its cachet meant that cavalry officers long held a disproportionate number of senior army posts. And so, from 1914 to 1918, five hundred years after Agincourt and in combat unimaginably different, it would be two successive cavalrymen who served as commanders in chief of British troops on the Western Front in the most deadly war the country would ever know.

The army career of one of those men began forty years earlier, in 1874, when, at the age of 21, after pulling the appropriate strings, he found himself a lieutenant in the 19th Regiment of Hussars. John French had been born on his family's estate in rural Kent; his father was a retired naval officer whose ancestors came from Ireland. French's short stature may not have fit the image of a dashing cavalryman, but his cheerful smile, black hair, thick mustache, and blue eyes gave him an appeal that women found irresistible. His letters also displayed great warmth; to one retired general who needed cheering up, French wrote, "You have the heartfelt love of every true soldier who has ever served with you and any of them would go anywhere for you to-morrow. I have constantly told my great pals and friends that I would like to end my life by being shot when serving under you." What French could not do, however, was hold on to money, an awkward failing given a cavalryman's high expenses. He spent lavishly on horses, women, and risky investments, running up debts and then turning to others for relief. A brother-in-law bailed him out the first time; loans from a series of relatives and friends soon followed.

Officers of the 19th Hussars wore black trousers with a double gold stripe down the side and leather-brimmed red caps with a golden badge. From April to September they drilled during the week and then marched to church together on Sundays, spurs and scabbards clinking, black leather boots smelling of horse sweat. During the autumn and winter, French and his fellow officers spent much of their time back on their estates, enjoying round after round of hunting, steeplechases, and polo.

Like many an officer of the day, French idolized Napoleon, buying Napoleonic knickknacks when not out of funds and keeping on his desk a bust of the Emperor. He read military history, hunting stories, and the novels of Charles Dickens, long passages of which he learned by heart. Later in life, if someone read him a sentence plucked from anywhere in Dickens's works, he could often finish the paragraph.

Soon after French joined the regiment, the 19th Hussars were sent to ever-restless Ireland. The English considered the island part of Great Britain, but most Irish felt they were living in an exploited colony. Recurrent waves of nationalism were fed by tension between impoverished Catholic tenant farmers and wealthy Protestant landowners. During one such dispute, French's troops were called in — on the landlord's side, of course. An angry Irish laborer rushed at French and sliced his horse's hamstrings with a sickle.

French was soon promoted to captain. An impulsive early marriage came to a quick end and was omitted from his official biography, for Victorian society looked on divorce with stern disapproval. At 28, French married again, this time with much fanfare. Eleanora Selby-Lowndes was the daughter of a hunt-loving country squire, the perfect mate for a rising, well-liked cavalryman. He seemed genuinely fond of his new wife, although this would not stop him from embarking on an endless string of love affairs.

In the army in which French was making his career, an important military virtue was sportsmanship. On his death, one officer left more than £70,000 to his regiment, in part for the encouragement of "manly sports." Some regiments kept their own packs of foxhounds, so officers did not need to take a day's leave to hunt. A book from the era, *Modern Warfare* by Frederick Guggisberg, who was later to become a brigadier general, likened war to rugby, which the British call football: "An army tries to *work together* in battle . . . in much the same way as a football team *plays together* in a match. . . . The army *fights* for the good of its country as the team *plays* for the honour of its school. Regiments *assist* each other as players do when they . . . *pass the ball* from one to another; exceptionally gallant *charges* and heroic *defences* correspond to brilliant *runs* and fine *tackling*." War's resemblance to another sport, cricket, was the theme of one of the most famous poems of the day, Sir Henry Newbolt's "Vitaï Lampada" (The Torch of Life):

> There's a breathless hush in the Close to-night—
>   Ten to make and the match to win—
> A bumping pitch and a blinding light,
>   An hour to play and the last man in.
> And it's not for the sake of a ribboned coat,
>   Or the selfish hope of a season's fame,
> But his Captain's hand on his shoulder smote—
>   "Play up! play up! and play the game!"
>
> The sand of the desert is sodden red,—
>   Red with the wreck of a square that broke;—
> The Gatling's jammed and the Colonel dead,
>   And the regiment blind with dust and smoke.
> The river of death has brimmed his banks,
>   And England's far, and Honour a name,
> But the voice of a schoolboy rallies the ranks:
>   "Play up! play up! and play the game!"

The poem would last; when Lieutenant George Brooke of the Irish Guards was mortally wounded by German shrapnel at Soupir, France, in 1914, his dying words to his men were "Play the game."

To the young John French, that desert red with blood long seemed out of reach. Except for the sickle-wielding Irish farmhand, he passed the age of 30 without seeing battle. Then, to his delight, in 1884 he was ordered to an outpost that promised action: a colonial war in the Sudan. At last French experienced the combat he had long dreamed of when troops he led successfully repulsed a surprise attack by an enemy force that surged out of a ravine, armed mainly with swords and spears. This was the real thing: hand-to-hand fighting, rebellious "natives" vanquished in textbook fashion by disciplined cavalry and British martial spirit. He returned to England with praise from his superiors, medals, and a promotion, at the unusually young age of 32, to lieutenant colonel. Only a few years later, a bit bowlegged from more than a decade on horseback, he took command of the 19th Hussars. Through the wall of the commanding officer's quarters, John and Eleanora French and their children could hear the growls and roars of the regimental mascot, a black bear.

For an ambitious young officer, it could be a career advantage to get your ticket punched on several continents. And so French was pleased when, in 1891, the 19th Hussars were ordered to India. In this grandest and richest of Britain's colonies many officers spent the defining years of their careers, convinced that they were carrying out a sacred, altruistic mission.

Enjoying a peacetime routine of polo field, officers' mess, and turbaned servants, French saw no military action. He busied himself instead training his horsemen to a high pitch in close-order drill, sending them trotting, galloping, and wheeling across the spacious Indian *maidans,* or parade grounds, raising clouds of dust behind them. With his family left behind in England, he spent his spare time in pursuit of another officer's wife, with whom he slipped away to one of the hill stations where the British fled the summer heat of the plains. The angry officer then sued for divorce, citing French as a co-respondent. There were rumors that he had also been involved with the daughter of a railway official, and with his commander's wife.

When French returned to England in 1893, word of these episodes slowed his career. On half pay, as officers often were between assignments, he, Eleanora, and their three children were forced to move in with a forgiving older sister. Far more humiliating, the cavalryman tried to resort to a bicycle as a less expensive alternative to a horse, a substitute steed he never fully mastered. Fellow officers observed French hopping down the road beside it, unable to mount. And yet his freespending ways continued, and he had to pawn the family silver. In disgrace, he waited restlessly for a new posting, or, better yet, a war.

In John French's England, the boulevards along which Victoria's Jubilee parade marched were splendid indeed, but large stretches of London and other cities were less glorious, for little of the wealth the country drew from its colonies ever reached the poor. In a cramped row house near a coal mine, a hungry family might occupy a single room, and the dwellings of an entire unpaved street might use a single hand-pumped water faucet; in the vast slums of London's East End, one boarding house bed might be shared by two or three impoverished workers sleeping in eight-hour shifts. Children's growth was stunted by malnutrition; their teeth already rotting, they might eat meat or fish only once a week. The poorest of the poor ended up in the workhouse, where they were given jobs and shelter but made to feel like prisoners. Barefoot workhouse children shivered through the winter in thin, ragged cotton clothes, often with only backless benches to sit on. In the worst slums, with some 20 of every 100 babies failing to survive their first year, infant mortality was nearly three times that for children of the wealthy. Just as combating the empire's enemies in distant corners of the world would shape the likes of John French, so combating injustice at home and wars abroad would shape other Britons of this generation—even, in some cases, those who sprang from French's own class.

Among them was a woman now remembered by her married name, Charlotte Despard. As girls, she and her five sisters would slip through the fence around their estate's formal garden to play with children in the closest village, until their parents discovered and put a stop to it. This—in Charlotte's memory at least—ignited a rebellious spark, and at the age of ten she ran away from home. At a nearby railway station, she later wrote, "I took a ticket to London where I intended to earn my living as a servant." Although caught after one night away, she was "not tamed." Her father died the same year, and her mother, for reasons we don't know, was confined to an insane asylum a few years later. Charlotte, her sisters, and a younger brother were then raised by relatives and a governess, with Charlotte lending a hand in caring for the younger children. The governess taught them a hymn:

> I thank the Goodness and the Grace
> That on my birth hath smiled,
> And made me in these happy days
> A happy English child.
>
> I was not born a little slave
> To labour in the sun,
> And wish that I were in the grave,
> And all my labor done.

"That hymn was the turning-point," Charlotte would claim. "I demanded why God had made slaves, and I was promptly sent to bed."

When she was a little older, she visited a Yorkshire factory and was horrified to see ill-paid women and children picking apart piles of old cloth to make rope from its threads. In her early twenties, she saw the slums of the East End: "How bitterly ashamed I was of it all! How ardently I longed to speak to these people in their misery, to say, 'Why do you bear it? Rise. . . . Smite your oppressors. Be true and strong!' Of course I was much too shy to say anything of the sort."

In 1870, at the age of 26, Charlotte married. Maximilian Despard was a well-to-do businessman, but like his new wife he favored home rule for Ireland, rights and careers for women, and many other progressive causes of the day. Throughout their married life, he suffered from a kidney disease of which he eventually died, and there are hints that his relationship with his wife remained unconsummated. The two traveled widely together for 20 years, however, several times going to India, and for decades afterward she spoke of how happy a time it had been. Whatever the frustrations of a marriage without children and possibly without sex, Charlotte Despard enjoyed something rare for her time and class: a husband who respected her work. And this meant being a novelist. Modern readers should not feel deprived that Despard's seven enormous novels (publishers made more money on multivolume works) have long been out of print. Abounding in noble heroines, mysterious ancestors, Gothic castles, deathbed reunions, and happy endings, they were the Victorian equivalent of today's formula romances.

If the country gentleman's role in life was to be on horseback, the upper-class Victorian woman's was to be mistress of a grand house, and so the Despards bought a country home, Courtlands, standing amid fifteen rolling acres of woods, lawn, stream, and formal gardens overlooking a valley in Surrey. A dozen servants handled the indoors alone. Living on an even grander estate nearby, the Duchess of Albany recruited Charlotte for her Nine Elms Flower Mission, a project in which wealthy women brought baskets of flowers from their gardens (also tended by servants) to Nine Elms, the poorest corner of London's overcrowded Battersea district. This was as far as a proper upper-class woman of the era was expected to go in response to poverty.

After her husband died in 1890, however, Despard startled everyone by making Battersea the center of her life. Using money she had inherited from him as well as from her parents, she opened two community centers in the slum, grandly called Despard Clubs, complete with youth programs, a drop-in health clinic, nutrition classes, subsidized food for new mothers, and a collection of layettes and other baby supplies that could be loaned out as women gave birth. Most shockingly to her family, she moved into the upper floor of one of her clubs, although for a time still retreating to Courtlands on weekends. Despite her background, Despard evidently had a knack for dealing with the children of Battersea. "She does not find them unmanageable," reported one observer, the social reformer Charles Booth. "They submit readily to her gentle force. 'You hurt me,' cried a big, strong fellow, but he did not resist when she took him by the arm in the cause of order."

It was said that you could smell Battersea long before you reached it, for its air was thick with smoke and fumes from a large gasworks, an iron foundry, and coal-burning railway locomotives on their way to Victoria and Waterloo stations. Coal dust coated everything, including the residents' lungs. Many women took in washing from the wealthier parts of the city. Dilapidated houses and apartments swarmed with rats, cockroaches, fleas, and bedbugs. Urban manufacturing areas like Battersea lay at the heart of Britain's Industrial Revolution, and in the great war to come their factories would mass-produce the weapons, and their crowded tenements the manpower, for the trenches.

Battersea was then a battlefield of a different sort, Despard quickly discovered, a center for radical politics and the growing trade union movement. Its gas workers had gone on strike to win an eight-hour day; later the borough council would refuse to accept a donation for the local library from the Scottish-American magnate Andrew Carnegie because his money was "tainted with the blood" of striking U.S. steelworkers. The part of Battersea where Despard worked reflected the empire's ethnic hierarchy, for like many of England's poorest neighborhoods, it was largely Irish, filled with evicted tenant farmers or families who had fled even more impoverished parts of Dublin in search of a better life in London.

In identification with Battersea's Irish poor, thumbing her nose at the upper-crust Protestant world of her birth, Despard converted to Roman Catholicism. She also developed a passion for theosophy, a woolly, mystical faith that includes elements of Buddhism, Hinduism, and the occult. Nor was this all: "I determined to study for myself the great problems of society," she would later write. "My study landed me in uncompromising socialism." She befriended Karl Marx's daughter Eleanor, and in 1896, representing a British Marxist group, was a delegate to a meeting of the federation of socialist parties and trade unions from around the world known as the Second International. An oddly assorted bouquet of belief systems this might have been, but one thing shone through clearly: a desire to identify with those at the bottom of Britain's class ladder and to offer them something more than baskets of flowers.

Just as she left behind the life she had been expected to lead, so Despard left behind its dress. She now clothed herself in black, and instead of the elaborate upper-class women's hats of the day that clearly telegraphed leisure, she covered her graying hair with a black lace mantilla. In place of shoes she wore open-toed sandals. She dressed this way at all times, whether on a lecture platform or cooking a meal for a group of slum children at one of her community centers. Eventually she would also wear these clothes to jail.

Before long she was elected to a Poor Law Board, whose job was to supervise the running of the local workhouse. Among the first socialists on one of these boards, she protested valiantly against the rotten potatoes given to inmates and fought to expose a corrupt manager whom she caught selling food from the kitchen while the workhouse women were on a bread and water diet. Despard was now devoting her copious energy to the women she called "those who slave all their lives long . . . earning barely a subsistence, and thrown aside to death or the parish when they are no longer profitable."

In every way, the lives of Charlotte Despard and John French form the greatest possible contrast. He was destined to lead the largest army Britain had ever put in the field; she came to vigorously oppose every war her country fought, above all the one in which he would be commander in chief. He went to Ireland to suppress restive tenant farmers; she ministered to the Irish poor of Battersea, whom she called "my sister women" (although they might not have spoken of her quite the same way). They both went to India, but he drilled cavalrymen whose job was to keep India British; she returned committed to Indian self-rule. At a time when a powerful empire faced colonial rebellions abroad and seething discontent at home, he would remain a staunch defender of the established order, she a defiant revolutionary. And yet, despite all this, something bound them together.

John French and Charlotte Despard were brother and sister.

More than that, for almost all of their lives they remained close. She was eight years senior to "Jack," as she called him, and he was the beloved little brother whom she taught his ABCs after their parents had disappeared from their lives. His sexual adventuring and reckless spending, which dismayed other family members, never seemed to bother her. When he went off to soldier in India, it was she who welcomed his wife Eleanora and the children to Courtlands, turning her house over to them while she lived in gritty Battersea. And when French returned from India under a cloud of debt and scandal, Despard took him in as well, lending him money long after his exasperated other sisters ceased to do so.

Their two very different worlds met when Despard periodically loaded some of Battersea's poor into a horse-drawn omnibus for a Saturday or Sunday at Courtlands, away from the grime and coal smoke of the city. French's son, Gerald, who would later follow his father into the army, remembered one such group of Battersea visitors, and his tone hints at what the rest of the family must have felt about Despard:

It certainly was amusing to some extent, but it had its trying side. For instance, they came equipped with several barrel-organs, which, of course, they never ceased playing from the time of their arrival until their departure. Their womenfolk accompanied them, and dancing went on during the greater part of the day, on the lawns and on the drive.

My father . . . threw himself nobly into the breach, and helped to organize sports for the men. . . . I think he was more amused than anyone at the extraordinary antics of the invaders of our peace and quietness. They swarmed all over the place, and when the evening came and they set off on the return journey to London, we, at any rate, were not sorry that the entertainment had at last come to an end.

John French's family might have resented the "invaders of our peace and quietness," but Courtlands was, after all, Despard's estate, although she now occupied only a small cottage on the grounds for her weekend visits. French remained fond of the sister who had helped raise him. When as a Poor Law Board member she gave her first public speech at Wandsworth town hall, he accompanied her. And when she was overcome at the door by stage fright, he encouraged her with the comment: "Only nervous people are ever of any real use."

Despite their disparate views of the world, the warmth and loyalty between this brother and sister would continue for several decades, through a grim, divisive colonial conflict about to break out, and then a global war that would leave more than 700,000 of their countrymen dead. Only events after that great watershed would finally break the bond between them.

2

A MAN OF NO ILLUSIONS

JUST AS SOME of the major commanders and protesters of the First World War came onstage well before it began, so too did one of the war's key weapons. It made a spectacular early appearance the year after Victoria's Diamond Jubilee.

The site was Omdurman, in the Sudan, the vast African territory whose inhabitants, in London's eyes, did not understand their proper role, which was to be loyal subjects of the British Empire. Under a militant Muslim leader, Sudanese Arabs had overrun an occupation force and beheaded the British general who led it. Thirteen years later, in 1898, Britain sent a large body of troops up the Nile to the Sudan under the command of legendary Major General Sir Horatio Herbert Kitchener, who had served in various corners of the empire, from Palestine to Cyprus to Zanzibar, and whose mission now was to teach the Sudanese their place, once and for all.

An adventurous young soldier with this force was peering through his binoculars at a hillside, crossed by what he thought was a defensive barricade of tree branches. "Suddenly the whole black line . . . began to move. It was made of men, not bushes. . . . We watched, amazed by the wonder of the sight, the whole face of the slope become black with swarming savages. Four miles from end to end."

Marching toward him from Omdurman, the headquarters of the

Sudanese, were some 50,000 troops carrying spears, swords, horns, drums, and antiquated rifles. "The whole side of the hill seemed to move. Between the masses horsemen galloped continually; before them many patrols dotted the plain; above them waved hundreds of banners, and the sun, glinting on many thousands of hostile spear-points, spread a sparkling cloud."

The witness was 23-year-old Winston Churchill, who was both correspondent for the London *Morning Post* and an officer in Kitchener's forces. As the scion of a well-placed family, he was, of course, in the cavalry. With the decisive battle about to begin, "standing at a table spread in the wilderness, we ate a substantial meal," he wrote. "It was like a race lunch before the big event."

The future prime minister was hardly the only ambitious Briton who had lobbied hard to be here for the showdown—or who ate well while awaiting glory. Consider a youthful major named Douglas Haig. Before setting off across the Sudanese desert, he had asked his sister to send him from home "jams, tinned fruits, cocoa, vegetables, haddock in tins, tongue, biscuits, some hock and a bottle or two of brandy," all of which, along with extra silk underwear, Haig would transport by the three camels that were at his disposal, along with four horses, a donkey, a goat (for milk), a cook, a valet, and various servants to look after the animals.

Haig came from a Scottish family famous for its whiskey distillery; funds from that fortune ensured that he would never have John French's money problems. Like French, he was on horseback from his early years, keeping two horses and a full-time groom while at Oxford and later becoming a member of the British national polo team. Entering the army, he soon acquired a reputation as a short-fused martinet who displayed no lack of imperial pride. "I am not one," he would declare later in life, "who is ashamed of the wars that were fought to open the markets of the world to our traders." It was at a cavalry camp in India that Haig first met French, nine years older, senior in rank, and in personality his opposite, for Haig was puritanical, incapable of small talk, and as stiff as the high collar of his dress uniform. Nonetheless, in an army laced with networks of patrons and protégés, he had a keen eye for strategic friendships.

Although French was now stuck at a post back in England, Haig had used family connections to win himself a place at Omdurman, where he was eagerly awaiting his first taste of combat. An hour after dawn on September 2, 1898, the day following Churchill's first sight of them, the Sudanese launched a frontal attack on the British position. Over their *jibbahs,* loose robes with colored patches, some of them wore chain mail and they outnumbered the British Empire troops by nearly two to one. But as British fire tore into the Sudanese line, the bloodshed was immense — and nothing was more devastating than the latest models of Hiram Maxim's machine gun.

For decades, military inventors had been struggling to make an effective rapid-fire weapon, but the results had been cumbersome in the extreme: generally a gunner had to turn a crank, and, to keep a single barrel from overheating, a series of them fired in succession — one early model had 37 barrels, another 50. Only in 1884 had Maxim finally perfected the first such gun that was both single-barreled and fully automatic: it used the energy of its own recoil to eject each spent cartridge and pull the next one into place — and it kept shooting as long as a soldier squeezed the trigger. A jacket of water, refilled as the liquid boiled away, kept the barrel from getting too hot. The Maxim could fire 500 rounds a minute.

No one was watching the Sudan fighting more closely than Britain's major imperial rival, Germany. "The enemy went down in heaps," wrote a German newspaperman with the British forces, "and it was evident that the six Maxim guns were doing a large share of the work." Indeed, thanks to the Maxims, in a few hours the British were able to fire an extraordinary 500,000 bullets at the hapless Sudanese.

It was a historic slaughter. When the Battle of Omdurman was over later in the day, some 10,800 Sudanese lay dead on the desert sand beneath a brilliantly clear sky. At least 16,000 more had been wounded, and were either bleeding to death or trying to drag themselves away. The British lost only 48 dead. A Union Jack was raised, the assembled empire troops gave three cheers for the Queen, and General Kitchener wept as a regimental band played "Abide with Me."

Britain's wars, the jubilant victors at Omdurman expected, would continue to be just such lopsided victories — or massacres, as a dissenter like Charlotte Despard might say — against poorly armed Arabs, Africans, and Asians. This assumption, and the confidence that weapons like the Maxim gun would always give Britain superiority, underlay a sort of ecstasy about battle that shines through the writing of this period. Lord Wolseley, army commander in chief at the time of Omdurman, wrote of "the rapture-giving delight which the attack upon an enemy affords. I cannot analyse nor weigh, nor can I justify the feeling. But once experienced, all other subsequent sensations are but as a tinkling of a doorbell in comparison with the throbbing of Big Ben."

Both the British and Germans had already experienced that rapture while wielding Maxim guns to deadly effect elsewhere in Africa. This, to Europeans, seemed the machine gun's logical use: "It is a weapon," declared the *Army and Navy Journal,* "which is specially adapted to terrify a barbarous or semi-civilised foe." No one imagined that either British or German soldiers would ever find themselves in the role of Sudanese Arabs, experiencing their own Omdurmans in the very heart of Europe.

The next war was clearly going to be quite far from Europe. For even as Kitchener's Maxims were swiftly mowing down the Sudanese, Britain's relentless imperial march was running into unexpected problems at the other end of the African continent. The war about to begin there would be the country's last before 1914. In ways no one understood at the time, it would offer additional glimpses of the great cataclysm ahead. And among the actors would be several destined to play major roles in fighting—or resisting—the world war to come.

With its temperate climate and fertile river valleys, the southern tip of Africa had attracted Europeans for several hundred years, and immigrants from Holland, Britain, and elsewhere had wrested a large expanse of land from the indigenous inhabitants. By the late nineteenth century, what today is South Africa was divided into four parts: two British territories, Natal and the Cape Colony—which included vastly lucrative diamond mines—encompassed all the coastline and much of the interior, while inland were two landlocked autonomous states, the Orange Free State and the South African Republic, which lay across the Vaal River and so was known as the Transvaal. These two territories were controlled by Boers, descendants of early European settlers, whose language derived from seventeenth-century Dutch. After some decades of friction, the British had been content to leave the Boers alone, for their wide stretches of empty veldt seemed to offer few enticements for conquest.

Everything had changed in 1886, however, when at the small town of Johannesburg an itinerant prospector stumbled upon a rock that turned out to be an outcrop of the world's largest underground deposit of gold ore. This staggeringly rich lode extended downward thousands of feet into the earth and spread for more than a hundred miles sideways under the Transvaal plains. Fortune hunters from Europe and North America flocked to Johannesburg, at first living in tents. On their heels came builders, merchants, brewers, distillers, pimps and prostitutes, and the tiny settlement was swiftly transformed into a large city with gaslit streets. Within a dozen years, this patch of dry grassland was producing one-quarter of the world's gold, and, exasperatingly for the British, the Transvaal controlled it all.

At first Britain hoped that mere demography would conquer the Transvaal, since most of the gold-rush miners and deep-level mining companies were British. It was unthinkable that the Transvaal's black majority would ever have the right to vote, and so surely it would be just a matter of time before the new immigrants outnumbered the Boers. Then they could elect a government that would bring the Transvaal into the empire—and in the process reduce taxes on the mining barons. To the total frustration of London, however, the republic's president, Paul Kruger, a man of great bulk, enormous jowls, and a fringe of white beard, denied the new immigrants full citizenship. That Britons had a right to rule other people seemed the most obvious of global truths, but that uncultured farmers led by an ugly-looking man said to believe the earth was flat should rule over Britons seemed outrageous. In 1897, the year of the Diamond Jubilee, the British government turned to one of the brightest stars in the imperial firmament to deal with the stubborn Boers.

Sir Alfred Milner was only 43—young to be appointed high commissioner to South Africa, in effect the British viceroy for the region. He had, however, already proven himself one of his country's most versatile administrators, and, at this moment of greed for gold, his imperial idealism provided a much-needed gloss of lofty purpose. "It is the British race which built the Empire," he typically proclaimed, "and it is the undivided British race which can alone uphold it. . . . Deeper, stronger, more primordial than material ties is the bond of common blood."

Milner was a man of driving ambition, in part to regain a lost family position on the steep British class ladder. His grandfather had been a major general and colonial governor, but his ne'er-do-well physician father failed to establish a successful practice in England and had to take a job teaching English in Germany, where Milner was born and spent part of his childhood. He never completely lost the trace of a German accent, and secret embarrassment about this may help explain his fierce, almost religious devotion to the "British race."

That he seemed to have no woman in his life gave an air of mystery to this austere, stern-looking man with a long, somber face and high forehead. Hard-driving and supremely efficient, he was once described by Churchill as "the man of no illusions." Unknown to almost everyone, however, he kept an aspiring actress, Cécile Duval, as a mistress for almost a decade, maintaining her for some £450 a year in South London and slipping away with her for secret boating, cycling, and card-playing holidays. He sometimes stayed at her home, but never she at his. Evidently because she was not of the right class, he seems never to have introduced her to any of his friends.

Milner served in high government positions dealing with finance and taxes, at home and in colonial Egypt. He earned a reputation for being able to quickly absorb the information in a complex mass of documents and for effortlessly understanding numbers—a balance sheet for him, an admiring aide once said, was "as lucid as a page of print." Milner was the ideal colonial civil servant, equal parts technocrat and prophet of empire, and both the British government and the mining magnates thought him the perfect man to bring the arrogant Boers into the empire where they obviously belonged. Queen Victoria gave him a personal sendoff from Windsor Castle, and some 140 dignitaries threw him a farewell dinner at the Café Monico in Piccadilly Circus, where he replied to effusive toasts by vowing to do his best as "a civilian soldier of the Empire." Then, he recorded in his diary, he went "to Brixton . . . to see C." He wrote three words, crossed them out, and finally scribbled them in the margin: "to say goodbye."

The brisk, purposeful man who settled into Government House, his official residence in Cape Town beneath the brow of the city's famous mountain, faced a huge challenge. Successfully bringing the Transvaal and its gold under British rule would be an imperial coup of the first order, but it would not be easy. Although European opinion accepted the conquest of Africans as normal, it would never tolerate the overt seizure of African territory controlled by white people.

Meanwhile, a growing rivalry in Europe began to shadow events in southern Africa. The Transvaal was importing rifles from Germany, which had itself jumped into the great race for African land, staking out several colonies. To the fury of the British public, Kaiser Wilhelm II sent the Transvaal's President Kruger a telegram congratulating him on maintaining his independence. With Germany making friendly overtures like this, Milner had no time to waste. For two years, he criss-crossed the southern end of the continent by train, wagon, and horse, tending his realm while negotiating with Kruger, whom he privately referred to as "a frock-coated Neanderthal." Demands, ultimatums, and refusals volleyed back and forth. Far more hawkish than the cabinet members who had dispatched him from London, Milner craved a war, as a "great day of reckoning" that would settle for good the "great game between ourselves and the Transvaal for the mastery of South Africa." Could the Boers, he wondered, somehow be manipulated into firing the first shots? As he put it to the colonial secretary in a letter marked VERY SECRET that left Cape Town with the weekly mail ship, "Will not the arrival of more [British] troops so frighten the Boers that they will take the first step and rush part of our territory?" By doing so, "they would put themselves in the wrong and become the aggressors."

While impatiently awaiting war, Milner allowed himself a few relax-ations: cycling, hunting for jackals, and archery, which he practiced on the lawn of Government House. He also took solace from a new arrival in Cape Town, Rudyard Kipling. In his early thirties and already a best-selling poet, novelist, and journalist, the writer sensed that South Af-rica was the next battleground for the expansion of the British Empire, and so had come for the first of what would be several lengthy visits.

Both Kipling's grandfathers had been Methodist preachers, and there was an almost evangelical fervor to his celebration of imperialism and to some of the countless phrases he added to the language, from "east of Suez" to "the white man's burden." Born in India, he later worked there as a newspaper reporter, spending long hours in the Brit-ish army barracks in Lahore. Absorbing soldiers' stories, he had come to relish feeling part of a small elite of bold, resourceful Britons — weeks away from home by ship and, when Kipling was born, out of reach by telegraph — carrying out the lonely task of governing a vast population of Indians. There was "no civilizing experiment in the world's history," he said, "at all comparable to British rule in India." In the nobility of this work he could believe fully because, as George Orwell wrote of him after his death, the poet never acknowledged "that an empire is primarily a money-making concern." Although India was unusually free of wars during his time as a journalist there, no one has ever written more lovingly and sympathetically about the British soldier than this man with his distinctive thick spectacles, heavy eyebrows, and bushy mustache, who never served in uniform.

Kipling was the last great writer in English whose work was equally beloved across the class spectrum; privates and generals alike knew many of his seductively melodious poems by heart. In the seamless universe of his writing, adventurous schoolboys turned into brave soldiers, loyal natives were always grateful for British rule, and the magnificent empire was untroubled by any undercurrents of dissent. Although well read in English, French, and Latin, and friendly with many of the leading writers of the day, Kipling nonetheless preferred the company of army officers, of bold empire builders like the business tycoon Cecil Rhodes and America's Theodore Roosevelt, of men willing to provoke war for what they believed in, like Alfred Milner. He and Milner hit it off and would remain fast friends the rest of their lives.

New detachments of troops sent from England at last had the effect Milner wanted. Seeing that hostilities with Britain were inevitable, the two Boer republics decided that their best hope was a series of swift attacks before yet more British troops arrived. And so, on October 11, 1899, to Milner's delight, they declared war. In London, British politicians were equally happy that their enemy had been maneuvered into appearing the aggressor. Another cabinet member wrote to the colonial secretary: "Accept my felicitations."

Slaughters like Omdurman aside, what today we call the Boer War was Britain's first in nearly half a century, and the public greeted it almost as if it were a continuation of the Diamond Jubilee. Everyone expected Milner's War, as some referred to it, to be gloriously won by Christmas. As a bonus, this decisive victory would send a strong warning to Germany, just then launching an ominous shipbuilding program to double the size of its navy.

British officers talked of combat as so much sport. Men ordered to advance against Boer positions, called "beaters," were to flush the quarry from their hiding places as in pheasant hunting. A captain in the Imperial Yeomanry declared that chasing Boer horsemen across the veldt was "just like a good fox hunt." The first British commanding general in South Africa, the paunchy, double-chinned Sir Redvers Buller, ordered his soldiers not to be unsportsmanlike "jack-in-boxes" who ducked after standing up to fire their rifles.

The war, however, failed to unroll like the good hunt it was supposed to be. A succession of Boer ambushes and humiliating British defeats left the public stunned. Even more shocking, Rhodes, the richest man in the British Empire, who had grandly gone to the Cape Colony diamond center of Kimberley to tend to the protection of his mines, was trapped there, along with some 50,000 civilians and 600 British troops, when the Boers surrounded the town. From Rhodes's luxurious quarters in the town's red-brick Sanatorium hotel and spa, which he owned, he managed to send an angry message to Milner in Cape Town: "Strain everything. Send immediate relief to Kimberley. I cannot understand the delay."

Because Kimberley produced 90 percent of the world's diamonds, breaking the siege was a top priority. As a British force fought its way closer to the town, in the vanguard were cavalry detachments, followed by supply wagons, artillery, and a cart that unreeled telegraph wire as it rolled along. Joyfully in command, reclaimed by war from a cloud of scandals past and now a general, was John French.

At his side as chief of staff, fresh from Omdurman, was his old friend from India days, Major Douglas Haig. The two had left England for South Africa on the same ship, and when French saw that Haig had not been allocated a cabin, he invited Haig to share his own on the top deck. As usual, French was in financial trouble, this time having speculated unwisely on South African gold stocks. Although it was almost unheard of for a commanding officer to be in debt to a subordinate, French borrowed a hefty £2,000 from Haig, the equivalent of more than $260,000 today, to stave off angry creditors.

On February 15, 1900, French's scouts finished reconnoitering the last enemy stronghold between his troops and the besieged Kimberley, fortified positions held by some 900 Boer soldiers on two ridges about three-quarters of a mile apart. Then, surrounded by snorting horses, the jangle and creak of boots and spurs, and the smell of saddle leather, the impetuous general gave the order that all cavalrymen dreamed of: Charge!

Successive waves of shouting British troopers in tall sun helmets galloped up the gently rising valley between the two ridges: first the lancers with pennants flying, their khaki-clad chests crisscrossed by diagonal straps, proud swordsmen next, horse-drawn artillery in the rear. French himself led the second wave of troops. It was a bold move, and it worked. Some 3,000 cavalrymen suffered fewer than two dozen casualties. "The feeling was wonderfully exciting, just as in a good run to hounds," said a British officer. "An epoch in the history of cavalry," enthused the London *Times* history of the war; the Boer foot soldiers "availed nothing against the rushing speed and sustained impetus of the wave of horsemen. . . . This was the secret French had divined."

There was, however, less to this rushing speed and sustained impetus than met the eye. To begin with, the Boer defenders on these ridges had no machine guns. Also, in the scorching Southern Hemisphere summer the British horses charging across the bone-dry veldt raised such masses of dust that Boer marksmen couldn't see a thing, and most of them fired too high. Only after the great dust cloud slowly dissipated did the bewildered Boers realize that the cavalry had thundered past them almost entirely unscathed. Most important, the Boers had neglected to use something that was quite plentiful in South Africa and which, a decade and a half later, would prove the simplest and most effective defensive weapon of all time.

Between their two ridges they had not strung any barbed wire.

Press descriptions of the cavalry charge were so exhilarating that millions of Britons ignored the fact that it wasn't exactly a classic dash that overran terrified enemy soldiers; rather, the charge was *between* two groups of dust-blinded Boer troops who were unharmed by it. Not a single cavalryman's sword or lance was bloodied. But no matter: when word reached the London stock exchange, applause burst out and the price of South African gold mine shares shot up; at a murder trial in Liverpool, when the judge broke into the proceedings to announce that Kimberley had been relieved, jury and spectators erupted in cheers.

"The Cavalry—the *despised* Cavalry I should say—has saved the Empire," the petulant Haig wrote to a friend. "You must rub this fact into the wretched individuals who pretend to rule the Empire!" For both French and Haig, the relief of Kimberley made their reputations and immeasurably advanced their careers. Particularly impressed were Germany's military observers on the scene, who were watching the combat closely, suspecting that someday soon they might be fighting these very commanders. "The charge of French's cavalry division was one of the most remarkable phenomena of the war," a German general staff report said, adding that "its staggering success shows that, in future wars, the charge of great masses of cavalry will be by no means a hopeless undertaking even against troops armed with modern rifles."

Germans and British alike were thinking of this war on the African plains as a rehearsal for a larger conflict. But it was not just about cavalry where they missed the mark, for they failed to pay attention to the machine gun. This was still thought of as a weapon mainly useful against large frontal attacks by Africans, Arabs, or other "natives." Both Boers and British had a small number of Maxim guns but, mounted on 400-pound carriages with steel-rimmed wheels nearly five feet high, they proved difficult to maneuver and were seldom used.

Although the war was not yet over, everyone on the British side was glad to have a victory to celebrate, no one more so than the bellicose Rudyard Kipling. He was the figure every nation waging a war of aggression sorely needs: the civilian celebrity who honors the warriors. Everywhere he went in South Africa he was wildly cheered by soldiers who knew his stories that celebrated their derring-do and his poetry that made music of their slang. At one banquet honoring his friend Milner, he made an ironic toast to the Boer leader Kruger, "who has taught the British Empire its responsibilities, and the rest of the world its power, who has filled the seas with transports, and the earth with the tramp of armed men." For several years now, Kipling had been sprinkling his prose and poetry with anti-German barbs. He believed this war would do "untold good" for his beloved British tommies, preparing them for the inevitable clash with Germany. The Boer War, said a character in a story he wrote at the time, was "a first-class dress-parade for Armageddon."

3

A CLERGYMAN'S DAUGHTER

IN BRITAIN'S WEALTHY, aristocratic families, the first son would inherit the title and usually the land, while a younger brother often went into the army. One of those now fighting the Boers, for example, was Major Lord Edward Cecil, who had grown up in the palatial Hatfield House, on a historic estate where Queen Elizabeth I had spent part of her childhood. Along paved paths, Cecil's eccentric father exercised on a large tricycle, a young coachman trotting beside him, pushing him up hills and then jumping on behind for the downhill slopes. For the 21st birthday of an older brother, a special train had brought London visitors to a banquet at which they consumed 240 quarts of soup, 60 partridges, and 50 pheasants, served by white-gloved footmen in blue-and-silver uniforms. After private tutoring and Eton, Edward was commissioned as an officer in one of Britain's most fashionable regiments, the Grenadier Guards. In 1898, befitting someone of social prominence, he had been on hand to watch the Maxim guns in action at Omdurman.

As with many British officers, when he was ordered to South Africa the next year, Cecil's attractive young wife, Lady Violet, accompanied him. After he had joined his army unit far in the interior, she stayed on in Cape Town, the command center of the war effort. As loyal to the empire as someone like Charlotte Despard was rebellious, Violet busied herself working with the Red Cross, while frowning on the British women who arrived in Cape Town "without evening dress of any kind." A drawing of her from this time shows a stunning woman who could turn many a man's head: slender, full-lipped, with dark curly hair and doe eyes set wide apart. And turn one head she did, for here in the seaside city, beneath the spectacular flat-topped Table Mountain with its "tablecloth" of fog rolling off the top, she and Sir Alfred Milner were falling in love.

Decades later, after the world war that would upend both their lives, she combed through Milner's papers and her own, making sure that no intimate details were left to history. But we do know that their passion was mutual, intense, and, for many years, furtive. In Victorian high society, there was no question of Violet and Edward divorcing. And for Violet, who had left their four-year-old son in the care of nannies and her in-laws in England, to be known to have a romance on the side while Edward was under Boer fire would have meant betraying not just her husband but the British Empire itself. Nor could Milner afford the appearance of the slightest impropriety, since as high commissioner to South Africa, in a mansion with portraits of Queen Victoria on the walls, he was the moral embodiment of that same empire.

And there was yet a further reason why public scandal was unthinkable: Edward Cecil's father was prime minister of Britain.

In fact, it was he — Robert Arthur Talbot Gascoyne-Cecil, the Marquess of Salisbury, to give him his full name — who had suggested that Violet accompany his son to South Africa. Edward's father's position was known to everyone, including the Boers. When Edward's mother died of cancer, they allowed a courier under a white flag to pass through their battle lines surrounding Mafeking, a town where Edward and his contingent of British troops had become trapped under siege, with the news.

Violet was a woman of style, wit, and elegance. Her father was an admiral, and a brother would become a well-known general. As a teenager she had lived two years in Paris, studying music and art, meeting the impressionist painter Edgar Degas, taking in the opera and the Comédie Française, and often seeing a family friend — the French politician, journalist, and future wartime prime minister Georges Clemenceau. It would be good for Edward, his mother wrote to a family member, "to have a clever wife." Violet and Edward had known each other less than six months before they married, but to both it must have seemed the perfect match: to him, Violet appeared suitably well-born, cultured, and dazzlingly beautiful; as for her, she was marrying someone whose social position promised a glamorous life near the pinnacle of imperial power.

It took little time, however, for the first problems to appear. Violet was the life of any party; Edward had a melancholy streak. She cared passionately about the arts; the Cecils had little use for them. Attending three Anglican services each Sunday, the Cecil family was devoutly religious; Violet was an atheist. At her first Christmas at the intimidatingly gloomy Hatfield House, she recorded dryly that four clergymen had come to dinner, "one, so to speak, to each daughter-in-law." Above all, the recessive Edward never fully emerged from the shadow of his famous father.

Alfred Milner, on the other hand, was a commanding public figure, confident of his destiny. "I wish Milner had a less heroic fight to make," Violet wrote to one of her brothers from Cape Town, adding that the high commissioner "telegrams *all day,* up at seven and generally not to bed until 2. . . . He is well, alert and cheerful, absolutely fearless."

Violet's privileged position gave her opportunities denied to other officers' wives, such as being invited to the front to inspect a contingent of guardsmen, and being asked by Rhodes to stay at his spacious Cape Town estate, Groote Schuur. She accepted both invitations, sometimes caring for wounded soldiers recuperating under Rhodes's roof—officers only, of course. Rudyard Kipling and his wife, Carrie, were frequent guests at the mansion's polished mahogany dining table, and became fond of Violet. An eight-person band of Rhodes's servants played on the steps for half an hour every night after dinner, while, from the long, columned porch facing Table Mountain, a herd of zebras could often be seen roaming an adjoining forest. A pet lion cub lived on the grounds. "One day I know he will break his chain and I shall find him in my bedroom," Violet wrote. "What shall I do?"

The imperial lion of Cape Town, Milner, lived a short carriage ride away. Like him, she rejoiced in how the war had made visible "the solidarity of the British people, wherever they were, and of the native races who lived under our flag. From Australia, Canada, India, New Zealand and other parts of the Empire, offers came of help in men, money and material. The Empire had found itself." A continent away at Hatfield

House, her little son, George, was given a miniature cannon that could shoot peas at toy Boer soldiers.

Avidly interested in politics, Violet watched debates in the Cape Colony's all-white parliament from Milner's private box in the visitors' gallery. The two of them also found time to stroll in the gardens of Groote Schuur and go riding together several times a week on the beach or up the slopes of Lion's Head, a hill with one of Africa's most breathtaking views. She joined him at a New Year's Eve party on the last day of the old century and at many official dinners. A sparkling, high-spirited conversationalist, she could be counted on to charm whichever visiting general or cabinet minister she might be seated next to. For Milner, it was a coup to have the prime minister's daughter-in-law as his unofficial hostess at Government House, where dinner dress for his aides-de-camp was black tuxedos with lapels of scarlet silk.

She was even included in a carefully posed photograph of Milner and his staff. He is seated, with watch chain, vest, morning coat, striped trousers, and the frown of a leader with no patience for trifles. Violet, in a long skirt, her curls tucked under a hat, stands behind him, her hand resting comfortably on the back of his chair.

Her effect on him was noticeable to others. "Sir Alfred is very happy and full of jokes, and chaffs everyone. One sometimes can hardly believe he is the same man as [before her arrival] last July," a friend wrote after Violet had been in Cape Town for a year. Some assume that the couple became lovers in South Africa, but in their book about this love triangle, Hugh and Mirabel Cecil—he is a collateral descendant of Edward's—are convinced that this did not happen until later. All we know is that on the evening of June 18, 1900, Violet Cecil and Alfred Milner dined alone at Government House and something happened that made her forever after fondly mark this anniversary in her diary. "Was it a declaration of love?" the authors ask. "A more than usually tender expression of affection? We shall never know."

For all the Britons engaged in the fight against the persistent Boers, whether civilians like Milner or officers like John French and Douglas Haig, something made this war disturbingly different from the other colonial conflicts they had known. Many people in Britain thought their country shouldn't be fighting at all.

One, naturally, was French's own sister. When Charlotte Despard first addressed a peace rally at the town hall of Battersea, angry hecklers tried to shout her down. But this left-leaning community already felt at war with Britain's upper classes and appreciated underdogs, and anti-war sentiment was not long in growing. Soon there was even a street renamed after Piet Joubert, a Boer commander whose soldiers fought several battles with the troops of Charlotte's brother. (Joubert Street still exists, not far from Charlotte Despard Avenue.)

Despard's denunciations of the war did not dampen her affection for the man she still called Jack. She seemed to think of him mainly as the little boy she had helped raise, not as anyone responsible for "the wicked war of this Capitalistic government" which she fulminated against from lecture platforms. Sister and brother dismissed the other's political opinions as forgivable quirks.

Many of the war's opponents in England were on the political left and saw the Boers as innocent victims. Such dissidents were frequently attacked by angry mobs; one group of antiwar socialists escaped harm only by fleeing to the upper deck of a horse-drawn London omnibus, where they could stamp on the hands of their pursuers, who had to climb a steep ladder to reach them. The youthful David Lloyd George, a Welsh member of Parliament and skilled orator, was one of the war's boldest critics. When he tried to speak in Birmingham, a brass band played patriotic tunes outside the hall and a street vendor sold half-bricks, "three a penny, to throw at Lloyd George." In the uproar, one man was killed by a baton-wielding policeman, and 26 people were injured. Lloyd George escaped the mob by slipping out a side exit disguised in a badly fitting policeman's uniform. At an antiwar meeting in Bangor, Wales, less lucky, he was clubbed on the head and momentarily stunned. Citizens of his own parliamentary constituency burned him in effigy.

Milner often came in for special attack as the man who had almost single-handedly started the conflict in order to seize the Transvaal's gold. Many of the "pro-Boers," as they were called, linked the war to injustice at home, foreshadowing later peace movements: every shell fired at the Boers, Lloyd George thundered, carried away with it an old-age pension. Though they did not prevail against the war fever, the Boer War protests proved an embarrassing—and enduring—crack in the imperial façade. They raised a question that would resound even more contentiously in the next decade, in a war whose costs, human and financial, were astronomically higher: was loyalty to one's country in wartime the ultimate civic duty, or were there ideals that had a higher claim?

Nowhere was opposition to the war stronger than in Ireland, where the spectacle of English troops occupying Boer land evoked the island's own history. Many Irish saw the Boers as Davids ground down by the English Goliath and reaching for their slingshots. Irish sports teams took on the names of Boer generals. Much of the world also viewed the Boers as noble underdogs, and several thousand foreign volunteers made the long journey to South Africa to fight beside them. To British outrage, one of the largest contingents came from Germany.

Given Britain's overwhelming military might, defeating the Boers was only a matter of time, and more battle victories soon came, French and Haig getting credit for several of them. After the grand prize—the gold mines—fell under British control in mid-1900, various honors were handed out, with French awarded a knighthood for his relief of Kimberley. Another siege, the seven-month one at Mafeking that Edward Cecil had endured, was also broken at last. At Hatfield House, four-year-old George Cecil planted a tree, the Mafeking Oak, and lit an enormous bonfire to celebrate the liberation of his father at the other end of the world. When news of the relief of Mafeking reached Cape Town, however, Violet Cecil took to bed with a headache.

Several months later, after she had been reunited with Edward, she returned to England, having been away from young George for fourteen months. Her departure left Milner feeling "very low indeed," he wrote in his diary. "Still feeling profoundly depressed," he added the next day. Violet suggested to Edward that they return to South Africa, where the family could help build the new, British-dominated country envisioned by Milner, and she urged the same on her two brothers. But Edward, by now aware of his wife's feelings for Milner, refused. Instead, he remained in the army and applied, successfully, for service in Egypt.

Like the Cecils, other Britons naturally assumed the war was essentially over. After all, the Union Jack now fluttered over South Africa's towns and cities, garrisoned by hundreds of thousands of tall-helmeted troops who outnumbered the remaining Boer fighters more than ten to one. But, exasperatingly, Sir John French and Douglas Haig, like the rest of the British army, found themselves pursuing elusive, bearded warriors in civilian dress who refused to acknowledge that they had been beaten.

Mounted Boer guerrillas raided British outposts and railway lines, ambushed British troops, and then disappeared into South Africa's endless plains. A proper cavalry charge, like that at Kimberley, was no use if you couldn't even find the enemy. In response, the British decided to cut the roaming bands of Boer raiders off from their food and supplies. This meant that wherever the guerrillas attacked, British soldiers ruthlessly destroyed Boer farm buildings, crops in the field, and food stocks for dozens of miles in all directions. From some 30,000 farms, black pillars of smoke rose into the sky and flocks of vultures swooped down to feast on more than three million slaughtered sheep. French, Haig, and other commanders ordered troops to cut down fruit trees and poison wells, to use their bayonets to slash open bags of grain, and to torch families' furniture and possessions along with their homes. No one imagined that 15 years later this would be the face of war in Europe as well, or that armies would sow vastly wider swaths of deliberate devastation, or that it would be not only farms but centuries-old cities reduced to smoking rubble.

As British troops continued their ruthless farm-burning, what was to be done with the more than 100,000 civilians—almost all of them Boer women, children, or elderly, plus African farmhands—now left homeless? Here, too, came an eerie glimpse into the not-so-distant future, as the British opened a network of guarded concentration camps, row after row of white tents, often surrounded by barbed wire. The largest of these held more than 7,000 Boers, brought in by soldiers in high-wheeled covered wagons or railway flatcars, the grim-faced women clothed in long dresses and bonnets with neckcloths against the sun. Milner ordered all news of these camps censored from press telegrams leaving Cape Town, fearing that it would supply "the mad men at home with their most valuable material."

One day, however, at the beginning of 1901, a visitor arrived to see him bearing a letter of introduction from a member of her family in England whom he knew. He invited her to lunch at Government House, where Emily Hobhouse found herself the only woman among eight male guests, her surroundings indelibly stamped by the image of the British crown—on lamps, writing paper, and even the servants' livery. When Milner asked what brought her to South Africa, she said that she would rather discuss it with him in private. He politely promised her 15 minutes after lunch. She took more than an hour.

In that private session, Milner quickly realized that despite her impeccable dress and prominent family, his visitor was just the sort of person he referred to in confidential correspondence as a "screamer." Hobhouse was the founder of a group called the South African Women and Children's Distress Fund, and she had already joined Lloyd George and others in speaking against the war at public meetings in Britain. But that was not enough for her, and so she had come in person to distribute clothes, food, and blankets to war victims, including the very Boer women and children — as she had discovered to her horror on arriving in Cape Town — whom British troops were now herding into Milner's concentration camps.

Sharing a sofa in the Government House drawing room with his most unwelcome guest, Milner did not want to appear to have something to hide, and reluctantly he agreed to her request to visit the camps and distribute her relief supplies, which filled two railway freight cars. "He struck me as . . . clear-headed and narrow," Hobhouse wrote to her aunt in England. "Everyone says he has no heart, but I think I hit on the atrophied remains of one."

Blue-eyed and fair-haired, Emily Hobhouse was 40 years old. In most of the photographs we have of her, she looks at the camera with unusual directness for a woman of her time, as she must have looked at Milner that day. We can only guess at what opened her mind to the injustices of a world far wider than the one she had been raised in. Possibly it was the way her father, an Anglican minister, angrily broke up a romance she had with a local farmer's son whom he considered beneath her — a relative of his had worked as a maid in their house. Or possibly it was the time she spent, some years later, studying child labor conditions with the encouragement of a liberal-minded aunt and uncle, well-known reformers. It was only after the death of her widowed father, whom she cared for through many years of illness in his rural parish, that she felt free to go her own way in life. She traveled to Cape Town on a cheap steamboat, second class, and apparently expected to do no more than put her organization's relief supplies in the right hands. That was before she found out about the concentration camps and went toe-to-toe with Milner.

On a bright moonlit night, Hobhouse boarded a train in Cape Town for a 600-mile journey into the interior. At the first camp she visited, the heat was overwhelming, flies covered everything, and in the tents where destitute, traumatized families were living, the nearest thing to a chair was often a rolled-up blanket. In the chaos of being rounded up by British troops, she discovered, some of the Boer women had gotten separated from their children. The food was terrible, drinking water came from a polluted river, and up to a dozen people were crowded, sick and well together, into each tent. When it rained the tents flooded. While she was interviewing one woman, a puff adder slithered into the tent. As everyone else fled, Hobhouse, no more intimidated by a poisonous snake than by a viceroy, tried to kill it with her parasol. Elsewhere, she saw corpses being carried to mass graves. "My heart wept within me when I saw the misery." (When a final tally was made after the war, it would show that 27,927 Boers—almost all of them women and children—had died in the camps, more than twice the number of Boer soldiers killed in combat.)

As the days went by and she continued touring the archipelago of camps, the scenes of horror only multiplied: "a little six months' baby gasping its life out on its mother's knee," she wrote to her aunt. ". . . Next, a girl of 24 lay dying on a stretcher." Furious, she issued demands to startled British officers: for milk, for a boiler for the drinking water, for nurses, clothing, medicines, soap. None of the camp commandants were quite sure who this well-dressed, well-connected woman was, but they knew she was angry and they were not about to say no to her. "I rub as much salt into the sore places of their minds as I possibly can," she wrote, blaming the outrages she saw on "crass male ignorance, stupidity, helplessness and muddling." It was not only to her aunt that she sent letters. Thanks in part to a stream of them Hobhouse sent to English newspapers, the existence of the camps rapidly burgeoned into an international scandal. Antiwar members of Parliament denounced them in the House of Commons, leaving an alarmed Milner seeing this as the war's main public relations problem: "If we can get over the Concentration Camps," he told the colonial secretary, "none of the other attacks upon us alarm me."

To read the many letters Emily Hobhouse sent from South Africa is not only to see a war's hidden toll on civilians; it is to see, in this age that was so restrictive for women, one finding herself. Quickly Hob-

house discovered how to make her way around a country at war, learning from soldiers, for example, which valve you could open on the side
of a stopped steam locomotive if you wanted hot water for tea. She
slept in a missionary's home, railway cars, a stationmaster's quarters,
and in a tent in one of the concentration camps. Once she even spotted
a troop of Boer guerrillas galloping across the veldt. To be among so
many who were homeless, dying, or at war matched nothing in her up-
bringing, but beneath the outrage and compassion in what she wrote
home is a current of restrained exuberance as this country clergyman's
daughter fully encounters the world for the first time.

After some five months, Hobhouse decided she could accomplish
more by returning to England, and she booked a shared cabin on the
mail ship *Saxon* from Cape Town in May 1901. Once on board, she discovered, in grander accommodations, none other than her archenemy.
Sir Alfred Milner kept to himself, but Hobhouse, with typical determination, managed to corner him as he sat alone on the upper deck
and immediately launched into a tirade about the camps. He heard her
out, polite as always, then jarred her by indicating that he had received
some 60 reports on her activities. "What an army of informers to pay!"
she wrote later.

Milner was returning to London to dampen what he called the "pro-
Boer ravings" against the war that Hobhouse had helped stoke, and to
have a series of secret rendezvous with his mistress, Cécile Duval. He
would also meet with Violet Cecil many times, in public and in private; as the prime minister's daughter-in-law, she had become his eyes
and ears inside the British government. On arriving at London's Waterloo station, he was driven off in an open carriage to receive a peerage
from King Edward VII, whose mother, Queen Victoria, had died earlier in the year.

Hobhouse had her own agenda in England. She went to see the secretary of state for war and lectured him, too, about the camps — for
nearly two hours. She produced a three-penny pamphlet on the subject
and had it distributed to members of Parliament, then embarked on a
lecture tour, speaking at 26 public meetings and moving audiences to
tears. At Southport, hecklers shouted "Traitor!" In Plymouth, they
threw summer squash, and in Bristol, chairs, sticks, and stones. Hobhouse kept some of the missiles as souvenirs. Colonial Secretary Joseph
Chamberlain called her a "hysterical spinster."

After nearly half a year of political agitation in England, Hobhouse quietly set sail on a return mission to the camps. Despite her efforts to get her name removed from her ship's passenger list, Milner, himself now back in Cape Town, found out and had soldiers meet the ship when it dropped anchor, to bar her from coming ashore. The following day the local military commander appeared and demanded that she return to England. She refused. A few days later, she was ordered onto a troopship bound for home. She refused again. This time, soldiers picked her up and carried her. She struggled so vigorously, however, that the colonel in charge had to order her arms tied, "like a lunatic," he said. "Sir," Hobhouse replied, "the lunacy is on your side and with those whose commands you obey." Later, the colonel was asked, in this most unusual arrest of a lady, had there not been a danger that her petticoats might have become visible? "I had thought of that," the colonel replied, "and when she was picked up I threw a shawl over her feet." From the troopship, Hobhouse managed to send a last letter to Milner. "Your brutal orders have been carried out," it began, "and thus I hope you will be satisfied." Two officers' wives on board refused to speak to her for the entire voyage.

In putting the camps on the world's front pages, Emily Hobhouse had shown that she had the courage to defy public opinion in wartime, and in a far more destructive war, much closer to home—in which she would again encounter Alfred Milner—she would not hesitate to do so once more.

The guerrilla war in South Africa dragged on, to end only in mid-1902, when an uncompromising Lord Milner accepted the surrender of the last Boer fighters. Now established in a majestic, sprawling red-brick and half-timber mansion in the city of the gold mines, Johannesburg, he saw the next phase of his task as nothing less than "restarting the new colonies [the two conquered Boer republics] on a higher plane of civilization," and molding them and the two existing British colonies into one entity, which would soon take its honored place as part of the British Empire. It was taken for granted—on this alone the British and Boers had always agreed—that in the new South Africa the black majority would be powerless. "The white man must rule," Milner declared, "because he is elevated by many, many steps above the black man; steps which it will take the latter centuries to climb." More than anyone else, he was the architect of twentieth-century South Africa as a unitary state under white control.

If the new country taking shape was to be a shining example of British rule, it would need the best of rulers. And so Milner recruited from England a dozen or so bright, eager aides to help him run the unified territory. All his life, Milner's dynamism and air of high, noble purpose made him a magnet for ambitious and talented young men. Most of those he chose now were graduates, like him, of Oxford, and in their youthfulness they became known collectively as Milner's Kindergarten. His new personal secretary, for instance, was a profoundly upbeat Scot named John Buchan. Buchan found it thrilling to meet in a railway compartment a wounded hussar who had won Britain's highest military honor, the Victoria Cross, or to be sent on a mission to deliver some dispatches to his fellow Scot Douglas Haig. That occasion, incidentally, may be the only time that the laconic Haig is on record as making a joke. Buchan had taken a night train, overslept, and managed to get off just in time, throwing an army greatcoat over his pajamas. Taking in his dishabille, Haig told him not to worry: Brasenose—the Oxford college both had attended—had never been a dressy place.

Buchan had taken up his post before the final surrender, and referred to the Boer guerrilla commanders still on the loose as sporting adversaries. Echoing Newbolt's famous poem, he wrote that they "play the game like gentlemen, and must be treated as such." Once the game ended, he helped Milner with what he called the "fascinating and most hopeful work" of resettling Boer survivors on their ravaged farms. For this ever-cheerful man just three years out of college it was a heady experience to draft laws ("I must say I am rather proud of my Land Act"), supervise a hundred officials, and be responsible for shepherding around a visiting British cabinet minister ("not so big a man as Lord M"). Buchan shared a house with three other members of the Kindergarten. Dressed in black tie for dinner every night, they told Oxford jokes and the others teased the good-natured Buchan for almost buying himself a farm on the veldt that turned out to have no water supply. It was all excellent experience for a talented young person eager to rise in the world, and having Lord Milner as one's patron could ensure a faster climb. To be not yet 30 and helping run an entire country—could any other job better destine a man for still greater things ahead?

Milner and his Kindergarten got the gold mines working again at full tilt, directed the building of some 800 miles of new railway lines, established insane asylums and leper colonies, and drew up regulations covering everything from taxation to the "light corporal punishment" that could be applied to unruly workers. After eight years of war and peace, Milner finally returned to England in 1905.

Douglas Haig and Sir John French had already gone home, where they were amply rewarded for their military triumphs: Haig soon became the youngest major general in the British army, and French was promoted to lieutenant general. He presented Haig—to whom he still owed £2,000—with a gold flask inscribed, "A very small memento, my dear Douglas, of our long and tried friendship." The high-spirited French was delighted to collect honorary degrees from Oxford and Cambridge, but was most pleased by his next job: commanding Britain's 1st Army Corps at Aldershot, Hampshire. Aldershot was considered the home of the British army, and its commander traditionally had influence in military circles well beyond his rank. "I daresay that he is not the cleverest man," one official wrote of him, "but he is the most successful soldier we could find."

"This is certainly a great piece of luck for me," French wrote to a friend. "I think it ensures my participating in the next war."

4

HOLY WARRIORS

N O O N E K N E W when Britain's next war would come, but everyone knew with whom it would be. The mercurial Kaiser Wilhelm II was both expansion-minded and resentful that Germany had gotten into the race for African and Asian colonies so much later than Britain. All his life he looked back fondly at his youth as an officer in an elite regiment, and he loved all things military, seldom wearing civilian clothes except when hunting. His keen, anxious ambition echoed that of many other Germans, whose country had the largest population in Western Europe, but not yet, it seemed, proportional prestige in the world. Since the end of the 1890s, Germany had been engaged in a polite but determined naval arms race with Britain, while the British worked to maintain their strong advantage in the heavily armored battleships and faster battle cruisers that had allowed the Royal Navy to so long dominate the world's oceans. The contest between the two nations to mobilize shipyards, foundries, and machine tools to build these fearsome vessels gave a hint of something new in the military trade: warfare that might be decided not by bravery, dash, and generalship, but by industrial might.

Not everyone saw it that way, however. Moving up the career ladder in 1907 to the influential army post of inspector general, Sir John French had no doubt what one of his top priorities was: the cavalry.

He found much sympathy from King Edward VII, whom he met frequently at dinners, receptions, and military ceremonies, and with whom he corresponded about cavalry matters. Disturbing anti-cavalry voices, he soon discovered, were to be heard all around him, such as that of a British military observer at the Russo-Japanese War of 1904–1905, who reported that the only thing cavalrymen could do when faced with entrenched machine guns was to cook for the infantry. French fought back against such heretics, who ignored the example of his glorious charge at Kimberley. The most outrageous move of the naysayers was to persuade the army high command to abandon the lance as a cavalry weapon. If the lance went, could the next casualty, heaven forbid, be the sword? For several years French fought a fierce bureaucratic battle, through memos, whispers in the King's ear, articles in the press, and the recruitment of Boer War heroes as behind-the-scenes lobbyists. Finally, in 1909, he won, and the lance was officially restored to the cavalry's arsenal.

In his leisure time, the diminutive general could be seen furtively squiring around London various elegant women married to other men. He frequently crossed the English Channel on military business; when sent to observe German army maneuvers, he got on well with the Kaiser, who awarded him the Order of the Red Eagle. To French, however, peacetime felt like waiting. "In the campaigns I've been in during my life," he once wrote, "I've never felt satisfied at the end of any and have looked forward to the next."

At the Cavalry Club on Piccadilly, he often dined with his old friend Douglas Haig. Both men lived in a world of comfortable certainties: of ranks of cavalry trotting smartly on parade with boots polished to a high gloss, of the nobility of Britain's imperial mission, of their own guaranteed steady rise through the army's senior ranks. Haig, naturally, was a comrade-in-arms in the great battle to restore the lance, testifying before a high-level commission, "I am thoroughly satisfied from what I have seen in South Africa that the necessity of training cavalry to charge is as great as it was in the days of Napoleon." In print, Haig attacked a skeptic who dared question the usefulness of a cavalry charge in the age of the machine gun and the repeating rifle. It was as strong a tactic as ever, Haig was certain, since the "moral factor of an apparently irresistible force, coming on at highest speed . . . affects the nerves and aim of the . . . rifleman." The horse, after all, had been central to warfare since the earliest recorded history, a position of dominance unshaken by every advance in weaponry from the crossbow to breech-loading, rapid-firing artillery. Why should it not remain central in the next war?

Haig played polo for his old regiment's team, befriended wealthy and influential people like the banker and racehorse breeder Leopold de Rothschild, and served as aide-de-camp to King Edward VII, who in due course would give him a knighthood. He also formed a lasting bond with someone of his own generation, the Prince of Wales—the future King George V, who had spent more than a decade of his youth in the Royal Navy and took a great interest in military matters. Even though Britain's was a constitutional monarch with little direct power, his voice carried weight in the making of key military appointments, so being in royal favor could be of crucial help to an officer's career. Well aware of this, Haig never failed to note in his diary, after dinners and banquets, whenever he sat next to, or across from, the King. In 1905, when he was on leave, Edward invited him to Windsor Castle the week of the Ascot races, and Haig found himself playing golf with the Honorable Dorothy Maud Vivian, a lady in waiting to Queen Alexandra. He proposed to the well-placed Dorothy within 48 hours. "I have often made up my mind on more important problems than that of my own marriage in much less time," he would later say. The couple were married in the private chapel of Buckingham Palace, a privilege apparently without precedent for someone not a member of the royal family.

Haig then returned to his current post as inspector general of cavalry in India. As he traveled about the subcontinent in a special railway car, every crease and campaign ribbon in place on his uniform, he established a new cavalry school and pushed the Indian mounted regiments through a rigorous training schedule, including mock combat designed to mimic the great cavalry battle that, military theorists agreed, would open the next war. In his 1907 book, *Cavalry Studies,* Haig declared that "the rôle of Cavalry on the battlefield will always go on increasing," thanks, in part, to "the introduction of the small bore rifle, the bullet from which has little stopping power against a horse."

Except in the distant, always troubled Balkans, Europe had been enjoying nearly half a century of peace. But there were disturbing undercurrents, even beyond the escalating naval arms race. Most ominous was the existence of a pair of rival blocs, tightly tied together by mutual security treaties, which virtually guaranteed that, should an armed clash break out between two countries, others would be sucked in as well.

Fifty percent larger in land area than today, Germany was the continent's economic powerhouse and was closely allied with the sprawling Austro-Hungarian Empire, where a German-speaking elite in Vienna dominated an array of restless ethnic groups. France, where nationalists still smoldered over the mortifying loss to Germany of the border provinces of Alsace and Lorraine in the Franco-Prussian War of 1870–1871, had made a treaty with the vast, unstable empire of Tsar Nicholas II. The Franco-Russian alliance inflamed German paranoia, since both countries bordered Germany, promising that the next war would be a two-front affair. Moreover, Russia's economy was expanding rapidly and its railway network, critical for moving troops to the front, was the fastest-growing in the world. German generals and politicians feared its population—more than twice Germany's—and its huge army, which, completely mobilized, could reach an intimidating six and a half million troops. For more than a decade, some German generals had quietly talked of launching a war against Russia before its power grew too great.

Periodically, Germany needled its rival to the west, France. In 1904, as the last colonial spoils in Africa were being divided up, France made a secret treaty with Spain sharing Morocco between them; the following year, the German Kaiser visited the territory, and from his yacht declared his support for Moroccan independence. It took a months-long international conference of colonial powers to calm the roiled waters.

No formal alliances bound Britain, but a looser set of understandings left no doubt that if the country did join hostilities, it would be on the side of France, and therefore of Russia too. The British government on no account wanted the Germans in control of the continental side of the English Channel, the crucial narrow-necked funnel through which ships going to or from London and many other English ports passed. For this reason Sir John French and other high military officials regularly talked with their counterparts in France about plans for what he believed was the "eventual certainty" of war with Germany. Then, at last, great cavalry charges would strike fear into the German army, while the Royal Navy's powerful battleships pounded German vessels and ports to smithereens.

While French, Haig, and other officers waited for the next conflict to start overseas, another war seemed to be breaking out on the very streets of London. And those waging it were, of all people, women.

Take, for example, the crowd that surged into Parliament Square on a cold, rainy February 13, 1907. To the tune of "John Brown's Body," some 400 women, marching four abreast, lustily sang:

> Rise up women! For the fight is hard and long,
> Rise in thousands, singing loud a battle song. . . .

Leading the march was none other than French's sister. "I asked myself," Charlotte Despard wrote this year, "'Can this be the beginning? Is this indeed a part of that revolutionary movement for which all my life long I have been waiting?'"

The cause was votes for women, and into it, with the thrill of a new love affair, Despard poured all her energy. To many horrified Englishmen, the new movement did indeed seem revolutionary. Foreigners and the lower classes could always be expected to cause trouble, but *women?* A double line of policemen was waiting in front of the Parliament buildings while to one side the horses of "London's Cossacks," as the mounted police were known, neighed impatiently.

On similar occasions in recent months, the police had been reluctant to arrest the sister of a famous war hero, and so today Despard had taken the precaution of not wearing her trademark lace mantilla. Instead she donned a "motoring hat," tied on with a headscarf, meant for a woman to wear in an open automobile. As she strode down the wet pavement her face was further disguised by a long veil. When the women, brandishing umbrellas, came up against the phalanx of police, a younger marcher cried out in alarm, seeing Despard squeezed between officers on horseback. "I'm quite safe," Despard yelled back. "I love horses!" To intimidate the crowd, the policemen made their mounts rear. "The women began to fight like tigers and they received and inflicted many bruises . . . ," reported one newspaper. "A dense mass of people swayed and heaved." Some younger women tried to surround Despard protectively, but she angrily waved them off. Amid the shouts of women knocked down and the clatter of horses' hooves on the pavement, a constable grabbed at Despard, ripping off her coat sleeve. Finally, much to her satisfaction, she was arrested, and, along with more than two dozen other women, sentenced to jail. As the leader of the march, she received a longer term than most of the others: 21 days in solitary confinement.

Two days later, her brother was at the Savoy Hotel to chair the officers' banquet that took place each year on the anniversary of the Kimberley cavalry charge—and he was not happy. "If she insists on joining in with these people she must expect it," Sir John told the press. "We have tried all we could to keep her from mixing up with these foolish women. . . . I wish she wouldn't do these things, but I can't prevent her."

Progressive Britons had long called for women's suffrage, but only in the new century had the cause caught fire. Activists were eager to have the well-known Despard in their camp, and the previous year she had been recruited by a new organization, the Women's Social and Political Union, or WSPU, and began traveling the country giving speeches on its behalf. She called for equality for women not just at the ballot box but in the workplace and in pensions. She even demanded wages for housework. When working-class women finally flooded the country's polling booths, Despard believed, the socialist state she had long dreamed of would burst into being. And just as soldiers form strong bonds in war, so in this new kind of battle Despard felt an electric excitement and solidarity. "I had sought and found comradeship of some sort with men," she wrote. "I had marched with great processions of the unemployed. . . . [But] amongst all these experiences, I had not found what I met on the threshold of this young, vigorous Union of Hearts."

The "young, vigorous Union" she had joined was, however, less of a mass movement than it appeared, for the Women's Social and Political Union was by no means democratically controlled by its thousands of members; rather, the organization was run by one family, the formidable Pankhursts. They brought to their cause flamboyance, fervor, and daring when it came to tactics, and a knack for infuriating friends as well as enemies, all of it unmatched in British politics in this era—indeed, in politics almost anywhere.

Emmeline Pankhurst had been widowed at 40, when her older, lawyer husband died suddenly, leaving her with debts to pay off and four children under the age of 18. She accepted money from friends, and took a job as registrar of births and deaths in a working-class district of Manchester. The work proved eye-opening, as it included tabulating the many illegitimate births to poor women raped or seduced by older male relatives. As a member of the Manchester school board, she was outraged to discover that teachers were paid more if they were male. "I began to think about the vote in women's hands," she wrote, "not only as a right but as a desperate necessity."

When the Boer War broke out, she and her children were outspoken in condemning Britain as the aggressor. As a result, her son Harry, whose health was fragile (he would die of polio at 20), was attacked after school and knocked unconscious. A schoolmate flung a book in the face of her youngest daughter, Adela, and a fellow student of another daughter, Sylvia, threatened to break the windows of their house. Already, the Pankhursts were anything but armchair radicals.

When, a few years later, Emmeline formed the Women's Social and Political Union, its membership was limited to women, and its leadership, it seemed, to Pankhursts. Emmeline and her three daughters, for example, were four-fifths of the WSPU's five-woman speakers' bureau. They militantly carried the gospel of votes for women, *now,* to debating societies, labor unions, and mass demonstrations. When Charlotte Despard was arrested in that 1907 march on Parliament, so were Emmeline and her daughters Christabel and Sylvia.

Approaching 50, Emmeline Pankhurst moved into the public eye as a powerful speaker who seemed made for the stage. The voice with which she rallied crowds, one friend remembered, was "like a stringed instrument in the hand of a great artist . . . from which sprang all the scorn, all the wrath, all the tenderness in the world." Her words seemed to come straight from her heart, for she never spoke from notes. An ethereal, delicate beauty that can be seen in photographs of her as a young woman had now turned into a steely middle-aged majesty. Her authoritative presence was somehow only emphasized by her modest, almost fragile-looking stature and impeccable dress. Also indisputably feminine, in traditional terms, was her favorite hobby, sewing. In another ladylike touch, she disliked saying how old she was—and on at least one occasion refused to do so in court. While in the dock at one trial, she held a bouquet of flowers.

Christabel Pankhurst, the oldest daughter and her mother's favorite, also appeared the picture of elegance; her lithe figure and dreamy, silent-film star's good looks surely helped her win headlines. "She was slender, young, with the flawless colouring of a briar rose," wrote the middle daughter, Sylvia, "and an easy grace cultivated by her enthusiastic practice of the dance." Like her mother, Christabel usually wore one of the huge women's hats of the period, with a precarious array of feathers, ruffles, lace, and artificial flowers that was so top-heavy the whole assemblage often had to be anchored in place with a ribbon tied under the chin—all the more necessary if you were expecting to be rudely dragged off to a paddy wagon. As the WSPU's chief tactician, she plotted such actions as driving a furniture mover's truck to the entrance of the House of Commons and then flinging open its doors so that some two dozen women could burst forth and rush the building. At Christabel's instigation, women infiltrated all-male meetings of the ruling Liberal Party: they hid underneath the speakers' platform, rappelled down from skylights, climbed through windows, always shouting "Votes for women!" The Pankhurst family had declared war, and a new style of battle was born—radically different from the war many Britons thought their country should be preparing for, with Germany.

In contrast to her older sister, Sylvia Pankhurst, with her prominent nose, slightly bulging cheeks, and heavily lidded eyes, was not one to fit conventional images of beauty. Heedless of her appearance, she paid no attention to fashion and never wore makeup. "She was one of those people whom it was impossible to keep tidy; her hair was always tumbling down," remembered a colleague. "One day I . . . noticed that she had her blouse on inside out. I got her behind some packing cases and helped her change it." Sylvia wrote prolifically and also studied art in both England and Italy, putting her skills to work designing suffrage posters, banners, calendars, and a medal for women who had gone to prison for the cause. Ultimately she would spend more time behind bars than anyone else in this oft-arrested family.

When they weren't in jail, the Pankhursts and their followers sometimes appeared at demonstrations in prison uniforms—surprisingly demure long skirts, white caps, and white aprons. On other occasions they wore the WSPU colors: white dresses decorated with green and purple, meant to signify, respectively, purity, hope, and dignity. On an American speaking tour, Emmeline displayed the colors by wearing a necklace of pearls, emeralds, and amethysts.

In the long run, larger and more moderate suffrage groups would be more responsible for actually winning women the vote. But the Pankhursts contemptuously dismissed all other activists, and, in the stormy decade before 1914, they and their confrontational politics edged the others out of the spotlight. Although it was the right-wing *Daily Mail* that scoffingly coined the term "suffragette," Pankhurst followers proudly adopted it as their own. "We are soldiers engaged in a holy war," Emmeline declared after one arrest, "and we mean to go on until victory is won."

This holy war, however, appeared to threaten Britain as a military power. Not only had Emmeline Pankhurst been a vocal opponent of the Boer War, but she now implied that *all* war was the mere byproduct of male stupidity. "We leave that to the enemy," she declared to a mass meeting at the Royal Albert Hall. "We leave that to the men in their warfare. It is not the method of women." If women won the vote and followed her lead, would the country still be able to fight its wars?

Many feared it would not be. Among them was Rudyard Kipling, now living in a majestic sandstone house bristling with chimneys in the Sussex countryside, who often spoke of the inevitable "Great War" to come. Member of an anti-suffrage league, he was convinced that the suffragettes were dangerously weakening the empire's martial spirit. "I wish that a sensible suffragette (if there be one)," he wrote to a friend, "could hear how much and how confidently the Germans count on the 'feminism' of England. . . . And confidence is an ill weapon to bestow on a possible enemy."

Women had no role in politics, he firmly believed:

And Man knows it! Knows, moreover, that the Woman that God gave him
Must command but may not govern—shall enthrall but not enslave him.

For someone whose writing was so widely loved, the poet and novelist was a man of many dislikes. Among them were Germans, democracy, taxes, labor unions, Irish and Indian nationalists, socialists, and, near the top of the list, the women he called "suffragines." Women were fated for the gentle role of wives and mothers to Britain's fighting men; enfranchising them would only open the way to further horrors, Kipling feared, such as women becoming ministers and bishops. When family and guests played charades, the Kiplings' young son, John, would mockingly pantomime a "suffragine."

A friend once described Kipling as "a short, wiry, alert man with steely blue eyes peering through his spectacles under bushy eyebrows and bald head, firm chin poked forward. His glasses were part of him, as headlights are part of a car." Central to the writer's life were his beloved children, John, Elsie, and the eldest, Josephine, for whom he began writing the *Just So Stories,* which would become a part of so many British and American childhoods. Along with his unmatched ability to imagine himself into the mind of a child went a love for everything military: one family photo shows a grinning four-year-old John Kipling shouldering a rifle taller than he is.

Kipling played with his children endlessly; he and his American wife, Carrie, were indulgent, hands-on parents, quite different from the conventional image of emotionally distant upper-class Edwardians, content to put all child care in the hands of a nanny. His love for his children was all the greater because of the devastating impact of losing the six-year-old Josephine to pneumonia on the eve of the Boer War. The affectionate letters he wrote to John and Elsie are sprinkled with spontaneous poems and limericks, with even parental admonitions couched gently: a drawing of a toothbrush and set of teeth to remind John to brush his, and some friendly joshing of John's erratic spelling: "Howe wood yu lick it if I rote you a leter al ful of misspeld wurds?" When John worried that his nearsightedness, apparently inherited from his father, might prevent the naval career he dreamed of, Kipling wrote, "Don't you bother too much about your eyes. They will come all right."

Among the visitors who strolled through Kipling's rose garden was Alfred, Lord Milner, whom the poet declared he admired more than anyone on earth. The two men took turns spending Queen Victoria's birthday, an occasion for fireworks and bonfires called Empire Day, in each other's houses.

After his return home in 1905, feeling his labors in South Africa underappreciated, Milner shunned politics, a brooding lion in exile. He put his financial skills to work on the boards of a mining company and several banks, all of which brought him a good income, but for a man who had started a war and run a country, the business world was a comedown. At home and abroad he continued to write and speak about the great cause of "imperial unity" among Britain, her many colonies, and her grown-up former colonies, like Australia, which were now called dominions. The future French leader Georges Clemenceau described the British as *un peuple planétaire,* but what would they do, he joked, if another Lord Milner appeared who wanted to control yet another continent, and there weren't any left?

Sharing Milner's enthusiasm for imperial unity were the former members of his South African Kindergarten of young aides, most of whom had returned to England and were fast rising in the world. His ambitious former private secretary John Buchan, for instance, although failing in attempts to gain a high post in the colonial service in Egypt or a seat in Parliament, began to find considerable success as a journalist and novelist. The empire needed praise-singers as well as civil servants, and the genial Buchan was ideally suited for that role. In his 1906 novel *A Lodge in the Wilderness,* a celebration of British rule in Africa, one character is modeled on Milner, and another defines imperialism in distinctly Milneresque terms: "It is a spirit, an attitude of mind, an unconquerable hope. . . . It is a sense of the destiny of England."

England's destiny, however, seemed to many to be under threat from a fast-rising Germany. Milner and Kipling were vigorous advocates of strengthening Britain's volunteer professional army with conscription. No longer, they felt, could the country rely for protection primarily on having the world's mightiest navy. "Do ye wait for the spattered shrapnel ere ye learn how a gun is laid?" Kipling asked in one poem. It chafed at both men that young Britons, unlike their counterparts in France, Germany, and Russia, were not required to undergo army service. They worried particularly about a Germany that could easily mobilize millions of well-trained reservists.

Milner's view of the world changed not at all in these years leading up to 1914, but this was not true of his nemesis from Boer War days, Emily Hobhouse. After that war ended, she returned to South Africa for several years to work helping Boer women rebuild their shattered lives. During the war she had paid scant attention to the territory's black and brown majority, but now her outlook was broadening. She met a young lawyer named Mohandas Gandhi, who was battling for the rights of Indians in South Africa, and was profoundly impressed by his philosophy of nonviolence. When a monument to the concentration camp victims was unveiled, she sent a message to be read at the occasion, gently warning the assembled Boer leadership against "withholding from others in your control, the very liberties and rights which you have valued . . . for yourselves." Coming home to Britain in 1908, she developed into an ardent socialist and campaigner for suffrage, both for women and for the millions of British men kept from voting by property qualifications.

A woman who had been in Milner's life in a different way, his mistress Cécile Duval, evidently had had enough of waiting. She married and moved to Canada. Milner showed momentary interest in one or two other women, but in the end no one took the place in his heart of Violet Cecil. With the mores of the time making divorce out of the question, she made one last attempt to breathe life into her marriage, moving to Egypt, where Edward was now stationed. But after the excitement of Milner's orbit in wartime Cape Town, she found colonial society in Cairo dry and constricted. Deeply ambitious, in an age in which a woman's aspirations had to be expressed through her husband, Violet had expected that Edward would leave the army and go into politics. Wasn't that the proper role for a former prime minister's son? In such circumstances, with her charm and gift for conversation, she would certainly have thrived. Yet Edward was determined to remain in Egypt, on what to her was the distant periphery of all that mattered. After some months, she returned to England. Their marriage, Edward's sister-in-law wrote years later, had been "a fatal mistake . . . for never were two people more hopelessly unsuited."

In 1906, she settled in a stone manor house southeast of London that dated from 1635, named Great Wigsell, and the following year Milner found an elegant country home not far away. She helped him decorate his house, and they exchanged many visits, sometimes with others, often alone. Friends surely understood, and with Milner no longer in government and Violet's father-in-law now dead, they were out of the public eye and there was no more danger of scandal.

Whatever the frustrations of not being able to marry the man she loved, Violet had her children—her son George now had a younger sister. They lived only a short carriage ride from the Kiplings, which meant that George often played with John Kipling. And when "Uncle

Alfred" Milner came to visit Great Wigsell, or they drove to his house, the talk would often be of the farther reaches of empire. Perhaps Violet felt badly about having left George behind for so long when she went to South Africa; in any event she was now closely attached to him, and when he went off to boarding school at age 14, she wrote to him as often as twice a day. Her time in South Africa remained so vivid to her that on the anniversaries of Boer War battles, she headed her letters with their names.

Growing up on the stories of that victorious war, George decided early on an army career, entering the Royal Military College at Sandhurst, the British West Point, where "gentleman cadets" whose families could pay their tuition were trained to become infantry or cavalry officers. After visiting Sandhurst and taking George out to dinner, Kipling reported to Violet, as one parent to another, that her son "looks well, a bit thinner, but more in possession of his body. . . . Of course one must always trouble about them but as far as one can see he is happy and all is well." Many of the army's top generals—Douglas Haig among them—had graduated from Sandhurst, and it would be a fine item for a new army officer to have on his résumé as he awaited the next war.

The war at home was the one Charlotte Despard saw herself fighting, and when she emerged in 1907 from her 21 days in Holloway Prison, an imposing stone structure with turrets and crenelated ramparts, there was no doubt in the public's mind that this venerable figure, now in her sixties, was on the front line of the struggle for women's suffrage. Her alliance with the Pankhurst family, however, would prove short-lived.

Suffragettes had already begun to disagree vociferously over how much they should consider themselves part of a larger left-wing movement. Despard was a supporter of the Independent Labour Party, or ILP, the leading party on the British left and an ancestor of today's Labour Party, which she saw as socialism's best hope. Sylvia Pankhurst privately agreed, but in public remained loyal to her mother and older sister—who no longer had any use for a party that did not put votes for women at the top of its agenda in the manner they demanded. Emmeline Pankhurst and Despard clashed in public at an ILP meeting, after which Emmeline and her daughter Christabel resigned from the party, and declared that the Women's Social and Political Union would not support parliamentary candidates—all male, of course—of any party.

Despard was not about to let someone else decide such matters for her, and she and other WSPU members angrily protested that the Pankhursts' sudden change of policy violated the WSPU constitution. To this Emmeline replied, "I shall tear up the constitution." A revolutionary movement, she added, had no time for formal niceties; decisions had to be made on the spot.

The WSPU promptly split, Sylvia staying, however uneasily, with her mother and sister, while Despard in September 1907 gathered dissidents at her house to form a rival group, the Women's Freedom League. By the following year, it would have 53 branches across the country. Although somewhat more democratically run, the organization's telegraph address was simply "Despard, London."

Meanwhile, the Pankhursts went their own way. The same boldness and intransigence that made them willing to endure arrest and prison also meant that Emmeline and Christabel brooked no opposition. Charlotte Despard would be only the first of the people they would leave scattered behind them in what they saw as a life and death struggle for the vote. Of their allies in this first rift, they would lose many in the years ahead. And eventually, under the pressure of war, the most bitter and permanent rupture of all would take place within the Pankhurst family.

5

BOY MINER

LONG AFTER THE BOY became a man, the day remained seared into his memory.

Young Jamie's stepfather was out of work. A younger brother lay ill at home, with a fever that would soon prove fatal. His mother was nine months pregnant. The entire family, with four children, lived in a single room in a packed Glasgow slum. Christmas, just passed, had been spare and grim, for ten-year-old Jamie was the family's sole source of income, working twelve and a half hours a day, seven days a week, delivering bread for a baker. Twice during the week after Christmas, helping care for his sick brother while his stepfather was away job hunting, he had been fifteen minutes late for work. On a rainy weekend, he arrived at the bakery to start another workday.

"When I reached the shop I was drenched to the skin, barefooted and hungry. There had not been a crust of bread in the house that morning. But [it] was pay-day." He was told that his employer wanted to see him in his flat above the bakery. A servant then asked him to wait while the baker's family finished their morning prayers. "At length the girl opened the door. . . . Round a great mahogany table sat members of the family, with the father at the top. . . . The table was loaded with dainties. My master looked at me over his glasses . . . 'Boy . . . my customers leave me if they are kept waiting for their hot breakfast rolls. I therefore dismiss you, and, to make you more careful in the future, I have decided to fine you a week's wages." Jamie wandered the Glasgow streets for hours before he could bring himself to go home and give his mother the news. "That night the baby was born, and the sun rose . . . over a home in which there was neither fire nor food."

The next job he found was in a coal mine.

For James Keir Hardie—who stopped using his first name as he grew older—the imprint of those early experiences would be stamped upon his life as if with a red-hot brand. Hardie's intensely Christian rage against the dirt-floor poverty he knew firsthand would never flag. When elected to the House of Commons, he would be the only member who spent nights helping dole out food at a soup kitchen to those who had none. Even as an MP, he rushed to the scene of a Scottish mining disaster, down the shaft, into the tunnel, to see what could be done for the trapped men, for he knew what it was like to see fellow miners killed. In portraits, his thick beard is dark red when he is young, white as a shroud when, in his fifties, he saw the war he had long feared shatter his dreams. His hauntingly sad, heavy-browed eyes seem to stare out at you so piercingly from any photo that they might as well be staring beyond Hardie's own life, into an entire century of world wars and crushed hopes.

Hardie had been born out of wedlock, as had his mother, a farm servant near Glasgow; several years after his birth she moved into the grimy industrial city, notorious for its slums crowded up against shipyards, locomotive works, and factories. There she married a ship's carpenter. Hardie had no formal schooling and the family could not afford books, so he read discarded newspapers he picked up off the street or the pages of books propped open in bookstore windows. At eight he went to work as a messenger boy. After that came a job as a riveter's assistant in a shipyard, where he worked on a narrow platform slung over a ship's side; once a boy working next to him slipped off and fell to his death.

After losing his bakery job, he labored in a coal mine for eleven and a half hours, six days a week—which meant that in winter he saw no daylight except on Sunday, when the workday was four hours. Before long he was driving one of the "pit ponies," which hauled coal on rails underground. "We were great friends, and drank cold tea from the same flask." One day, he and the pony had to be rescued after part of the mineshaft caved in; Hardie always remembered the splintering creak of the wooden supports collapsing, the thunder of falling earth, the sobs of panicked miners. When he was older he became a hewer, digging and shoveling coal from the advancing end of a mine tunnel in the dim light of a lamp on his helmet, often standing ankle-deep in water. By 21, he had spent more than half his life in the mines.

When he became an organizer for the miners' union, the role seemed to him fully of a piece with his work as a lay preacher in the Evangelical Union, a working-class Protestant sect that was one of the "dissenting," or non-Anglican, churches from which so many English and Scottish radicals sprang. "The rich and comfortable classes have annexed Jesus and perverted His Gospel," Hardie declared. "And yet He belongs to us." Hardie rallied miners to press for better pay and safer conditions, and for this he and two of his brothers were fired. An elevator in which they were descending underground was recalled to the surface by the mine manager, who told them, "We'll hae nae damned Hardies in this pit."

Soon he became secretary of the Scottish Miners' Federation, began to think of himself a socialist, and found that he was as persuasive with his pen as with his voice. Although he turned 30 before he left Scotland for the first time, his horizons rapidly broadened beyond the mines and the Glasgow slums. A founder of the Independent Labour Party in 1893, he became the editor of its paper, the *Labour Leader,* whose office windows were smashed by an angry crowd when Hardie denounced the Boer War as an imperialist land grab. More jeering mobs dogged his steps as he toured the country speaking against the war, sometimes from a lecture platform, sometimes from the back of a wagon in a muddy field.

For congresses of the Second International, Hardie began crossing the English Channel. For him, as for many other delegates, socialism was less a matter of workers owning the means of production—although he firmly believed in that—than a moral crusade for a society that put workers before profits, public good before private wealth, and, above all, peace before war. Like the spirit of the times, it was an optimistic creed. Sylvia Pankhurst once wrote of "a longing, profound and constant, for a Golden Age when plenty and joy should be the gift of all." And at this point in history, before the bloody battlefields of 1914–1918, the Golden Age seemed within reach. If journeys that once took weeks had shrunk to hours through the miracle of steam power, why could not all injustice be eradicated by the miracle of socialism? If determined campaigners a half century earlier had managed to abolish British Empire slavery, why not abolish poverty too? Socialism, said Jean Jaurès of France, should allow people, however they chose, to "walk and sing and meditate under the sky." Hardie became fast friends with the plump, unkempt Jaurès, leader of the French socialist party, with whom he shared a dread of a future war in Europe that could set working people against each other.

The final goals of the socialist revolution to come might be hazy, but the world's wrongs were pressingly real, and Hardie's passion for justice knew no national boundaries. He barnstormed the United States for two months in one of the presidential campaigns of his socialist friend Eugene V. Debs, speaking at 44 rallies and meetings, including one at a mining camp in Colorado. Visiting India, he spoke out forcefully for self-government and refused to enter any building if Indian friends with him were barred. After the Boer War, he traveled to South Africa to demand political rights and decent farmland for the territory's voteless majority, declaring that to allow no Africans to sit in the new country's legislature was like inscribing, above the portals of the British Empire, "Abandon hope all ye who enter here." His hotel was stoned, and a meeting he addressed in Johannesburg was broken up by a white mob.

When Hardie arrived to take a seat in Parliament for the first time, a hired trumpeter played the tune of the socialist anthem, "The Internationale":

> Arise ye workers from your slumbers,
> Arise ye prisoners of want . . .

Instead of the usual ceremonial garb of parliamentarians — starched wing collar, black tailcoat, and black silk top hat — he wore Scottish tweed and a Sherlock Holmes–style deerstalker cap. Once, entering the House of Commons, he was stopped by a policeman who did not recognize him but knew the building's roof was under repair. "Are you working here, mate?" he asked.

"Yes," Hardie replied.

"On the roof?" asked the policeman.

"No," said Hardie. "On the floor."

On that floor, Hardie voted against the usual extravagant appropriations for the royal family. He rose, outraged, to protest when MPs spent hours making speeches celebrating a royal birth while ignoring the 251 Welsh miners killed in an accident the same day. After fiercely criticizing an exchange of visits between King Edward VII and Tsar Nicholas II — whose absolute rule was the epitome of tyranny for the European left — he was not asked to the King's annual summer garden party, to which the entire House of Commons was routinely invited.

Hardie's wife, Lillie, cared for and made all the clothes for their four children — one of whom died in childhood — remaining in Scotland when for parliamentary sessions he went to London. In the capital he lived frugally in a one-room apartment, decorated with busts of Walt Whitman and Robert Burns and a photograph of Karl Marx. At one point he was forced to auction off his beloved library to keep the *Labour Leader* publishing. When he was stricken with appendicitis, family and friends had to raise funds for his operation and convalescence. He used the same pocket watch he had had as a boy in the mines, which bore the teeth marks of his pit pony, and he often stopped in the street to talk to horses. In Parliament, Hardie never ceased demanding support for those who had little, whether this meant free meals for schoolchildren, help for the poor who were suffering through a winter so bitter that the Thames froze over, or better pay and conditions for the waiters and messengers at the House of Commons itself. He worked hard to ensure that the beneficiaries of workmen's compensation insurance included illegitimate children.

Although his own marriage was quite traditional, the breadth of Hardie's sense of justice made him, far more than most male radicals, an ardent backer of votes for women. For years he had been a regular visitor to the dinner table of Emmeline Pankhurst, who became his comrade in opposing the Boer War, and her crusade for suffrage resonated with all he had seen of the difficult lives of his own mother and the mothers and wives of other Scottish miners. He supported suffrage in Parliament, raised money for the WSPU, and repeatedly intervened on behalf of imprisoned suffragettes. After one of Christabel's arrests, he telegraphed, "Can I do anything?"

Above all else, ever since he had seen the raw face of British jingoism whipped up over the conflict with the Boers, Hardie feared war — its frightening atavism, its destructiveness, the way it could make people forget the fight for social justice. His hope, always, was that organized working people would simply not let their nations go to war. Attending the 1904 congress of the Second International in Amsterdam, while the Russo-Japanese War was under way, he was profoundly moved when the Russian and Japanese delegates spied each other on the platform and rushed to embrace, to fervent applause. This, he felt, was a moment "worth having lived to see."

At a later congress of the group, in Copenhagen, Hardie, supported by Jaurès, proposed that in the event of war, workers in all countries immediately declare a general strike. His anxiety only grew as he watched Parliament funnel money that might have gone for social welfare programs into the naval arms race with Germany, centered on the powerful new *Dreadnought*-class battleships, whose high-speed steam turbines and long-range 12-inch guns made previous warships obsolete. When an American journalist asked him what he thought would be the twentieth century's major danger, his one-word answer was "militarism."

The British public knew Hardie as the leading voice of labor, and they knew the Pankhurst family as the defiant embodiment of the fight for women's suffrage. But there was another story they did not know. It began, as far as we can tell, one day in 1906 when Sylvia Pankhurst was sick, short of food and money, and moving into a new flat. She had only 25 shillings to her name, scarcely more than two weeks' rent, because she had chosen not to be on the WSPU payroll and so become dependent on her mother and older sister. "I sat among my boxes, ill and lonely," she wrote many years later, "when, all unexpected, Keir Hardie came knocking at my door. He took command of the situation. He lifted heavy things into position and when all was in order, took me out for a meal."

Sylvia was 24, and Hardie about to turn 50. She had known him as a family friend ever since she was a small girl, and had long admired him. But now they were both at low moments in their lives, and they turned to each other.

Hardie was a hero to thousands around the world, but his was not the happiest of households. He had married Lillie as a 22-year-old coal miner, but from the age of 35 on, he spent most of his time in London. While he frequently visited Scotland, where the children were in school, he rebuffed his wife's wish to join him permanently in the capital. Hardie felt undervalued by her, writing a friend that Lillie did not seem to know "what a terribly important body her man is in other folks' opinion." Around the same time, the friend cryptically recorded Hardie's being upset at Lillie's "strange behaviour to him," adding that Hardie "feels . . . Mrs. Hardie's ways keenly." For her part, she may well have resented having to run a household and raise the children while her husband was away most of the time, becoming a world figure. In any event, others noticed that she was given to long, stony periods of silence.

Where he found Lillie reticent and unappreciative, the far younger Sylvia Pankhurst was supportive, warm, and uninhibited. "We are for free sexual union contracted and terminated at will," she wrote later in life, a thought that would have horrified her more straitlaced mother. "We are for free love because love is free and no one can bind it." Until Hardie arrived that day to help her move, however, such ideas of hers were purely theoretical; he was almost certainly her first lover. In a poem she wrote for him, she spoke of how his love "woke the tender buds that slept before." She respected him not just for his politics but for the way he cooked and cleaned for himself in London, polished his own shoes, worked so hard, and wrote so constantly. They exchanged their favorite books, he read Robert Burns's love poetry aloud to her, and they wrote many letters. One poem she sent him ran:

> Last night when all was quiet you came to me.
> I felt in the darkness by my side
> Waiting to feel your kisses on my mouth,
> The clasping of your arms, and your dear lips
> Pressing on me till my breath came short . . .

What he wrote to her was only somewhat more restrained:

> Sweet,
>   All the night I have been working and thinking about you
> and hoping that all was going well with you.

In one letter, written in 1911 when she was on a lecture tour of the United States, he spoke of how she would continue his work—an acknowledgment of their age difference but also, in a way that must have thrilled her, of their equality: "I like to think of you going over the same ground, speaking in the same halls, & meeting the same people as

I have. I can think of myself as . . . smoothing the pathway for the coming of my little sweetheart. May it ever be so."

"They did not hide their attraction," recalled a friend of Hardie's. ". . . I remember her sitting on his knee with her arms around his neck." As he worked long hours in the evening, Sylvia drew or painted portraits of him, and soon two of her paintings would be hung in his room. That their bond was intense is clear, but it may have felt precarious as well, as love affairs between people of very different ages often do. Theirs, also, was love on the run between two busy activists, and her frequent arrests brought other complications.

Hundreds of jailed suffragettes were now trying to provoke the government by launching hunger strikes in prison. In response, the authorities ordered that they be force-fed. Hardie denounced force-feeding in Parliament and more than 100 doctors signed a protest, all to no avail. He desperately tried to persuade Sylvia to stop going on hunger strikes. As an agitator, he understood the tactic, but as her lover, he was horrified. "He told me," Sylvia later wrote, "that the thought of forcible feeding was making him ill." Weren't there enough martyrs to the cause already, he asked. "Of what use to make one more?"

Sylvia wanted to be a martyr for the cause, however, and repeatedly pushed her body to the limit. And there could be no question of her breaking ranks with her hunger-striking mother or WSPU comrades. On one occasion, she was so weak on being released from jail that she had to be carried on a stretcher to a suffrage rally, where she managed to say only a few words before being taken home by ambulance. Once she smuggled a desperate message out to the mother whose love and esteem she craved: "I am fighting, fighting, fighting. I have four, five and six wardresses every day as well as the two doctors. I am fed by stomach tube twice a day. They prise open my mouth with a steel gag, pressing it in where there is a gap in my teeth. I resist all the time. My gums are always bleeding. . . . My shoulders are bruised with struggling whilst they hold the tube into my throat."

Nothing Sylvia did or said, however, could change the emotional balance in the Pankhurst family. As long as she could remember, she had felt in the shadow of her famous mother and the favored elder sister with the china-doll good looks, whose face had even been sculpted for the famous Tussaud waxworks. Given that history, Keir Hardie's love and respect must have felt doubly affirming, and given her desire to be in the public eye, it must have been heady to find that several issues she had suggested were raised by Hardie in the House of Commons.

Both of them had strong reasons to keep their love concealed. Hardie was, after all, a married man, with powerful right-wing enemies who would have been delighted to see him enmeshed in public scandal over an affair with a woman half his age. To make things more thorny for them both, it was soon after Hardie took up with Sylvia that the Pankhursts left his Independent Labour Party, vociferously spurning all alliances with male MPs. Sylvia remained one of the WSPU's most outspoken campaigners, so for the Pankhursts any disclosure of the affair would have proved politically as well as personally embarrassing, guaranteed fodder for anti-suffrage cartoonists. Emmeline, who carefully balanced her militance by always presenting herself as a well-dressed, respectable widow, was particularly dismayed. Once when Sylvia was on a hunger strike in prison, she smuggled out to Emmeline a letter for Hardie that her mother did not deliver. Sylvia never forgave her.

Although the war Hardie feared did not yet seem imminent, suspicion of Germany pervaded popular culture. In 1906, a novel called *The Invasion of 1910* was serialized in the *Daily Mail;* the newspaper advertised it by sending men in spiked Prussian helmets, wearing sandwich boards, through the London streets. The book was a sensation and helped launch a whole fantasy literature of invasion. Another novel depicted the imperial German black-eagle banner flying over Buckingham Palace, the British King exiled to Delhi, and signs declaring it *verboten* to walk on the grass in Hyde Park. A play about an invasion by "the Emperor of the North" opened in London in 1909 and was still running 18 months later. So many invasion novels flooded the bookstores that the humorist P. G. Wodehouse satirized them with one of his own, *The Swoop! or How Clarence Saved England,* featuring an attack by the Swiss navy and the Chinese seizure of the Welsh port of Lllgxtplll.

Meanwhile, preparations for possible war ratcheted up dramatically: between 1908 and 1913, total arms expenses by the six largest countries of Europe rose by 50 percent. Almost all the great powers were now spending between 5 and 6 percent of their national incomes on their armed forces, even though the usual motives for conflict were relatively few. For example, no major European country, at least in public, claimed a piece of another's territory.

The best counterweight to war, Keir Hardie and millions of other men and women believed, was the socialist movement. The Second International's membership came from more than 30 nations; its first co-presidents had been a Frenchman and a German; all conflicts between countries seemed forgotten by those who rallied under its red flag. Workers thronged streets across Europe to march under that banner every May Day. German generals might bluster, but the German socialists, the Social Democrats, despite a long history of harassment by the authorities, were the biggest party in the national legislature. The Social Democrats were envied by leftists everywhere for their more than 90 newspapers, their large staff of professional organizers, and their welfare programs that almost seemed the embryo of a socialist state within a capitalist one. Hardie attended one congress of the German party and was impressed by how many of the delegates were women—who kept a constant peace demonstration going outside the meeting hall for the duration of the congress. The German government was clearly afraid of the party, for it banned Social Democratic literature from army barracks, and party members from the officer corps. In almost every other European country, socialists were also increasing their share of the vote. Even in the resolutely anti-socialist United States, Hardie's friend Eugene V. Debs, campaigning on his Red Special train with red banners flying, won more than 400,000 votes for president in 1908, and more than doubled the total, to 900,000, in 1912.

An advance in one country was greeted with delight in all the others; a setback in one was pain shared: when the Tsar's Cossacks shot down workers marching in St. Petersburg, for example, British trade unionists meeting in Liverpool quickly raised £1,000 for their families. And even when disagreements broke out among socialists, there was still friendship and respect. At one congress of the Second International, the fiery Polish-German Rosa Luxemburg vigorously criticized a statement by Jean Jaurès. When Jaurès rose to answer, he asked who would translate his reply into German. "I will, if you like, Citizen Jaurès," said Luxemburg. Between such trusting comrades, could there ever be war?

Of course, a skeptic might have claimed that the proletarian desire for peace was only a mere dream in the eyes of middle-class intellectuals. But Hardie believed in it fervently, and he *was* working class — in fact, one of only two major leaders in the Second International who could claim that distinction. The other, the German August Bebel, was far less sanguine about the peaceful instincts of his fellow workers. "Look at those fellows," he once remarked while watching a military parade. "Eighty per cent of them are Berliners and Social Democrats but if there was trouble they would shoot me down at a word of command from above."

6

ON THE EVE

A T EVERY POINT on their journey, the new King and Queen
were greeted with thunderous cheers. As their ship sailed
from Portsmouth, it was flanked by 15 vessels of the Royal
Navy's Home Fleet—mighty ships with names to match: *Indefatigable,
Invincible, Indomitable, Superb.* Several days' travel brought the royal
liner and its escorts to Cape Trafalgar on the Spanish coast, the scene of
Britain's epochal triumph of naval arms in the Napoleonic era—proof
again that in warfare, daring and discipline would always carry the
day—and then, after night fell, to the colony of Gibraltar. The town
beneath the great rock that controlled the entrance to the Mediterranean was lit up in welcome. In the morning, sailors on ten ships of
the Atlantic Fleet gave the royal couple—the King in his white admiral's uniform—three lusty cheers as they sailed onward. At Port Said
the Khedive of Egypt, wearing the star and ribbon of the Order of the
Bath, came to pay tribute. As the monarchs' ship steamed through the
Suez Canal, relays of troopers from the Egyptian Camel Corps can-
tered along the banks as an escort. At Suez, fireworks filled the sky. At
Aden, more British warships fired off a 121-gun salute. King George V
and Queen Mary, crowned in Westminster Abbey only a few months
before, were on their way to be formally installed as Emperor and Empress of India. Their voyage, in November 1911, marked the first time a

British sovereign had left Europe since Richard the Lion-hearted had set off to capture Jerusalem in the Third Crusade.

The pageantry of the six-week visit surpassed anything the British Raj in India had ever seen. There were trumpet fanfares, a Punjabi war dance, a Scottish sword dance, and a championship polo match; in Calcutta, crowds of Indians broke through a line of soldiers to seize clumps of earth the King's feet had stepped on and press them to their foreheads. Gone—at least from British press coverage—was all memory of the long history of Indian uprisings against the colonial regime, some of them fairly recent. In the foothills of the Himalayas, a maharaja assembled 645 elephants to take His Majesty and a large party of guests and gamekeepers on a tiger hunt. In Bombay, the normally reticent King George was so overwhelmed by the warmth of the welcoming crowd that his voice broke and for a few moments he was unable to speak.

The climax came at a grand ceremony in Delhi, the Durbar, in which George V and Mary were proclaimed Emperor and Empress. Dust filled the air as 100,000 people assembled in the open, while on raised crimson-and-gold thrones under a canopy the imperial couple took their seats. He wore a robe of purple velvet and a crown glittering with diamonds; more diamonds sparkled in her coronet, and her white satin dress was bordered with gold. Escorting them to their thrones were men of the Life Guards and Indian Lancers, Scottish Archers and Gurkha Rifles, and 12 British and 12 Indian trumpeters on white horses. Sixteen hundred military bandsmen played triumphal music. Fourteen bemedaled Indian attendants in scarlet, with white turbans, carried maces; four more bore fans of yak tails and peacock feathers, to whisk away any insect arrogant enough to approach. Swords, helmets, and bugles glinted in the sunlight; the air was filled with fluttering pennants and smoke from the booming artillery. For a full hour, British officials and Indian nobility came forward to bow in homage, then respectfully back away: the viceroy; the chief justice and judges of the High Court; the governors and lieutenant governors of the provinces; the Nizam of Hyderabad, the Begum of Bhopal, the Nawab of Rampur, the Khan of Kalat, and too many maharajas to count.

Only one curious episode marred the proceedings. An Indian nobleman, the Gaekwar of Baroda, was thought not to have shown the proper respect. "When he came up to do homage," huffed the London

Times, "he walked up jauntily swinging a stick in his hand — in itself a gross breach of etiquette — and as he passed before their Majesties he saluted in the most perfunctory manner. Very few people believe that his discourtesy was not deliberate." In vain, later, did the distraught Gaekwar repeatedly protest that he was simply nervous and confused. Wild rumors began to fly: he was even said to admire the United States for breaking free of Britain. London crowds hissed when they saw him in a newsreel. Keir Hardie, however, eagerly seized on the event: "His fellow-rulers had been taught to grovel low before the Throne, as becomes all who go near such a symbol of imbecility," he wrote. "But he . . . kept erect, and then, horror of all horrors, when leaving the dais, he actually turned his back upon the King." Hardie looked forward to the day when more citizens of India would refuse "to add to her abasement by kissing the foot of the oppressor."

The British officials who proudly attended the Durbar, of course, considered themselves anything but oppressors. Prominent among them, sitting in the front row, was Sir Douglas Haig. An assignment in India as military chief of staff had come to an end, but he had strategically delayed his departure until after the royal visit. He filled his diary with satisfied comments on his soldiers' role performing for the monarchs. "A perfect parade. Men stand like rocks. . . . I have never seen troops march past better, or Cavalry gallop in better order." As much a royal favorite as ever, he was honored with an additional knighthood and sailed for home as Knight Commander of the Indian Empire. Like John French before him, his next post would be commanding the 1st Army Corps at Aldershot, now a force slated to be immediately sent to the Continent in the event of hostilities.

Displays of imperial might like the Durbar did far more than satisfy the vanity of those who took part. They underlined to any potential adversary that if war did break out, Britain would have the strength of its entire empire to draw on. In any war in Europe, the message was, soldiers from the British Isles would be joined by those from illustrious units like the Royal Deccan Horse, the King's African Rifles, or the West India Regiment. In every corner of the empire, loyal subjects saw coming to Britain's aid as their duty. "Schools are like munitions factories," proclaimed the Reverend Percy Kettlewell, headmaster of a private boys' school in Grahamstown, South Africa, in 1913, "and ought to be turning out a constant supply of living material." He would get his wish: in the war that began the next year, nearly 1,000 graduates of his own munitions factory donned uniforms; 125 of them were killed.

The same year as the Durbar, Germany precipitated a second international crisis over Morocco, sending a warship to the port of Agadir during an uprising, supposedly to protect German citizens. (Embarrassingly, there turned out to be none on hand, but to make reality match the Kaiser's rhetoric, a startled German businessman was hastily summoned to Agadir from a Moroccan town 75 miles away.) Helmuth von Moltke, the bellicose chief of the German general staff, hoped privately that his country would "pluck up the courage to make an energetic demand which we are prepared to enforce with the sword." In response to the German move, Britain put the Royal Navy on a rare peacetime alert. Like other disputes in Africa, this one was settled by a division-of-the-spoils agreement: France consolidated its hold over most of Morocco; Germany won a slice of French territory in central Africa.

In the face of mounting tension between their countries, French and German socialists redoubled their statements of solidarity: a leading German socialist promised a congress of the French party, to great applause, "We will never fire on you"; Jean Jaurès addressed comrades in Berlin and returned home to sing the praises of the German Social Democratic Party. When the German party won more than a quarter of the seats in the country's parliament in early 1912, the leading French socialist newspaper was ecstatic, calling the results "a victory of the proletariat as a whole. It is an expression of the universal desire for peace." And, indeed, German socialist parliamentarians, rosettes of revolutionary red in their lapels, continued their long practice of voting against the country's military budget—a budget that was now increasing.

Later that year, 555 delegates from 23 countries assembled for an unusually fervent congress of the Second International in Basel, Switzerland. Children dressed in white singing socialist songs led the participants through the streets to the city's cathedral. The next year, Hardie's Independent Labour Party staged a campaign against the danger of war, which climaxed in a large London demonstration addressed by, among others, his friend Jaurès. This short, rotund, heavily bearded man, who trembled with emotion, gestured dramatically, and threw back his head as he spoke ("Jaurès thinks with his beard," commented one person who knew him), was an orator of legendary power, and though he spoke in French, no one could miss his meaning. When he placed his hand near the platform and steadily lifted it, the British crowd cheered him wildly, recalled a witness, because "we all knew he was talking about the rise of the working class."

In high places more voices were predicting war. Von Moltke pushed for a hefty enlargement of the German army and bluntly told the country's chancellor, "All sides are preparing for European War, which all sides expect sooner or later." Not only were all sides preparing, but the high commands had detailed plans for how the war would unfold. Should Germany attack France, British and French officers had already worked out which French ports British troops would disembark at, how many French railway cars and interpreters would meet them, and where their jumping-off points for combat would probably be. Little of the preparations, however, took into account that weapon meant to slaughter "natives," the machine gun. As British, French, and German generals spread their maps on war ministry tables, they spent inordinate amounts of time planning where to place their cavalry divisions.

Where were the Germans likely to attack? Obviously not across the frontier they shared with France, where they would run up against heavy French fortifications. They were expected instead to sweep through neutral Belgium, making use of the country's well-developed rail system and sturdy, granite-block roads, and then turn south toward Paris. In fact, the British and French were counting on it. Only an assault on Belgium could make Britain's entry into the war easy to justify, for all the major powers had signed a treaty recognizing Belgian neutrality. On no account, one high British official warned a French colleague, "let the French commanders be led into being the first to cross the Belgian frontier!"—for then the British public would never countenance going to war.

Since all of the nation's wars in living memory had been victorious, many influential Britons expected that a brisk campaign in Europe would be a welcome spine-stiffener for a country in danger of going soft. "Peace may and has ruined many a nationality with its surfeit of everything except those tonics of privation and sacrifice," wrote a commentator in the *Daily Mail* in 1912. "But the severest war wreaks little practical injury."

Others were less sanguine about the nature of the war, but very certain it would come. Charles Beresford, a member of Parliament and former admiral of the Channel Fleet, began each day with the greeting "Good morning, one day nearer the German war." Beresford was a friend of Kipling, whose writing pulsed with exasperation at those who did not see that war was imminent. Kipling fretted about the German naval buildup, complained loudly that his fellow Britons were "camping comfortably on the raw edge of a volcano," and began speaking of Germans as "Huns" or "Goths." In his poetry he fulminated against a government that was spending money on social reforms instead of more arms:

> And because there was need of more pay for the shouters and marchers,
> They disbanded in face of their foemen their bowmen and archers.

His son John's bad eyesight had defeated his hopes for joining the navy, but Kipling began pulling strings to see if he could get John into Sandhurst, sending him to a "crammer" to prepare for the military academy's entrance exam, in hopes that he could make an army career instead.

A century later, it is easy enough to see the incremental steps that primed an entire continent for war. But to Britons at the time, the bloodshed that seemed most likely lay at home. Labor union membership was surging and militance on the rise: in 1911 a transport workers' strike stopped traffic for weeks in most ports, and more strikes followed. During that year and the next, the government called out a total of 50,000 troops in response, and even sent two warships to Liverpool. In that city alone, in battles with soldiers 200 strikers were wounded and two killed.

With such threats to the status quo came a rise in surveillance. At Scotland Yard, the job of tracking potential troublemakers was taken over by Basil Thomson, an ambitious, deeply conservative former colonial official with a flair for self-promotion. In photographs, with his mustache, wing collar, and white handkerchief nattily tucked in his breast pocket, he looks more a dapper boulevardier than a detective. His agents were soon attending strike meetings, opening suffragettes' mail, and keeping close watch on Hardie's Independent Labour Party. Thomson remarked to a friend that "unless there were a European War to divert the current, we were heading for something very like revolution." He was not alone in feeling this way. "A good big war just now might do a lot of good in killing Socialist nonsense," one army officer confided in a letter, "and would probably put a stop to all this labor unrest."

When it came to eye-catching destruction, however, labor unionists were outstripped by the militant suffragettes. After Parliament failed to pass a women's suffrage bill in 1911, Christabel Pankhurst urged WSPU members to violence. In two spectacular raids, suffragettes rampaged through central London with hammers hidden in their muffs, breaking windows at newspapers, hotels, the Guards' Club, a host of government offices, and nearly 400 shops. Fearing arrest, Christabel fled to Paris, where she continued to edit the WSPU newspaper and call for ever more vandalism. Her mother and two other women made a surprise raid by taxi on 10 Downing Street, the prime minister's residence, and smashed two windows. (Emmeline managed to wrench herself away from policemen long enough to throw a rock through a Colonial Office window as well.) Britain had seldom seen anything like this.

WSPU supporters, shrinking in number but ever more extreme, set on fire an orchid house at Kew Gardens, a London church, and a racecourse grandstand; blew up a deserted railway station; and smashed a jewel case at the Tower of London. They cut the telephone wires linking London and Glasgow, and slashed the words NO VOTES, NO GOLF! into golf course greens and then poured acid in the letters so grass would not grow. One newspaper estimated that suffragettes had inflicted £500,000 worth of property damage, some $60 million in today's money. By now, more than 1,000 of them had gone to prison, and one spectacularly sacrificed her life before a huge crowd and newsreel cameras in 1913 — Emily Wilding Davison, a WSPU member who ran onto the racecourse in the midst of the Epsom Derby and grabbed at the bridle of the King's horse, which struck her while galloping at full speed. She died of her injuries four days later. Queen Mary referred to her as "the horrid woman." Emmeline Pankhurst called her "one of our bravest soldiers."

Pankhurst's embrace of violence was striking for someone who had always taken such care to present herself as a woman of utmost propriety. Any WSPU members who opposed the new extreme tactics or her autocratic control found themselves expelled from the ranks. One person ejected not just from the WSPU but from England was Emmeline's emotionally unstable youngest daughter, Adela. Furious that Adela supported striking workers and other left-wing causes that had nothing to do with women's suffrage, Emmeline gave her a ticket, £20, and a letter of introduction to a suffragette in Australia, and firmly insisted that she emigrate. Deeply hurt, conflicted, yet still under her mother's spell, Adela obediently boarded a ship and never saw her mother or sisters again.

Behind their show of militance and unity, similar tensions were brewing between Emmeline and Sylvia, her middle daughter. For Sylvia, too, women's suffrage was always part of a broader battle for the dispossessed, as it was for her lover, Keir Hardie; she was also quietly dismayed by the newfound zeal for violence of her mother and the self-exiled Christabel.

After 1912, Sylvia increasingly went her own way, moving into the festering slums of London's East End to work with the poor. For the time being, she and the East End women she started organizing remained formally, if uneasily, affiliated with the WSPU. Living with a couple who were shoemakers, she continued to stage the dramatic confrontations that were the Pankhurst trademark. She arranged, for instance, for a woman to be hidden in a large padded box, which was delivered as freight through the service entrance of the House of Commons. Once inside, the woman slipped out of the box unobserved, and from the visitors' gallery dumped the contents of a three-pound bag of flour over the head of the anti-suffrage prime minister, Herbert Asquith. But despite her love of the limelight, the organization Sylvia built did far more than such stunts. Among other things, it offered classes or lectures on public speaking, the legal position of women, child care, and, unusual for the time, sex education. Many women she helped train later went on to leadership positions in trade unions or elective office.

During a long, bitter dock strike, she organized women to help feed the dockers' children, and in return hundreds of East End labor unionists joined a solidarity march to Holloway Prison in support of a hunger-striking suffragette. After all, many working-class men also did not have the right to vote, since roughly 40 percent of Britain's adult males were too poor to qualify. Basil Thomson's men at Scotland Yard kept Pankhurst and her new allies under close surveillance.

A police inspector who arrested her in 1913 reported to his superiors that he had had a narrow escape from "a hostile crowd" of men, some of whom "were armed with . . . docker's hooks . . . and were going to make every possible effort to prevent Sylvia Pankhurst being arrested." For a brief few years, her East End work seemed a living embodiment of that always elusive socialist dream: solidarity among society's have-nots. And at one point it seemed as if another dream of Sylvia's might be fulfilled when her mother came to visit her while she was bedridden after a prison hunger strike. Could she finally be winning a place equal to Christabel's in Emmeline's heart?

Charlotte Despard, of course, had long preceded Sylvia into London's slums. Although of different generations—Despard was 38 years older—the two women now found themselves political allies, often speaking from the same platform. Oratory, in this pre-television era, was the primary way for radicals and dissidents to get their message out,* and Despard was as at ease on a street-corner soapbox as in a lecture hall. Crowds in the hundreds, sometimes thousands, turned out to hear her. The writer Christopher St. John described her talking suffrage to a rally in Hyde Park: "The arms were raised Cassandra-like; the whole thin, fragile body seemed to vibrate with a prophecy, and, from the white hair, the familiar black lace veil streamed back like a pennon."

Despard and many of her followers refused to pay taxes, declaring, like the American rebels of 1776, "no taxation without representation!" In response, the government seized her household furniture. Now nearing 70, she felt so energized by the battles for women's suffrage and the rights of labor that she declared, "I was older at twenty than I am now." However much Despard identified with the dispossessed, she never lost her aristocratic sense of entitlement, even on the four occasions she went to prison. "I was thrilled to see that stately and commanding figure enter," another prisoner wrote. ". . . Her first act was a calm refusal to take the medicine the doctor had prescribed. 'I have never taken medicine in my life—I do not propose to begin now.' Her word was immediately taken as law. All the officers appeared to be in awe of her."

---

* One Liverpool agitator used to gather a sidewalk crowd by shouting, "I've been robbed! I've been robbed!" Once people surrounded him, he would explain that the robbers were the capitalists.

Another inmate remembered: "I have never heard of [another] prisoner before or since who slept soundly through the first night of sentence."

"News in the Paper . . . makes one think that the class war has already begun," Despard wrote hopefully in her diary in early 1914. If there was a revolution in Britain, someone destined by his position to play a central role in suppressing it was her brother, who had just been promoted to field marshal, the British army's highest rank. Sir John French continued to keep his wife Eleanora and their children tucked away in Hertfordshire while he carried on his London love affairs from a pied-à-terre he shared with George G. Moore, an American railway magnate and financier as well as the solution to French's chronic money problems. An ardent Anglophile, Moore idolized French and gladly paid for the house and the lavish expenses the men incurred in wining and dining their lady friends. Despard remained on friendly terms with "my dear old Jack," and, as she told her diary, he paid her a "delightful" visit in the spring of 1914. What did French make of his sister's many passions? He certainly shared none of them, but she still mattered to him enough that he visited her again a few months later, bringing along his latest mistress, a former actress now the wife of an earl. The thought that brother and sister might someday find themselves on opposite sides of some revolutionary barricade apparently did not bother either of them.

Despite the accelerating military buildup of the previous half-dozen years, the first six months of 1914 felt like an unusual interlude of calm, unbroken by any international disputes. More than 50,000 Germans were working in Britain, where they could often earn higher wages than at home. Britons who went to Germany were pleased to find how many Germans now spoke English; German artists and intellectuals were so admired in England that the majority of honorary doctorates awarded by Oxford this year went to Germans.

The major powers of Europe seemed to be getting along splendidly, as well they might, since King George V, the look-alike Tsar Nicholas II, and Kaiser Wilhelm II were all kin. George was a first cousin of Nicholas on one side of his family, and of Wilhelm on the other; he was also related to the wives of both. The three future monarchs had met as children, moored their royal yachts next to each other on holidays in the Baltic, and had all been together in Berlin for the wedding of the Kaiser's daughter the previous year. Wilhelm was godfather to one of Nicholas's children and had been at the bedside of his grandmother Queen Victoria when she died. In late June, a squadron of British battleships and cruisers were welcome guests at Germany's annual Elbe Regatta. Loving medals and epaulets as much as ever, the Kaiser proudly donned his gold braid as an honorary British admiral of the fleet, and British and German officers attended races and banquets together. When the Royal Navy warships weighed anchor and sailed for home, their commander signaled his German counterpart: "Friends in past, and friends for ever." And why not? The conflict that dominated English newspaper headlines and political life this spring and early summer was not with the Germans, but close by.

After long centuries of seeing its taxes and landowners' profits drained away to England, Ireland was ablaze. A compromise version of an Irish home rule bill, granting autonomy over most domestic issues to a new Irish legislature, was scheduled to be implemented later in the year. Appalled by the prospect of falling under the sway of the island's impoverished Catholic majority, activists in wealthier, largely Protestant northern Ireland vowed to form a rebel provisional government of their own. Quietly supported by Protestant landowners in the rest of Ireland, they set up a militia for which they imported 30,000 rifles. In response, Irish nationalists in Dublin formed their own paramilitary force and also began arming. Delighted by this potential warfare in England's backyard, the Germans secretly sold weapons to both sides.

For months, the crisis consumed a British government already on edge from labor turbulence and from not knowing where militant suffragettes were going to attack next. That Ireland and England were inseparable was an article of faith for imperial-minded Britons—wasn't the country's very name the United Kingdom of Great Britain and Ireland? Many of those at the very top of British society—Sir John French, for example—proudly boasted family roots in Ireland. Hadn't the United States fought a civil war to remain united? Some in Britain were prepared to risk the same, and among them was Alfred Milner. In early 1914, he decided drastic action was needed—action, he hinted ominously, "falling short of violence or active rebellion, or at least not beginning with it." To Violet Cecil he wrote: "For the last 3 or 4 months *I have really worked hard*—at public things—for the first time since

South Africa." In Milner's view, the Irish were no better than Boers, and like them belonged firmly under British control; Rudyard Kipling agreed, considering Irish Catholics "the Orientals of the West."

Milner began traveling England making speeches and skillfully mobilizing other opponents of Irish home rule on the political right. Publicly, he and his allies gathered some two million signatures on a manifesto threatening civil disobedience. Secretly, he raised funds to buy arms for the Protestant militia, with Kipling contributing an astonishing £30,000, the equivalent of well over $3 million today. Violet Cecil firmly supported their campaign. After all, if the subversive idea of home rule spread, there would soon be no British Empire left for her son George—now a newly minted officer in the Grenadier Guards—to defend.

As the summer of 1914 began, the authorities worked desperately to resolve what seemed the gravest national crisis in a century. The Royal Navy recalled some ships from overseas. King George V convened an unprecedented emergency conference of all sides at Buckingham Palace, somberly declaring, "Today the cry of Civil War is on the lips of the most responsible and sober-minded of my people." The conference collapsed in discord. Widespread violence seemed to draw yet closer when British troops opened fire on protesters in Dublin, killing three and wounding many more, one of whom died. Carrie Kipling began assembling supplies of clothing for the beleaguered Irish Protestant refugees who were certain to soon flood England.

The Kiplings, Milner, Despard, French, the Pankhursts, and almost everyone else in Britain were so focused on the looming conflagration in Ireland that they paid little attention to the news, at the end of June, that Archduke Franz Ferdinand of Austria-Hungary and his wife, Sophie, had been killed by an assassin's bullets in the provincial city of Sarajevo.

II

1914

7

A STRANGE LIGHT

THERE HAD BEEN plenty of pomp and circumstance on the schedule, but not much else. Archduke Franz Ferdinand's visit to Sarajevo, capital of one of the outlying provinces of the Austro-Hungarian Empire, was largely ceremonial. Fifty years old, overweight and ill-tempered, he was not on the best of terms with his elderly uncle, the Emperor, whose throne he was due to inherit. Unusually for a member of European royalty, however, he had a happy marriage, and his pregnant wife had come along from Vienna for the trip. During two days of rain, she visited schools and orphanages while, in his role as inspector general of the army, Franz Ferdinand observed military maneuvers. At the suburban spa where they were staying the couple gave a dinner dance for local officials and army officers; a military band played *The Blue Danube* and other waltzes. The next morning, June 28, 1914, the sun came out and Franz Ferdinand and Sophie headed into the city in a convoy of cars flying the black and yellow Hapsburg dynasty flag for a 24-gun salute, a welcoming ceremony, and a formal celebration of their 14th wedding anniversary.

The very headgear of the dignitaries who greeted them in Sarajevo reflected the crazy quilt of this ungainly empire that threatened to come apart at the seams: homburgs, yarmulkes, miters, fezzes, turbans, plus cavalry helmets and brimmed military caps in different shapes for regiments of different ethnicities. The empire was a wobbly agglomeration of nearly a dozen minorities, almost all of them restless under Vienna's autocratic domination. The region around Sarajevo included many ethnic Serbs, among them a faction of militant nationalists. Living next door to the independent nation of Serbia, they dreamed of a Greater Serbia encompassing all Serbs. Gavrilo Princip was one of them, a 20-year-old aspiring poet. Small, ascetic, and tubercular, fired up by the writings of Friedrich Nietzsche and Russian anarchists and aided by a shadowy group of sympathizers across the border in Serbia, he conceived the idea of assassinating the heir apparent on his visit to Sarajevo, and with several fellow conspirators planned a suicide mission. On the morning of June 28 they set off with pistols, bombs, and poison tablets they would swallow after their task was accomplished.

Relations between the empire and Serbia were already touchy. Austro-Hungarian officials considered that country's very existence a threat, and were flexing their military might with the army exercises that the Archduke had come to watch. They were looking for any possible excuse to invade, dismantle, and partition Serbia. Waiting in the crowd on a sunny Sarajevo street for the Archduke's motorcade, Gavrilo Princip was about to provide one.

Making things even more combustible was Kaiser Wilhelm II, the staunchest backer of Vienna. A world industrial colossus, Germany was like an impatient, overbearing big brother to Austria-Hungary. For 35 years the two empires had been bound together by a military alliance, each committed to support the other if attacked. The hot-blooded Kaiser, enthusiastic about flaunting Germany's power but for the moment deprived of opportunities to do so, frequently encouraged his ally to take on little Serbia.

In the background was Russia, another rickety empire and longtime rival of Austria-Hungary for control of the Balkans. The Russians' emotional ties to the Serbs, fellow Slavs and fellow Eastern Orthodox believers, went far back in time (and, indeed, would be a factor in the Balkan wars of the 1990s). Vienna always suspected, sometimes correctly, that any expression of Greater Serbian nationalism had covert Russian support. If Austria-Hungary invaded Serbia, the Russian government would face overwhelming pressure from its own people to come to the aid of their Slavic brethren. Helmuth von Moltke of the German general staff had already assured his Austrian counterpart that if this ever happened, Germany would gladly join a war against Russia.

Like so many German military men, he was eager for the inevitable war to come, in which, he felt, "the issue will be one of a struggle between Germandom and Slavdom." The Kaiser agreed, optimistically assuming that in the long run the British could not remain allied with the "Slavs and Gallics," and would come over to the side of their Teutonic cousins. Racial paranoia about Russia ran deep. "This unorganised Asiatic mass," declared the head of Germany's Royal Library, "like the desert with its sands, wants to gather up our fields of grain." Sometimes high German officials and industrialists talked privately of annexing a slice of western Russia and of turning other parts of it into vassal states.

It was into this powder keg of jostling empires, just as Franz Ferdinand's open touring car unexpectedly stopped on the street in front of him, that young Gavrilo Princip fired two point-blank pistol shots. One hit the Archduke, who was wearing a sky-blue tunic and a helmet with green peacock feathers, in the jugular vein; the other struck the Duchess, dressed in white silk. Both were dead within half an hour.

Outside the Balkans, the assassinations made the headlines for a few days, then dropped from sight. In England, the early summer of 1914 was warm and bright, perfect for tennis at Wimbledon and for the upcoming Henley Regatta; the cloud that threatened to spoil everything was the growing likelihood of civil war in Ireland. The Continent seemed far off. It was "difficult to discuss foreign affairs freely," said one member of the House of Commons, "when our home affairs were in such a particularly evil plight."

In France, President Raymond Poincaré was at the races at Longchamp, where the Baron de Rothschild's horse Sardanapale won the Grand Prix, when he received news of the killings, and did not bother to leave. The French had something far more intriguing to distract them: the sensational murder case against Henriette Caillaux, wife of a former prime minister. She had shot and killed a newspaper editor who threatened to publish love letters she and her husband had exchanged when both were still married to others. At her trial the next month, the murder would be judged a crime of passion for which a woman, by definition not in control of her emotions, could not be held accountable. She was acquitted.

Even today it seems extraordinary how swiftly Princip's two bullets, fired in a city most people had never heard of, set in motion events that would so profoundly reshape our world. Few periods have been as intensively studied as the six weeks that followed the moment Princip squeezed off his shots, unsuccessfully swallowed his poison capsule, and was wrestled away from an angry crowd by sword-wearing policemen. (He would die of tuberculosis in prison four years later.)

If the Archduke and his wife had not been assassinated, might the war have been avoided? Possibly, but given Austria-Hungary's impatience to crush Serbia and Germany's ambitions to dominate Europe, it is hard to imagine a conflict of some sort not taking place—not when we listen, for example, to the Kaiser, at a court ball in 1913, pointing out the general designated "to lead the march on Paris," or asking, fruitlessly, two successive Belgian kings for the right to begin that march through Belgium, or when we read General von Moltke, in 1915, writing to a friend about "this war which I prepared and initiated."

Princip's bullets may have provided the spark, but—German and Austro-Hungarian aggressiveness aside—three other factors steepened Europe's plunge toward the abyss. First was the pair of rival alliances that obligated some countries to come to the aid of others in case of war. Second was the pressure felt by all the major Continental powers to mobilize their large forces of trained reservists who could triple or quadruple the size of any peacetime army. Mobilizing an army in 1914 required several weeks: reservists had to be called up, get to their bases, and collect their rifles and equipment; then millions of men, their weapons, and tens of thousands of tons of food and supplies had to be laboriously deployed by train and horse-drawn wagon to wherever the fighting was expected to be. The very time necessary for mobilization, however, was something inherently destabilizing, for if the other side looked about to mobilize, and you didn't do so, you would be at a fatal disadvantage. A third dangerous factor was the tremendous advantage gained by any country that attacked first, for this guaranteed that the fighting would at least begin on another country's territory.

In Vienna, Emperor Franz Joseph seemed remarkably unperturbed by the death of the nephew he disliked. What he and his advisers saw in the assassination of the heir apparent was something they had long sought: an excuse to attack Serbia. Anti-Serbian riots soon broke out on Vienna's streets. In Germany, when a launch raced out from shore to bring news of the murders to his yacht off Kiel, Kaiser Wilhelm II, who had been a close friend of Franz Ferdinand and impatient for him to succeed his aging, side-whiskered uncle, was crushed. A few days later at his palace, he told Vienna's ambassador to Berlin that he would back any Austro-Hungarian move against Serbia—and he urged that the upstart Serbs be taught a lesson with no delay. In effect, the Kaiser, who had far more power than a constitutional monarch like Britain's, gave Austria a secret blank check to invade.

Was anyone in the Serbian cabinet aware of the plans of Princip and his tiny band? No proof of this has ever surfaced, but it hardly mattered now that Austria had the perfect pretext to wipe Serbia off the map.

July was the month when Europe's emperors, kings, and prime ministers began their summer vacations, so the steps toward the cataclysm were taken in slow motion. In Berlin and Vienna, although messengers and telegraph wires were kept busy, no break in the normal routine that might hint at an impending attack on Serbia was allowed. Even General von Moltke, more impatient for war than ever ("We are ready," he had said some weeks earlier, "and the sooner the better for us"), conspicuously went to take the waters at the famous spa in Carlsbad. The Kaiser departed for a cruise off Norway. Germany's chancellor headed for his country estate. Austro-Hungarian officials, from the Emperor on down, similarly took their holidays. The Kaiser sent birthday greetings to the King of Serbia because, the German Foreign Office advised, "the omission of the customary telegram would be too noticeable." All over Europe those of a class who could afford to take July off were doing so: young George Cecil, home on leave from the army at his mother's country house, Great Wigsell, whiled away his time playing cricket with the Kiplings.

The Kaiser had convinced himself that if Austria-Hungary promptly attacked Serbia, there would be no risk of Russian intervention: Tsar Nicholas II's own grandfather had been murdered by terrorists, so how could he come to the aid of a nation possibly implicated in the assassination of two members of another Emperor's family? Furthermore, if the attack were immediate, as the Kaiser urged, Russia would not even be able to intervene. Unlike industrialized countries with dense rail networks, Russia, with its more primitive infrastructure and vast distances, would need some six weeks to fully mobilize. By then, Austria should long have Serbia fully occupied.

Even though the Austro-Hungarian general staff had already been planning moves against Serbia several weeks before the assassinations, it was unable to follow the Kaiser's urging to strike quickly and without warning. To their dismay, Austrian officials discovered that large numbers of army troops had been granted leave to go home and help their families with the summer harvest. Recalling them would tip the government's hand. As a result, only on July 23, 1914, almost four weeks after the killings, did the Austro-Hungarian envoy present an ultimatum to the Serbian finance minister—the prime minister was out of town—who refused to accept it. The diplomat finally left the document on a table and departed. By design, the ultimatum was composed of demands that Serbia could never accept, such as the removal of government officials to be specified and a carte blanche for Austro-Hungarian police to operate on Serbian territory. It was this warlike document, not the assassinations, that rang out like a warning bell across the continent, signaling that, for the first time since the Battle of Waterloo nearly a century earlier, Europe was facing an all-engulfing war.

Winston Churchill, now First Lord of the Admiralty, was in a cabinet meeting about the Irish crisis when a messenger arrived with news that the foreign secretary shared with his colleagues: "The quiet grave tones of Sir Edward Grey's voice were heard," he later wrote, "reading a document which had just been brought to him from the Foreign Office. It was the Austrian note to Serbia. . . . The parishes of Fermanagh and Tyrone faded back into the mists and squalls of Ireland, and a strange light began . . . to fall and grow upon the map of Europe."

Prime Minister Asquith was optimistic his own country could avoid the dangers of the strange light. He sometimes penned letters during meetings, and from that same cabinet session he wrote to his confidante, Venetia Stanley, "We are in measurable . . . distance of a real Armageddon." But about Britain he added reassuringly, "Happily, there seems to be no reason why we should be anything more than spectators." Famous for enjoying his leisure, the following weekend he went to play golf.

Desperately mobilizing its small army, Serbia sent an urgent appeal asking the Russian Tsar, "in your generous Slav heart," for help. In St. Petersburg, the Russian capital, the general staff ordered the first steps toward mobilization. France, bound to Russia by treaty, recalled all generals to active duty and canceled all army leaves. Then some 40,000 French troops stationed in Morocco were ordered home.

The moves and countermoves succeeded each other ever faster. On July 28 Austria-Hungary declared war on Serbia and the following day Austrian gunboats on the Danube began shelling the Serbian capital, Belgrade—the first actual shots of the First World War. Kaiser Wilhelm II returned from his seagoing holiday, boiling with exasperation that the bumbling Austrians had not done this weeks earlier. In his erratic way he was having an attack of cold feet, for now France and Russia were mobilizing against him. And Britain took an ominous step.

As a long-planned test of its reserve system, in mid-July the Royal Navy had called up reservists from all over the country to man more than 180 warships—the most powerful armada that had ever been assembled in one spot—for exercises off the great south coast naval base at Spithead. Thrilling spectators onshore and in boats, an endless line of vessels, studded with huge *Dreadnought*-class battleships like the *Audacious* and *Colossus,* had steamed past the royal yacht for six hours, the sailors on board returning King George V's salute with rousing cheers. The government then decided to keep the reservists on duty. On July 29 Churchill secretly ordered the core of the fleet to move north to its protected wartime base. From the English Channel, an 18-mile line of battleships and battle cruisers, running at top speed and with lights out, tore through the night up the North Sea to safe anchorage at Scapa Flow, in the Orkney Islands north of Scotland, where a tight circle of fogbound islands would protect them from enemy ships and submarines.

Meanwhile, the British ambassador in Vienna sent a telegram to London: "This country has gone wild with joy at the prospect of war with Serbia." In Berlin, General von Moltke, his eyes no longer on paltry Serbia but on France and Russia, was convinced that Germany should strike. Its army, Europe's best, was prepared. "We shall never hit it again so well as we do now," he said impatiently. The German foreign minister told the Russian ambassador that, with Russia mobilizing, Germany would be "likewise obliged to mobilize . . . and the diplomatists must now leave the talking to the cannon."

Indecisive and fatalistic, Tsar Nicholas II waffled, issuing contradictory orders, now for full mobilization, now for partial mobilization. Trying to halt the momentum toward war, he exchanged telegrams with the Kaiser—in English, which they both spoke fluently. But his top generals, like the German ones, were eager to let the cannon do the talking. "I will . . . smash my telephone," said one, so that he could not "be found to give any contrary orders for a new postponement of general mobilization." Having humiliatingly lost a war to Japan a decade earlier, the Russian high command felt anxious to prove its mettle. If France were attacked, the generals felt, for Russia to refuse to go to war, as its treaty commitments required, would be an intolerable loss of face. Outside the British embassy in St. Petersburg, an enormous crowd rallied late into the night, excited that Britain's all-powerful fleet might join the war on Russia's side. Nearby, as the Tsar and Tsarina appeared on the balcony of their palace, a great mass of Russians sank to their knees and fervently sang the national anthem.

Although both sides made proposals for mediation, the mobilizations and ultimatums rolled inexorably onward. In Britain, however, most people still hoped the country would not be drawn into the maelstrom. No formal treaties bound it, and despite left-wing rhetoric, most of Britain's industrialists and financiers were not eager for war: after all, Germany was Britain's largest trading partner. In addition, all those monarchical family ties seemed to promise that Europe could step back from the cliff's edge. "Czar, Kaiser and King May Yet Arrange Peace," ran an optimistic headline in the *New York Times*.

This was the moment that Keir Hardie and his comrades had so long feared, and they hoped desperately that they could call on labor and socialist movements across the continent to reverse the drift toward war. These forces had grown remarkably strong. The number of socialist parliamentary deputies had been rising rapidly, not only in Germany, but in Italy, Belgium, and France. In the past five years, British trade union membership had nearly doubled, and for some time there had been talk of staging a general strike in November 1914. Russian workers were the most militant of all: 1,450,000 of them had gone on strike in the first seven months of the year; in St. Petersburg this July, strikers were smashing shop windows and, in one working-class district, had put up street barricades.

Hardie, who was now talking about the need for a "United States of Europe," had spent the early part of the year railing against war on a speaking tour of Britain. Besides his many supporters in the trade union movement, there was a wider circle of possible sympathizers as well, such as the network of Britons who, like him, had once opposed the Boer War. Even though his comrade in that struggle, Emmeline Pankhurst, had spurned male allies in her suffrage campaign, hadn't she also declared that the WSPU had no use for war? And Christabel, the daughter she was so close to, had, as recently as June, echoed her mother in an article in the organization's newspaper, referring to "men's wars" as "savage and cruel and violent" and "a horror unspeakable . . . a mechanical and soulless massacre of multitudes of soldiers, mere boys some of them." Another opponent of the Boer War, David Lloyd George, was now in the cabinet as chancellor of the exchequer — and in public statements, even after the assassinations at Sarajevo, seemed to go out of his way to play down the possibility of war with Germany. Might this new crisis find all of them campaigning together once again?

At the end of July, Europe's socialist parties called an emergency meeting in Brussels at the Maison du Peuple, the headquarters of Belgium's trade unionists, whose café, theater, and cooperative shops hinted at the enlightened social order that united workers might soon bring into being. On a rainy day, their journeys slowed by railways newly clogged with mobilizing soldiers, Hardie came from Britain, Jaurès from France, the diminutive, chain-smoking Rosa Luxemburg from Germany, and more comrades from other countries. To Hardie's disappointment, not all endorsed his call for a general strike against the looming war. The delegates did, at least, approve an antiwar resolution, and called for a full emergency congress of the Second International in Paris ten days later. Jaurès would preside there; perhaps, Hardie hoped, with his great eloquence he could steer the delegates toward a general strike. He was known as a charismatic speaker no matter what he was talking about. "The walls of the room seemed to dissolve: we swam in the ether," wrote one listener after hearing Jaurès mesmerize a dinner party with a discourse on astronomy. "The women forgot to re-powder their faces, the men to smoke, the servants to go in search of their own supper."

Alarming the delegates, the news that Austria had declared war on Serbia arrived during the Brussels meeting — but so did dramatic proof of opposition to German militarism: a telegram from Berlin reporting an antiwar demonstration of 100,000 people on the Unter den Linden, the city's great boulevard. That evening Jaurès stood before a rally of Belgian workers with his arm around Hugo Haase, co-chair of the German Social Democrats—just the sort of public gesture that enraged ultranationalists in France. He spoke with all the passion of someone who had feared the coming of this moment his whole life; when he finished, the crowd of some 7,000 poured through the streets of Brussels, singing "The Internationale" and chanting "*Guerre à la guerre!*" (War on war!)

"It is impossible that matters will not be settled," Jaurès told a Belgian socialist leader the next morning. "Come, I have a few hours before my train. Let's go to the Museum and see the Flemish primitives." Once back in Paris, Jaurès hurried to the Chamber of Deputies to lobby his fellow legislators against war. The French socialists were encouraged when a special envoy from their sister party in Germany rushed to Paris to assure them that the socialist bloc in the German parliament would vote against the war credits the Kaiser was about to ask for. If socialists in France and Germany worked together, could not the conflict be prevented?

Events outraced them. "The sword is being forced into my hand," Kaiser Wilhelm II declared on July 31. Playing the role of the aggrieved victim of Russia's mobilization, he promptly ordered Germany's own first steps in the process. (Tsar Nicholas II would use similar words a few days later: "I have done all in my power to avert war. Now . . . it has been forced on me.") Britain then asked both France and Germany for guarantees that they would honor Belgian neutrality. France said yes within the hour. Germany did not reply.

That night, returning home from dinner, Hardie found a crowd of journalists gathered outside his London flat. They had terrible news from Paris: a fanatical young nationalist had fired two shots into Jean Jaurès as he was dining with some comrades at the Café Croissant on the Rue Montmartre. Slumped across the table, he was dead within minutes. Crowds swept toward the restaurant in such numbers that it took the police a quarter of an hour to clear the way for an ambulance. The French cabinet feared a working-class uprising might occur just as war was about to begin. Politicians who had had no use for Jaurès when he was alive rushed to comfort his widow and to proclaim to all that, at this moment of crisis, the great man surely would have called for national unity.

A German ultimatum to Russia demanding a halt to mobilization brought no answer. On August 1, Germany called up all troops; officers waving handkerchiefs and shouting "Mobilization!" stood in open-topped cars that raced through the streets of the capital. Outside the Kaiser's palace, crowds broke into a hymn of thanksgiving. That evening, Germany declared war on Russia. So eager were its officials that the German government had telegraphed its ambassador in St. Petersburg two declarations of war to be delivered to Russia's foreign minister: one if Russia did not reply to its ultimatum, the other rejecting the Russian reply as unsatisfactory. In his haste and confusion, the ambassador handed over both messages.

That same day, France began preparing for the German attack that clearly was inevitable. At a tea dance at the fashionable lakeside Pavillon d'Armenonville in the Bois de Boulogne, the manager halted the music, announced "Mobilization has been ordered," and asked the band to play "La Marseillaise." By evening, Paris restaurant orchestras were playing the British and Russian national anthems as well.

Across Europe, crowds pulsed with an eerie excitement that few people had experienced in their lifetime. "I must acknowledge that there was a majestic, rapturous, and even seductive something" in the air of Vienna, recalled the Austrian writer Stefan Zweig, a pacifist. "In spite of all my hatred and aversion for war, I should not like to have missed the memory of those first days. . . . All differences of class, rank, and language were swamped at that moment by the rushing feeling of fraternity. Strangers spoke to one another in the streets, people who had avoided each other for years shook hands, everywhere one saw excited faces. Each individual experienced an exaltation of his ego, he was no longer the isolated person of former times."

In Berlin, exuberant masses of well-dressed people, who expected the war to be finished quickly, surged along the boulevards. After all, in the Franco-Prussian War of 1870–1871, victory had come in a matter of months. With motor transport and the vast expansion of railways, an even swifter triumph was surely at hand. Leading figures from across German society declared their support for war: university rectors, prominent intellectuals, avant-garde artists, Protestant and Catholic bishops, rabbis, even the heads of groups working for women's suffrage and the rights of homosexuals. "The victory of Germany," wrote the novelist Thomas Mann, the country's greatest living writer, "will be a victory of soul over numbers." Many pacifists, too, were carried along by the current. "Every German friend of peace must fulfill his duty towards the fatherland exactly as any other German," urged the German Peace Society.

In the capital alone, as reservists prepared to rush off to their units, 2,000 marriages were performed at short notice. "I run to the War Ministry," one official recorded in his diary. "Beaming faces everywhere. Everyone is shaking hands in the corridors: people congratulate one another for being over the hurdle." The congratulations were especially fervent because, with Russia already mobilizing, the war could be presented to the world as a defense against aggression. "The government has managed brilliantly," wrote the chief of the Kaiser's naval staff, "to make us appear as the attacked."

Although August 2 was a Sunday, the British cabinet met three times. The Conservative opposition in Parliament was turning up the heat, saying that any British delay in supporting France and Russia was a sign of national weakness; some hawks among the governing Liberals, like Churchill, felt this way as well. Despite such pressure, 12 of 18 cabinet members opposed giving France a guarantee that Britain would send troops. This majority had a strong argument that the conflict was other countries' business. Only a German invasion of Belgium, whose neutrality Britain had guaranteed, could change that.

One person in England who knew firsthand how much death and suffering for civilians could lurk behind headlines about military triumphs was Emily Hobhouse. Over that weekend, she fired off desperate letters to everyone she could think of, including her onetime ally Lloyd George. Thirteen years earlier, she had personally briefed him for his excoriating attacks in Parliament on the British scorched-earth campaign against the Boers. Could he be persuaded to speak out once again? "Few English people have seen war in its nakedness," she wrote to the *Manchester Guardian,* backing the newspaper's plea for British neutrality. ". . . They know nothing of the poverty, destruction, disease, pain, misery and mortality which follow in its train. . . . I have seen all of this and more."

Crowds gathered outside newspaper offices, where in these pre-radio days the latest information was to be had. Extra editions poured off the presses and hired taxis supplemented regular delivery vans in rushing bundles of papers to street corners across London. Labor unions and left-wing parties organized protest marches that converged for a giant Sunday afternoon antiwar rally in Trafalgar Square, the largest demonstration there in years. Charlotte Despard and other speakers addressed the crowd, which was really waiting for one man, Keir Hardie. To wild cheering, he called for a general strike if Britain declared war. "You have no quarrel with Germany!" he roared. "German workmen have no quarrel with their French comrades. . . . We are told international treaties compel us [but] who made those? The People had no voice in them!" As he spoke, the sky over London blackened with storm clouds, and before he finished, they burst in a torrential downpour.

That evening, Germany demanded from Belgium passage for its troops. The long-prepared German plan was being put into action. Asquith ordered the British army mobilized. Although several government officials resigned in protest, they included no senior cabinet ministers like Lloyd George, who, to Hardie's dismay, in short order would declare in a fiery speech that "we are fighting against barbarism." All Europe was on a downward slope toward the inevitable, and few were those on either side who cared to press on the brakes.

Hardie spoke again the next day, this time in the House of Commons. During his speech, like a mocking dirge for his lifetime of work to stave off this moment, he heard the national anthem being softly sung—from the Labour benches behind him.

That same day, August 3, Germany declared war on France. Of some two million German troops now being mobilized, one and a half million were heading for France and Belgium, the rest for the Russian frontier. Germany expected to move quickly through Belgium and northern France to capture Paris. The plan, worked out over many years, was based on a precise estimate of the time needed to knock France out of the war: exactly 42 days. Then the victorious army would turn on the real enemy, Russia. In the west, however, Belgium rejected Germany's demand and started blowing up railway tunnels and bridges on its border. Berlin, now infuriated and vowing vengeance, had never factored this possibility into its planning.

In the German capital, as reserve soldiers marched to the railway station amid cheering crowds, Social Democratic parliamentary deputies urgently debated whether to oppose war credits for the government. The argument was stormy and agonizing; one legislator wept. Could they refuse if their country was about to be attacked by despotic

Russia? And if they did refuse, would the government then shut down socialist newspapers and imprison party activists? Older socialists had painful memories of such repression in the not-so-distant past, and the Social Democrats still suffered annoying official restrictions that did not apply to other parties. If, on the other hand, they supported the government in this moment of crisis, might it put a stop to long years of being labeled subversives and traitors? Could this be, as one socialist put it, the chance to show "that the fatherland's poorest son was also its most loyal"?

In the end, most German socialists were, like everyone else, carried along on the unstoppable torrent of emotion. Two parliamentary deputies taking the train to Berlin had been startled to hear socialist songs—being happily sung by uniformed reservists heading for war. When the party caucus finally took a straw vote on war credits, of 111 deputies, only 14 voted no, among them Hugo Haase, whom the now murdered Jaurès had embraced at Brussels. The next day, following party discipline, they all cast ballots for war credits along with the rest of the German parliament. Delighted to get his financing, the Kaiser declared, "Henceforth I know no parties, I know only Germans."

Echoing him unawares, the president of the French Chamber of Deputies said, "There are no more adversaries here, there are only Frenchmen." In St. Petersburg, too, war fever spread. Strikers pulled down their street barricades and joined the enthusiastic crowds waving flags with the double-headed tsarist eagle outside the French, Belgian, and Serbian embassies.

Countries vied with each other to declare the war a crusade for the most noble goals. *Le Matin*, a big French daily, on August 4 called the conflict a "holy war of civilization against barbarity." In Germany the next day, a Social Democratic Party newspaper charged that tsarist Russia "wants to crush the culture of all of Western Europe." In Russia, the leftist writer Maxim Gorky was one of many who signed a statement supporting the fight against the "Germanic yoke." When Ottoman Turkey shortly joined the war on the German side, its sultan declared it was fighting a sacred struggle, or *jihad*.

On both sides, also, governments were delighted to discover that they had feared the left too much. French authorities, for example, worried by socialist anti-militarism, had estimated that 13 percent of reservists would fail to report for duty—but only 1.5 percent did not show

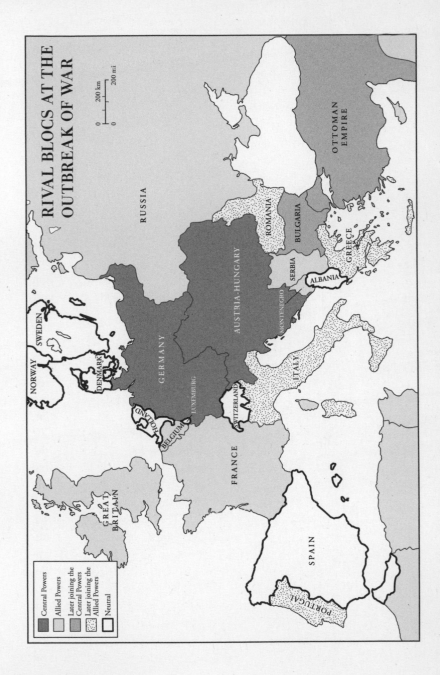

RIVAL BLOCS AT THE
OUTBREAK OF WAR

0   200 km
0   200 mi

RUSSIA

NORWAY

SWEDEN

DENMARK

GERMANY

HOLLAND

BELGIUM

LUXEMBURG

SWITZERLAND

AUSTRIA-HUNGARY

ROMANIA

BULGARIA

SERBIA

MONTENEGRO

ALBANIA

GREECE

OTTOMAN
EMPIRE

ITALY

FRANCE

GREAT
BRITAIN

SPAIN

PORTUGAL

Central Powers

Allied Powers

Later joining the
Central Powers

Later joining the
Allied Powers

Neutral

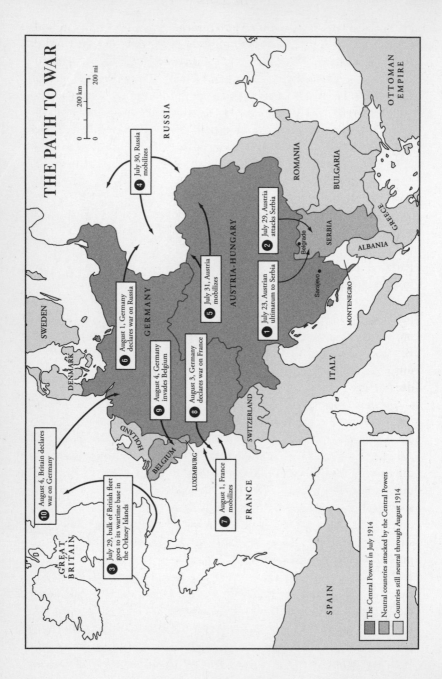

THE PATH TO WAR

200 km
200 mi

RUSSIA

④ July 30, Russia mobilizes

⑤ July 31, Austria mobilizes

⑥ August 1, Germany declares war on Russia

① July 23, Austrian ultimatum to Serbia

② July 29, Austria attacks Serbia

AUSTRIA-HUNGARY

GERMANY

SWEDEN

DENMARK

ROMANIA

BULGARIA

GREECE

SERBIA

ALBANIA

Belgrade

Sarajevo

MONTENEGRO

OTTOMAN EMPIRE

⑨ August 4, Germany invades Belgium

⑧ August 3, Germany declares war on France

HOLLAND

BELGIUM

LUXEMBURG

SWITZERLAND

ITALY

⑦ August 1, France mobilizes

FRANCE

⑩ August 4, Britain declares war on Germany

③ July 29, bulk of British fleet goes to its wartime base in the Orkney Islands

GREAT BRITAIN

SPAIN

The Central Powers in July 1914

Neutral countries attacked by the Central Powers

Countries still neutral through August 1914

up. Socialist leaders soon joined governments of national unity in both France and Belgium. The French minister of the interior sent word to local police chiefs *not* to arrest anyone listed in Carnet B, the government's secret roster of several thousand people it considered dangerous subversives. He guessed right: 80 percent of them would eventually do military service. Even in Austria-Hungary, with its restless mix of ethnic groups to whom mobilization orders had to be issued in more than half a dozen languages, the authorities were amazed that so few men refused the call-up. In the end, as the historian Barbara Tuchman wrote, "The working class went to war willingly, even eagerly, like the middle class, like the upper class, like the species."

"A wide road leads to war," goes a Russian proverb. "A narrow path leads home."

Early on the morning of August 4, German troops crossed the Belgian frontier. Opinion in the British cabinet, in Parliament, and among the public now swung overwhelmingly toward intervention. With Belgium invaded, the Liberal government would be accused by its parliamentary opponents of failing to uphold the national honor if it did not respond. Britain immediately delivered to Germany the final ultimatum of these ultimatum-filled weeks: halt the invasion by midnight or Britain would declare war.

With German soldiers flooding into Belgium, few people in England were in the mood to remember that British troops had been equally uninvited and unwelcome in the various parts of Africa and Asia they had invaded over the last century or two. Belgium seemed a different matter: it was inhabited by white people and less than 100 miles away. The nation, in fact, had virtually been created under the sponsorship of Britain, which had long wanted a friendly power on the other shore of the eastern approach to the English Channel. Belgium's strategic importance mattered most to the government; the British public reacted more emotionally, for citizens of a great imperial power always like to think of themselves as anointed protectors of the weak. But even many anti-imperialists on the left were shocked by the spectacle of hundreds of thousands of German troops in spike-topped helmets shooting their way into a small country that had done nothing to provoke them.

Throughout Europe the summer weather had been unusually warm, enticing people into the streets. As the evening of August 4 ticked by with no German reply to the British ultimatum, thousands gathered in front of Buckingham Palace and in Parliament Square, less exuberant than the crowds in Berlin, perhaps, but equally loyal to their country, and equally eager to cheer the newly mobilized soldiers in uniform marching through the streets. As Big Ben tolled 11 P.M. — midnight in Berlin — and Britain declared war, thousands of voices began to sing "God Save the King."

Observing formalities to the last, the Kaiser sent a message to his first cousin King George V, resigning his honorary posts as field marshal in the British army and admiral of the fleet in the Royal Navy. In Parliament, meanwhile, with astounding swiftness — helped by the fact that victimized Belgium, like Ireland, was heavily Catholic — the Irish crisis evaporated. All sides agreed to put home rule on hold.

Throughout Europe, men were fearful not of being killed, but of not getting a chance to fight before the war was over. "A single worry tormented me at that time, as with so many others, would we not reach the Front too late?" wrote a young corporal from Austria, Adolf Hitler. The British novelist Alec Waugh recalled how he and his friends "joined with our elders in the discussions about peace, but we kept to ourselves the consideration that weighed most with us. We did not want the war to end before we had reached the trenches; we dreaded having to sit silent after the war when men only a few months older than ourselves compared front-line experiences."

The day after its declaration of war, Britain, too, declared that the very fundaments of civilization were at stake. The country was fighting, Asquith told the House of Commons, "not for aggression or the advancement of its own interests, but for principles whose maintenance is vital to the civilised world." Unfortunately for him, however, the two sides in this war, as in most, did not conveniently break down into the forces of enlightenment and darkness. One of Britain's allies, after all, was Russia. "Semi-barbarians," Emily Hobhouse called the Russians, in a letter to a Boer friend, when the war began. "Pretty bedfellows indeed!" Nor would Germany's invasion of Belgium be the only case of a great power assuming the right to march across the territory of a neutral one: within weeks, British troops would cross Chinese soil to attack the German colony of Tsingtao.

With reservists summoned to active duty by telegrams, church bells, and even bugle calls, some six million soldiers were flowing in trains, wagons, on horseback, and on foot across Europe and the British Isles toward various battlefronts. It was the largest mass movement of men and arms ever seen. Between countries in the world's industrial heartland, limited war was no longer possible. Total war, of a sort not seen before, was about to begin.

Two days after Britain entered the fray, a despairing Hardie took a train to Wales, to appear at a long-planned public meeting in his parliamentary constituency in the coal-mining town of Merthyr Tydfil. Having been a strong supporter of a local miners' strike some years before, he was a popular figure in the district. Here, in the bedrock of British labor militance, he believed public opinion would be with him. But the miners' union official who was to chair the meeting took Hardie aside, and—he would later write—never forgot the "look of surprise and astonishment . . . on his face when I told him that the feeling was intensely in favour of war." When someone taunted Hardie about why his sons had not enlisted, he replied, "I would rather see my two boys put up against a wall and shot than see them go to the War." In response came hoots and jeers.

The meeting dissolved in pandemonium, with Hardie and his supporters drowned out by a much larger group who sang the national anthem and "Rule Britannia." When he left the hall, jostled by an angry crowd, shots were fired, apparently into the air. "We walked up the street followed by a howling mob," a colleague remembered. "He looked neither left nor right, his head erect, grey haired, grey bearded chieftain, one of the grandest men that had ever braved the rabble." He spent the night in the house of the local schoolmaster, surrounded by a mob shouting, "Turn the German out!"

Compounding Hardie's grief was a more personal sorrow, for at some unknown point not long before the war that engulfed Europe, his love affair with Sylvia Pankhurst had quietly come to an end. We can only guess at the reasons. Some difficulties were there from the beginning: the great difference in their ages, their all-consuming work. In the previous few years, she had come into her own on the national political stage and perhaps no longer felt the same need for the affirmation Hardie's attention had given her, or perhaps Hardie was put off by her streak of martyrdom. Or perhaps she simply grasped that Hardie was never going to leave his wife. In any case, the love letters and poems ceased. Although the two remained friends, and on one or two occasions spoke from the same platform, Hardie now faced the most painful moment of his political life alone.

Although some generals knew enough to fear otherwise, most people were confident the war would be short. The explorer Sir Ernest Shackleton, about to set out from England to attempt the first full crossing of the Antarctic continent, patriotically telegraphed the Admiralty offering to cancel his plans and put his ship and crew at its service. Within an hour he received a one-word telegram: "Proceed." The very day that Britain joined the war, the King sent for Shackleton and handed him a Union Jack to carry on the expedition. By the time Shackleton got to Antarctica, crossed it, and returned, all expected, the war would be long past and the country ready to celebrate the British flag's being raised over yet more new places on the globe.

Two who cared about keeping that flag flying, Alfred Milner and Rudyard Kipling, welcomed their country's taking part in the great fight. Both had been restlessly anticipating this moment for years. Even before Britain declared war, Milner had been pressing friends in the government to send troops to France. When the declaration finally came he said, "It is better to have an end of the uncertainty." Kipling claimed to have only two frustrations now: that he was too old to fight, and that John, just turning 17, was too nearsighted. But perhaps if the war lasted long enough that barrier could be overcome.

An everyone-at-your-posts order meant that Violet Cecil's husband, Edward, back in England on leave, was promptly recalled to Egypt, which would leave her free to spend more time with Milner. But her 18-year-old George, unlike John Kipling, was heading for the front, his battalion of the Grenadier Guards among the first British units ordered to France. Violet and her daughter Helen handed baskets of fruit through a window as the troop train began to move; soldiers cheered; a band played "Auld Lang Syne"; and his mother had one last glimpse of George's "flushed, excited face thrust out of the window." For the first time ever in Helen's sight, Violet burst into tears.

Milner soon went to stay with her at Great Wigsell; the army had requisitioned his own country house as an officers' barracks. (Enlisted men slept in rows of tents in his fields.) We do not know what he said to her, but he may well have reassured her that at least George was in the best of hands, of officers who had proven their mettle in the Boer War, where he had known them. For in charge of the corps of two army divisions of which George's battalion would be a part was Sir Douglas Haig. And commanding the entire 75,000-man British Expeditionary Force being rushed across the English Channel was Sir John French.

8

AS SWIMMERS INTO
CLEANNESS LEAPING

T HE NEWS THAT armies were on the march spread instantly
throughout the continent, from Trafalgar Square to Nevsky
Prospekt. At Saint-Malo on the coast of France, a picturesque
walled city in Brittany, townspeople and summer vacationers gathered
somberly to hear the mayor read Germany's declaration of war. Among
the crowd was a fugitive from British justice.

In the preceding months, Emmeline Pankhurst had tangled with
the authorities more furiously than ever, and they had begun using a
new legal tool against her. To deprive suffragettes on hunger strikes of
their martyrdom, the government was applying a law called the Prisoners (Temporary Discharge for Ill Health) Act, which everyone immediately rechristened the Cat and Mouse Act. Any hunger-striking
suffragette would be released when she became weak, allowed to recover, and then rearrested as many times as necessary for her to serve
her sentence.

A court had sent Pankhurst to prison the previous year because
one night several suffragettes had slipped into a country house being
built for Chancellor of the Exchequer David Lloyd George and planted
a bomb, whose blast destroyed five rooms. Pankhurst had not known
about the bombing beforehand but promptly gave it her enthusiastic

blessing. As a result, she was found guilty of "wickedly and maliciously" inciting "persons unknown" and given three years' penal servitude.

Declaring herself to be "a prisoner of war," she repeatedly went on hunger strikes, and the government repeatedly released and rearrested her. During her most recent imprisonment she had reached a new peak of defiant fury, and was put into solitary confinement for a week, accused of insubordination, using offensive language, and striking a prison officer. Released, she was ordered to return to prison once again on July 22, 1914. Instead, pale and emaciated, she had fled across the Channel to recuperate in the company of the exiled Christabel. British officials must have expected both mother and daughter to be ardent opponents of the war; indeed, on its very eve, as ultimatums filled the air of Europe, Christabel was quick to declare that war would be "God's vengeance upon the people who held women in subjection."

But as soon as actual fighting began, everything changed: Emmeline ordered all Women's Social and Political Union activity to halt. The British government, meanwhile, unconditionally freed all imprisoned suffragettes. (The amnesty was greeted with relief at Scotland Yard's Special Branch, where it released many of Basil Thomson's agents for new duties, including the 12 who earned a bonus of three shillings a week for knowing shorthand. They had often been kept busy recording suffragette rallies.) Although the next issue of the WSPU's fiery newspaper, the *Suffragette,* had already been printed, Emmeline and Christabel canceled its distribution and embarked for home. As the ferry took them across the Channel to England, tens of thousands of John French's soldiers were on troop transports steaming in the other direction. Emmeline was heading toward a battle of her own — with her daughter Sylvia.

Just before the war began, Emmeline and Christabel had pushed Sylvia out of the WSPU. But the rift was about to deepen. True to her socialist convictions, Sylvia passionately opposed British participation in the war. A public clash with her mother and sister seemed inevitable.

Voices like Sylvia's were few. Even Charlotte Despard, who had spoken against "this criminal war" to a rally of more than 2,000 women on the night Britain declared hostilities, fell uncharacteristically silent; it was hard to oppose the war when her beloved younger brother was now commander in chief at the front. Keir Hardie, who continued to call the war a catastrophe, found himself jeered on the street in London. A fellow MP came upon him sitting on the terrace of the House of Commons, gazing despairingly at the Thames. Although he roamed the country speaking his mind, one comrade described him as "crumpled in body and broken in spirit." In the euphoria of mobilization, press coverage of his speeches was scanty, and few people seemed to notice when his Independent Labour Party issued a defiant proclamation: "Across the roar of guns, we send sympathy and greeting to the German Socialists. . . . They are no enemies of ours, but faithful friends."

Hardie faced a dilemma common to peace activists then and now: how do you oppose a war without seeming to undermine the husbands, fathers, and brothers of your fellow citizens whose lives are in danger? Occasionally he equivocated, at one point speaking of pushing German troops back across their borders. His heart went out to the families who soon started receiving tragic news from France, sometimes those who were his political enemies. After the only son of a wealthy, stridently chauvinist Conservative MP was killed at the front, Hardie wrote to a friend that he wanted "to go up to him and put my arms around his neck."

For a country that, until almost the last minute, had looked as if it might not join the conflict, the transformation was stunning. Military recruiters were warmly welcomed everywhere, as streets were cordoned off so that men waiting to enlist could practice bayoneting dummies. Newly enlisted soldiers marched off to railway stations singing. On August 1 only eight men had signed up at the army's principal recruiting office in London. Three days later, the crowd trying to get in was so large that 20 policemen were needed to force a path for the officer on duty to reach his post. Three days after that, to accommodate all applicants, the Edinburgh recruiting office had to remain open all night.

In London alone, 100 new recruits were sworn in every hour. Some two dozen plays on patriotic themes, with titles like *Call to Arms,* were rushed into West End theaters, and during intermissions recruiters signed up men from the audience. At Knavesmire, Yorkshire, delighted spectators filled the stands at a racecourse to watch squadrons of the Royal Scots Greys practice the cavalry charges they planned to use against German troops in France. Everywhere, recruiters found that one thing above all was certain to draw a torrent of eager men: music from a military band. Some units were so flooded with would-be recruits that they began charging an entrance fee; others had to drill with umbrellas or broomsticks for lack of rifles. Tens of thousands of men were turned away on grounds of age or health, among them the imperial-minded novelist John Buchan, who was deeply disappointed. Within a year or two, the need for soldiers would be so great that those barriers would diminish, but at the beginning men felt them keenly: when Edgar Francis Robinson, a 33-year-old London lawyer, was turned down by the army for health reasons, he shot himself.

Similar fervor was to be found around the world. In Canada, Australia, and New Zealand, among the white population of South Africa and British settlers in colonies throughout the empire, men rushed to sign up, and battalions of those who were already trained began boarding ships for Europe, to support the mother country in its hour of need.

In Britain itself, labor unrest came to an almost complete halt; plans for a general strike in November were shelved; union leaders spoke at recruiting rallies and so many members of the coal miners' union joined up that the government, worrying about coal supplies for the navy, forbade more from enlisting. Emrys Hughes, a 20-year-old college student who would later marry Keir Hardie's daughter, was appalled to find a group of soldiers recruiting in his mining town in the Welsh hills. "I thought that in the Westphalian villages [of Germany] the same appeal was being made, and that the miners there would leave their homes among the hillsides . . . to fight . . . in exactly the same spirit."

The national mood was summed up by the 27-year-old poet Rupert Brooke, newly commissioned in the Royal Navy:

> Now, God be thanked Who has matched us with His hour,
> And caught our youth, and wakened us from sleeping,
> With hand made sure, clear eye, and sharpened power,
> To turn, as swimmers into cleanness leaping,
> Glad from a world grown old and cold and weary . . .

Brooke would die early the next year, on board a hospital ship. His feeling of joy and gratitude that war had come at last was echoed in Germany. The war meant "purification, liberation," said Thomas Mann, from the "toxic comfort of peace."

Gray-uniformed German troops now headed for Belgium in 550 trains a day, some with "To Paris" chalked on their sides and bedecked with flowers by enthusiastic crowds. "You will be home before the leaves have fallen from the trees," the Kaiser told his soldiers. The far smaller Belgian army, however, put up an unexpectedly stiff fight. Just as horse-mad as the British, the Germans had included in their invasion force eight cavalry divisions — each with more than 5,000 horses — the largest body of horsemen ever sent into war in Western Europe. But they quickly discovered that the lances and sabers of their famed Uhlans were useless against massed quick-firing Belgian rifles. Hundreds of Uhlans were shot out of their saddles. A ring of Belgian forts surrounding Liège, near the German border, further delayed the invasion until they were finally pounded into submission by giant siege guns, each so large it required 36 horses to pull. Explosions from their shells flung earth and masonry 1,000 feet into the air.

Exasperated by the resistance, the Germans soon imposed a regime of terror, in town after occupied town setting houses aflame, some with families inside. They shot Belgian hostages by the thousands on the pretext — for which there was no clear evidence — that civilians were sniping at German troops. By late August, German forces had taken the capital, Brussels, pushed the remnants of the Belgian army out of the way, and were moving, if considerably behind schedule, into northern France. Still anticipating quick victory, Kaiser Wilhelm II proposed to his generals that, after the war, Germany should permanently take over border areas of France and Belgium, clear them of inhabitants, and settle them with German soldiers and their families.

The French army proved incapable of containing the Germans flooding across the Belgian frontier, and to the southeast, an offensive of their own, where France directly bordered Germany, was disastrous. French prewar planning had centered on the mystique of the attack: great masses of men filled with élan rushing forward in shoulder-to-shoulder bayonet charges or thunderous cavalry assaults that would strike fear into German hearts. Furthermore, France's troops went into battle in the highly visible blue coats and bright red trousers that had long made them the most flamboyantly dressed of Europe's foot soldiers. At a parliamentary hearing two years earlier, the minister of war had shouted down a reformer who wanted to eliminate the red trousers. "Never!" he declared. *"Le pantalon rouge c'est la France!"* Cuirassier cavalrymen in tall brass helmets with horsehair plumes made conspicuous targets in a different way: they were, commented a British officer wryly, "easy to see at long distances, as the sun flashed in all directions from their shining breastplates. As the latter were not bullet-proof, it was difficult to understand their exact function." Zouave troops from France's North African colonies were easy to spot in red caps and baggy trousers of brilliant white. The French officers commanding Algerian cavalry were singled out by their bright red tunics. And in case sight was not enough to guide enemy marksmen, there was sound as well: brass bands led many French infantry units on the attack (a practice also sometimes followed by the Germans). Massive French bayonet charges stalled in the face of German machine-gun and point-blank artillery fire that left shattered body parts, still clad in red, blue, and white, littering the battlefield. In less than a month, nearly 300,000 of those well-dressed soldiers would be dead or wounded. No indication whatsoever of this toll appeared in the British press.

Meanwhile, every soldier in the British Expeditionary Force was given a personal message from Lord Kitchener, the victor of Omdurman and now secretary of state for war, an exhortation about honor, duty, and country that reflected his famous puritanism—and the army's fear of venereal disease: "Keep constantly on your guard against any excesses. In this new experience you may find temptations both in wine and women. You must entirely resist both temptations, and, while treating all women with perfect courtesy, you should avoid any intimacy."

The army Britain fielded in France was not large—when war broke out there were more soldiers on active duty in India than in the British Isles—but the men who began landing on August 9, 1914, in Boulogne and Le Havre were met with a delirium of cheers, ships' whistles, showers of blossoms and candy, and mugs of cider brought by some of the women with whom "intimacy" was to be avoided. Some troops who had served in India greeted the French in the only foreign language they knew, Hindi. Soldiers were rushed to the front by freight train and even by red double-decker London buses that had crossed the Channel with them. The positions they were ordered to defend against a much larger German attacking force were around the Belgian city of Mons, where the Germans had not yet crossed the frontier into France.

The very surroundings hinted that a new, industrialized kind of war was in the offing, for this would be the first time the British army fought in an industrial region. Enlisted men from the working class found themselves surrounded by exactly the world—blast furnaces, factories of grimy brick, drab workers' housing, coal miners emerging from underground with blackened faces—that many of them had joined the army to escape.

Sir John French caused consternation when he impulsively suggested deploying his troops not according to plans British and French generals had carefully worked out over the years, but at the Belgian port of Antwerp, where the remnants of that country's army had retreated. He was overruled, but cabinet ministers were left shaking their heads in dismay. It had not occurred to him that the sea approach to Antwerp, up the Scheldt River, required a long transit through the waters of neutral Holland. Nor, it soon became apparent, was he going to have an easy time getting along with his French counterparts. "They are a low lot," he wrote to Kitchener, "and one always has to remember the class these French generals mostly come from." Worse yet, in the excitement of leaving London for the first British military expedition to the mainland of Western Europe since Waterloo, French's headquarters left its codebooks behind.

All this made no difference to his troops. They loved the short, buoyant field marshal, who wandered around his headquarters after hours in a blue dressing gown, whistling. Their confidence in him was not shared, however, by an ambitious subordinate, General Sir Douglas Haig. "In my own heart," Haig confided to his diary just a week after the war began, "I know that French is quite unfit for this great Command." He strategically voiced the same "grave doubts," he recorded, to someone he had lunch with that day, King George V.

The British Expeditionary Force included four infantry divisions of up to 18,000 men each, and one cavalry division of some 9,000 men. Officers' swords were freshly sharpened. Because of their horses, which had to be hoisted into and out of the holds of vessels in slings, the cavalry took up a disproportionately large amount of space in ships crossing the Channel, and then trains heading to the front. Newly landed in France, his bowlegged gait visible in newsreel films, French inspected two of his infantry units, which he thought looked "well and cheery." In Paris, shouts of "*Vive l'Angleterre!*" came from thousands of throats when he arrived at the Gare du Nord. President Poincaré was disappointed to discover, however, that despite his name, the jovial British commander spoke little French. (The field marshal himself believed otherwise. Reportedly, he was addressing one group of French officers when he heard several of them call out, "*Traduisez!*" [Translate!] He tried to explain that he was already speaking their language.)

While inspecting his units, French was happy to run across men who had served under him in the Sudan, India, and South Africa. His gray mustache and ruddy face became a familiar sight as he spoke before ranks of soldiers, sometimes supporting his short, 61-year-old figure by leaning on a gold-plated walking stick. Kitchener, who was receiving intelligence on a huge buildup of German troops, peppered French with anxious messages. But the field marshal was not worried. "I think I know the situation thoroughly," he replied, "and I regard it as quite favourable to us." After dining at the Ritz in Paris, Sir John noted in his diary, "The usual silly reports of French 'reverses' were going about. All quite untrue!"

In these early weeks he remained remarkably focused on the appearance of his troops—and little else. "I saw the 4th Brigade (Scott-Kerr) file by on the march," he recorded, "—they looked splendid." Among the soldiers marching past in that unit was George Cecil. His battalion had landed at Le Havre to cheers from local fishermen, marched through sunbaked cobblestone streets, then boarded a train for Belgium. Although George doubtless would have been deeply embarrassed, his mother had written to his commander, Brigadier General Robert Scott-Kerr. She was more fearful of her son's health, Violet Cecil told him, "than I am of the bullets," and asked that an older officer keep an eye on him. "At 18 to undergo such a strain as *this* campaign seems to me excessive," she complained. By August 23 his battalion had moved into position among the slag heaps and coal-mining machinery near Mons—sights that were surely as exotic to him as they were familiar to many of his unit's enlisted men. German observation planes could be seen in the sky and the roads were crowded with refugees. Charged with defending a bridge, George's company pulled up paving stones to build barriers against the German attack expected at any moment. In one of the weekly letters she dutifully wrote to his father, Edward, in Egypt, Violet passed on news from George: "He said that up to date it had all been the most glorious fun."

On the other side of the English Channel, a different sort of conflict loomed. Until now, England had known Emmeline and Christabel Pankhurst as the most radical of firebrands. Some weeks after the war began, however, the two of them called a large WSPU rally at the London Opera House on "The Great Need of Vigorous National Defence Against the German Peril." The theater was decorated with the flags of the Allies, including that anathema to the left, the double-headed eagle of tsarist Russia. For Christabel, it was her first public appearance since fleeing the country several years before, and the enthusiastic crowd sang "For She's a Jolly Good Fellow." Sylvia, torn and dismayed by the widening political gulf between them, was in the audience: "The empty stage was hung with dark green velvet. She appeared there alone, lit by a shaft of lime-light, clad in her favourite pale green, graceful and slender. Her W.S.P.U. adorers filed up and presented her with wreaths. She laid them in a semicircle at her feet." Militant women, Christabel told the crowd, should now turn their energy to arousing the spirit of militance in men. When someone shouted "Votes for women!" she retorted, "We cannot discuss that now." She called on the government to mobilize women for the economy in order to free men for the front.

"I listened to her with grief," Sylvia wrote, "resolving to write and speak more urgently for peace." Afterward, she gingerly went backstage to see her sister, but it felt as if "an impenetrable barrier lay between us." When their mother joined them, Emmeline and Sylvia "exchanged a brief greeting, distant as through a veil," before parting ways. From the crowd waiting outside the opera house, as divided as the Pankhurst family, rose competing cheers of "Christabel!" or "Emmeline!" and "Sylvia!"

Before an audience in Glasgow a few weeks later, Sylvia became one of the first suffragettes to speak out against the war. She also published in *Woman's Dreadnought,* the newspaper she had been putting out in the East End in competition with Christabel's WSPU paper, a proposal for a thousand-strong "Women's Peace Expeditionary Force" that would march under a white banner with a dove on it into the no man's land between rival male armies. She also reprinted part of a speech by the antiwar German socialist Karl Liebknecht on how imperialist rivalry had caused the war. And she was one of more than 100 British women who signed an open letter, circulated by Emily Hobhouse, addressed to German and Austrian women. "Do not let us forget our very anguish unites us. . . . We must all urge that peace be made. . . . We are yours in this sisterhood of sorrow."

The other two Pankhursts took quite a different path. With the full blessing of the British government, Christabel set off on a six-month lecture tour of the United States, aimed at persuading Americans to join the war on the Allied side. Emmeline, meanwhile, took to the lecture circuit in England, putting the power of her commanding presence behind the war effort. "I want men to go to battle like the knight of old," she demanded, "who knelt before the altar and vowed that he would keep his sword stainless and with absolute honour to his nation." In Plymouth she told a cheering crowd, "If you go to this war and give your life, you could not end your life in a better way—for to give one's life for one's country, for a great cause, is a splendid thing."

For someone who, only two years before, had thrown rocks through the windows of 10 Downing Street and talked contemptuously of war as something male, this was the most dramatic of transformations. Scarcely less astonishing was the ferocity of the split within a family that for years had campaigned and gone to jail together and, in the case of Emmeline and Sylvia, shared the excruciating hardships of prison hunger strikes. What accounts for it?

Sylvia's antiwar stance was certainly of a piece with her socialist politics and with the beliefs of her former lover, Hardie, but her mother's newfound ardor as a British patriot was more mysterious—and, indeed, it shocked many of her WSPU followers. One reason for Emmeline's war fervor was undoubtedly personal: as a teenager, she had spent several years at a girls' school in Paris, gaining a lifelong love of all things French and a suspicion of Germany. But beyond any such feelings and the tribal allure of wartime patriotism lay another motive for her and Christabel's *volte-face*. To embrace the war wholeheartedly, and publicly place themselves at the service of the British government, was a once-in-a-lifetime opportunity to leave the political fringe where their unpopular campaign of rock throwing and arson had put them and step into an honored position at national center stage. In this grave crisis, they knew, the government would be delighted to have the country's most conspicuous dissidents rally round the flag. And, to give them their due as political crusaders, they surely also knew that doing this could bring them closer to their great goal of winning women the vote.

In late 1914 it was easy enough for a reasonable person to support a war against Germany, which seemed bent on dominating Europe. Stopping Germany might seem a moral imperative, albeit a tragic and regrettable one, given the inevitable bloodshed. Millions of quite unmilitaristic people in Britain felt this way. But now that Emmeline and Christabel had decided to back their country's war effort, to do so with the slightest ambivalence or nuance was for them unimaginable. Theirs was a world of good and evil, with neither subtleties nor paradox, and they had only withering scorn for anyone who didn't agree with them. In the next four years they would take their full-throated vehemence to lengths that would startle even their allies.

When the family divided, no one suffered more than Sylvia, for whom her mother's new patriotic zeal seemed a betrayal of everything the Pankhursts had once believed in. To Emmeline, of course, what was deplorable was Sylvia's position—which she shared with her exiled sister Adela in Australia: "I am ashamed to know where you and Adela stand," Emmeline wrote to her daughter. They would seldom communicate again.

For weeks after the war began, the British public read few details about the actual fighting. Many people simply went about their business as if it were peacetime; Charlotte Despard, for example, noted in her diary having "tea and conversation" with Mr. and Mrs. Gandhi at a London hotel. The first real news came like lightning flashes in a darkened sky on August 30. In a special Sunday edition of the *Times,* its correspondent wrote of

> a retreating and a broken army. . . . Our losses are very great. I have seen the broken bits of many regiments. . . . Some [divisions] have lost nearly all their officers. . . . The German commanders in the north advance their men as if they had an inexhaustible supply. . . . So great was their superiority in numbers that they could no more be stopped than the waves of the sea. . . .

To sum up, the first great German effort has succeeded. We have to face the fact that the British Expeditionary Force, which bore the great weight of the blow, has suffered terrible losses and requires immediate and immense reinforcement. The British Expeditionary Force has won indeed imperishable glory, but it needs men, men, and yet more men.

That final paragraph had actually been written by the nation's chief press censor, and it had just the effect he intended: over the next two days alone, recruiters swore in 30,000 new volunteers.

British soldiers, George Cecil among them, first came under heavy German fire at Mons on August 23. Faced with infantry attacks and a colossal rain of artillery shells, Sir John French ordered his troops to withdraw after a day in which the British suffered 1,600 dead and wounded. Many a single hour later in the war would claim far more casualties than that, but to the newly arrived army, the toll was unexpected and staggering. Since transport was mostly horse-drawn, the battle also left fields and roads strewn with panicked, wounded horses. For the next 13 days, the British did little but retreat through the scorching summer heat—a chaotic, precipitous flight back across the Belgian border, through northern France, and finally to the southeastern outskirts of Paris. Soldiers slept a few hours a night, if at all, by the roadside or in farmers' barns. Desperate to get rid of anything that slowed them down, officers ordered the disheartened troops to abandon excess equipment and supplies; pursuing Germans were thrilled to come upon large piles of ammunition, new boots, canned food, clothing, sides of beef. The long retreat was one of the most drastic in British military annals.

While it was under way, French repeatedly squabbled with his subordinates. "Sir John as usual not understanding the situation in the least," wrote his deputy chief of staff in his diary. "A nice old man but absolutely no brains." He spent comparatively little time at his headquarters, leaving its officers frustrated as he dashed about by car or on horseback, seeking the personal contact with soldiers that he craved. "I met the men and talked to them as they were lying about resting," French recorded. "I told them how much I appreciated their work and what the country thought of them. . . . The wonderful spirit and bearing they showed was beyond all praise — ½ a million of them would walk over Europe!" Nothing daunted the field marshal, not even news of new German divisions appearing nearby. He remained almost farcically ebullient in the face of disaster: "Perhaps the charm of war lies in its glorious uncertainty!"

No one on either side was prepared for the fighting's deadliness. Like the British, recent German and French experience of war had been of minor colonial conflicts with badly armed Africans and Asians: Erich von Falkenhayn, soon to be chief of the German general staff, had helped suppress the Boxer Rebellion in China, and Joseph Joffre, the French commander in chief, had led an expedition across the Sahara to conquer Timbuktu. Neither side had spent much time on the receiving end of fire by machine guns or other modern weaponry. The new generation of long-range, fast-loading artillery, for instance, could leave your troops under a downpour of shells from guns miles away and out of sight. "Louder and louder grew the sound of the guns," wrote one British officer of the German attack, ". . . under a sky of brass, shaking with the concussion of artillery, now a single heavy discharge, then a pulsation of the whole atmosphere, as if all the gods in heaven were beating on drums the size of lakes." Even as they rolled back the British, the Germans, too, seemed totally surprised by the effect of massed fire from clip-loading repeating rifles directed at them. The 15 rounds a minute these weapons could fire took a fearsome toll among dense rows of troops. "The Germans just fell down like logs," remembered a British soldier of one skirmish.

Worrying about her brother, Charlotte Despard tried to see the news from France in the best possible light: "It is with keen admiration but a constriction of heart that I read of my Jack's splendid despatch of the retreat," she wrote in her diary. British cabinet members, on the other hand, saw nothing splendid and felt that French had retreated farther and faster than necessary. They were shocked to find that the field marshal now wanted to pull back more than a hundred miles from the line of battle, to refit and reorganize his battered divisions. French's compassion for his bloodied and exhausted men had overwhelmed his already limited sense of military strategy. To withdraw from the front now would leave a desperate France feeling abandoned by its ally at its moment of greatest danger. Kitchener hastily boarded a British cruiser

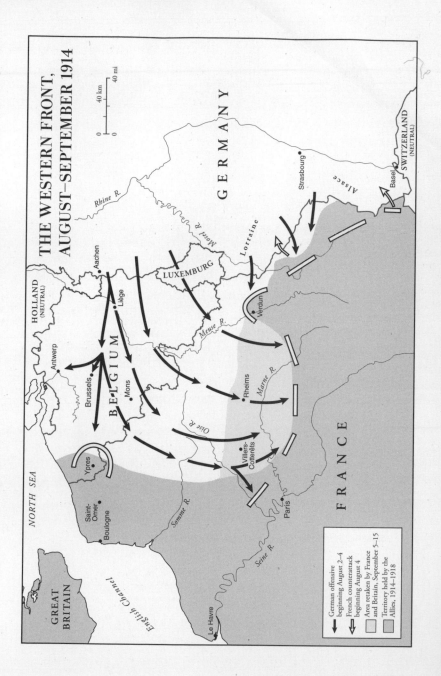

THE WESTERN FRONT,
AUGUST–SEPTEMBER 1914

GERMANY

Rhine R.

HOLLAND
(NEUTRAL)

Aachen

Liège

LUXEMBURG

Moselle R.

Lorraine

Strasbourg

Alsace

SWITZERLAND
(NEUTRAL)

Basel

BELGIUM

Antwerp

Brussels

Mons

Meuse R.

Verdun

NORTH SEA

Ypres

Oise R.

Rheims

Marne R.

Saint-Omer

Boulogne

Somme R.

Villers-
Cotterêts

Paris

FRANCE

GREAT
BRITAIN

English Channel

Seine R.

Le Havre

40 mi
40 km

German offensive
beginning August 2–4

French counterattack
beginning August 4

Area retaken by France
and Britain, September 5–15

Territory held by the
Allies, 1914–1918

for an urgent meeting with his erratic commander at the British embassy in Paris.

Kitchener's post as secretary for war had traditionally been occupied by a civilian. But in this time of need, Alfred Milner and other influential figures had quietly maneuvered a reluctant prime minister into giving the job to the hero of Omdurman, regarded as the country's greatest living military man. It was the first time a serving soldier had been in the cabinet in more than 250 years. French felt threatened by Kitchener, with whom he had never been close, and was insulted that Kitchener wore his field marshal's uniform to Paris—undermining, as French saw it, his own authority as field commander. During a contentious meeting, Kitchener bluntly forbade French to remove his troops from the battlefront.

As dismayed Britons tried to absorb the disastrous news from France, a curious rumor swept the country. This retreat would not matter, because Russians—hundreds of thousands of them, millions of them—were coming to Britain's aid. They had been seen, in vast hordes, pouring off ships at night, filling hundreds of trains which secretly whisked them through England to the Channel ports. They sang, played balalaikas, sported fierce beards, wore fur hats, and called out for vodka in deep voices; their rubles had jammed the slots of railway station vending machines built for pennies; they still had the snow of Russia on their boots. The rumors were so persistent and convincing that a German spy in Scotland urgently reported to Berlin that Russian soldiers had landed at Aberdeen; he himself had seen them heading south in high-speed trains with window blinds drawn.*

The British reverses were especially painful for those who felt their country should not be fighting at all. None of them wanted a German victory; but, few as they were, they felt the war would not be worth the high casualty counts that seemed certain to come. One distinguished dissenter was 42-year-old Bertrand Russell, a Cambridge logician and mathematician. Not only was the pipe-smoking Russell his country's

---

* Russia figured in wild rumors that swept Germany as well. In the war's first week, it was reported that 25 French automobiles were stealthily transporting 80 million gold francs across Germany to Russia. Hundreds of towns set up roadblocks, and a total of 28 people, who were thought to look suspicious or who failed to stop quickly enough, were killed by trigger-happy guards.

best-known philosopher, but his broad forehead, aquiline nose, piercing blue eyes, ramrod posture, and arresting shock of hair, now turning gray, made him one of the most striking-*looking* philosophers of all time. A young woman who fell in love with him wrote to him about "your heathery hair . . . looking robustious and revolutionary"; decades later, in her memoirs, she recalled that Russell's hair "seemed almost to give off sparks like a heath fire."

The grandson of a prime minister, whose earldom he would eventually inherit, Russell explored the abstruse heights of theory—his greatest work, the co-written *Principia Mathematica,* takes 347 pages before reaching a definition of the number 1—but he also wrote fluently and widely for the general public. Over his long life dozens of books flowed from his pen as easily as letters: a popular history of philosophy still read today, collections of essays, a sprinkling of fiction, volumes about China, happiness, politics, socialism, and educational reform. He denounced conventional marriage but had an irresistible attraction for women (one came all the way from the United States to pound on the door of his flat); he hated organized religion but felt moments of spiritual ecstasy; he came from the ruling class yet spent most of his life on the political left. During this greatest crisis of his generation, he loved his country deeply but believed from the start that the war was a tragic mistake.

Part of Russell's intellectual bravery lay in his willingness to confront that last set of conflicting loyalties. He described himself poignantly in the autumn of 1914 as being "tortured by patriotism. . . . I desired the defeat of Germany as ardently as any retired colonel. Love of England is very nearly the strongest emotion I possess, and in appearing to set it aside at such a moment, I was making a very difficult renunciation." What left him even more anguished was realizing that "anticipation of carnage was delightful to something like ninety per cent of the population. . . . As a lover of truth, the national propaganda of all the belligerent nations sickened me. As a lover of civilization, the return to barbarism appalled me. As a man of thwarted parental feeling [he as yet had no children], the massacre of the young wrung my heart."

Over the more than four years of fighting to come, he never yielded in his belief that "this war is trivial, for all its vastness. No great principle is at stake, no great human purpose is involved on either side. . . .

The English and French say they are fighting in defence of democracy, but they do not wish their words to be heard in Petrograd or Calcutta." He was dismayed to see two-thirds of Cambridge and Oxford undergraduates enlist in the war's opening months, their powers of reasoning "swept away in a red blast of hate." These convictions, expressed in an unceasing blizzard of articles and speeches, would soon land him in the forefront of a slowly growing antiwar movement, while losing him old friendships, his Cambridge lectureship, and his passport. Eventually, they would put him behind bars.

Antiwar beliefs were severely tested by the mass patriotic hysteria of the war's first months. "One by one, the people with whom one had been in the habit of agreeing politically went over to the side of the war," as Russell put it, "and as yet the exceptional people . . . had not yet found each other." How hard it was, he wrote, to resist "when the whole nation is in a state of violent collective excitement. As much effort was required to avoid sharing this excitement as would have been needed to stand out against the extreme of hunger or sexual passion, and there was the same feeling of going against instinct."

While dissenters like him tried to make their voices heard against the torrent, generals and cabinet ministers feverishly debated strategy, and men thronged recruiting stations, messages from the War Office were reaching thousands of British homes. On September 8, 1914, Violet Cecil received the news that, following an infantry battle in a French forest, her son George was reported wounded and missing.

9

THE GOD OF RIGHT WILL
WATCH THE FIGHT

WHILE BLOODIED BRITISH and French forces retreated, filling the roads of northern France with haggard troops and ambulances and open wagons full of wounded men, their commanders could at least take comfort that, unlike them, the Germans had to battle on two fronts. For Russia, with its bottomless reserves of manpower, was attacking Germany from the east. Russian armies were already well across the border, heading for the medieval Teutonic city of Königsberg on the Baltic, and had won a battle with German troops on the way. Since so many Germans had been sent west, the advancing Russian forces outnumbered their adversaries by three to one, and, in cavalry, by eight to one. On August 23, 1914, the same day as the battle at Mons, a titanic clash began on the Eastern Front.

Unfortunately for the Allies, though Russia's army was the largest on earth, it was also one of the most inept. There were, for example, little more than half as many rifles available as soldiers who needed them, a matter to which no one seemed to have given much thought. The army had only one battery of antiaircraft guns — which were protecting the Tsar's summer palace. Many Russian generals were elderly and overweight; the nerves of one corps commander proved incapable of withstanding the sound of rifle fire. Higher-ranking officers had been promoted largely by seniority and connections at court; the main claim to renown of the army's chief, Grand Duke Nicholas Nikolaevich, was being the Tsar's cousin. His most visible asset, along with royal blood, was commanding height. At six feet six inches, he towered impressively above all others; in his headquarters, aides pinned pieces of white paper over door frames built for ordinary mortals, to warn him to duck. He had no battlefield experience, and upon being appointed commander in chief he wept, believing himself not up to the job. Furthermore, he and the minister of war were barely on speaking terms, and he was also out of favor with the Tsarina, who connived ceaselessly to weaken his position in the eyes of her husband.

In the Russian military supply services, corruption was the norm. When a major general led a purchasing mission to buy war materiel in the United States, according to a New York businessman, "He and his officers quickly became notorious in the metal trade as grafters. The General himself was less interested in the prices his government had to pay than in trying to get the companies to add a concealed commission for him."

Western suppliers discovered the same expectations when they went to Russia. "A French businessman, seeking a contract to supply ten thousand platoon tents, was duly placing his bribes in the Ministry of War," the historian Alan Clark has written. "Finally he came to the highest point, the minister's personal secretary. . . . To the businessman's alarm the private secretary insisted on a personal 'gratuity' equal in size to all the lesser disbursements which he had been obliged to make on the way up. He protested that, if this last sum were paid out, he would have no profit left on the order. 'Ah,' replied the secretary with a silky smile, 'I understand. But why deliver the tents?'"

When the Grand Duke met his supply staff for the first time, his words to them were "Gentlemen, no stealing."

Russia was a peasant country and roughly one-third of its millions of conscripts were illiterate. Unfamiliar with modern technology and in need of cooking fuel, soldiers sometimes chopped down telegraph poles for firewood. Exasperated commanders then resorted to the radio, but as codebooks had not been properly distributed, the Germans could simply listen in. In these early days, Russian soldiers tended to fire on any airplane, including their own. Not having seen one before, they assumed such an exotic invention must be German.

For the upper classes, the war was still an adventure. Wealthy women sponsored their own private hospital trains, in which their daughters did the nursing, at least when marriageable officers were involved. Such volunteer nurses, however, were allowed to treat only "cases of light wounds, above the belt." Observers noticed that these hospital trains tended to migrate to the rear of the Imperial Guard regiments, whose officers were likely to come from the most eligible layer of St. Petersburg society.

This, then, was the army that went into battle in the swamps and forests of East Prussia on August 23, with a German force whose size and position were unknown. In the inscrutable ways of the Russian bureaucracy, the commanding general, Alexander Samsonov, had just finished seven years as governor of Turkestan when, less than two weeks earlier, he had been placed in charge of troops and staff he had never seen before. As his tired, ill-fed soldiers blundered forward through unfamiliar terrain, they were set upon by large detachments of well-supplied German troops, who—thanks to overheard radio transmissions—knew exactly where to find them. Largely unaware, Samsonov was at his headquarters in a town behind the lines having dinner with a British military attaché when a whole division of panicked retreating troops came pouring down the street. As the sound of German artillery fire drew closer, Samsonov commandeered some Cossack horses and headed to the front to take on-the-spot command of whatever forces remained. Urging the British attaché to get away while he could, the general rode off, saying, obscurely, "The enemy has luck one day, we will have luck another."

Samsonov had no luck. The Russians who were not captured tried to retreat, only to find that the Germans now controlled all passable roads. From one entire army corps (well over 25,000 soldiers) under Samsonov's command, only a single man returned to Russia. When the battle was over, although the Germans had suffered 13,000 casualties, the Russians had lost more than 30,000 men killed or wounded, plus 92,000 taken prisoner—60 German trains were needed to transport them to POW camps. Like his army's remnants, Samsonov, too, ended up fleeing. With their horses unable to cross marshy ground, he and some aides slogged through the night on foot. When their supply of matches was exhausted, they could no longer read their compasses. Shortly after midnight, Samsonov moved apart from the rest of the group and shot himself.

Soon after this debacle, the Germans crushed a second invading Russian army. The Russian general commanding it lost his nerve and fled home by car. All in all, during a month of fighting, the Russians lost 310,000 men killed, wounded, or taken prisoner, as well as 650 artillery pieces. Industrial war had taken an instant and devastating toll of their half-industrialized country. For the rest of the conflict, Russia's armies would never again pose a threat to Germany.

In November, sensing that the winds were blowing in Germany's favor, a longtime rival of Russia, the Ottoman Empire, joined the Central Powers, as the alliance between Germany and Austria-Hungary was now called. This opened up a new front in the rugged mountains and valleys of the Caucasus, where the Turkish and Russian empires met. As if they had not heard enough bad news already, toward the end of 1914, Russian officials began receiving troubling secret-police reports of revolutionary agitators spotted talking to wounded soldiers, and to fresh troops heading for the front on the Trans-Siberian Railway. Antiwar leaflets were also found. In several units, including those that ran the crucial railroads to the front, the army discovered cells of the most militant underground revolutionary faction, the Bolsheviks. In the more developed countries of Western Europe the lower classes had stopped talking of revolution and patriotically joined the fighting, but in Russia, it seemed, their loyalty was not so certain.

That prospect did not trouble the Tsar and Tsarina. Long after Russian casualties started streaming home from the front, she still ordered special trains each week to rush fresh flowers more than a thousand miles northward from the Crimea to the capital, to decorate the imperial palace.

The Russian defeats were so massive they could not be kept hidden, but the British press preferred to emphasize instead the news from a less important front where the Russians were having success against the only major army that was even more incompetent than their own. Reflecting the power structure of the Austro-Hungarian Empire, three-quarters of its officers were of German-speaking stock, while only one enlisted man in four understood the language. Throughout late 1914 until they were halted by winter, Russian troops advanced steadily, inflicting great casualties as they pushed the Austro-Hungarians back into the rugged Carpathian Mountains, where wounded men stranded on the battlefield faced an additional terror: prowling wolves, already gorging themselves on the bodies of the dead.

Austrian cavalrymen made excellent targets in their brilliant blue-and-red uniforms (which, unlike the French, they would not abandon for several years). One of many Britons who took heart from this Russian advance was Sir Ernest Shackleton, who had his last news of the war that autumn as he set sail for Antarctica. "The Russian Steam-Roller was advancing. According to many the war would be over within six months."

In England, enthusiasm remained strong. "I would not be out of this glorious delicious war for anything the world could give me," Churchill told Margot Asquith, the prime minister's wife. Most people were so confident that it would be over quickly that brokers began offering "peace insurance": if you paid £80, you would receive £100 if the war hadn't ended by January 1, 1915 — and you could more than quadruple your money if the war wasn't over by September 15, 1915.

At soccer matches, army recruiters patrolled outside the gates with sandwich boards saying "Your Country Needs You"; patriotic speakers addressed crowds before the games started; players themselves stepped forward as volunteers, to great bursts of applause. Fans followed their example, so these games proved the single best venue for recruiters. One poster, taking a phrase from Newbolt's poem, invited volunteers to "Play the Game!" and showed Kitchener, French, Haig, and others lined up in different positions on a team for another sport, rugby. The first correspondent sent to cover the fighting in France by the proprietor of the *Daily Mail,* Lord Northcliffe, was the paper's sports editor. The *Times,* which Northcliffe also owned, published these verses:

> Come, leave the lure of the football field
> With its fame so lightly won,
> And take your place in a greater game
> Where worthier deeds are done. . . .
>
> Come, join the ranks of our hero sons
> In the wider field of fame,

> Where the God of Right will watch the fight,
> And referee the game.

Eagerness to fight was not the full story behind soaring recruitment figures, however. When London trolley workers went on strike, for instance, the city council simply fired all males of military age and urged them to join up. Young men working for local governments and businesses often found themselves "released" from their jobs so they could volunteer. Although a bumpy economy had thrown hundreds of thousands of people out of work and was raising food prices, the government quietly asked charities not to aid jobless men eligible to enlist. The bull-necked, immensely wealthy "King of Lancashire," Lord Derby, who owned 68,000 acres of land and employed more than 75 servants and gardeners at his manor house alone, declared that after the war he intended to hire only men who had been at the front. Hundreds of other landowners and employers followed his example — especially after Derby was appointed director general of recruiting.

Young John Kipling once again was crushed when he failed the army medical exam. But this time, making use of the new climate of national urgency, his father called upon a friend for help, the renowned Field Marshal Lord Roberts, a hero of many nineteenth-century colonial wars, whom he had first known in India. Roberts pulled the necessary strings and, to Rudyard Kipling's delight, got John a commission in the Irish Guards. Kipling proudly identified with his son, writing to a friend that "he's rather like what I was, to look at, at his age." Just turned 17, John began training with the regiment in Essex. His father, meanwhile, suggested that Oxford should close down and that all undergraduates should be sent into the military. His poetry throbbed with martial fervor:

> For all we have and are,
> For all our children's fate,
> Stand up and take the war,
> The Hun is at the gate!

But Kipling was not all blood and thunder. Trying to assuage a shaken Violet Cecil, he carefully tracked down wounded survivors of the battle where young George had last been seen, and interviewed them in their hospital beds. None knew George's fate, but Kipling was able to sketch for Violet a map of the fighting. The Germans had been surging down a forest road near the French town of Villers-Cotterêts and George's unit, near a clearing in the woods, could hear their shouts and bugle calls. A German machine gun began spraying bullets into the clearing and surrounding forest, dotted with British troops. By one account, with enough of a storybook feel to make one skeptical, George ordered his men to fix bayonets and led them in a counterattack. When a bullet hit him in the hand, he stumbled, then drew his sword and shouted, "Charge lads, and we'll do 'em in yet!" The charge, it was said, delayed the Germans and helped other British troops escape, but left dozens of Grenadier Guardsmen dead or wounded, George among them, on the forest floor.

Milner found Violet "terribly distressed and looking very ill." The War Office could offer her no further details. Desperate for information, she turned to the American ambassador, as a representative of a neutral power, but he could not help either. She then wired a cousin working in neutral Holland, asking him to check whether George could be a prisoner of the Germans. Or might some French family, she wondered, be sheltering him behind enemy lines? After all, George spoke French well. "I have every reliance on George's resourcefulness and brain," she wrote. "But he may be too ill to think."

The Germans advanced well beyond the point where George had gone missing, and for a terrifying moment it looked as if Paris itself might fall. On September 5, 1914, German troops were only 23 miles away. Shops closed, traffic vanished, hotels emptied. Thousands of Parisians who had not fled were impressed into labor battalions to build barricades of felled trees and dig trenches on the main roads into town. To provide food in case the city was besieged, cattle were put to graze in the great park of the Bois de Boulogne. Ingloriously, in the dark of night, government ministries burned nonessential files and moved their offices hundreds of miles southwest, to Bordeaux. In a foretaste of the scorched earth that would become a hallmark of the war, retreating French soldiers destroyed bridges and railway lines behind them, slowing down the advancing Germans and their chain of supplies. Then an imaginative French general commandeered 600 taxis to rush some of his infantrymen to the front. After Kitchener laid down the law to Sir John French, the reluctant field marshal ordered British troops into action as well. The Germans were finally halted and in the end pushed back some 45 miles. Paris was saved.

The news was flashed around the world, bringing jubilant headlines — "Turn of the Tide," said the *Times*—and joy and relief to millions. It was soon followed by word that General von Moltke, whose mission had been to achieve a swift victory, had lost his job. For Violet Cecil, however, what mattered was something else: Villers-Cotterêts and the forest clearing where George was last seen had been retaken by the Allies. Although Milner tried to dissuade her, on September 19 she embarked for France.

There she promptly enlisted the help of her old family friend Georges Clemenceau, now a senator and newspaper editor, who made inquiries of hospitals and ambulance stations around Villers-Cotterêts. Trying to bolster her spirits, he told her that he believed George to be a prisoner. With a car and military attaché on loan from the American ambassador, she made her way to the town. "The Mayor had had instructions to facilitate my search. I found many relics picked up on the battlefield, some of them men's pocket books, and among them some signed by my boy." (Every soldier was required to carry a small brown leather-covered notebook showing his identification details, next of kin, inoculations, and other data. Each record of a wage payment bore an officer's signature.) Then, from a Grenadier Guards officer news reached her that George had last been seen lying in a ditch with a bad head wound.

Frustrated and despairing, she returned to England. Milner met her ship and they drove back to Great Wigsell together, too depressed to talk. Late the following day, however, came a telegram from her cousin in Holland: George, it said, might indeed be a wounded prisoner at Aachen, Germany. "It is *only a rumour*," she wrote to an army officer acquaintance. "I am not building any hopes on it."

Kipling was able to enlist former president Theodore Roosevelt in the search for George. "Mr. Roosevelt is asking the Kaiser to give him a list of our wounded," Carrie Kipling wrote. Nothing came of this either. "And so the horrible see-saw goes on," Rudyard Kipling told a friend. "She dying daily and letters of condolence *and* congratulation crossing each other and harrowing her soul. Meanwhile the boy's father thousands of miles away and cut off from all save letters and wires."

"I don't feel as if George could be dead," Violet wrote her husband in Egypt, "but that is simply because I saw him last so well and full of life. My instincts tell me he is alive—my reason that he is dead." A kind of numbness crept over her: "I write calmly—I eat, I walk, I talk, I sleep, I feel hot and cold, I write my letters. I have all the appearance of a live person." Further searching turned up nothing. Milner asked a friend to travel to Holland, where it was possible to contact German government officials in a way that couldn't be done from England, but a wire from him reported that the Germans had no record of George as a prisoner. Gradually Violet's hopes began to flicker out.

George Cecil was but one of hundreds of thousands of soldiers already missing, wounded, or dead only two months into the war, a chaotic and bloody period in which the fighting had not gone according to the orderly plans of either side. The battlefield was still one of movement, as huge armies tried to wheel and outflank each other, sometimes marching a dozen or more miles a day with thousands of supply wagons rumbling along behind and sending up choking clouds of dust. Short of military vehicles, the British mobilized everything at hand, from moving vans to beer trucks, and these, with their original signs promising less deadly contents, carried ammunition to the troops. There was still a role for the British cavalry: not the thousands-strong charges of the pre-machine-gun age, but occasional small skirmishes and, especially during bad weather that grounded spotter planes, reconnaissance forays to probe French lanes, fields, and forests, trying to find where the Germans were.

Sometimes the Germans themselves did not quite know where they were. Wars abound in chaos, but in the early stages of this one the confusion was of a new order of magnitude as millions of soldiers streamed along narrow country roads in the late-summer heat. In their wake came an array of problems that no commander had expected. This may have been the first industrialized war, but the industrialization was erratic and undependable. As the German army moved ever farther from its railway lines—an infantry division required some two dozen freight cars of supplies per day—other forms of transport became crucial. But automotive engines were in their infancy, and during the army's push into France, 60 percent of its trucks broke down. This left preindustrial horses to do the work. But they, too, required fuel: some two million pounds of feed a day, far more than the countryside could furnish. Eating unripe green corn from French fields, German horses sickened and began dying by the tens of thousands. And when horses pulling supply wagons gave out, soldiers started running low on food—and on artillery ammunition; it evidently had not occurred to planners on either side that the new quick-firing howitzers would use up shells so rapidly. In the end, the very size of the German juggernaut proved a liability: a full-strength German army corps on the move, for example, could stretch out over 18 miles of road, which meant that when the head of the column finished its day's march, the rear had barely begun. The longer the fighting continued, the less it resembled the tidy, forward-thrusting arrows that rival general staffs had long been used to inscribing on maps. The armies began to bog down.

By late October, neither side could make much headway against the other, so each began digging protective trenches. The war of maneuver was over—just temporarily, the generals thought—and the front line began to solidify. Two parallel rows of trenches faced each other on a wriggling, northwest-to-southeast diagonal beginning at the English Channel, then crossing a corner of Belgium, northern France, and finally a tiny sliver of its onetime province of Alsace (all France had been able to capture from Germany), some 475 miles in all, ending at the Swiss frontier.

Trench warfare was not new. The American Civil War had ended with a version of it, at the besieged Confederate capital, Richmond, and at nearby Petersburg, and more recently British troops had sometimes dug in to protect themselves against Boer fire. But it seemed such an ignoble sort of combat that hardly anyone in Europe planned for it, certainly not Sir John French, who concluded, almost incredulously, in a report to the King, that "the *spade* will be as great a necessity as the rifle." Nonetheless, his cavalryman's optimism remained undaunted. "In my opinion," he insisted to Kitchener in October, "the enemy are vigorously playing their last card, and I am confident they will fail."

As his men wielded their spades, French began dreaming of cavalry attacks that would make combat glorious once again. He proposed an aggressive thrust at the Germans, unfazed by the fact that his troops would have to cross a large swamp in the process, but his subordinate commanders and staff officers talked him out of it. "The little fool has no sense at all. . . . He cannot read a map in scale," one of them wrote. "It is really hopeless."

While France held most of the front line against the Germans, the British Expeditionary Force had moved to the end of the front closest to the English Channel. From late October through most of November, they and nearby French and Belgian troops were battered by repeated German attacks around the ancient Belgian weaving center of Ypres. Heavily reinforced with new men from England, the British held a bulge in the front line that included the town itself, a picturesque assemblage of Gothic arches, medieval ramparts, a spired cathedral, and the landmark Cloth Hall with a clock tower — almost all of which would soon be shattered into rubble by German artillery fire.

In their introduction to trench warfare, the British made all kinds of mistakes: they did not have enough spades, for instance, and sometimes had to dig with pitchforks taken from Belgian barns. But the German attackers proved even more maladroit. Masses of them advanced head-on into British rifle and machine-gun fire, young officer cadets walking to their deaths with flowers in their helmets, singing patriotic songs. Astonished British soldiers looking through their binoculars saw German troops advancing with arms linked, wearing caps with what appeared to be the badges distinct to university students. Nor did Germans with regulation helmets seem to realize that the little spikes on top only made the wearers better targets. (These would not be removed until 1916.) "When immediately in front of the enemy," ran the German army's infantry regulations, "the men should charge with bayonet and, with a cheer, penetrate the position." The regulations spelled out what drum rolls should accompany the assault, but not what to do when British machine guns started firing.

Although they greatly outnumbered the British, sometimes by as much as seven to one, the attackers made little headway as British fire slashed huge holes in their lines, leaving thousands of Germans dead. There should have been a clear lesson here about how strongly this strange new style of battle favored defenders, but it was a lesson that, in different ways, each side resisted learning. No general was ready to acknowledge that the machine gun had upended warfare as it had been known for centuries. A single such gun emplacement could stave off hundreds, even thousands of attackers. "I saw trees as large round as a man's thigh literally cut down by the stream of lead from these weapons," wrote an American journalist in Belgium.

Nor was anyone prepared for what the best defensive weapons

turned out to be. In times past, defenses had offered their own kind of glory: great turreted stone fortresses that took years to construct. Now, however, almost anything above ground could be smashed by heavy artillery in days or even hours, as the Germans had done to Belgium's forts. Could it really be that the best defensive position was *below* ground, in nothing more, in the end, than a deep, narrow slit in the earth? And that the most impenetrable fortification was something as mundane as cattle fencing?

It was an Illinois farmer and former county sheriff, Joseph F. Glidden, not a military engineer, who had used some of his wife's hairpins to construct the prototype of a new kind of fence he patented in 1874. Forty years later, unrolled at night in great coils and staked firmly to the ground, barbed wire turned out to be the barrier of all barriers. Cutting through it was hard enough for attackers under the best of circumstances, and almost impossible when bullets were flying. Paradoxically, the same tangle of wires, being porous, easily absorbed the blast of exploding shells, which made it remarkably difficult to destroy.

German barbed wire in particular would prove a nearly insuperable obstacle, spread out for miles in a dense maze 50 to 100 feet wide and anchored to long rows of six-foot-high wooden posts pounded into the ground. For both sides, as they dug in, trenches and wire only grew more elaborate. In case the first line of trenches was breached or captured, several backup lines remained, each with its own thick belt of barbed wire.

Although the generals had not yet grasped it, these multiple lines instantly rendered obsolete the time-honored attacker's goal: the breakthrough. In more old-fashioned combat, once a fortress had been taken, soldiers on foot or horseback could quickly stream many miles beyond it, because the enemy didn't have the months or years needed to build another. But now, if pushed out of one set of trenches, the enemy could simply take refuge in the next one and fight on—or could unroll dense coils of barbed wire in a matter of minutes and dig a rudimentary new trench in a few hours.

Despite machine guns and barbed wire, in these first few months the war sometimes still had a courtliness carried over from earlier times, when people observed a strict distinction between soldiers and civilians. At one point, for example, German troops captured an Englishman—but when they discovered he was a London *Times* correspondent and not a soldier, they let him go. Other civilians also won special treatment, among them Millicent, the Dowager Duchess of Sutherland, one of several aristocratic women who led or sponsored private medical teams in the war zone. When the Belgian city where she was nursing wounded troops was overrun by the Germans, it turned out that both the local German commander and his aide-de-camp were noblemen whom she had met before the war. The Duchess called at their headquarters, presented her card, and, among other demands, asked for transport to Mons so she and her nurses could care for wounded British prisoners there. The Germans dutifully complied, supplying a car and driver.

Many soldiers on both sides found combat thrilling. Julian Grenfell, the eldest son of Lord Desborough, had boxed, rowed, and won steeplechases while at Oxford. A keen shot, he recorded a successful day's bag of "105 partridges" in his "game book" in early October 1914. He took the book to France with him, and the very next entries, following raids on German trenches, are for November 16, "One Pomeranian," and November 17, "Two Pomeranians." "It is all *the* best fun," he wrote home. "I have never felt so well, or so happy, or enjoyed anything so much. . . . The fighting-excitement vitalizes everything, every sign and word and action." A piece of shrapnel would end his life six months later.

By late November, as winter blizzards started, both sides were mainly concentrating on keeping warm. Of the original British Expeditionary Force, one-third were now dead and many more seriously wounded. Before the end of 1914, 90,000 British soldiers would become casualties. Trainloads of maimed men flooded London, where they were rushed into the care of nurses in white, flowing, nun-like headdresses. Banners saying "Quiet for the Wounded" hung outside the city's hospitals, and nearby streets were covered with straw to muffle the sound of horses' hoofs.

For his headquarters, Sir John French had taken over a lawyer's house in Saint-Omer, a town in France some 20 miles inland from the English Channel. Parked outside could be seen a row of automobiles whose chauffeurs wore civilian black double-breasted uniforms and caps, for many well-to-do officers had brought their own cars and drivers to France. One young aide-de-camp, as dutiful about saluting superiors as any other junior officer, was the Prince of Wales, who, two decades later, before abdicating, would reign briefly as King Edward VIII. A steady stream of VIP visitors arrived from London, and one of French's aides was soon ordered to request that headquarters be given a larger entertainment allowance. The King came to award medals, look in on his son, and be assured by French that the war would be over by Christmas. Winston Churchill appeared—there were no nearby sea battles for him to observe as First Lord of the Admiralty, so he wanted to savor some combat on land. So did the venerable Field Marshal Lord Roberts, whose great desire was to visit Indian troops now on the front line. The 82-year-old Roberts was "enraptured by being amongst us," French reported to a lady friend, but then complicated his visit by catching pneumonia and dying.

Additional guests included George G. Moore, French's American playboy housemate from London, who essentially moved into headquarters despite the fact that he was a citizen of a neutral country, and Charles À Court Repington, a fellow womanizer and cavalry enthusiast who was a military correspondent for the *Times*. At this point journalists were not permitted at the front, but Sir John assured London that Repington was staying with him "in an entirely private capacity." Nor did French lack for female company; during these months a more puritanical general was heard to complain to him, "Too many whores around your headquarters, Field-Marshal!"

For others, the season was more grim. As 1914 drew to a close, Edward Cecil at his post in Egypt received a telegram: "Grave opened George believed identified broken hearted Violet." At Villers-Cotterêts, workmen had exhumed a mass grave that held 98 British soldiers. George's body was identifiable only by the initials on his vest. The bodies of 94 enlisted men were quickly reburied. George and the other three officers got coffins, flowers from the mayor, and a burial in the town cemetery, under a cross with the inscription "*Tombés au champ d'honneur*" (Fallen on the field of honor), with twenty French officers in attendance. Artillery fire could be heard in the distance.

Knowing where George was buried did little to ease his mother's grief. He had, she wrote, been "thrown like carrion into a pit. When I think of the inhuman waste of a beautiful life I can hardly endure myself or to be a part of a world where such things were possible." Nor did his death bring her any closer to her estranged husband. "You and I can't talk about any of the great vital things without my saying something which might touch upon your religious views," she wrote to him, "so I won't write about the Great Dissolver, Death—we have no common ground at all. . . . I had written and . . . then came your letter with a reference to 'future life' and I felt mine had better go into the fire and the whole subject remain untouched."

Like most Britons, Violet Cecil did not question the aims of the war. As a memorial to George, she wanted to donate something to his old boarding school, Winchester. Her gift was a rifle range. Rudyard Kipling, his bushy eyebrows still black though his hair and mustache were turning gray, gave a speech at the opening ceremony, fired the inaugural shot, and hit a bull's-eye.

After several months of war, the hopes of peace-minded socialists throughout Europe were all but gone. Their dream had dissolved in the face of an ancient and greater force: the deep, instinctive human impulse for solidarity with fellow members of one's tribe—a group most people defined, in this moment of crisis, not by class but by nation. Surprisingly haunting testimony to the strength of this feeling came from someone who largely resisted it, the prominent left-wing editor George Lansbury, who argued that it was nothing less than criminal madness for Europe's workers to be fighting each other at the behest of the ruling classes. Nonetheless, once it became possible for journalists to visit the front, he confessed that "every troop or regiment of troops on the march created a longing in me to get out and march with them. I had no sort of feeling about killing or being killed. There was a sense of danger and service—impersonal service—which, as men swung past, made me wish to be with them." If even a committed antiwar socialist could experience such longing, young Britons without leftist convictions felt it far more, and those speaking out against the war found themselves depressed and isolated.

Among them were Sylvia Pankhurst and Keir Hardie. Although no longer lovers, they still saw each other frequently. He was in despair that all his efforts against war had failed, and she was bruised by her final, very public rupture with her mother and sister. The written record is scanty, but they seem to have offered each other some solace during what must have been, for each, the worst winter of a lifetime. One night when Sylvia was giving a speech, she received a telegram from Hardie telling her to pay no attention to press reports that he was ill—which sounds like a desperate plea for her to do just the opposite. As soon as the meeting was over she rushed to his flat and found that he had been escorted home after having had a seizure in the House of Commons. Near the end of the year he suffered a stroke, as if his body were reflecting the grief he felt at the war. He was only 58, but, his writing arm now paralyzed, he had to compose by dictating. For a time he was not even able to take his daily walk.

Sylvia worked on in the East End, ceaselessly badgering officials at every level. In this time of emergency, why not impose government controls on prices? Why not nationalize food supplies? Immersed in the war of daily life, she saw the war in Europe as the enemy of all she had been trying to do. To read her autobiographical account of these years, *The Home Front,* is to enter the trenches of down-and-out London: women getting by on their husbands' paltry military pay and allowances (a mere extra twopence per day per child at the start of the war), women crowded out of hospital beds needed for wounded soldiers, a blacksmith with nine children and no work because so many horses had been commandeered for the army. The book is humorless, intense, and long-winded; you cannot imagine her bursting into song, as Hardie, in better days, had been wont to do.

Yet she did amass some solid accomplishments in a difficult time, when the nation was focused on war against Germany and not against poverty at home. She opened a garment workshop and a boot-making co-op, upending tradition by paying women the same wage as men. She took over a pub, the Gunmaker's Arms, renaming it the Mothers' Arms and installing a Montessori nursery school. Many of its pupils had fathers at the front; soon there would be others whose fathers were jailed war resisters. When women and children were evicted by their landlords, if no shelter could be found, she took them into her own home. On one occasion when no midwife was available, she assisted at a birth. And throughout this time she edited one of the few newspapers in Europe where voices dissenting from militarism could be heard.

The year's end brought no improvement to conditions in the East End—or at the front. Every British soldier, however, received an embossed brass box of cigarettes, pipe, and tobacco (or another gift for nonsmokers, such as spices for Indian troops) and a Christmas card from the royal couple, showing the Queen in broad choker necklace and crown and the King in his field marshal's uniform. In Haig's head-quarters, they celebrated Christmas well, with turtle soup and other delicacies; Leopold de Rothschild sent the general some prized 1820 brandy and more than 50 pairs of fur gloves for him to distribute as presents to his staff. In the trenches, however, a very different sort of Christmas was under way.

South of Ypres, where the British and Germans faced each other across the white-frosted fields of Flanders, as northern Belgium was known, Christmas morning dawned cold and foggy. Looking at one section of German trench, British soldiers noticed that a wooden board had been hoisted with the words "You no fight, we no fight." From another trench farther down the line, a German officer emerged with a white flag. On the British side, some soldiers of the Queen's Westminster Rifles climbed out of their trench, waved, then jumped back in. When no shots were fired, they emerged a second time and began a cautious, unarmed advance into no man's land. "Suddenly from the enemy hurrahing was heard," a German soldier wrote to a socialist newspaper in Berlin, "and, surprised, we came from our mouse-holes and saw the English advancing towards us. . . . They had no rifles with them, and therefore we knew it could only be a greeting." Soon a German NCO hauled a Christmas tree into no man's land.

These forays multiplied along more than two-thirds of the British-held section of the front. By that afternoon, thousands of British and German soldiers were trading cigarettes, helmets, canned food, and other souvenirs, taking pictures, and singing carols in both languages. One lieutenant, wielding barbed-wire clippers, snipped two buttons from a German officer's coat in exchange for two of his own. Some German soldiers turned out to speak English well, having worked in Britain before the war, often as clerks, barbers, or waiters. (British troops would sometimes shout "Waiter!" from their trenches.) A German soldier who had lived in Suffolk gave a lieutenant of the Scots Guards a postcard to mail to his girlfriend there. A member of the 3rd Battalion of the Rifle Brigade got a haircut in no man's land from a German who had been his barber on London's High Holborn.

One officer described the day almost as if it were the fraternization between teams following a soccer match. "The Germans came out . . . they're good fellows on the whole and play the game," he wrote to the *Times.* In several stretches of no man's land British and German troops played games of soccer, despite the half-frozen ground pocked with shell holes. "We marked the goals with our caps," wrote a German lieutenant, Johannes Niemann. "Teams were quickly established . . . and the Fritzes beat the Tommies 3–2." Where there was no ball, the two sides made use of a tin can or a sandbag stuffed with straw.

Later in the day, a German juggler who had been onstage in London before the war gave a bravura performance; soldiers from both sides chased and caught hares running between their trenches. Men from the Cheshire Regiment slaughtered a pig, cooked it in no man's land, and shared it with the Germans, and some Saxon troops rolled a barrel of beer over their parapet and into eager British hands.

The Christmas Truce, as it came to be called, has passed into legend, celebrated in books, poems, popular songs, short stories, and films. The truce represented, it is said, an outburst of spontaneous solidarity among ordinary, working-class soldiers that outraged higher-ups and militarists on both sides. Adolf Hitler, for example, at the front in an infantry regiment and much given to brooding alone in his dugout, strenuously disapproved: "Such a thing should not happen in wartime," he told his fellow soldiers. "Have you no German sense of honor?" But tempting as it may be to see the Christmas Truce this way, the Britons who strolled out between the lines to wish their German counterparts a Merry Christmas ranged as high as colonels. Sir John French seems to have learned of the truce only after the fact, and promptly issued orders that nothing of the sort should happen again. Looking back after the war, however, he wrote of the occasion as a valiant gesture within the warrior caste, and compared it to a Christmas in the Boer War when he had sent whiskey and cigars through the lines to an opposing general. "Soldiers should have no politics, but should cultivate a freemasonry of their own and, emulating the knights of old, should honour a brave enemy only second to a comrade, and like them rejoice to split a friendly lance [i.e., take part in jousting competitions] today and ride boot to boot in the charge tomorrow."

Keir Hardie, on the other hand, was eager to see the truce as anything but chivalry. Many descriptions of the event by soldiers appeared on newspapers' letters pages; still crippled by his stroke, he dictated a column quoting them and hailing the truce as an omen of revolutionary changes. "Why are men who can be so friendly sent out to kill each other? They have no quarrel. . . . When the war is over . . . each will realise that the lies told them by their press and their politicians had been deliberately concocted to mislead them. They will realise . . . that the workers of the world are not 'enemies' to each other, but comrades." The Christmas Truce, he felt, was essentially a matter of soldiers staging a one-day wildcat strike against the war. And if that could happen now, why not a general strike before the war went on much longer?

III

1915

10

THIS ISN'T *WAR*

SIR JOHN FRENCH still believed that some of his most "valuable" officers in France and Flanders were "county men of position and influence, accustomed to hunting, polo and field sports." But for others, the metaphor of war as sport was no longer convincing. At the beginning of 1915, if you were a British officer peering into no man's land, what met your gaze resembled the cratered surface of the moon more than any fox-hunting meadow or polo field. The only horses in sight were dead ones. Even to safely look out of your trench you had to use a special set of binoculars whose lenses could be raised above the sandbag parapet like twin periscopes. Between you and the German front-line trench, which might be anywhere from 50 to several hundred yards away, was a desolate landscape filled with rusted tangles of barbed wire, mercilessly pitted and gouged by hundreds of shell bursts. Now, in winter, it would usually be covered with snow, and the rainwater that collected in shell craters would be frozen. On warmer days, your trench would thaw into a muddy morass. Better-off soldiers begged their families to send them rubber waders. Otherwise, you stood in the cold slime day after day until your feet swelled, went numb, and began to burn painfully as if touched by fire. This was the dreaded "trench foot," which sent men crawling or being carried to the rear by the thousands.

If you turned to face the back of your trench, you would see a protective wall almost as high as the parapet, because exploding shells were as likely to drop behind you as in front. At intervals along the back of the trench, you could see the beginning of a communication trench that snaked its way to the rear, so that troops moving to or from the front line would have some protection from bullets and shrapnel. If you looked to either side, you would not see far, for soldiers were already learning to build narrow trenches with right-angle turns every ten yards or so. These zigzags better contained the blast of a direct hit from an artillery or mortar round, while also preventing any German raiding party from taking control of a long stretch of trench with one well-placed machine gun. If you looked down, you might see the entrance to one of many dugouts carved into the side of the trench and reinforced with planks and beams. These underground spaces for crude sleeping quarters, command posts, or emergency first aid would be the size of a small room at best, filled with clammy air smelling of mud, sweat, and stale food. Worse, you might be sharing your trench not just with your fellow soldiers but with the dead. When the poet Edmund Blunden first arrived at his front-line post in Flanders it was night; only in the morning did he notice that "at some points in the trench, bones pierced through . . . and skulls appeared like mushrooms." Later, Blunden came across "a pit, the result of much sandbag filling; among its broken spades and empty tins I found a pair of boots, still containing someone's feet."

By now it was clear to both sides that to defend yourself against attack you needed to dig ever deeper — or, when you couldn't dig more without hitting the water table, pile up sandbags. Each shell that hit a trench meant rebuilding with yet more of those sandbags, which were filled not with sand but with earth that oozed out in muddy rivulets when it rained. When the temperature dropped, waterlogged sandbags froze and burst. As 1915 began, Britain was shipping a quarter-million empty sandbags a month across the Channel; by May, the monthly total would rise to six million.

Because both ground water and freezing rain collected in your trench, a crude floor of boards might cover the deepest puddles and a pump would be going constantly. There were seldom enough pumps, and in the dreaded lower-lying areas, it felt as if you were living in a swamp. "Spent the morning trying to dry out our clothes," Corporal

Above: Charlotte Despard, suffragette, prison veteran, pacifist, communist, IRA supporter. *Right:* Her brother, "dearer to me than anyone else," Field Marshal Sir John French, cavalryman, commander in chief on the Western Front, viceroy of Ireland.

Horsemen en route to Kimberley, South Africa,
for Britain's last great cavalry charge, 1900.

Rudyard Kipling, staunch
patriot in his country's wars.

Above: Alfred, Lord Milner, the "man of no illusions." *Below:* His great love, Lady Violet Cecil (*left*); his nemesis, antiwar campaigner Emily Hobhouse (*right*).

The Pankhurst family, bitterly split by the war: Christabel (*left*), Sylvia addressing a public meeting (*opposite*), and their mother, Emmeline, under arrest (*below*).

Socialist leader (and Sylvia's secret lover) Keir Hardie speaks
against the coming war, Trafalgar Square, 1914.

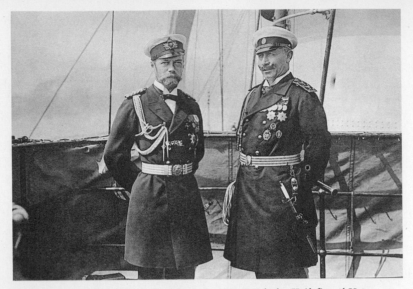

Above: Royal cousins before the storm: Tsar Nicholas II (*left*) and Kaiser Wilhelm II (*right*) on Wilhelm's yacht. *Below:* King George V and Queen Mary in Delhi as Emperor and Empress of India.

Basil Thomson, Scotland
Yard spycatcher

Field Marshal Sir Douglas Haig

John Buchan: novelist, officer,
chief propagandist

Bertrand Russell: resisting the
"red blast of hate"

Friends who met similar fates: John Kipling (*left*), George Cecil.

The tight Royal Navy blockade cut off food and fertilizer imports to Germany, hastening hundreds of thousands of deaths. A woman faints in a Berlin food line.

Alex Letyford of the Royal Engineers wrote in his diary on January 5, 1915. "We are all covered in mud from head to foot. At 6 P.M. I go with Captain Reed to the trenches and fix six pumps. Wading about in water to our waists until 2 A.M."

The sound of splashing, or the suck of a boot being pulled out of mud, or an inadvertent cry of rage when someone fell into a water hole often alerted the other side's snipers to troop movements. To the accompaniment of harmonicas, soldiers sang:

> I've a little wet home in a trench,
> Where the rainstorms continually drench,
> There's a dead cow close by
> With her feet towards the sky
> And she gives off a horrible stench.

In addition to the stink of decomposing bodies, which grew worse with the spring thaw, another smell came to be indelibly associated with the trenches: that of human waste. Many soldiers simply relieved themselves in the nearest shell hole. There were also pit latrines in small, specially built dead-end trenches, but if a shell struck one, it blasted the contents in all directions, leaving men covered with feces.

The barbed-wire moonscape of no man's land was no place for cavalry charges, which the German high command reluctantly recognized several months into the war, withdrawing cavalry units from the Western Front. But French optimistically kept masses of British horsemen on hand. The cavalry busied themselves with training and by staging competitions: the 12th Royal Lancers won several prizes at their Divisional Horse Show in early 1915, for example. Behind the lines, some officers pursued foxes and hares with hunting dogs they had brought to France. "This afternoon we went off to the hunt," one officer wrote to the *Times*. "Half a dozen couples of beagles and a good field went off after bunny at a fine pace, but, fortunately for bunny, there were plenty of wide ditches in this flat country, and she and all the rest got away scot free." After objections from infuriated local farmers the practice was banned, but some horse-loving officers continued to slip off for furtive hunts.

With thousands of impatient cavalrymen waiting in the wings, the generals were eager for the long-awaited breakthrough that would loose their horsemen into open country. The first British attempt of 1915 came at the French village of Neuve Chapelle, in the sector of the front under Haig's command. After the infantry smashed the German front line, British and Indian cavalry were to charge through. So went the plan, and French, who wore his spurs at headquarters, personally briefed the British officer commanding the Indian horsemen, a fellow Boer War veteran who, French wrote, "thinks he may be able to do some dashing cavalry work." On the damp, foggy morning of March 10, after a surprise artillery bombardment, the British unleashed an assault by some 40,000 British and Indian soldiers. Far outnumbering the Germans they faced, the infantry gained a mile or so of ground, at which point Haig ordered the cavalry forward to be ready to attack.

But the Germans rushed in reinforcements, and repeated, costly British attempts to advance farther came to a halt under snow flurries. Haig's subordinates, afraid of his well-known temper, never dared give him a crucial piece of information: on one key stretch of the German trench under attack, the British bombardment had failed to blast apart the barbed wire or knock out machine-gun emplacements. And so while British troops frantically tried to cut through the tangle of wire, a mere two German machine guns killed roughly 1,000 of them. "The Germans were shooting like mad while our lads were crouching down in the mud trying to breach it [the wire] with wire-cutters, and those that didn't have wire-cutters hacking at it with bayonets . . . ," recalled a stretcher bearer in the Scottish Rifles. "All the officers went, killed or wounded. By the end of three days we had just one subaltern left." On the third day, French called off the attack. His troops had lost 12,847 dead and wounded.

In winning their blood-soaked mile of earth, the British experienced yet another way in which trench warfare put the attacker at a painful disadvantage. If you had the rare luck to capture some ground, your supplies and reinforcements then had to advance through ground strewn with craters, barbed wire, and dead bodies, the air filled with bursting shrapnel, without communication trenches for protection. It was hard enough for a man on foot to make his way unscathed, much less a cavalry division.

In addition, the matter of sending messages — about, for instance, what terrain you held and where your artillery should fire — was staggeringly difficult. Telephone wires were invariably cut by enemy shells; primitive radios and their heavy batteries were too bulky to hand-carry onto the battlefield; and signal flags proved impossible to see through the smoke. This left runners, who, as they scrambled across the shell-blasted wasteland, were ideal targets for German snipers. The farther you advanced, the more out-of-date the runner's message—if he even survived the journey. On the first day at Neuve Chapelle, it took nine hours for front-line officers to send a message back to their corps commander and get a reply. (German commanders would complain of the same problem.) Generals had no way of knowing whether their troops a mile away, invisible in the dust and smoke, had captured an enemy trench or all been wounded or killed.

Trying to put a good face on this battle, French reported "the defeat of the enemy and the capture of his position" to London. Adjusting his predictions, he now was convinced that the war would end by June. His faith—and Haig's—in the cavalry remained as strong as ever. A month after Neuve Chapelle, Haig scoffed at two officers who were cavalry skeptics: "If these two had their way, Cavalry would cease to exist as such. In their opinion, the war will continue and end in *trenches*."

On one front, however, French had won an unusual victory: his exalted position had—for the moment—curbed his sister's long-standing pacifism. Charlotte Despard continued her relief work in Battersea, where many women were suffering from the economic dislocations of the war and the absence of husbands at the front. She helped them fight off debt collectors, distributed milk to nursing mothers, and set up a shelter for women recovering from childbirth. At a cafeteria that provided healthy meals at cost, she often ladled out soup herself (although some diners complained of her ardent vegetarianism). With Sylvia Pankhurst and others, she founded the League for the Rights of Soldiers' and Sailors' Wives and Relations. Military authorities had worked themselves into a misogynist dudgeon about army wives who might be tempted by romance while their husbands were off at war, and were using emergency powers to impose curfews on them, or, in some areas, on all women. A new regulation also made it a crime for a woman with venereal disease to have intercourse with a member of the armed forces. Despard and Pankhurst led protest delegations to the War Office and 10 Downing Street.

Out of loyalty to her brother, Despard visited military units in

France and England, formally presenting, for example, a set of fifes and drums to the band of the 5th North Staffordshire Regiment. In March 1915, she set up the Despard Arms, a teetotal pub, on Hampstead Road, near several of the big London railway stations through which troops passed on their way to France. Men heading for the front could find food, baths, a dormitory, a clubroom, artistic performances, and a soccer team—the Despard Uniteds. On a trip back to London, her brother visited the pub and exhibited his usual common touch in chatting with the soldiers.

But Despard could not be tamed for long. In April, along with Sylvia Pankhurst and some 180 other British women, she tried to attend the Women's International Peace Congress at The Hague in Holland. In the letters columns of newspapers, Britons thundered against this "pow-wow with the fraus." Among those most outraged at what she called "the peace-at-any-price crowd" was Emmeline Pankhurst: "It is unthinkable," she stormed in a magazine interview, "that Englishwomen should meet German women to discuss terms of peace while the husbands, sons and brothers of those women . . . are murdering our men."

Cleverly attempting to sow jealousy in the pacifist ranks, the British government granted passports only to some 20 "women of discretion" among the would-be delegates. But even this select group, arriving at the dock, found that their ship and all others had been suddenly banned from sailing to Holland. Only three British women, already out of the country, managed to join the 1,500 others—mostly from neutral nations—at the conference. Beneath the fronds of potted palms in an ornate hall in The Hague's Zoological and Botanical Gardens, the women passed resolutions calling for an end to the fighting and for peace by negotiation. The German delegates were given no less of a hard time by their government: 28 German women who managed to attend were arrested on their return.

Only 100 miles from the peace conference, a terrifying new weapon had made its appearance. On April 22, 1915, near the battered city of Ypres, French soldiers and troops from French colonies in North Africa noticed a strange, greenish yellow mist billowing out of the German positions and blowing toward them in the wind. An unfamiliar smell filled the air. When the acrid cloud reached them, it was so thick that they couldn't see more than a few feet. Soldiers quickly found themselves gagging and choking, yellow mucus frothing out of their mouths. Hundreds fell to the ground in convulsions. Those who could still breathe fled, staggering into first-aid posts blue from suffocation and coughing blood, speechless but pointing desperately to their throats. In the next few days, Canadian troops fell victim as well. Whatever this mysterious cloud might be, it was heavier than air and sank into the trenches, hugging the earth and forcing soldiers to stick their heads out into a hail of bullets. "The chaps were all gasping and couldn't breathe," a sergeant remembered later. "And it was ghastly, especially for chaps that were wounded—terrible for a wounded man to lie there! The gasping, the gasping!"

The spring leaves just coming out on the trees shriveled; grass turned yellow and metal green. Birds fell from the air, and chickens, pigs, cows, and horses writhed in agony and died, their bodies rotting and bloating. The ever-fatter rats that normally swarmed through the trenches, keeping men awake by running over them in the dark on the way to feast on soldiers' corpses, themselves died by the thousands.

This was the first widespread use of poison gas—chlorine—on the Western Front. Deadly and painful as it could be, later forms of gas would be still worse. Like so much else about the war, chlorine was the product of an industrial economy, in this case made by a complex of eight large chemical firms in Germany's Ruhr region known as the IG cartel. Chlorine and its compounds had a long history in manufacturing, but its new use in warfare was an ominous landmark, seeming to open up a range of horrifying possibilities that had previously existed only in the realm of early science fiction.

Allied generals and cabinet members railed against the Germans, accusing them of unprecedented savagery. Groping for the ultimate insult, Kitchener used the word by which the British had referred (incorrectly) to their Arab opponents at Omdurman: "Germany has stooped to acts which vie with those of the Dervishes." But, gruesome as choking on gas undoubtedly was, was it really any worse than having your body riddled with steel shrapnel? Or than having your lungs bruised to pulp by an artillery shell's blast even if the shrapnel missed you? What made gas warfare provoke such rage, the historian Trevor Wilson suggests, was something else. For all of recorded history, soldiers had believed that victory went to the manly, the fearless, and the daring. Now, with deadly gas brought to you not from the hand of an enemy you could see and slay, but by the very wind, all bravery seemed useless.

Not only had British and French generals been unprepared for gas, they had refused to even imagine it. Allied commanders around Ypres had had ample warning that a gas attack was coming: from an intercepted German message requisitioning 20,000 gas masks, from a deserter who, more than a week before the assault, brought one of the masks with him, and from captured German soldiers who told of masses of gas canisters lined up near their trenches. But they made not the slightest preparations, reluctant yet again to acknowledge that warfare could take a radically new direction.

The British generals' bewilderment at the war in which they found themselves was reflected in the very language they used. "An abnormal state of affairs," the director of military intelligence called trench warfare, while a major general termed it downright "peculiar." The chief of the Imperial General Staff thought conditions at the front "were not at present normal," although he hoped "they may become normal some day." "I don't know what is to be done," a despairing Kitchener said to the foreign secretary more than once. "This isn't *war*."

Gas added a new dimension to the fighting but did not break the deadlock. In a pattern that was to repeat itself with each new weapon introduced to the battlefield, the innovators seemed almost as surprised by their success as the other side. The Germans failed to take advantage of the fear, confusion, and temporary breach in the Allied lines their first gas attack caused.

As a defense against gas, the Allies began hastily improvising masks of tape and wet lint (chlorine dissolves in water). Not long after, all soldiers on both sides would be equipped with gas masks — as would tens of thousands of horses. This pattern, too, would become familiar as the years dragged on: for every weapon there would be countermeasures, and usually effective ones. Against the machine-gun bullet and the artillery shell there were ever deeper trenches; against airplanes, antiaircraft guns; against the periscope binoculars for seeing out of a trench, the well-aimed sniper's bullet, which could fill the viewer's face with ricocheting shards of glass.

In May 1915, the Allies staged another round of attacks from Haig's sector. Sir John French watched from a church tower as guns pounded the German positions with nearly 1,000 shells a minute, yet failed to break open paths through the enemy barbed wire, cleverly concealed in long, deep ditches up to 20 feet wide, or to destroy most of the German concrete-and-steel machine-gun bunkers. Germans sheltering in reinforced underground dugouts climbed back to the surface as soon as the British shelling ended, shouting across 150 yards of no man's land to the Scottish division about to attack them, "Come on, Jocks, we are waiting for you!" Before Haig called off the attack the next day, 458 officers and 11,161 men would be killed and wounded.

When disaster follows disaster, someone or something has to be blamed. Since he was the commander in chief and could not blame himself, French blamed a shortage of artillery ammunition. Haig, on the other hand, using his skills as a master of backroom maneuvering, blamed French. Both streams of recrimination flowed back to London, and gradually it dawned on French that Haig was gunning for him. His subordinate was well entrenched on some strategic high ground: both Kitchener and the King had asked Haig privately to keep them informed. Lady Haig supplemented his letters by typing up extracts from his diary and sharing them with the royal family. "Precious documents," one Buckingham Palace official called them.

As for artillery shells, French was not wrong: there was indeed a shortage, and some were defective. Haig blamed this on the British worker, who, he was convinced, had too many holidays and too much to drink—a notable argument for someone whose family fortune was based on whiskey. "Take and shoot two or three of them," he wrote to his wife, "and the 'Drink habit' would cease." In reality, no country had been prepared for a war of this length, least of all Britain, with its small professional army used to fighting ill-armed colonials. In the three-day Battle of Neuve Chapelle—a mere skirmish compared to the giant clashes to come—British artillery had shot off almost as many shells as in the course of the entire Boer War.

During this frustrating spring, French received an alarming telegram from the War Office ordering him to immediately ship much of his meager stock of ammunition to the British Empire forces on the Gallipoli Peninsula in western Turkey. There, a new campaign had been launched, aimed at skirting the impasse on the Western Front: an amphibious assault on the Ottoman army, which was thought to be far weaker and more vulnerable than Germany's. The attack, it was hoped, would seize Constantinople (today's Istanbul) and knock the Ottoman Empire out of the war. French was dismayed: not only would his supply of scarce shells be diminished further, but some other British general might get credit for turning the tide.

No more skillful at office politics than the new style of combat, French fought his campaign of blame too much in the open. His friend Repington, the *Times* correspondent and a veteran intriguer, weighed in with an article blazingly headlined: "Need for Shells: British Attacks Checked: Limited Supply the Cause: A Lesson from France." French then pressed his American millionaire housemate, George Moore, into service to urge newspapers to attack Kitchener for the shell shortage. Believing—quite incorrectly—that he had the confidence of Prime Minister Asquith, he claimed that everything was the fault of the secretary for war. In his erratic way, he evidently forgot that earlier in the spring he had sent Kitchener two separate messages declaring his stock of shells adequate.

Had he plenty of high-explosive shells, Sir John wrote to his latest mistress, he would be able at last to "break thro' this tremendous *crust* of defence . . . once we have done it I think we may get the Devils on the run. How I should love to have a real good 'go' at them in the open with lots of cavalry and horse artillery and run them to earth. Well! It may come." French's correspondent, like almost every woman he was drawn to, was married to someone else. The tall, elegant Winifred "Wendy" Bennett was the wife of Percy Bennett, a diplomat whom she referred to as "Pompous Percy." Most unusually for French, this affair, begun in early 1915, would last more than half a decade. The two of them were, he told her, "shipwrecked souls who have found one another." The best she and French could do was to snatch an afternoon or evening at his lodgings on his short trips to London to consult with the War Office, but they wrote almost daily—sometimes using a younger sister of hers as a go-between—and nearly a hundred of his letters survive, in a hasty, forward-slanting, almost unreadable scrawl. With startling indiscretion, he describes military operations and troop movements, as well as his contempt for the French generals ("you can't trust them"), for his superior ("I devoutly wish we could get rid of Kitchener. . . . It is so hard to have enemies both in *front* and *behind*"), and for War Office burcaucrats ("While they are fiddling Rome is burning").

In one letter he mentions a curious episode that reflected his assumption, and that of his era, that marriage was permanent and love sacred, but that the two would never coincide. Of a couple he knew, he wrote:

> They've been married some 17 or 18 years. A few years ago they found out the same old story that they weren't *meant* to be in love with one another—so each went his and her way but they remained together and are the best of friends. The wife found what she thought was her "alter ego" in a Guardsman who is serving out here. About a year or two ago he gave her up and *married*. The husband then wrote to him and told him he had behaved like a cad to his wife and that he should always cut him in future and he has always done so.
>
> Now I call that husband a real good fellow. Don't you? He saw no reason why his wife shouldn't be made happy simply because she happened to be his wife.

No doubt French hoped for the same generosity of spirit from his long-suffering Eleanora, and from "Pompous Percy." But that may have been no less wishful thinking than his expectation of a quick end to the war.

Haig had long since ceased to have any use for French as a commander. "He is so hot tempered and excitable," he wrote to his friend Leopold de Rothschild, "—like a bottle of soda water in suddenness of explosion." And again: "French seems to have that scoundrel Repington staying with him as his guest!" It was "most unsoldierlike," Haig fumed, ". . . to keep one's own advertising agent." After a private visit with George V in July to receive a medal, Haig happily noted in his diary that the King "had lost confidence in French."

The field marshal's position only weakened. Cabinet ministers were disturbed by his mood swings and his promises of victories that looked ever more improbable as, month after month, millions of men faced each other across a front line that barely moved. Worse yet, in technology, if not miles gained, the Germans seemed to be making breakthroughs, for on July 30 they made the first major use of another frightening new weapon, devised by a reserve army captain who in civilian life had been the fire chief of Leipzig: the flamethrower, which shot a jet of burning gasoline like a fire hose spraying water. Although its range was only about 75 feet, it thoroughly panicked British soldiers.

All French and Haig now shared was a relentless optimism that, somehow, the war would end quickly. "The enemy . . . can't go on after January," Haig wrote to his wife on August 10, 1915, "and I would not be surprised to see him give in by November." Which, of course, made the goal of supplanting French as commander all the more urgent. Otherwise, who would be honored for the victory? Meanwhile, French, sensing his stock falling, began planning a decisive blow at the Germans to prove his critics wrong.

11

IN THE THICK OF IT

JUST AS WARFARE on an industrial scale required the mass production of new weapons like poison gas, so this new kind of conflict required the mass production of public support. In earlier British wars this had not been a problem. Despite some opposition to the Boer War, dramatic victories had come along swiftly enough to keep people cheering and to keep jingoist poets and magazine illustrators busy. Not so this time. Nor was there good news to celebrate from Britain's allies: the badly bloodied army of France, like its British counterpart, was hunkered down in trenches; in its early invasion of eastern Germany, Russia's army had suffered the war's largest and most humiliating defeat; little Serbia was being overrun by the Central Powers; and Italy, which in the spring of 1915 had been cajoled onto the Allied side by the promise of chunks of Austro-Hungarian territory, soon became bogged down in its own costly trench-bound stalemate. And the joint Allied invasion of the Gallipoli Peninsula in Turkey, involving troops from Britain, France, Australia, New Zealand, and Newfoundland, was, ominously, proving anything but the triumph the generals had hoped for.

From the beginning, key British officials had grasped that this war would require propaganda of unprecedented sophistication and scope — something all the more important in a country where, without conscription, attracting the necessary millions of army recruits depended on public enthusiasm. Until now, nations had not seen the need for government bureaus or departments devoted to stoking popular emotions. To supervise this novel and delicate task, the prime minister turned to Charles Masterman, chancellor of the Duchy of Lancaster, an ancient title that had come to mean, in effect, cabinet minister without portfolio. And so, on a sunny September day only a month after Britain entered the war, Masterman secretly brought together, around a large blue conference table in an inconspicuous health insurance office, some two dozen of the nation's most prominent authors, including Thomas Hardy, James Barrie, John Galsworthy, Arthur Conan Doyle, and H. G. Wells. For the creators of figures as varied as Peter Pan and Sherlock Holmes it was a rare experience to be asked to serve their country with their pens, and they all quickly agreed to do so. They spoke to colleagues, and within days 52 writers had signed an open letter calling on "all the English-speaking race" to fight for the "ideals of Western Europe against the rule of 'Blood and Iron.'" One of the few major authors not to sign was Bertrand Russell.

Dissenters like him were rare. Far more common were those like the biographer, critic, and poet Sir Edmund Gosse. War, he wrote, "is the sovereign disinfectant, and its red stream of blood is the Condy's Fluid [a popular antiseptic and deodorant] that cleans out the stagnant pools and clotted channels of the intellect." Many authors were enlisted by the new War Propaganda Bureau, which launched a flood of books, pamphlets, newspapers, posters, postcards, slide shows, and films for consumption in Britain and abroad—since the government wanted to win over public opinion in neutral nations, especially the powerful United States. The bureau was never identified as the source of this material, and Parliament had little idea what it was doing. Pamphlets and books bore the imprimatur of well-known publishing houses, and the government secretly agreed in advance to buy copies, which it then distributed for free.

The initial focus of the campaign was German atrocities in occupied Belgium. The actual killings and destruction carried out by the Germans were by no means enough for the newborn propaganda mill. Instead, every thirdhand story or wisp of rumor was treated as the truth, and articles, books, and an influential official report spoke in shocked tones about German troops bayoneting babies, hacking off people's hands, and crucifying Belgian peasants by nailing them to the doors of their cottages. Cartoons, drawings or posters showed a giant German soldier with children speared on his bayonet, the Kaiser cavorting with a skeleton, and three pigs in spiked helmets laughing over a woman's body.

A star of the literary war effort was the novelist John Buchan, who had gained a wide public following since his days in Milner's South African Kindergarten. For Thomas Nelson, an Edinburgh publisher, he put his agile pen to work writing a series of short books that constituted an instant history of the war as it was unfolding. They downplayed British reverses, emphasized acts of heroism, evoked famous battlefield triumphs of times past, scoffed at pacifists, predicted early victory, and overestimated German losses. The first installment of *Nelson's History of the War* appeared in February 1915; within four years, with some assistance, Buchan would produce 24 best-selling volumes totaling well over a million words—by far the most widely read books about the war written while it was in progress. Like the best propagandists, he was not just a manipulator but a believer, for his sunny personality allowed him to imagine the upside of absolutely anything. The inevitable British victory, he claimed, would produce a more democratic society, and so "this war may rank as one of the happiest events in our history."

Rudyard Kipling also lent his skills to the war effort, and gave speeches at recruiting rallies and elsewhere. His unbounded rage at Germany overwhelmed even his fiction, as in "Swept and Garnished," a story about a well-to-do Berlin matron whose elegant home is disturbed by the ghosts of murdered Belgian children. Nonfiction flowed from his hand as well, including a series of pamphlets singing the praises of the infantry, the artillery, the navy, and other troops. And no soldiers sparked Kipling's enthusiasm more than those arriving on the Western Front from his beloved India. Like colonialists everywhere, he prided himself on knowing what the natives were thinking, which was, he assured readers, that "it is a war of *our Raj*—'everybody's war,' as they say in the bazaars." Nothing in his work, of course, even hinted at the degree of official anxiety over the growth of Indian nationalism. All armies censor mail coming from soldiers at the front, but the British had a special postal unit of Urdu-speakers censoring mail going *to* Indian soldiers, to screen out letters or pamphlets supporting independence.

Kipling had only scorn for anyone who shirked the glorious task of war. "What will be the position," he asked, "in years to come of the young man who has deliberately elected to outcast himself from this all-embracing brotherhood?" No such shame lay in wait for his son, whose battalion shipped off to the front in August 1915. John Kipling went to war, his mother wrote, looking "very straight and smart and brave and young," and sporting a small, newly grown mustache. Because John was only 17, his father had to give the army consent for his son to be sent overseas. "*This is the life,*" John exuberantly told his parents after a destroyer had escorted his troopship across the Channel. More letters followed, one of them exulting over food given the officers: "Bread, sardines, jam Whisky & water, A-1!"

Were John's parents as cheerful as Kipling's endless stream of rousing articles and stories suggests? The novelist Rider Haggard did not think so: "Neither of them look so well as they did. . . . Their boy . . . is an officer in the Irish Guards and one can see that they are terrified lest he should be sent to the front and killed, as has happened to nearly all the young men they know."

From 20 miles behind the lines, John reported that the Irish Guards were billeted "in a splendid little village," himself in the house of the mayor, "a topping old fellow who can't speak a word of English, but the kindest chap you ever met," with a pretty daughter. He seemed amazed to find himself, now just turned 18, censoring his men's mail and sitting as a judge in a court-martial. Then, schoolboy fashion, it was back to talk of packages from home: "The cigarettes, tobacco, chocolate, clean shirts socks etc were *most* acceptable." He was lucky to have an experienced commanding officer, John wrote: "What he doesn't know about the game isn't worth knowing."

Back home, volunteers still crowded recruiting offices but the euphoria of the war's opening weeks had dissipated, and a hard-edged social pressure to enlist was in the air. A London theater put on a play called *The Man Who Stayed at Home.* Women stood on street corners handing out white feathers, an ancient symbol of cowardice, to young men not in uniform; Fenner Brockway, editor of the *Labour Leader,* the newspaper Keir Hardie had started, who would soon go to jail for his antiwar convictions, joked that he had been given so many he could make a fan. Recruiting posters, too, appealed to shame: one showed two children asking a frowning, guilty-looking father in civilian clothes, "Daddy, what did *YOU* do in the Great War?" (Hardie's friend Bob Smillie, leader of the Scottish mineworkers, said his reply would be: "I tried to stop the bloody thing, my child.")

Ferocity about the war could be heard everywhere. "Kill Germans! Kill them!" raged one clergyman in a 1915 sermon. ". . . Not for the sake of killing, but to save the world. . . . Kill the good as well as the bad. . . . Kill the young men as well as the old. . . . Kill those who have shown kindness to our wounded as well as those fiends who crucified the Canadian sergeant [a story then circulating]. . . . I look upon it as a war for purity, I look upon everybody who dies in it as a martyr." The speaker was Arthur Winnington-Ingram, the Anglican bishop of London.

In Parliament, Hardie kept up a stream of critical questions, though he had never really recovered from his stroke. Several times he collapsed from exhaustion, and physician MPs had to come to his aid. At home in Scotland he tried a favorite cure of the day, hydrotherapy, but being dipped in cold baths did little to revive him. He kept on writing and speaking against the catastrophe that was steadily eviscerating his life's work. How, he asked, could Britain say it was fighting for freedom when it was allied with tsarist Russia?

Despite weakening physically, he went to Norwich for a conference of his Independent Labour Party. The streets were filled with soldiers and the city was blacked out at night. Suddenly permission to use the meeting halls the party had booked was denied. Dissenting churches stepped forward, and local Unitarians and the breakaway Primitive Methodists offered their buildings instead. On the last evening, Fenner Brockway remembered, "The little hall was crowded to suffocation and the lights were dimmed. Hardie's bushy white hair and his white beard shone out in the darkness with almost phosphorescent radiance. His head was held high, defiantly; his voice was strong and deep. . . . His voice nearly broke when he spoke of the tragedy of Socialists murdering each other."

Resolutions passed at the conference had no effect, for most other left-wing and labor groups in Britain backed the war—as did many ILP members. One former comrade who turned against Hardie was the Scottish suffragette Flora Drummond, though before the war she had named her son Keir Hardie Drummond. Ruptures with old friends and his worsening health were too much for him. He would, Hardie announced, no longer attend parliamentary debates and was returning to Scotland. "Ten million Socialist and Labour voters in Europe," he lamented, "without a trace or vestige of power to prevent war!"

Still unable to use his hand, he dictated a letter to Sylvia Pankhurst, saying that he was clearing out his London lodgings. There was a painting of hers, he said, that he could not bring himself to part with, but he wanted to return her letters to him. "They are well worth preserving . . . ," he wrote, seeming to look ahead to his own death. "You could use your discretion as to which are most worthy of being kept and published, and which should be destroyed. I have not now the capacity for dealing with such a matter."

They saw each other one last time, at Hardie's tiny London flat. She found his voice "low and muffled. . . . We were tongue-tied as never before, I struggling dumbly, desperately, to maintain my slender self-control. . . . Keir in his agony, mysterious, unkenned, seemed to loom over us like some great tragic ruin." As Sylvia tried to keep back tears, Hardie said to her, "You have been very brave." In the end, she did not destroy the letters; both of them, it seems, wanted posterity to know of their love.

Sylvia's mother and sister, meanwhile, had become a kind of private War Propaganda Bureau of their own, incessantly beating the drum for battle and demanding that the government put women to work in the jobs of men who had left to join the army. An article of Christabel's on the subject caught the King's eye, and his secretary wrote to David Lloyd George, now the country's first-ever minister of munitions: "His Majesty feels strongly that we ought to do more to enlist women-workers. . . . The King was wondering whether it would be possible or advisable for you to make use of Mrs. Pankhurst." Lloyd George quickly arranged to meet her at the house of a mutual friend. Each had a very clear agenda: Lloyd George wanted more munitions workers and a club to use against labor unions; Emmeline wanted equal wages for women (she would win this for piecework but not for hourly wages) and, ultimately, the vote. But for the moment they would work together.

Once again Emmeline found herself grandly leading a mass procession of women and marching bands through London to demonstrate before a government ministry. Despite wind and rain, some 60,000 people turned out. This time, however, the British treasury was providing more than £4,000 to cover the cost. Two miles of women in raincoats carried signs such as SHELLS MADE BY A WIFE MAY SAVE A HUSBAND'S LIFE. Costumed women represented different Allied nations; conquered Belgium marched barefoot, carrying a half-shredded flag. Along the route were tables where women could sign up for war-related work. Only a year earlier Emmeline Pankhurst had been in prison for inciting the blowing up of Lloyd George's house, but now both were smiling as they appeared together before the cheering crowd. For months afterward, newspapers celebrated the odd new couple. As one headline put it: "The Ablest Woman, the Ablest Man in England, Once They Were Enemies, War Has Made Them Friends."

The war not only brought poison gas to the Western Front, it brought another previously unimaginable weapon to London itself. When fighting each other in the past, Europeans had generally observed the distinction between soldiers and civilians. Indeed, part of the traditional ideal of a soldier's gallantry was that he should respect even the enemy's women and children. Now, however, with war ever more dependent on the strength of an entire economy, the morale of civilians became a key target.

The first, shocking sign Londoners had that the old rules no longer applied came on May 31, 1915, when incendiary bombs began raining down on the city from the night sky. They were dropped from a zeppelin—a giant airship nearly two football fields long, held aloft by huge bags of hydrogen within its steel frame and floating too high for most British fighter planes to reach. By the end of the war, German raids over England—by more zeppelins and soon by airplanes as well —would kill about 1,400 people and wound some 3,400. Although these numbers pale before the aerial bombardments of later wars, the very idea that explosives could be dropped through the clouds onto homes, farms, streets, and schools hundreds of miles from the nearest battlefield seemed to represent an unprecedented level of savagery. "Barbarous weapons," the *Times* called the bombs (although few people in Europe had thought it barbarous—or so much as noticed—when before the war France and Spain had bombed rebellious Moroccan villages from the air). No one was emotionally prepared for it, not even soldiers back from the front. An officer on leave in London who took a woman to the theater found himself back at war when a bomb landed nearby, shaking roof plaster onto the audience. "It's no business to happen here, you know," he exclaimed, unnerved. "It's no business to happen here."

One night Bertrand Russell heard a "shout of bestial triumph in the street. I leapt out of bed and saw a Zeppelin falling in flames. The thought of brave men dying in agony was what caused the triumph in the street." Such moments of war hysteria made him feel "the agonizing pain of realizing that that is what men are." In poorer parts of London, crowds rioted after air raids and smashed the windows of merchants of German or Austrian origin, or whose names simply sounded Germanic. German bakers, rumor had it, were putting poison in their bread. The press only fanned the flames of xenophobia. Newspaper headlines screamed about "The Enemy in Our Midst." One article warned, "If your waiter says he is Swiss, ask to see his passport."

In the East End, Sylvia Pankhurst watched in horror as a mob hustled a baker through the street, his clothes still white with flour but his mouth dripping blood. Another crowd tore off a woman's blouse and beat her unconscious. In vain, Sylvia pleaded with the police to intervene. One night she heard banging on her door. "A man in his shirt sleeves, white and haggard, fell in, a small man with one leg deformed, so that he limped badly. He blurted a plea to telephone, and as I took him upstairs, told me he was from the baker's shop a few doors away, and born in London, though his old parents had come from Germany half a century before."

She went out into the street intending to speak to the crowd, but faltered before the scene of frenzied looting of the baker's home. "The air was filled by . . . the noise of knocking and splintering wood. Men were lowering a piano through the window. . . . [A] woman ran by, dragging a polished table. She rammed it against the pavement in her haste—a leg of the table was smashed, the top was split. Discarding the broken trophy she ran back to secure another."

A locomotive of the London and North Western Railway named Dachshund was quickly rechristened Bulldog. A flurry of tabloid press articles pointed out that Alfred Milner had been born in Germany. One store bought ads to explain that the eau de cologne it sold did not come from Cologne. The hysteria spread into scholarship of centuries past: the editors of the *Cambridge Medieval History* announced that they would drop all German contributors from their volumes.

Civil liberties eroded. The Defence of the Realm Act, rushed through Parliament with no debate at the start of the war, was continually expanded until it blanketed daily life, from limiting pub hours to allowing censorship of information "likely to cause disaffection or alarm." People could be arrested, have their homes searched and documents seized, all without a warrant. Moreover, a civilian charged with violating certain parts of the act could be tried by military court-martial. In mid-1915, police raided the offices of Hardie's Independent Labour Party, searched its files, and charged the organization with publishing seditious matter. Though the government failed to win a conviction, it did manage to bar the press and public from the trial.

Under the impact of a series of small strokes, Hardie's brain was starting to go. He sent a note to Sylvia Pankhurst from his latest hydrotherapy spa, misspelling her name and saying that he was leaving shortly "with no more mind control than when I came." His family began to fear letting him go out for walks alone. But Sylvia's sister Christabel showed him no mercy. In a July 1915 issue of her WSPU newspaper, she printed a cartoon showing Kaiser Wilhelm II giving "Keir von Hardie" a bag of gold. Sylvia turned to her mother, begging her to stop such attacks. "He is dying," she wrote. Emmeline did not answer.

At sea, as on land, the proper war of the textbooks was nowhere to be found. The mighty guns of the behemoth dreadnoughts that Britain had invested so many billions in building, and their tens of thousands of sailors, were useless against the real naval threat from Germany, which turned out to be a weapon that neither side had previously paid much attention to, the submarine. (Various pre-1914 British admirals had grumbled that submarines were "un-English," or "the weapon of cowards who refused to fight like men on the surface," or "an underhanded method of attack"; one had called for captured submarine crews to be hanged as pirates.) Germany's small but state-of-the-art fleet of U-boats sent 227 British merchant ships to the bottom of the ocean in 1915. The Royal Navy searched desperately for a counter-weapon.

More bad news also came from the Gallipoli Peninsula, where the Turks were not playing their expected role as Orientals who could be conquered with ease. They had German arms, good discipline, and fine generalship. Many of the Allied soldiers killed by Turkish machine guns never made it out of the small craft landing on Gallipoli's beaches; they were packed into the boats so tightly that they remained sitting up even after being shot dead. The troops who did manage to come ashore never managed to advance more than five miles in from the coast. All told, the Allies suffered well over 200,000 killed and wounded. Before the end of the year they decided to abandon the campaign.

Things were even worse in Russia. In May 1915, on the one section of the front where the Tsar's armies had won substantial territory, from the lackadaisical Austro-Hungarians, the Germans stiffened their ally with a strong infusion of troops and artillery and began methodically pushing the Russians far back into their homeland. Avoiding major attacks in the west, Germany poured all its offensive effort for the year into expanding eastward, and the Central Powers advanced steadily some 300 miles until cold weather and swampy ground finally halted them. The new front line left a wide swath of the Russian Empire — much of what today is Poland, Ukraine, Belarus, Latvia, and Lithuania — in enemy hands. During the six months of the relentless offensive, the Russian army lost an estimated 1.4 million men, or more than 7,500 a day. By July, the general staff had alerted all commanders to watch for Bolshevik propaganda leaflets concealed in packages sent to the troops from home, and the army was hit by its first large wave of desertions. In August, capturing a besieged fortress, German troops took 90,000 Russian prisoners in a single day, including 30 generals.

As the Russian army slowly retreated on a front more than 600 miles long, its troops destroyed crops, houses, railways, entire cities, anything that might be of use to the enemy. In western Russia a zone of destruction gradually spread for hundreds of miles, where no food grew and few buildings stood. It was the Boer War's scorched-earth policy all over again, but on an immeasurably vaster scale. From this wasteland the retreating Russians also forcibly removed huge numbers of people. Targeted above all were non-Russian ethnic minorities, who the tsarist government feared would cooperate with the German occupiers. After bayoneting and hanging some people to start with, pillaging, whip-wielding Cossacks and other troops drove at least half a million Jews from their homes. Three-quarters of a million Poles were also forced to move east, and, in total, roughly the same number of Lithuanians, Latvians, and ethnic Germans. As these terrified refugees began their flight, they could often look back and see Russian soldiers setting fire to their homes or farms. A British military attaché with the Russian army passed a column of refugees 20 miles long. "Whole families with all their little worldly belongings piled on carts; two carts tied together and drawn by a single miserable horse; one family driving a cow; a poor old man and his wife each with a huge bundle of rubbish tied up in a sheet and slung on the back." By the end of 1915, Russia had well over three million homeless refugees—in caravans on the roads, packed into freight trains, or crowded into makeshift shelters in fields, forests, towns, and cities. A year later, there would be some six million. No one imagined that in a second global conflict less than three decades later the numbers would be so much higher, the expanse of blackened rubble so much wider.

The commander of the retreating Russian army, Grand Duke Nicholas Nikolaevich, let it be known that after-dinner conversation at his headquarters should be on "diversionary themes not concerning the conduct of the war." In September he was gently eased into another job. The dreamy and indecisive Tsar Nicholas II himself took personal command of his armies. The Tsar, the British ambassador once observed, was "afflicted with the misfortune of being weak on every point except his own autocracy." He moved in at army headquarters in grand style, watched parades, toured the nearby countryside in his Rolls-Royce, played dominoes, read novels, and issued odd orders, at one point promoting all the officers who happened to attend a ceremonial dinner. "My brain is resting here . . . no troublesome questions demanding thought," he wrote to his wife.

For the troops, however, rifles remained in short supply, and some infantry units moved up to the front carrying only axes. In December, part of Russia's 7th Army would march to their front-line positions without winter boots. Here and there, Russian soldiers began talking of mutiny, and, once the front line stabilized for winter, they started fraternizing with the Austro-Hungarians, visiting the enemy trenches, trading caps and helmets, and posing for photographs. In a desperate attempt to keep the troops disciplined, the Russian army's high command legalized flogging.

If Russia collapsed, it would mean that the full weight of German manpower and munitions would fall on Allied forces in the west. This only increased the pressure on Sir John French, who noticed grimly that VIP visitors like Prime Minister Asquith always made a point of visiting Haig's headquarters as well as his own when they came to France.

Meanwhile, plans were drawn up for the decisive battle, Sir John's final chance. Although the field marshal surely wished it could be otherwise, in the sector of the front where Britain and France had agreed the attack was to be launched, Haig was his subordinate commander. For his part, Haig assured everyone that this time they would reach the German rear areas and cut their lines of communication. He told a visiting French general that his men "were never in better heart and longing to have a fight." Among the units moved into advance positions was the Irish Guards battalion in which Lieutenant John Kipling eagerly awaited his first battle. Ominously, the attack was to take place near the northern French village of Loos, another coal-mining district where slag heaps offered protection to the German defenders and pithead elevator towers provided perfect observation posts.

In the preceding weeks, John's father had toured the Western Front, thanks to the War Office. Out of this came a bellicose series of newspaper articles, quickly turned into a book, *France at War*. Kipling termed the Germans "outside of all humanity," rejoicing when he saw a charred patch on the floor of a dressing station where a wounded German major had been burned alive when the building was set on fire by shelling. Noble France, he found, was without "human rubbish" like British pacifists. French soldiers and civilians he met echoed his righteous fury. "It is against wild beasts that we fight," said one Frenchwoman he quoted, or perhaps invented.

Although father and son were at one point within 20 miles of each other, the writer was sensitive enough to know that his son "wouldn't like to have me tracking him." John followed his father's movements through newspaper articles and the letters Rudyard wrote to him almost every day, which included bits of advice he picked up from British and French soldiers: put up wire netting to keep grenades out of your trenches; equip a man with a whistle to warn of falling mortar shells; when interrogating enemy prisoners, believe the private rather than the officer. Just as in the letters he had written John when he was a

THE EASTERN
FRONT AND THE
BALKANS, 1915

SWEDEN
(NEUTRAL)

DENMARK
(NEUTRAL)

BALTIC SEA

Riga

Vilna

Minsk

Danzig

Königsberg

GERMANY

Berlin

RUSSIA

Pinsk

Lodz

Warsaw

Brest-Litovsk

Lublin

FRONT LINE IN SEPTEMBER

Cracow

Lemberg
(Lviv)

FRONT LINE IN JANUARY

Czernowitz
(Chernivtsi)

CARPATHIAN MOUNTAINS

Vienna

Budapest

Jassy

AUSTRIA-
HUNGARY

Trieste

Trieste

ROMANIA
(NEUTRAL)

BOSNIA

AUSTRIAN FORCES

GERMAN
FORCES

Belgrade

Bucharest

BLACK SEA

ADRIATIC SEA

MONTENEGRO

SERBIA

BULGARIAN FORCES

BULGARIA

ITALY

Sofia

ALBANIA

Constantinople

OTTOMAN EMPIRE

Salonika

Dardanelles

Corfu

GREECE

AEGEAN SEA

0   100 km
0   100 mi

Area gained by Germany
and Austria, January–July

Area gained by Germany
and Austria, August–September

Central Powers' assault on
Serbia, October

Allied landings at Gallipoli

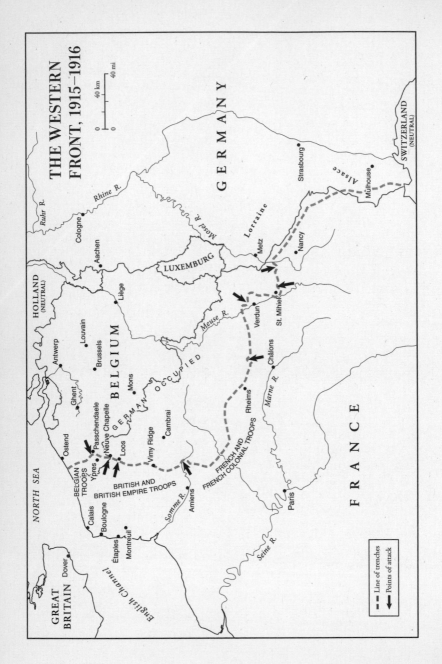

THE WESTERN
FRONT, 1915–1916

40 mi
40 km

NORTH SEA

GREAT
BRITAIN

English Channel

Dover

Étaples

Montreuil

Boulogne

Calais

HOLLAND
(NEUTRAL)

Ostend

BELGIAN
TROOPS

Passchendaele

Ypres

Neuve Chapelle

Loos

BRITISH AND
BRITISH EMPIRE TROOPS

Amiens

Somme R.

Vimy Ridge

Cambrai

Mons

GERMAN

Ghent

Antwerp

Brussels

Louvain

BELGIUM

Liège

OCCUPIED

LUXEMBURG

Aachen

Cologne

Ruhr R.

Rhine R.

Moser R.

Meuse R.

GERMANY

Rheims

FRENCH AND
FRENCH COLONIAL TROOPS

Châlons

Marne R.

Seine R.

Paris

FRANCE

Verdun

St. Mihiel

Metz

Nancy

Lorraine

Strasbourg

Alsace

Mulhouse

SWITZERLAND
(NEUTRAL)

Line of trenches

Points of attack

child, Kipling sometimes made little drawings: a skirt worn by a music hall performer, a scene from a film, a diagram of how to put up that chicken wire. John replied with a story about a French farmer's pig that had got into his platoon's food supply and had to be chased away: "I don't think I have ever laughed so much in my life." In the midsummer heat, "my visage is the colour of a well smoked briar pipe," John reported. "We look like a Colonial regiment, we are so sun burnt. . . . I don't think I have ever felt so fit before."

As the battle at Loos approached, Sir John French, Haig recorded contemptuously in his diary, looked "older and fatter." This would be the biggest land offensive in British military history, and French knew his job was on the line. "Whatever may happen I shall have to bear the brunt of it," he wrote to his mistress Winifred Bennett on September 18, 1915, "and in cricket language they may 'Change the bowler.'"

Writing home a few days later, John Kipling asked for "a really good pair of bedroom slippers (fluffy & warm with strong soles)." Then, after an 18-mile march through rain: "Just a hurried line as we start off tonight. The front-line trenches are nine miles off from here so it wont be a very long march. This is THE great effort to break through & end the war. . . . One will be in the thick of it tomorrow."

12

NOT THIS TIDE

MORE THAN ANY previous war, this one depended on huge quantities of industrial products and the raw materials needed to make them. The Germans soon coined a word for it, *Materialschlacht*, the battle of materiel. Among the more important goods was precision optical equipment—aerial reconnaissance camera lenses, periscopes, rangefinders, telescopic sights for sniper rifles, and binoculars. All were essential, particularly the last: when the lives of his men on the battlefield could depend on locating an enemy sniper or machine-gunner, every officer or NCO needed a reliable pair of binoculars hanging from his neck. The British military, however, was running disastrously short of binoculars. An appeal to the public brought in some 2,000 pairs (including four each from the King and Queen), but not the tens of thousands needed. Manufacturing high-quality lenses requires special glass that is difficult to make: it must transmit light without flaws, dimming, or distortion, yet be strong enough not to crack or shatter when ground and polished. Optical factories in England were capable of increasing their output only slowly.

And so, in mid-1915, just as preparations were getting under way for the big attack at Loos, British authorities turned to the world's leading manufacturer of precision optics: Germany.

Before the war, German companies, like the famous firm of Carl

Zeiss in Jena, had been major exporters of top-of-the-line optical goods. From London, an agent of the Ministry of Munitions was quietly dispatched to neutral Switzerland to propose a deal. The answer from Germany was prompt and positive, and the outlines of an agreement were sketched out. The German War Office would immediately supply 8,000 to 10,000 each of two types of binoculars, one for infantry officers and one for artillery officers. "For the future," reads the dry official record of the *History of the Ministry of Munitions,* "they were prepared to deliver, six weeks after the signing of the contract, 10,000 to 15,000 [of each type] and they were even prepared to demobilise special workmen from the Army to enable these orders to go through quickly." Of lower-grade binoculars for NCOs, Germany could supply 10,000 to 12,000 immediately and 5,000 a month thereafter. It would also be happy to supply 5,000 to 10,000 telescopic sights per month "and to provide as many rangefinders as the British Government required. In order to obtain samples of the instruments, it was suggested that the British Forces might inspect the equipment of captured German officers and artillery."

And what did Germany want in return for this astonishing bounty of tools that would better aim British rifles and howitzers at German troops? One treasured commodity, vital for everything from telephone wires to factory machinery to the tires and fan belts of motor vehicles, a commodity unavailable to Germany because of a tight blockade imposed by the Royal Navy, but abundant in the Allies' African and Asian colonies: rubber. Without rubber the Germans, among many other problems, faced the prospect of using steel tires on their army trucks, which rapidly chewed roads to bits. The rubber, it was agreed, would be delivered to Germany at the Swiss border.

During August 1915, the first month of this top-secret devil's bargain, the Germans delivered to the British even more than first agreed to: some 32,000 pairs of binoculars, 20,000 of them the higher-quality types for officers. Records that would show how long the trade continued, or how much rubber the Germans received in return, have disappeared. More frustrating, there seems to be no written trace of what was in the minds of the men who negotiated this extraordinary agreement. Did each side think it was getting the better deal? Were both British and German business executives so eager for profit that nothing else mattered? Or did the war have such all-encompassing momentum that, to better fight it, anything at all seemed justified, even trading with the enemy?

Looking through exactly these kinds of high-grade binoculars late on the morning of September 26, 1915, German officers at the front near Loos could not believe what they saw. On the second day of a major battle, roughly 10,000 British troops were walking toward them across more than half a mile of no man's land. This was not a case—as had happened before and would happen again—in which a preliminary bombardment had failed to destroy German machine-gun nests. Before this day's British attack, there had been no bombardment. The German machine guns were in protected bunkers, behind long, intact rolls of barbed wire, in belts sometimes up to 30 feet thick.

The British, according to a German account, moved forward in ten columns, "each about a thousand men, all advancing as if carrying out a parade-ground drill. . . . Never had machine guns had such straightforward work to do . . . with barrels becoming hot . . . they traversed to and fro along the enemy's ranks; one machine gun alone fired 12,500 rounds that afternoon. The result was devastating. The enemy could be seen falling literally in hundreds, but they continued to march." Some British officers were mounted on horseback, and so made even more conspicuous targets. German riflemen stood on the parapets of their trenches to fire at the fast-diminishing ranks that kept moving until they reached the first row of unbroken barbed wire. "Confronted by this impenetrable obstacle the survivors turned and began to retire."

These British troops, most of them volunteers who had joined the army after the war broke out, had arrived in France only weeks earlier. As the survivors retreated, the Germans, in a moment of mercy rare for either side, held their fire. "My machine gunners were so filled with pity, remorse and nausea," a German commander later said, ". . . that they refused to fire another shot."

The battle at Loos had begun the previous day, after Kitchener himself had reviewed the soldiers and congratulated them on the honor that had fallen to them. For Sir Douglas Haig, commanding the troops involved, it was a promising opportunity: if the attack succeeded, he would win great glory; if it failed, the person blamed would likely be the already precarious Sir John French. The two feuding generals did not even have a telephone line connecting their temporary command posts. Meanwhile, the Germans, knowing some sort of an attack was coming, had strengthened their defenses. In photographs from before the attack, the chalky soil around Loos gives the parapets of German trenches the ghostly look of long rows of snowdrifts stretching across the summer fields.

This was the first assault in which British troops used poison gas. For in scientific, industrialized warfare—as would be true four decades later with the atomic bomb—no nation would have a new weapon to itself for long. Haig ordered 5,000 six-foot-long cylinders of chlorine, weighing 150 pounds each, to be transported to the British front line by night, to maintain secrecy. For the last part of the way each of these had to be carried through communication trenches slung from a pole resting on the shoulders of two men. More pairs of soldiers carried lengths of pipe, to be attached to each cylinder, in order to spray the gas over the parapet of the trench and into no man's land. One pipe carrier's memories are a reminder of how much of the war's torment lay in merely getting supplies to the front: "The communication trench is zig-zag from beginning to end. The result was that we had to carry the pipes right above our heads in order to get them along the trench, otherwise at every corner they would get stuck. The communication trench is 3½ miles long and the journey took us between 7 and 8 hours. Rain was falling during the whole of the journey. In many places the trench was over a foot deep in water."

When September 25, the day for the attack, dawned, Haig ordered the gas released. The wind, however, was very slight. In some places the gas made it to the German lines, where soldiers had already donned their masks. In others, it drifted into no man's land and stayed there—which meant that British troops had to attack through it as they tried to pierce what, in some places, were seven to ten rows of German barbed wire. In a few spots, the breeze blew the gas back into the British trenches. All told, the British suffered more casualties from their own gas than the Germans. The surprise gas release was supposed to substitute for a massive artillery bombardment, which would have signaled an attack was imminent, and in any case, shells were still in short supply. But neither Haig nor French seems to have given much thought to one crucial fact: gas does not cut barbed wire.

The British forces far outnumbered the Germans, and, almost miraculously, in one spot a division did break open a three-quarter-mile gap in the German first and second trench lines. How to exploit this opportunity? Although French had plenty of infantry in reserve, he had erred badly in stationing them too far from the front, having forgotten that what appeared on a map as a quick few hours' march could take several times that long when troops had to funnel single file along narrow country roads clogged with ambulance wagons of wounded men heading in the other direction, and then through narrower, winding communication trenches and a ragged morass of shell holes, all under a torrential rain.

By the time his two reserve divisions arrived at their attacking positions after an exhausting all-night march, the gap had closed and the Germans had moved up their own reserves. British and German corpses and body parts from the first day's fighting littered the ground and the air was rank with the smell of death. It was then, on the second day of the battle, that Haig ordered the fateful advance by the two weary, inexperienced reserve divisions directly against hilltop German machine guns and uncut barbed wire. This was the sight, and the slaughter, that German officers observed with such amazement.

To Captain Graham Pole of the Northumberland Fusiliers, one of the advancing units, his commander dispatched this message: "The C.O. wishes the attack to be carried out with bayonets in the true Northumbrian fashion." How did it feel to be one of the men in this doomed attack? Private Harry Fellows, who had been ordered to carry the message to Captain Pole, remembered:

> The whole slope in front of me and as far away to the left as one could see was crowded with cheering men moving forward as fast as they could. And still the enemy had not fired a shot. . . .
>
> The leading men would have been about 100 yards from the German wire . . . when all hell was let loose. As if from some predetermined signal the enemy machine guns opened up with a murderous fire, both from the front and enfilading fire [i.e., from the sides] from some buildings which had been out of sight behind some trees. Men began to stumble and fall, then to go down like standing corn before a scythe. The cap from the head of the lad in front of me flew from his head and he fell — I stumbled over him — and even to this day I feel no shame when I say that I stayed where I was: my face buried in the grass, and never had the good earth smelled so sweet. . . . The firing seemed to go

on for hours. I afterwards learned that it was not even ten minutes. Bullets were cracking overhead and then it ceased . . .

After a few more minutes I rose to my knees and should I live to be a hundred I shall never forget the sight that met my eyes. The whole slope was one mass of prone figures; some even lying on top of one another. . . . Many, like the lad I had stumbled over, would never move again. Many men, even though wounded themselves, were helping their wounded comrades back. Still the Germans held their fire. . . . Assisting a lad who had a bullet wound in his foot, I arrived back at the trench near where the Scots had their machine gun. . . . One of the team offered me his water bottle: water was extremely scarce. I still remember the emotion in his voice as he said, "Ye nae had a chance."

. . . It was nerve racking to hear the cries of the men lying wounded on the slope. Even if the Germans had allowed us to help them—which I believe they would—we had no stretchers. . . .

Looking around I was pleased to see that Captain Pole was safe and remembering the message I still had for him I handed it to him with an apology for the delay. After reading it he said, with a tremor in his voice, "It doesn't matter now. But isn't that just what we tried to do?"

In this brief spasm of carnage, out of 10,000 British officers and men, more than 8,000 were killed, wounded, or missing.

As with many episodes from this war, it is hard for us to see the attack on September 26, 1915, as anything other than a blatant, needless massacre initiated by generals with a near-criminal disregard for the conditions their men faced. Strikingly, however—and this is especially typical of the war's early battles, when all soldiers were professionals or volunteers—few survivors talked of it in this way. For them to question the generals' judgment would have meant, of course, asking if their fellow soldiers had died in vain. From the need to avoid such questions are so many myths about wars born.

One of the units ravaged that day, for instance, was the 8th Battalion of the Queen's Own Royal West Kent Regiment. Of its 25 officers, 24 were casualties in little more than an hour, along with 556—a majority—of its enlisted men. The battalion commander, Colonel Eden

Vansittart, who had spent most of his long army career in India, witnessed much of the killing before being himself severely wounded. But in a long report on the battle he wrote two years later, he revealed not the slightest anger at the suicidal position he and his men were put in, only praise for their good form. "They advanced as if on parade, and under perfect discipline, till they reached the enemy's undamaged barbed wire entanglements, beyond which they were unable to go, and here our losses were very great." A decade later, when he was retired, he still did not question the decision to attack; his main concern remained that the authors of the multivolume official history of the war, for whom he prepared another report, "bring out more sharply the gallant conduct" of the battalion.

The fighting at Loos continued sporadically for several weeks more. Among the British soldiers killed whose bodies were never found was Captain Fergus Bowes-Lyon of the 8th Black Watch, whose sister, when she was married a few years later in Westminster Abbey, placed her wedding bouquet on the Tomb of the Unknown Warrior in his memory. She would survive into the next century as Queen Elizabeth the Queen Mother.

Riding a white horse, Sir John French visited the troops several times, at one point spending two hours talking to injured men at a first-aid station near the front. "Dead, dying and badly wounded all mixed up together," he wrote to Winifred Bennett. "Poor dear fellows they bear their pain gloriously and many of them gave me a smile of recognition."

In the end, the Allies gained a mile or two of ground, but once again, the losses were overwhelmingly on the attackers' side, with more than 61,000 British casualties. "It was impossible to bury them all. . . . You'd go along the trenches and you'd see a boot and puttee sticking out, or an arm or a hand, sometimes faces," remembered one soldier. "Not only would you see, but you'd be walking on them, slipping and sliding. . . . But if you ever had to write home about a particular mate you'd always say that he got it cleanly and quickly with a bullet and he didn't know what had happened." Bloated to the size of cats, rats feasted on the bodies left in no man's land, beginning with the eyes, the softer flesh of the face, and the liver, then working their way onward as the days passed, leaving only skeletons draped in scraps of khaki. At night, soldiers in their trenches could hear a constant rattling, as rats nosed their way among the tin cans and canteens around the skeletons, looking for bits of food.

Still, British generals denied the awesome power of the chief weapon involved. "The introduction of the Machine Gun," declared a memo from French's headquarters to the Ministry of Munitions two months after the battle, "has not, in the opinion of the General Staff, altered the universally accepted principle that superior numbers of bayonets closing with the enemy is what finally turns the scale." Even some two and a half years later, in May 1918, the British forces would have only one machine gun for every 61 men. The Canadians would have one for every 13, the French one for every 12.

Day after day the size of the British death tolls sank in, and "Roll of Honour" listings spread across the columns of the *Times,* with officers' names in slightly larger type. A volley of recriminations quickly began over who was to blame: French, who had stationed the reserves too far away, or Haig, who had launched the troops directly against undamaged German wire and machine guns. With the *Times* correspondent Repington on French's side, some of this argument again spilled into the press. French got the *Times* to publish a dispatch of his that misleadingly implied that the reserves were closer to the front than they really had been. But the battle that counted was within the government, and there the winner was foreordained. Haig simply wrote to Kitchener laying all the blame on French: "My attack, as has been reported, was a complete success," he said nonsensically, ". . . and reserves should have been at hand *then*."

Kitchener demanded an explanation of the Loos debacle from French, and in Parliament several speakers attacked the beleaguered field marshal, one mentioning the presence of women at his headquarters. Milner, frustrated and on the sidelines, spoke acidly in the House of Lords of the official "furtive admissions" and "laboured explanations" for the terrible casualty toll. The King himself crossed the Channel to sample military opinion firsthand. "Douglas Haig came to dinner and I had a long talk with him afterwards," he wrote in his diary. "He . . . said the C-in-C was a source of great weakness to the Army, and no one had any confidence in him anymore." In a railway dining car in England, an officer overheard Asquith, Lloyd George, and the foreign secretary debating French's removal.

Compared to previous wars, at Loos, as in earlier battles, a strikingly high proportion of casualties were simply listed as "missing." Men might be mowed down by German fire in patches of ground not held long enough to recover the bodies, or there might not be any body to recover after a high-explosive shell blew someone into unrecognizable bits—and also killed any comrades who witnessed his end. Many of the British casualties counted as missing at Loos came on the day after the catastrophic slaughter of the reserve divisions. New troops were then thrown into the battle, among them the 2nd Battalion of the Irish Guards, John Kipling's unit, whose men had not slept or had much to eat during the preceding 48 hours. But despite their exhaustion, Lieutenant Kipling led his platoon through rubble at the pit head of a mine, shouting "Come on boys," and managed to capture at least one building occupied by German defenders. Late that afternoon, he vanished from sight. According to one account, he was wounded at a place the soldiers called Chalk Pit Wood and crawled into a building later seized by the Germans, but there was no additional news. A War Office telegram to his parents reported him missing in action.

The day the reserve divisions were mowed down at Loos thousands of people assembled in London's Trafalgar Square, long a favorite spot for protest rallies. They had come to raise their voices against conscription—which, it was clear, was soon going to be imposed to meet the army's insatiable demand for men. Charlotte Despard, no longer able to hold her antiwar feelings in check, was one of those who addressed the crowd—as was Sylvia Pankhurst. After she spoke, Pankhurst noticed boys hawking newspapers and carrying large placards. She could not make out what they were shouting, but finally one came close enough for her to read his placard: DEATH OF KEIR HARDIE.

She collapsed and had to be helped offstage. "I was not faint but stunned and stricken. . . . I felt as they who had lost their dearest in the War," she later wrote, "for the War had killed him, as surely as it had killed the men who went to the trenches." Hardie died in a Glasgow hospital, his failing health worsened by pneumonia. Supporters gathered for his funeral in that city a few days later, as the bullets continued to fly at Loos. Along the path of the procession, workmen, and sometimes soldiers, stood solemnly, their heads bared. With Hardie's family in attendance, Sylvia did not come, but she sent a wreath of laurel, with ribbons in the suffragette colors of purple, green, and white, as well as revolutionary red. The muffling chill of the times extended even to the funeral service, for the vicar said nothing of Hardie's long battle against war, speaking only of his youth in the Evangelical Union church.

In London, Sylvia put out a special issue of her *Woman's Dreadnought* filled with tributes to him, including her own passionate goodbye: "He was built for great strength, his head more grandly carved than any other; his deep-set eyes like sunshine distilled, as we see it through the waters of a pool in the brown earth." She called him the "greatest human being of our time." As in all the tens of thousands of words she wrote about Hardie over her lifetime, she did not mention his wife.

He remained a beacon for her, and in maintaining her own unremitting opposition to the war, she saw herself as carrying on his legacy. But making others feel the same way while men in their families were at the front proved as difficult for her as it had been for the man she loved. At one point the playwright George Bernard Shaw asked her, "How can you expect to convert the public when you cannot even convert your mother and Christabel?" Indeed, there was no hope of that. In October, Christabel renamed the *Suffragette*, the WSPU newspaper, *Britannia*, with the motto "For King, for Country, for Freedom." Its pages would from now on be filled with patriotic prose and poetry accompanied by images of Joan of Arc and other women warriors. The paper's nationalism became so extreme that one article attacked the Foreign Office for being "corrupted . . . by Germanism, German blood, German and pro-enemy ties and sympathies. [It] must be CLEARED OUT and its whole staff replaced."

Seeking an ally, Christabel wrote to Alfred Milner, sharing with him her suspicions of secret Germanophiles hidden in high posts. "I absolutely agree with your criticism of the conduct of the war," he replied. But, he added, "where I differ from you is imputing evil motives to our rulers. . . . I think them incompetent—extremely so— . . . but I do not think that any of them is otherwise than anxious to do the best for his country." And he gently chided her for suspecting "everybody who has any foreign blood in his veins," pointing out that Queen Victoria was half German and that he himself had a German grandmother.

Christabel was not alone in her paranoia about German spies and sympathizers. As 1915 drew to a close there was an ever-greater hunger to find traitors or scapegoats whose actions would explain the lack of battlefield victories. During the war years, more than 90 plays about spies were performed in British theaters, abounding in sinister German servants in unsuspecting British homes, poisoned reservoirs, and secret radios sending messages to lurking U-boats. Scotland Yard was overwhelmed with an average of 300 tips a day about possible spies. Soldiers were dispatched on hundreds of missions to isolated homes and fields to check out reports of mysterious flashes at night thought to be signals to German airships. Woe to any homing pigeon fancier seen with his birds, which might be about to carry vital state secrets straight to Berlin. Actual German spies in Britain proved remarkably few. Most of them, in fact, were rounded up in the first days of the war, but the publicity-hungry Basil Thomson of Scotland Yard made sure that any such arrest or trial, no matter how minor, was trumpeted in the press.

In breaks from writing his multivolume history of the war and from sending optimistic dispatches to the *Times* from the Western Front, John Buchan lent a helping hand to the spy mania. In October 1915, just after Loos, he published what became his best-known book (later brought to the screen by Alfred Hitchcock), *The Thirty-Nine Steps.* In this novel and its sequels, Buchan essentially invented the most popular form of the modern spy story: a daring, athletic hero, chase scenes, friends who turn out to be enemies, enemies who turn out to be friends, coded messages, and grand conspiracies that will destroy everything if the hero cannot escape from a castle dungeon in time. With Britain's soldiers dug in below ground on a front that barely moved month after bloody month, the public was relieved and delighted to read stories like these, in which individual feats of boldness carried the day.

In *The Thirty-Nine Steps,* Buchan's hero, Richard Hannay, foils the machinations of a whole network of German spies. Hannay is a colonial who has returned from various adventures in southern Africa just in time to help the "Old Country" in its hour of need. Significantly, the Old Country is not an industrialized nation of drab, crowded urban tenements and factories belching coal smoke, but a serene, pastoral landscape of moors and hills. Pursued by the evil Germans, Hannay races "through little old thatched villages and over peaceful lowland streams, and past gardens blazing with hawthorn and yellow laburnum. The land was so deep in peace that I could scarcely believe that somewhere behind me were those who sought my life; ay, and that in a month's time, unless I had the almightiest of luck . . . men would be lying dead in English fields." In the novel's happy ending, Hannay, of course, nabs the spies just before they can spirit away stolen military plans on their yacht. The book, which sold more than a million copies in Buchan's lifetime, contributed to an upsurge of volunteers to become special police constables—a job in which many a middle-aged Briton too old for the trenches could still imagine himself catching a German spy.

No spies or conspiracies could explain the British failure at Loos, however, so the commander in chief was doomed. As French had predicted, they changed the bowler. To save face, he was given command of the Home Forces—all troops in Britain and Ireland, who were mainly in training—which was a bitter comedown. When the prime minister's emissary tried to soften the blow by telling him he would be ennobled as well, French wryly suggested he could become "Lord Sent-Homer." In recognition of his role in withstanding the German attacks at Ypres and of his Irish ancestry, he was made Viscount of Ypres and of High Lake, County Roscommon. But because Ypres became associated with so much lost British blood, the name never fully stuck, and contemporaries as well as later writers generally continued to refer to him as Sir John French. He remained popular with British troops, thousands of whom lined the road, cheering wildly, when he left his headquarters for the last time in December. At the dockside in Boulogne, there were more cheers from his old regiment, the 19th Hussars. For French, it was farewell to this front, but, as it would happen, the play was not over; one major act was yet to come.

His successor, of course, was Haig, who was fully confident that he could succeed where the capricious French had failed. "DH never shines at dinner," recorded an officer on his staff at this time, "but he was obviously in very good spirits, and kept silence merrily."

In the trenches, the Christmas season was anything but merry. "A high wind hurtled over the Flemish fields," remembered the war correspondent Philip Gibbs, "but it was moist, and swept gusts of rain into the faces of men marching through the mud to the fighting-lines and of other men doing sentry on the fire-steps of trenches into which water came trickling down the slimy parapets. . . . They slept in soaking clothes, with boots full of water. . . . Whole sections of trench collapsed into a chaos of slime and ooze."

At a point where British and German lines were so close that each side could hear the squelching of the other's boots, Gibbs reported a conversation in shouts over the parapets:

> "How deep is it with you?" shouted a German soldier. . . .
> "Up to our blooming knees," said an English corporal, who was trying to keep his bombs dry under a tarpaulin.
> "So? . . . You are lucky fellows. We are up to our belts in it."

As Christmas Day approached, all British units were given strict orders that there be no repeat of the spontaneous fraternization of the previous year. But even without a truce, something else had already started to happen, without reference to any holiday. At a number of places on the front where Allied and German trenches had been fixed in place for so long, there evolved a tacit system of "live and let live." If, for example, you fired trench mortars at the Germans while they were having lunch or dinner, they would do the same to you, so sometimes firing stopped at mealtimes. At a safe moment like this, a soldier might even signal the other side—perhaps by climbing briefly above the parapet and pointing to his shoulder, where an officer's insignia would be—when a commander was about to visit. Then troops on both sides would begin a barrage of rifle and machine-gun fire, and British and French infantrymen quickly learned that if they aimed too high, the Germans would do the same. A similar informal understanding sometimes also covered no man's land, where soldiers were ordered to go on dreaded night patrols to repair barbed-wire barricades and reconnoiter enemy defenses. One young British officer typically described leading several men on such a mission when "we suddenly confronted, round some mound or excavation, a German patrol . . . we were perhaps twenty yards from each other, fully visible. I waved a weary hand, as if to say: what is the use of killing each other? The German officer seemed to understand, and both parties turned and made their way back to their own trenches. Reprehensible conduct, no doubt."

In some places, the front-line trenches were far apart and the cratered expanse of no man's land might be several hundred yards wide. This allowed the rise of a curious and persistent legend. No man's land was not empty, some soldiers claimed, but populated by deserters who found shelter in shell holes and caves as well as abandoned trenches and dugouts. After every skirmish, when darkness fell, they would come out to rob the dead and dying of their food and water. As time passed these spectral survivors grew long beards and their uniforms turned to rags—until they took new ones from the dead. They were the source, it was said, of mysterious noises heard at night. And this roving community in no man's land was international, men were convinced, with deserters from both sides. The generals had forbidden fraternization, but they couldn't prevent it from happening in myth.

No war in history had seen so many troops locked in stalemate for so long. The year 1915 had begun with the Germans occupying some 19,500 square miles of French and Belgian territory. At its end, Allied troops had recaptured exactly eight of those square miles, the British alone suffering more than a quarter-million casualties in the process. Still an endless stream of wounded flowed home, and still the newspapers were filled with lists of those killed or missing.

For Rudyard and Carrie Kipling, messages of sympathy arrived from all over the world, from Theodore Roosevelt, Sir Arthur Conan Doyle, and other friends at home and abroad. "They tell me John is reported missing," said a letter from a fellow Irish Guards officer wounded in the same battle, "but I feel sure that it will all come right as . . . I myself was officially reported missing." Others also tried to be optimistic: "We can but trust he is a prisoner," wrote the Prince of Wales.

The distraught Kipling doggedly questioned a succession of Irish Guardsmen, but in vain. The War Office had listed John as "wounded and missing"; Kipling was enraged when a newspaper referred to him as "missing, believed killed." He and Carrie clung to the hope that John might be alive, in a hospital or prison camp in Germany. With survivors of the battle eager to comfort the stricken parents with any possible scrap of news or rumor, conflicting information began to pile up: that John had a leg wound, that he had been shot in the neck, that he had been seen alive after the time he was reported missing. Even though he despised governments that had remained neutral in what he saw as a titanic struggle between good and evil, Kipling turned to the American ambassador, asking that a description of his son be sent to the U.S. embassy in Berlin: "He is dark with strongly marked eyebrows, small moustache, thick brown hair (straight), dark brown eyes with long lashes. Height about 5.7½. . . . He is short-sighted and is most probably wearing gold spectacles."

Now it was Violet Cecil's turn to offer sympathy and compassion to her friends, as they had to her. Milner, ever the realist, wrote in his diary, "We fear he is killed." Carrie Kipling had rushed to see Violet the day after John was reported missing, and sometimes wrote to her twice a day. Violet herself interviewed one wounded Irish Guards officer in the hospital to see if she could find out anything, and, in hopes that another neutral power could help, sent a letter to the Crown Princess of Sweden. "No news," Carrie wrote to her, "—a great darkness seems to be settling down on it all. But who should know better than you."

Kipling wrote on, but on occasion now his martial voice was muted, and it almost seemed a different person speaking:

> "Have you news of my boy Jack?"
>   *Not this tide.*
> "When d'you think that he'll come back?"
>   *Not with this wind blowing, and this tide.*
>
> "Has any one else had word of him?"
>   *Not this tide.*
> *For what is sunk will hardly swim,*
>   *Not with this wind blowing, and this tide. . . .*

IV

1916

13

WE REGRET NOTHING

B Y THE BEGINNING of 1916, in response to recruiting drives, posters ("Don't Lag! Follow Your Flag!"), and music hall songs ("Oh, we don't want to lose you, but we think you ought to go"), an impressive two and a half million men had enlisted. One historian has called Britain's volunteer army "the greatest expression of enthusiasm for war in all history." That enthusiasm, however, was not evenly shared. Although members of the working class never opposed the war on anything like the scale Keir Hardie dreamed of, they showed less zeal than the better-off, volunteering for the army at a noticeably lower rate than professionals and white-collar workers.

War-minded Britons who worried about lingering pockets of working-class internationalism were heartened, however, in March 1916, by the birth of a new organization, which became known as the British Workers' League. The group, made up mostly of trade union officials, issued statements that sounded vaguely socialist, calling for better wages and pensions as well as for "national control of vital industries." But it was also vigorously prowar. "All-British from the core," it proclaimed itself, vowing victory over "Germans and Austrians who are now doing their best to destroy us." Unusual then, this combination — support for social welfare measures and strident nationalism — would become far more familiar as fascism rose in the 1920s and '30s.

As in the fascist labor movements to come, several of the League's leaders were distinctly thuggish. Followers of one of them, Joseph Havelock Wilson of the National Sailors' and Firemen's Union, set fire to the office of an antiwar rival, with the man still inside. When he fled the fire, they tried to throw him back in.

It was clearly a great boon to the government to have an organization of "workers" attacking the Independent Labour Party and other antiwar groups, which officials of the new League quickly did, at public meetings and in its vociferously chauvinist weekly, the *British Citizen and Empire Worker.* For every demand the League made for better pay or public ownership of key industries, there were louder attacks on "shirkers" from the war effort and on traitors to the empire. The prowar press was delighted; the *Times* described one League demonstration as "beyond all question . . . the authentic voice of the working classes." Less than a year after its founding, this surprisingly well-financed organization would claim 74 branches around the country, staging 100 patriotic mass meetings a week.

There were, of course, millions of working-class Britons who were genuinely prowar. The League, however, was the brainchild of someone who was anything but proletarian: Alfred, Lord Milner. "I am trying, very hard, but quietly," he wrote to a friend just before the League went public, "to further a purely working-class movement which I hope will knock out the ILP . . . among Trade Unionists [and] which will make Imperial Unity and Citizens' Service [i.e., conscription] planks in its programme." The enthusiasm of the *Times* for this "authentic voice of the working classes" was also Milner's doing, for the paper's editor was a close friend and disciple, a former member of the South African Kindergarten.

"It would be difficult to imagine," a biographer comments, "anyone less suitable than Milner to inspire a working class movement." But the League was his creation and his alone: he had found the perfect person to run it, Victor Fisher, an experienced socialist journalist, and then quietly lined up the necessary funders: Waldorf Astor, MP, a young member of a famously non-working-class family, and later the shipping magnate Sir James Knott. The cash was put into a special account at the London Joint Stock Bank, from which Milner personally doled it out to Fisher, checking his expense reports. "Shall we call the a/c the 'Imperial Fund'?" Astor asked. Milner replied: "It would not be necessary or perhaps desirable, to give it any name. . . . I am a Director of that Bank, so no questions would be asked, and nobody need know anything about it except ourselves."

Fisher himself received a full-time salary plus £1,000 a year for expenses, with a remarkable guarantee that his salary would be paid for three years even if the League ceased operations. Milner met with most of the speakers before the League's first big public meeting, but after that he kept a low profile, although he saw Fisher in private almost every week. He did not mind working with trade unionists, for he had always been open to what some Britons called "gas and water socialism." Public health? Better schools? Public ownership of electric power? No problem: such things were entirely tolerable if they made the economy more efficient and the working class more enthusiastic for the empire—and the war.

The month the new League was founded, conscription finally began. The mass-production slaughter on the fields of France and Flanders required it, to feed the army's relentless appetite for human bodies. A military draft was a radical change for Britain, and because even some prowar MPs were uncomfortable with it and needed persuading, the new law provided a surprisingly broad exemption for conscientious objectors, or COs, as they came to be called. Special tribunals were set up around the country, and if one of these boards agreed that a man had a principled objection to bearing arms, whether religious or secular, he could do alternative service—either in a Non-Combatant Corps within the army or in supervised work gangs doing farm labor, forestry, and other manual jobs that kept the wartime economy going at home. Those exempt from the draft included some skilled workers doing "work of national importance" in strategic industries—and all Irishmen. The last thing the government wanted was anything that might provoke a new nationalist uprising on that highly combustible island.

New conscripts filled training camps in Britain, most of them eventually destined for Haig's forces in France and Belgium. His subordinates at headquarters "all seem to expect success as the result of my arrival," the general wrote to his wife, "and somehow give me the idea that they think I am 'meant to win' by some Superior Power." Strait-laced, humorless, intolerant of off-color jokes, gambling, and ribald songs, Haig was convinced that he had been led to the Western Front by God's hand. He urged a visiting party of clergymen to "preach . . . about the objects of Great Britain in carrying on this war. We have no selfish motive but are fighting for the good of humanity."

"We lament too much over death," Haig approvingly quoted his own chosen army pastor, Reverend George Duncan of the Church of Scotland, whose services he attended. "We should regard it as a change to another room." Duncan's views fitted, chillingly, with the general's own thinking. "The nation must be taught to bear losses," Haig wrote, ". . . [and] to see heavy casualty lists for what may appear to the uninitiated to be insufficient object[s]. . . . Three years of war and the loss of one-tenth of the manhood of the nation is not too great a price to pay in so great a cause."

For manhood of prime military age, the price would prove far higher.

As the year began, Haig was as relentlessly optimistic as his predecessor, supremely confident that his tenacity and skill could succeed —and swiftly—where French had failed. "The Germans might bargain for peace before the coming winter," he told the King. Shortly after taking command, Haig urged renewed cavalry recruiting and ordered a fresh round of inspections of his five cavalry divisions, to put spine into "some officers who think that Cavalry are no longer required!!!" In a letter to the chief of the Imperial General Staff, he spoke of being prepared for a version of Murat's famous cavalry pursuit of the retreating Prussians at the Battle of Jena—in 1806. Haig's obsession was shared by British painters and illustrators, who filled canvases and magazine pages with heroic cavalry charges that bore little resemblance to reality. "Straight at the Guns the Lancers Rode," read a typical caption in the *Illustrated London News.*

At the front, most soldiers were focused on less glorious matters, such as the slimy mass of frogs and slugs that infested the trenches as the weather grew warmer and wetter with the spring thaw. One 36-year-old infantry officer wrote to a friend that "lately a certain number of cats have taken to nesting in the corpses, but I think the rats will get them in the end; though like all wars it will doubtless be a war of attrition." This observation came from Raymond Asquith, son of the prime minister and a widely admired lawyer and wit. Of trench life in winter, he wrote to his wife, he was trying to "take the same sort of interest . . . as an ill-tempered tourist may take in an uncomfortable hotel."

An unending stream of VIP visitors enjoyed far better lodgings when they called on Haig at his headquarters, which were spread among a military academy, a hotel, and other buildings in the medieval French town of Montreuil; the commander himself lived in a small château nearby. "Montreuil was a place to bring tears to the eyes of an artist. . . . The tiny walled town on a hill had that poignant fulness of loveliness, making the sense ache at it, like still summer evenings in England," wrote the author C. E. Montague, whose army job was to take journalists on tours of the front. "It was a storied antique, unscathed . . . weathered mellow with centuries of sunshine and tranquillity. . . . Walking among its walled gardens, where roses hung over the walls . . . you were not merely out of the war; you were out of all war."

For Haig's entourage, their uniforms marked by staff officers' distinctive red lapel tabs and hatbands as well as armbands in the red and blue of General Headquarters colors, there was a tennis court to play on and narrow cobblestone streets to stroll down. At the officers' club, a band played ragtime while customers were served by attractive young waitresses from the new Women's Army Auxiliary Corps in khaki stockings and skirts (no more than 12 inches off the ground, regulations required). The bows in their hair were in headquarters red and blue.

A man of strict routines, Haig stepped out of his bedroom at exactly 8:25 every morning, checked the barometer, went for the briefest of walks in the château's garden, and sat down for breakfast at 8:30. After a morning in his office, unless he was visiting one of his subordinate commanders, he would take a two-hour afternoon ride on horseback, accompanied by several aides-de-camp and an escort of lancers with fluttering pennons. Having returned to his desk, he stopped for dinner promptly at 8:00 P.M. and then worked again or talked with visitors until 10:45. When he inspected troops, he was particularly attentive to their appearance and discipline, noting disapprovingly in his diary one battalion's "slackness . . . in the matter of saluting."*

Haig and his staff ate well, enjoying the steady supply of foie gras,

---

*One of Haig's generals, the hot-tempered Edmund Allenby, equally a stickler in such matters, once let loose a tirade at a soldier he found wearing an incorrect uniform in a trench, only to discover, when there was no reply, that he had been berating a dead man.

fresh fish, and joints of lamb that his friend Leopold de Rothschild sent to Montreuil. "All the troops here are very fit and cheery," the general wrote to Rothschild. "Indeed . . . it is the troops in the field who write home to cheer their friends and not the other way!" The censors who read the soldiers' outbound mail collected only the most upbeat excerpts to show Haig. There can be no question, though, that in this honeymoon period soldiers did indeed project onto Haig their hopes for an early victory and a return home.

Haig's very uncommunicativeness allowed civilians and soldiers alike to read into the man the qualities they wanted to see. "Haig was a silent man. . . . You had to learn a sort of verbal shorthand made up of a series of grunts and gestures," wrote his aide-de-camp Desmond Morton. Of one such instance Morton recalled, "The briefing lasted about twenty minutes and consisted of Haig with a pointer in front of a large-scale map of the battle pointing at various spots and making grunting noises with a few words interspersed. 'Never believed . . . petrol . . . bridge gone . . . where cavalry?' and so on. Fortunately I knew the cipher by this time. I am sure Haig felt he had given me a long and lucid lecture on the whole affair."

In the subordinates Haig chose, loyalty and length of service were what counted, not initiative. "If by any chance failures are sent home," an officer at the Montreuil headquarters wrote to his wife, "they are put in charge of new divisions and re-appear in a few months to do further damage." As he had all his life, Haig vigorously defended the seniority principle, demanding that if someone was recommended for promotion, a list of any officers senior to the man had to be forwarded with the recommendation. Haig had risen through the military bureaucracy by attracting not those with talent or new ideas but rather those who would not outshine him. There was no shortage of mediocrity in the British army of this era, but he was unusual in openly endorsing the quality. Years before, when his sister wrote to him doubting that a certain officer joining his staff was "clever enough for the job," Haig replied: "The so called sharp people very often disappoint us or cheat or have some other drawback such as being disagreeable, bad-tempered, etc. All I require is people of *average* intelligence who are keen to do their work properly."

While Haig planned for a great breakthrough, it became painfully clear that the Germans were doing exactly the same thing, and they struck first. Their target was the French army, whose sector of the front line was anchored by the fortress city of Verdun and its surrounding double ring of smaller forts. The assault on Verdun began in late February 1916 with the largest and longest artillery bombardment yet seen. No one knew the extent of German casualties, but 90,000 French soldiers were killed or wounded in the first six weeks. The ferocious combat raged on, murderously but indecisively, into the spring, the German troops deploying their flamethrowers when they could get close enough to French positions. Not for the last time in this war, gaining a tiny piece of ground became an obsession for the attacking commander.

Anxious to see the Germans diverted from Verdun, the French high command urged its British allies to accelerate plans for a massive joint assault where the British and French sectors of the front met, near the River Somme, which meandered its slow and weed-filled way through a countryside of wheat and sugar beet fields. As ever more French troops were drawn into the bloody maw of Verdun, it became clear that the major work of the assault on the Somme would fall to the British army. July 1, 1916, was fixed as its date, and months of intensive preparations began.

In London, a measure of elite status was whether you had access to the latest uncensored news from the battlefields of the Western Front. Coded telegrams flowed from Montreuil to the War Office, and longer dispatches were carried by couriers known as King's Messengers. On Easter Monday, April 24, 1916, urgent telegrams about a surprise attack streamed in — but not from Haig's headquarters. Many of them landed on the desk of the shocked commander of the Home Forces, the new Viscount French, still angry over being kicked upstairs from his post at the front. At this worst of possible moments, the largest insurrection in a century had broken out in Ireland.

Some 1,750 nationalists had taken up arms, determined, after long centuries of English rule, to take Ireland out of the United Kingdom once and for all. Men carrying rifles on their shoulders, but sometimes wearing suits and ties, marched up Dublin's O'Connell Street. As they approached the majestic General Post Office, the column's leader, James Connolly — a self-educated socialist, friend of Keir Hardie, and military veteran — gave the order, "Left turn . . . charge!" Within a few minutes the rebels had occupied the building and decked it with a green flag sporting a gold harp and the words IRISH REPUBLIC. They soon came out on the front steps and announced, to a small scattering of surprised pedestrians, the establishment of a provisional government. "Irishmen and Irishwomen," their proclamation began. "In the name of God and of the dead generations from which she receives her old tradition of nationhood, Ireland, through us, summons her children to her flag and strikes for her freedom."

The rebels quickly cut telephone lines and occupied railway stations and other key buildings. Preparing for the British army counterattack that was sure to come, they began building barricades, organizing blockades of cars across major streets, and digging trenches in St. Stephen's Green. At the domed Four Courts building they used heavy law books as the equivalent of sandbag fortifications.

French immediately ordered two infantry brigades to Ireland and put other units on alert. After conferring with the prime minister, the King, and Kitchener, he dispatched yet more troops and a hard-line general to command them. The British soldiers surrounded rebel-held central Dublin, and the authorities declared martial law.

The Easter Rising, as it was termed, proved a dramatic blow at England's imperial *amour-propre,* but fell far short of the rebels' dreams. The nationwide revolt they hoped to ignite never materialized: popular support for such an extreme move proved weak, dissension broke out among the leaders, and weapons promised by the Germans were intercepted by the British. The Rising was largely limited to Dublin, where British forces soon outnumbered the insurgents 20 to 1. As the badly armed rebels in their fedoras and cloth caps fought on, however, their doomed revolt gained an aura of sacrificial tragedy that would make it a landmark in Irish nationalist mythology—looming far larger, paradoxically, than if the Rising had been better planned and executed.

As the British army closed in, a Royal Navy gunboat on the River Liffey shelled the rebels' temporary headquarters, which bore a big sign: WE SERVE NEITHER KING NOR KAISER, BUT IRELAND. Insurgents barricaded in shops and factories fought on stubbornly, evacuating their wounded, when they could, through back doors and holes smashed in walls. Hit by an incendiary artillery round, the General Post Office began to burn and soon became a blackened shell whose outer walls still bear the scars of bullets today. Flames soared into the sky day and night. Women accused of carrying ammunition to the rebels were seized and carted off screaming. The last headquarters of the Irish Republic's short-lived army was Hanlon's fish shop on Moore Street.

According to the official count, the week of bitter street fighting left more than 400 dead and 2,500 wounded—among rebels, bystanders, and British troops—although some estimates put the figures higher. British military authorities court-martialed the leaders of the revolt, sentencing 15 to be shot. Some feared this would provoke a new round of uprisings, but French, in London, refused to overrule the general he had dispatched to Dublin. In dealing with the suffragettes, the British government had been careful not to create martyrs; French's failure to do the same would prove a pivotal mistake. The last of the condemned to be brought before the firing squad was James Connolly, so badly wounded that he had to be carried on a stretcher and then tied to a chair to be shot. People throughout Ireland were enraged, as were English supporters of Irish freedom like Sylvia Pankhurst.

Her *Woman's Dreadnought* became a rare source of news about the Rising, for its correspondent, 18-year-old Patricia Lynch, scored a coup when she evaded a government news blackout and managed to slip into Dublin: on the way there she met a politically sympathetic army officer who got her through roadblocks by identifying her as his sister. The issue of the *Dreadnought* that carried her report, "Scenes from the Irish Rebellion," promptly sold out and had to be reprinted several times. "The hopeless bravery of it," Pankhurst wrote later of the Rising, "the coercion and the executions which followed, to me were a grief cutting deep as a personal sorrow."

With some blocks in Dublin as reduced to rubble as war-ravaged towns in France and Belgium, the Easter Rising was a sharp blow to all who hoped that the shared ordeal of war would strengthen the bonds holding together the British Empire. No one valued that dream more than Milner. Despite his prodigious administrative talents, he was not close to Asquith, and so the prime minister had given him only minor assignments. Milner chafed impatiently as admirers inside the government and the military told him how wartime bureaucrats were making a mess of things that he could have set right. ("I shall never be quite happy until I see you War Minister," wrote one general.) His one solace was his love for Violet Cecil.

She, however, was still consumed by grief. Like many bereaved women then, she tried to console herself by compiling a collection of letters from her son's final weeks, copying them by hand into an album, along with a list of the villages where he had spent each night during his short time in France and a hand-drawn map of the forest where he died. One by one she watched other families she knew receive the same terrible news about sons, husbands, or brothers.

An advisory committee Milner served on recommended that all possible land be farmed—to make Britain less dependent on imported food that had to cross an ocean patrolled by German U-boats. And so, adding to her own sense of a world turned upside down, Violet dutifully ordered her flower gardens at Great Wigsell converted to grow fruit and vegetables, and sheep were set to graze on the lawns. With farmhands called away to the front, the only laborers available were German POWs. "This place is polluted by German prisoners who are ploughing," she wrote to her husband. "I hate to see them in the field . . . George used to ride in." Servants, too, were hard to find, for young women flocked to jobs now open to them in munitions factories, just as Emmeline Pankhurst had wanted. Violet lost her maid, and for a time had to cook and sew for herself.

Meanwhile, at venerable Hatfield House, the seat of Edward Cecil's family, fields and the private golf course were filled with trenches and a man-made swamp to create a maneuvering ground for an experimental weapon under development, the tank. The King himself came one day to watch the enormous machines grind their way across ancestral Cecil land. Most of the great house itself, with its library of 10,000 leather-bound books, marble floors, gold leaf ceilings, and flags captured at Waterloo, had, like many similar homes, been transformed into a convalescent hospital for wounded soldiers, with remaining family members confined to one corner.

The same month as the Easter Rising, Sylvia Pankhurst and her supporters organized an antiwar rally in Trafalgar Square, to which she marched with a working-class group from the East End. Never strong on modesty, she wrote later, "I knew the dear London crowd loved me. . . . In their jolly kindness some shouted: 'Good old Sylvia!'" At the square itself, though, far less love was in sight. The demonstrators were set upon by right-wing thugs and soldiers wearing the broad-brimmed hats of the notoriously rowdy Australian and New Zealand troops.

They tore the marchers' banners to pieces and jeered so loudly that the speakers could not be heard. Other hecklers hurled red and yellow dye. Sylvia tried to speak over the uproar, but her voice was drowned out. Finally two policemen made her leave the platform before the violence got out of hand. From across the Atlantic, where she was in the midst of a North American speaking tour, her mother cabled Christabel: "Strongly repudiate and condemn Sylvia's foolish and unpatriotic conduct. . . . Make this public."

Sylvia's voice was not alone. A socialist named William Holliday had been sentenced the previous year to three months of hard labor for publicly insisting, "Freedom's battle has not to be fought on the blood-drenched soil of France but nearer home—our enemy is within the gates." Acquitted on appeal, he was arrested again on a pretext and died in prison. Others dared to speak out: the first men refusing the draft, a few trade unionists, a handful of MPs, and some intellectuals, of whom the most prominent—each would later spend months in prison for his opinions—were Bertrand Russell and the distinguished journalist Edmund Dene Morel.

A burly man of imposing dynamism, Morel, for more than a decade before 1914, had been the moving spirit of the century's first great international human rights campaign, against the forced labor system King Leopold II of Belgium had used to draw profits from the Congo, a system Morel had done more than anyone else to expose. He was Britain's most skilled practitioner of what today we would call investigative journalism. After the war began, Morel became a founder of the Union of Democratic Control, a coalition that drew together a number of liberal, socialist, and labor figures and groups who felt that Britain's participation in the war was a huge mistake, possible only because foreign policy was made outside of open, parliamentary control. By the war's end, organizations affiliated with the UDC, most of them local or regional labor union groups, would have a combined membership of more than 650,000. The UDC called for ending the war through a negotiated peace, based on several principles, one of which was that no territory should change hands in a peace settlement without a plebiscite of those who lived there.

Morel poured out an unceasing stream of books, articles, and pamphlets arguing that the war was not due to German aggression alone, but also to various secret treaties and agreements—including the understanding Britain had had with France—and to an uncontrolled arms race. For years before the war, he wrote, the leaders of every major country in Europe had been telling their people "that while they themselves were extremely anxious to keep the peace, the fellows next door were a quarrelsome lot, and that the only way to keep them quiet was to arm to the teeth." Writing in 1916, three years before the postwar Treaty of Versailles would virtually guarantee the rise of Nazism, he already grasped that the most dangerous outcome of the conflict would be the total victory of either side—"a war which enables one side to impose its unfettered will upon the other . . . a war closing amid universal exhaustion, followed by a sullen peace." Although Morel had won wide respect for his Congo muckraking, newspapers now fiercely attacked him as a German agent, and before long he would find his writings censored, his mailbox filled with hate letters, and the police raiding his home to carry away private papers from his study.

Conscription spurred the country's antiwar movement into new life. In 1916, for example, some 200,000 Britons signed a petition calling for a negotiated peace. Except for Russia when it erupted in revolution the following year, none of the other major powers would develop an antiwar movement as large and vocal. Nor, of course, did any of them have the deeply embedded tradition of civil liberties that allowed one to flourish in Britain. Before the end of the war, more than 20,000 men of military age would refuse to enter the British armed forces. Some accepted alternative labor as conscientious objectors, but—usually because they refused that option on principle or because they were denied CO status—more than 6,000 resisters spent time in prison. Today it is easy enough to look back and see the manifold tragic consequences of the First World War, but when the guns were firing and the pressure from friends and family to support the war effort was overwhelming, it required rare courage to resist.

As antiwar organizations carried on their uphill struggle, their offices were raided and searched, their mail was opened, and they were infiltrated by informers and *agents provocateurs*. Before long the authorities began raiding sports matches, cinemas, theaters, and railway stations to round up men who were not in uniform. Hysteria against pacifists rose everywhere. A pamphlet by "A Little Mother" typically declared that "we women . . . will tolerate no such cry as 'Peace! Peace!' . . . There is only one temperature for the women of the British race, and that is white heat. . . . We women pass on the human ammunition of 'only sons' to fill up the gaps." It sold 75,000 copies in a few days. "The conscientious objector is a fungus growth—a human toadstool —which should be uprooted without further delay," screamed the tabloid *John Bull.* The *Daily Express* declared that COs were financed by German money. Those against the war were so accustomed to being ostracized that they were sometimes startled when it didn't happen. When an old friend, now in uniform, warmly greeted E. D. Morel in the street, Morel was so moved that he burst into tears, exclaiming, "I did not think anyone would speak to me now."

In April 1916 the largest group backing resisters, the No-Conscription Fellowship, or NCF, drew some 2,000 supporters to a convention in a London Quaker meeting hall while an angry crowd milled about in the street outside. The organization's chairman, wrote the young editor Fenner Brockway, "did not wish to incite further attack by the noise of our cheering. He therefore asked that enthusiasm should be expressed silently, and with absolute discipline the crowded audience responded." When Bertrand Russell addressed the gathering, he was "received with thousands of fluttering handkerchiefs, making the low sound of rising and falling wind, but with no other sound whatsoever."

Russell continued to write articles, books, and letters to newspapers, in prose that rang with moral clarity. He hated German militarism, he always said, loved the tradition of English liberty, and would prefer an Allied victory to a German one. But the longer the war went on, the more it was militarizing Britain in Germany's image, while killing and maiming men by the millions and making certain an embittered and dangerous postwar world. He not only lent his enormous prestige to the No-Conscription Fellowship; for much of the war his thick shock of graying hair was a familiar sight at the NCF headquarters each day, for he became the group's acting chairman when its head went to prison for refusing the call-up. He attended the courts-martial of COs, visited them in prison, and devoted hours to the most mundane office tasks, writing numerous "Dear Comrade" letters to branches around the country, signed "Fraternally Yours, Bertrand Russell." And he made clear to all that he was as willing to sacrifice his freedom for what he believed as were the younger men and women around him. When the government began prosecuting people for distributing an NCF leaflet, he immediately wrote to the *Times:* "Six men have been condemned to varying terms of imprisonment with hard labour for distributing this leaflet. I wish to make it known that I am the author of this leaflet, and that if anyone is to be prosecuted, I am the person primarily responsible." For this he was fined £100 (which he refused to pay, forcing the authorities to seize some of his property), dismissed from his post at Cambridge, and denied a passport for a trip to lecture at Harvard. The government was still uneasy about the bad publicity in the United States that would come from throwing such a prominent intellectual in jail. Incidentally, like thousands of people in Britain at this time, Russell came from a divided family: his first cousin was a War Office official who at one point ordered a raid on the NCF headquarters.

Believing—correctly—that sooner or later most of its leaders would be arrested, the NCF set up a "shadow" structure modeled on that used before the war by the Pankhursts' WSPU. If any officer was jailed, someone else, designated in advance, would automatically take his or her job. Similarly, wrote one member, "in various secret places, buried in an orchard in Surrey, or locked in an unsuspecting city merchant's safe, or at the back of the bookshelf in the house of a remote sympathiser . . . were duplicates of every document likely to be seized." These included a daily bulletin on the numbers of men arrested, court-martialed, and imprisoned, and file cards showing the whereabouts of every CO. Any instance of their mistreatment was recorded and turned over to one of the small band of sympathetic MPs willing to ask questions in the House of Commons. Communications were often in code: if a telegram said that a meeting was to be at Manchester, it in fact meant Newcastle. Basil Thomson's Scotland Yard agents frequently raided the NCF office, so its staff took care to leave enough unimportant documents on the desks and shelves so that the police would think they were seizing something valuable.

The draft resisters in prison served their sentences at hard labor. For the first two weeks, a prisoner was given no mattress to sleep on in his seven-by-twelve-foot cell. Prison labor usually consisted of sewing a daily quota of thick canvas mailbags with a big, skewer-like needle. NCF members who were free organized relief for families of those behind bars, and groups gathered every week and on special occasions like Christmas Eve to sing hymns and labor songs outside prison walls. "The singers can have little idea how eagerly we looked forward to the evening when we imagined them due," a CO at Wormwood Scrubs

Prison wrote to the NCF's lively weekly newspaper, which at its peak had a circulation of 100,000. "I can never thank these unknown friends sufficiently."

Anyone claiming exemption from the draft for whatever reason, whether as a conscientious objector or because he was engaged in labor "of national importance," had to go before one of many special tribunals around the country. The military representative on one tribunal asked a socialist militant, "Are you doing work of national importance?" "No," came the reply, "but I'm engaged on work of international importance."

The NCF scored another rhetorical point when, in the course of one legal case, a lawyer on the government side, Sir Archibald Bodkin (best known to history as the man who later would get James Joyce's novel *Ulysses* banned from publication in postwar England), thundered accusingly that "war will become impossible if all men were to have the view that war is wrong." Delighted, the NCF proceeded to issue a poster with exactly those words on it, credited to Bodkin. The government then arrested an NCF member for putting up this subversive poster. In response, the NCF's lawyer demanded the arrest of Bodkin, as the author of the offending words. The organization's newspaper—named, with deliberate irony, the *Tribunal*—called for Bodkin to prosecute himself, and declared that the NCF would provide relief payments to his wife and children if he sent himself to jail.

In the spring of 1916, a succession of desperate telephone calls to the NCF office revealed a crisis that was no occasion for humor. When conscription first began, if a tribunal refused a man's application for CO status, he was considered to have been drafted into the army—where, once at the front, the wartime punishment for disobeying an order could be death by firing squad. One such group of COs found themselves forcibly inducted into the military and, when they refused to follow orders, were put in irons, fed bread and water, and locked up in the darkened rooms of a granite-walled fortress at Harwich, built by prisoners during the Napoleonic Wars. One day an officer told them that they were being sent to the front in France. "Once you are across the Channel," he said, "your friends in Parliament and elsewhere won't be able to do anything for you."

The 17 men were put on a train headed for the port of Southampton. As the train trundled through the outskirts of London, one of them tossed a note out the window. Luckily, it was found by a sympathetic member of the militant National Union of Railwaymen, who telephoned the NCF office, which promptly went into action. When questioned in Parliament two days later, Prime Minister Asquith swore he knew nothing of the case. Lord Derby, director of recruiting, gave the impression—rightly or wrongly—that he did, claiming that the army was fully justified in its actions, and that, as for the 17 hapless COs, "if they disobey orders, of course they will be shot, and quite right too!"

More protests came from liberal voices in the press, which the War Office countered with a propaganda barrage of its own. Bertrand Russell joined a delegation that visited Asquith to plead for the men's lives. "As we were leaving," Russell wrote later, "I made him a speech of denunciation in an almost Biblical style, telling him his name would go down in history with infamy. I had not the pleasure of meeting him thereafter." Meanwhile, horrified family members and fellow pacifists could get no news of the men's fate. The mothers of nine of them, desperate for help, visited Sylvia Pankhurst, who went to lobby on their behalf at the War Office. In late May, the army sent several additional groups of COs from different parts of the country across the Channel, some in handcuffs. It now appeared that almost 50 COs were in France, and could face firing squads if they refused to fight. As one cluster was taken out through the gates of an army camp in Wales, a band played a funeral march.

"In France a court-martial can be held and an execution carried out without the knowledge of the public at home," Russell wrote to a newspaper. "The name of the victim can be simply published in casualty lists, and the truth need not leak out until the war is over."

The families and supporters of the prisoners had no news of where they were. Then one day in early June 1916 the NCF received a clue: a Field Service Post Card, designed to save army censors the time it took to read mail. Tens of millions of these cards were issued to troops overseas, with half a dozen printed messages that a soldier could either underline or cross out. This postcard was signed by a 27-year-old schoolteacher named Bert Brocklesby, one of the missing men. All the messages were crossed out, except two. One was "I am being sent down to the base." The other was "I have received no letter from you for a long time." But Brocklesby had cleverly and lightly crossed out many individual letters, so that the message read, "I am being sent . . . to . . . b . . . ou . . . long."

The NCF immediately dispatched two clergymen to Boulogne.

But would they be in time? While the ministers were crossing the Channel, another message was smuggled out from France, reaching the mother of a Quaker CO named Stuart Beavis. "We have been warned today that we are now within the war zone," he wrote to her stoically, "and the military authorities have absolute power, and disobedience may be followed by very severe penalties, and very possibly the death penalty. . . . Do not be downhearted if the worst comes to the worst; many have died cheerfully for a worse cause." To the NCF's *Tribunal* he sent a brief message on behalf of himself and his comrades, ending, "We regret nothing."

While the COs imprisoned in Boulogne awaited their fate, the explorer Ernest Shackleton, long out of touch with Europe, unexpectedly appeared on one of the earth's southernmost islands, South Georgia. His ship had been trapped in Antarctic pack ice, then crushed and sunk. After months of drifting on the ice floes, he and his men had finally escaped to the Antarctic mainland. In search of a vessel to rescue them, he led a handpicked crew of half a dozen in an epic 800-mile journey by small boat across one of the world's stormiest patches of ocean to South Georgia, where there was a Norwegian whaling station. Shackleton had been cut off from the rest of the world for a year and a half. The first question he asked the startled station manager was "Tell me, when was the war over?"

"The war is not over," the Norwegian answered. "Millions are being killed. Europe is mad. The world is mad."

The madness was growing, and not just where rival armies did battle. In the Caucasus, for example, where Russia and Ottoman Turkey were fighting, the Turks had just carried out a forced deportation and genocide against one of their subject peoples, the Armenians, claiming they were in league with Russia. No one knows exactly how many Armenians perished, but most scholars estimate the number at one to one and a half million.

That mass murder stemmed from only one of many ancient ethnic rivalries inflamed by the war. The Ottoman Empire was also unleashing a reign of pillage, terror, and village-burning on its Greek population, leaving thousands dead and hundreds of thousands conscripted as forced laborers. And in the perennial tinderbox of the Balkans, old enmities among Serbs, Croats, Muslims, Bulgarians, and others helped Austria-Hungary carry out a ruthless occupation of Serbia. When the war ended, that tiny country would have proportionately the highest death toll, military and civilian, of any combatant, nearly one out of five of its people. Everywhere, it seemed, the war had undammed reservoirs of hatred long kept in check.

While fighting raged on many fronts on land, in the North Sea the British and German fleets met in the late spring of 1916 for the largest naval encounter of the war, the Battle of Jutland, involving some 250 ships and 100,000 men. "Had we used the Navy's bare fist instead of its gloved hand from the beginning," fumed Kipling, "we could in all likelihood have shortened the war." Yet despite Jutland's being the greatest maritime battle in more than 100 years, this long-awaited encounter between bare fists at sea was as bloodily inconclusive as those in the trenches of France.

Britain's navy suffered from the same peculiar mismatch as the army between firepower and communications. Its massive battleships and battle cruisers could fire salvos of staggering destructive power, each shell weighing nearly a ton. But when it came to sending orders and messages, the admirals remained in the previous century, inexplicably reluctant to use the new wireless sets their ships were equipped with. They preferred blinking lights at night, and, by day, the tradition-hallowed system of colored signal flags dating from the days of sail— both of which were difficult or impossible to see through rain squalls and the dense smoke from both funnels and guns. In foggy weather just before the battle, two British battle cruisers collided, a battleship ran into a merchant vessel, and three destroyers managed to collide. More confusion reigned as the main action began: the rival armadas of tall, lumbering ships shelled and sank one another; vessels exploded when their ammunition magazines were hit; thousands of men from both sides were blown to bits or carried to the bottom of the sea as their vessels became giant steel coffins. The Germans sank more ships and killed more enemy sailors than the British, but failed to cripple the Royal Navy enough to break its blockade of Germany. The scarred surviving ships steamed home in different directions as both sides claimed victory.

On more distant fronts in Africa, small contingents of British, South African, French, and Belgian troops—with far larger numbers of African conscripts—had fought German soldiers (with their own conscripts) everywhere from Cameroon on the west coast of the continent to German Southwest Africa near the southern tip to Tanganyika in the east. While exhausted troops succumbed to tropical diseases, the top commanders treated each other with an old-world courtesy: at one point, South African General Jan Smuts, commanding the British Empire forces in East Africa, sent a messenger under a white flag to congratulate his German counterpart, Paul von Lettow-Vorbeck, cut off from communications from home. The Kaiser had awarded him one of Germany's highest medals.

Just as Germany openly coveted the central African colonies of France and Belgium, which would give Berlin an unbroken belt of territory stretching across the continent—*Mittelafrika,* Berlin's strategists called it—so the Allies were maneuvering to seize Germany's African possessions. The British cabinet set up a group, the Territorial Desiderata Committee, to keep an eye out for precisely such acquisitions —and not just in Africa. The oil-rich land around the Persian Gulf, much of it under Ottoman control, looked attractive to an empire whose military was increasingly oil-powered. All this was glossed with high purpose by John Buchan. Germany ran its African colonies with "the lash and the chain," he wrote, while Britain generously allowed "ancient modes of life to continue side by side with the new."

Driven by similar ambitions, more countries were joining the war: Bulgaria, promised chunks of Serbia, had joined the Central Powers; Greece, promised pieces of Turkey; and Romania, its eye on Austro-Hungarian territory, would join the Allied side later in 1916. In the Pacific, Japan had jumped into the fray, helping itself to some of Germany's island colonies and, aided by British troops, to the German-controlled port of Tsingtao in China. Australia and New Zealand, which had sent troops to Europe and the Mediterranean to fight under British command, had taken over German Samoa, New Guinea, and the Solomon Islands. From desert and rain forest to remote atolls, the war was engulfing the globe.

Through the docks of French ports flowed a torrent of supplies for Haig's divisions as they prepared to smash through the German lines near the Somme. Half a million British troops, three times as many as had tried to break through at Loos, were concentrated along an 18-mile sector of the front; 120,000 of them would attack on the first day alone. This was to be the "Big Push," a concentration of manpower and artillery so massive and in such a small space that the German defenses would burst open as if hit by floodwaters. Once that happened, the generals believed, a key weapon in the hands of the soldiers pouring through would be the bayonet. The military's leading bayonet expert, the bushy-browed Major Ronald "Bloody" Campbell, an apostle of physical fitness whose broken nose and battered ears were proud evidence of his record as army middleweight boxing champion, traveled among British bases in France demonstrating the weapon and lecturing troops. "When a German holds up his hands and says: 'Kamerad — I have a wife and seven children,' what do you do? — Why . . . you stick him in the gut and tell him he won't have any more!" After the Germans had been bayoneted in their trenches, it would be a matter of what Haig called "fighting the Enemy in the open," and so battalions were trained intensively in maneuvering across trenchless fields and meadows. Finally, of course, charging through the gap in the lines would come horsemen from three cavalry divisions.

While such plans may have been rooted in centuries past, the scale of the preparations, at least, belonged to the age of mass production. Troops unrolled 70,000 miles of telephone cable. Thousands of soldiers unloaded and piled ammunition in huge dumps; others, stripped to the waist and sweating in the summer heat, dug endlessly to construct special roads and railways to speed supplies to the front. Fifty-five miles of new standard-gauge railway line were built for the Somme offensive, with track beds of scarce crushed stone imported from England. With as many British soldiers crammed into the launching area as the population of a good-sized city, wells had to be dug and dozens of miles of water pipe laid. Horses, tractors, and more sweating soldiers maneuvered heavy artillery pieces into position — no easy job when a single eight-inch howitzer weighed 13 tons.

British troops, the plan went, were to move forward across no man's land in successive waves. Everything was precise: each wave would advance in a continuous line 100 yards in front of the next, at a steady pace of 100 yards a minute. How were they to be safe from the machine-gun fire that had taken such a deadly toll at Loos? Simple: the preattack bombardment would destroy not just the Germans' barbed wire but the trenches and firing positions that sheltered their riflemen and machine-gunners. How could this not be when there was one artillery piece for every 17 yards of front line, which would rain a total of a million and a half shells down on the German trenches over five solid days? "Nothing," General Sir Henry Rawlinson, commander of most of the attacking troops, emphatically assured his subordinates, "could exist at the conclusion of the bombardment." And if that weren't enough, once British troops climbed out of their trenches, a final "creeping barrage" of artillery shells would precede them, a moving curtain of fire riddling with shrapnel any surviving Germans who emerged from underground shelters to try to resist the attackers.

The plan for the first day's assault was 31 pages long, and its map included the British names with which the German trenches scheduled to be captured had already been rechristened. Preparations this thorough were hard to conceal, and there were occasional unnerving signs that the German troops knew almost as much about them as the British. When one unit slated to take part in the attack moved into position, it found a sign held up from the German trenches: WELCOME TO THE 29TH DIVISION.

The Germans had staged no major attacks in the Somme sector for a year and a half, and had instead used that time to build up their defenses. Scattered clues suggested that these were disturbingly sturdy. From both sides, miners were now busily tunneling under the other side's trenches to plant explosive charges; some surprised British miners digging at a level they thought far below the German trench system found themselves unintentionally hacking through the wall of a German dugout. But this and other signs of how deep the Germans had built their shelters were brushed aside.

Several weeks before the attack, General Rawlinson joined 167 other officers for an Old Etonian dinner at the Hotel Godbert in Amiens, a nearby French city whose bars and brothels were doing a booming business with British troops awaiting the offensive. In Latin, Rawlinson and his fellow Eton graduates raised their voices in the school song, "Carmen Etonense," with its chorus:

> *Donec oras Angliae*
> *Alma lux fovebit,*

Floreat Etona!
  Floreat! Florebit!

(So long as kindly light cherishes the shores of England
May Eton flourish! She will flourish!)

Enlisted men waiting for the big day entertained themselves in other ways. A haunting piece of documentary film footage from these months, taken from a Red Cross barge moving down a canal behind the lines, shows hundreds of Allied soldiers stripped completely bare, wading, bathing, or sunning themselves on the canal bank in the warm summer weather, smiling and waving at the camera. Without helmets and uniforms, it is impossible to tell their nationality; their naked bodies mark them only as human beings.

Riding a black horse with his usual escort of lancers, Haig inspected his divisions as they rehearsed for the attack, on practice fields where white tapes on the ground marked the German trenches. On June 20 the commander in chief wrote to his wife, "The situation is becoming more favourable to us." On June 22 he added, "*I feel* that every step in my plan has been taken with the Divine help." For additional Divine help, he invited his favorite preacher, Reverend Duncan, to his forward headquarters. On June 30, the day before the attack began, as the great artillery barrage had been thundering for four days, Haig wrote in his diary, "The men are in splendid spirits. . . . The wire has never been so well cut, nor the Artillery preparation so thorough." For good measure, the British released clouds of deadly chlorine gas toward the German lines. Haig recorded only one note of caution, a complaint that two divisions at the northern end of the attack front had not carried out a single successful reconnaissance raid, something that should have been easy under cover of darkness if the British shelling actually had destroyed the German barbed wire.

As it grew close to zero hour, 7:30 A.M. on July 1, 1916, ten enormous mines were detonated deep underneath the German trenches. Near the village of La Boisselle, the crater from one that contained 30 tons of high explosives remains, a stark, gaping indentation in the surrounding French farmland; even partly filled in by a century of erosion, it is still 55 feet deep and 220 feet across.

Alfred Milner could hear the low thunder of the bombardment at his country house near the Kent coast, and when the barrage reached its crescendo, 224,221 shells in the last 65 minutes, the rumble could be heard as far away as Hampstead Heath in London. More shells were fired by the British this week than they had used in the first 12 months of the war; some gunners bled from the ears after five days of nonstop firing. At a forest near Gommecourt, entire trees were uprooted and tossed in the air by the shelling and the forest itself was set on fire. Soldiers of the 1st Somerset Light Infantry sat on the parapet of their trench cheering at the tremendous explosions. Officers issued a strong ration of rum to the men about to head into no man's land. Captain W. P. Nevill of the 8th East Surrey Battalion gave each of his four platoons a soccer ball and promised a prize to whichever one first managed to kick the ball to the German trench. One platoon painted on its ball:

THE GREAT EUROPEAN CUP
THE FINAL
EAST SURREYS V. BAVARIANS

14

GOD, GOD, WHERE'S THE REST OF THE BOYS?

PREPARATIONS FOR THE Somme offensive were already at high pitch when the first group of British conscientious objectors forcibly transported to France were taken to an army camp parade ground with other soldiers and given the order "Right turn! Quick march!" The other troops marched off; the 17 remained in place, unmoving. The army fined them five days' pay, something that amused them, since on principle they were already refusing to accept any military pay. There was little else to laugh about. Periodically they were summoned to hear announcements of men sentenced to death for desertion or disobedience. And, of course, they knew that in Ireland the Easter Rising leaders had just been shot by army firing squads. At times, they could hear the rumble of artillery from the front.

They refused to do any work. Angry sergeants punished them by administering what was known as Field Punishment Number One, which meant being trussed to a fixed object like a gun carriage wheel or prison fence for two hours at a time, arms held open in crucifixion position. "We were placed with our faces to the barbed wire of the inner fence," recalled one CO, Cornelius Barritt. ". . . I found myself drawn so closely to the fence that when I wished to turn my head I had to do so very cautiously to avoid my face being torn by the barbs. To make matters less comfortable, it came on to rain and the cold wind blew straight across the top of the hill." But the men's spirits held, for when officers weren't looking, ordinary soldiers showed them unexpected kindness. One gave his dinner to CO Alfred Evans, and when his superiors were gone for the evening, a sergeant of the Irish Guards spent his own money buying cake, fruit, and chocolate for the whole group at the post canteen. Evidently worried that the men's pacifism might influence the troops, the army moved them off base, to a fish market on the docks of Boulogne that had been turned into a punishment barracks. There, they were locked in group cells with no sustenance but water and four biscuits a day.

The men in one cell could talk to those in other cells only through knotholes in the wooden walls. As best they could, the entire group —which included a schoolteacher, a watchmaker, a student missionary, several clerks, and a Catholic from a trade union family—held debates: on Marxism, Tolstoyan pacifism, and the merits of the invented international language Esperanto. The Quakers among them held a Quaker meeting. For some, religious conviction had put them behind bars; for others, a belief in socialism; for many, both. The songs they sang included both Christian hymns—

> Trusting Him while life shall last,
> Trusting Him till earth be past

—and the famous labor song "The Red Flag":

> The people's flag is deepest red,
> It shrouded oft our martyred dead,
> And ere their limbs grew stiff and cold,
> Their hearts' blood dyed its every fold.

"Rats were not infrequent visitors," remembered Barritt. "They would sit on the edge of a fire bucket to drink the water and occasionally run up one's back during a meal. . . . There were now eleven of us in the one cell. . . . We could just lie six a side with our feet almost touching; but it was a problem to find room for the bucket placed in the cell for 'sanitary' purposes. The cells measured 11 feet 9 inches by 11 feet 3 inches."

Unable to comprehend so many people acting according to conscience, the military at first decided that Barritt and three other COs were the ringleaders responsible for the larger group's disobedience. They were court-martialed and found guilty. None of them knew whether the messages they had smuggled out had reached England — or would have any effect. On June 15, 1916, just two weeks before the Somme offensive was scheduled to start, the four "ringleaders" were taken to a nearby army camp for sentencing.

"I cast many a glance in the direction of the white cliffs of Dover," recalled one, "for this might be our last opportunity." They were brought to a large parade ground, and several hundred soldiers were assembled on three sides as witnesses. A command rang out for silence. "As I stepped forward I caught a glimpse of my paper as it was handed to the Adjutant. Printed at the top in large red letters, and doubly underlined, was the word 'Death.'"

As each man stepped forward, the adjutant read out his name and serial number and the charge, and intoned, "Sentenced to death by being shot." There was a pause. "Confirmed by General Sir Douglas Haig." Then a longer pause. "And commuted to ten years' penal servitude."

In the days that followed, while trains and truck convoys all around them sped last-minute supplies to the front for the great offensive, a total of 34 British COs in army camps in France were told that they had received the death sentence, commuted to ten years' imprisonment; some 15 others were given lesser sentences. None of them knew of the visit Bertrand Russell and others from the No-Conscription Fellowship had paid Asquith, but it was crucial in saving their lives, for immediately afterward the prime minister had sent a secret order to Haig that no CO was to be shot. Two weeks after the first sentences, the COs were returned to England and sent to civilian prisons — as would happen with all COs refusing alternative service from then on. Jeering bystanders threw eggs and tomatoes at them when they landed at Southampton. But the men knew that they had stuck to their beliefs even when threatened with death. "As I stood listening to the sentences of the rest of our party," one CO said later of that day on the parade ground, "the feeling of joy and triumph surged up within me, and I felt proud to have the privilege of . . . testifying to a truth which the world as yet had not grasped, but which it would one day treasure as a most precious inheritance."

Throughout the British Isles, millions of people waited tensely for news of the great attack. "The hospital received orders to clear out all convalescents and prepare for a great rush of wounded," remembered the writer Vera Brittain, working as a nurse's aide in London. "We knew that already a tremendous bombardment had begun, for we could feel the vibration of the guns. . . . Hour after hour, as the convalescents departed, we added to the long rows of waiting beds, so sinister in their white, expectant emptiness."

Haig waited anxiously in his forward headquarters at the Château de Beauquesne, ten miles from the battlefield. As dawn came on July 1, a Royal Flying Corps observer found himself looking down on a fogbank that covered part of the front, on which "one could see ripples . . . from the terrific bombardment that was taking place below. It looked like a large lake of mist, with thousands of stones being thrown into it." Then, after five days of nonstop explosions, the British barrage abruptly ceased, and silence settled over the battlefield.

When whistles blew at 7:30 A.M., the successive waves of troops began their planned 100-yards-a-minute advance. Each man moved slowly under more than 60 pounds of supplies — 200 bullets, grenades, shovel, two days' food and water, and more. But when those soldiers actually clambered up the trench ladders and over the parapet, they discovered something appalling. The multiple belts of barbed wire in front of the German trenches and the well-fortified machine-gun emplacements dotted among them were largely intact.

Officers looking through binocular periscopes had already suspected as much, and a handful of German deserters who made it through the barrage to the British lines reported the same. Plans for any attack, however, have tremendous momentum; rare is the commander willing to recognize that something is catastrophically awry. To call off an offensive requires bravery, for the general who does so risks being thought a coward. Haig was not such a man. The whistles blew, men cheered, Captain Nevill's company of East Surreys kicked off its four soccer balls. The soldiers hoped against hope to stay alive — and sometimes for something more: troops of the 1st Newfoundland Regiment knew that a prominent young society woman back home had promised to marry the first man in the regiment to win a Victoria Cross.

The bombardment, it turned out, had been impressive mainly for its tremendous noise. More than one out of four British shells were duds that buried themselves in the earth, exploding, if at all, only when struck by some unlucky French farmer's harrow years or decades later. Two-thirds of the shells fired were shrapnel, virtually useless in destroying machine-gun emplacements built of concrete, steel, or stone appropriated from nearby houses. Nor could shrapnel shells, which scattered light steel balls, destroy the dense thickets of German barbed wire unless they burst at just the right height above the ground. But their fuses were wildly unreliable, and often they exploded only after they had plummeted into the earth, destroying little and embedding so much metal in the ground that soldiers trying to navigate through darkness or smoke sometimes found their compasses had ceased to work.

The remaining British shells were high-explosive ones, which could indeed destroy a German machine-gun post, but only if it was hit with pinpoint accuracy. When guns were firing from several miles away, this was almost impossible. The many photographs from the Western Front of geysers of earth lifted skyward by a shellburst are usually evidence that the shell rammed itself into muddy ground and spent its energy pointlessly blowing dirt into the air. German machine-gun teams were waiting out the bombardment as much as 40 feet below the surface in their dugouts, supplied with electricity, water, and ventilation. For them, being underground for nearly a week, largely sleepless and at times in gas masks, had been grossly unpleasant but seldom fatal. In one of the few places where British troops did reach the German front line on July 1, they found the electric light in a dugout still on. And when, after tens of thousands of British deaths, more of the German front-line trench had finally been captured, a soldier reported, "I did not come across a single dugout which had been broken into from the roof by our artillery fire."

Unaccountably, an underground mine exploded beneath the German lines ten minutes before zero hour, a clear signal that the attack was soon to begin. Then, like a final warning, the remaining mines went off at 7:28 A.M., followed by a two-minute wait to allow the debris—blown thousands of feet into the air—to fall back to earth before British troops climbed out of their trenches to advance. Those two minutes gave German machine-gunners time to run up the ladders and stairways from their dugouts and man their fortified posts, of which there were roughly a thousand on the sector of the line under attack. Ominously, during the two minutes, the British could hear bugles summoning the gunners to their positions.

Even before the British left their trenches, some machine guns had begun firing, streams of German bullets knocking bits of dirt and grass into the air as they grazed the tops of the British parapets, a horrifying warning that the five-day artillery barrage had been for naught. Elsewhere the Germans held their fire as the British moved forward. With some exceptions, the attacking units had been ordered to walk, not run. "They came on at a steady easy pace as if expecting to find nothing alive in our front trenches," recalled a German soldier facing them. ". . . When the leading British line was within 100 yards, the rattle of [German] machine guns and rifle fire broke out from along the whole line. . . . Red rockets sped up into the blue sky as a signal to the artillery, and immediately afterwards a mass of shells from the German batteries in [the] rear tore through the air and burst among the advancing lines." The Germans, like the British, had plenty of artillery pieces; these were under camouflage netting and had not been used during the weeks leading up to the attack, so as not to reveal their positions to British aircraft. Now they fired their deadly shrapnel shells, whose effects the Germans could see: "All along the line men could be seen throwing their arms into the air and collapsing never to move again. Badly wounded rolled about in their agony . . . with . . . cries for help and the last screams of death."

The Germans were just as much prisoners of traditional ideas of military glory as their opponents, and this account of the first day's slaughter, like so many British descriptions, ends by noting not the suicidal nature of the attack, but the soldiers' bravery. "It was an amazing spectacle of unexampled gallantry, courage and bull-dog determination on both sides."

Plans for the orderly march forward in line abreast were quickly abandoned as men separated into small groups and sought the shelter of hillocks and shell holes. But there was no question of the hard-hit British troops' turning back, for each battalion had men designated as "battle police," herding any stragglers forward. "When we got to the German wire I was absolutely amazed to see it intact, after what we had been told," remembered one British private. "The colonel and I took cover behind a small bank but after a bit the colonel raised himself on his hands and knees to see better. Immediately he was hit on the forehead by a single bullet." Because artillery had destroyed so little barbed wire, British soldiers had to bunch up to get through the few gaps they could find—making the battlefield even more of a shooting gallery. Many soldiers died when their clothing, especially the loose kilts of the Scotsmen, caught on the wire and pinned them in positions exposed to fire. "Only three out of our company got past there," recalled a private of the 4th Tyneside Scottish Battalion. "There was my lieutenant, a sergeant and myself. The rest seemed to have been hit in no-man's-land. . . . The officer said, 'God, God, where's the rest of the boys?'"

The vaunted "creeping barrage," which was supposed to force German machine-gunners and snipers to keep their heads down, accomplished little. It crept forward according to the prearranged timetable—and then continued to creep off uselessly into the far distance long after British troops who were supposed to be following it had been pinned down by the tangles of uncut wire. The troops had no way to tell their artillery in the rear to change the plan. The cavalry waited behind the British lines, but in vain. Those who survived in no man's land sometimes waited until after dark to crawl back to their own trenches, but even then the continual traversing of German machine-gun fire sent up showers of sparks as bullets hit the British barbed wire.

Of the 120,000 British troops who went into battle on July 1, 1916, more than 57,000 were dead or wounded before the day was over—nearly two casualties for every yard of the front. Nineteen thousand were killed, most of them within the attack's first disastrous hour, and some 2,000 more who were badly wounded would die in hospitals later. There were an estimated 8,000 German casualties. As usual, the toll was heaviest among the officers, three-quarters of whom were killed or wounded. These included many who had attended the Old Etonian dinner a few weeks before: more than 30 Etonians lost their lives on July 1. Captain Nevill of the East Surreys, who had distributed the soccer balls, was fatally shot through the head in the first few minutes of combat.

The 1st Newfoundland Regiment, awaiting its Victoria Cross winner and the young woman who had promised herself as his reward, was virtually wiped out. The regiment's 752 men climbed out of their trenches to advance toward the skeletal ruins of an apple orchard covered by German machine-gun fire; by the day's end 684 were dead, wounded, or missing, including every officer. The German troops the Newfoundlanders attacked did not suffer a single casualty. Only in the far south of the attack area, on three miles of front, did the British advance a significant distance—roughly one mile. It was one of the bloodiest days any army suffered in this war.

Attacking soldiers had been ordered not to tend injured comrades but to leave them for stretcher bearers who would follow. The dead and wounded, however, included hundreds of stretcher bearers themselves, and there were nowhere near enough men to carry the critically injured to first-aid posts in time. Stretchers ran out; some wounded were carried off two to a stretcher or on sheets of corrugated iron whose edges ravaged the bearers' fingers. Many wounded who lived through the first day never made it off the battlefield. For weeks afterward their fellow soldiers came upon them in shell holes, where they had crawled for shelter, taken out their Bibles, and wrapped themselves in their waterproof ground sheets to die, in pain and alone.

In other ways, too, the terrible day took its toll after the fact. One battalion commander, Lieutenant Colonel E.T.F. Sandys, having seen more than 500 of his men killed or wounded during that day, shot himself in a London hotel room two months later, after writing to a fellow officer, "I have never had a moment's peace since July 1st."

On the second day of the battle, Haig was told that the casualties had been over 40,000 so far—a gross underestimate but still an appalling figure. "This cannot be considered severe," he wrote in his diary, "in view of the numbers engaged, and the length of front attacked."

As fighting continued, the gains were minimal: a half mile here, a few hundred yards there, and in some places nothing at all. Haig's optimism never wavered. A week into the carnage, he wrote to his wife, "In another fortnight, with Divine Help, I hope some decisive results may be obtained." A few days later he told her, "If we don't succeed this time, we'll do so the next!"

Haig's supporters, even today, argue that the Battle of the Somme carried out its primary mission, to relieve the pressure on the French at Verdun, and to some extent this was true. The Germans, however, had already lost whatever chance they had of capturing that strongpoint with an all-out assault that failed miserably a week before the Somme offensive began—and for many of the same reasons the British experienced in this war that so relentlessly favored defenders over attackers. Despite the diminished threat to Verdun, Haig doggedly, unyieldingly sent out order after order for more attacks on the Somme, and these would continue for an astonishing four and a half months.

The Germans' best weapon remained barbed wire. They were bringing 7,000 tons of it up to the front every week, in long rolls stacked on railway cars two layers high, and both sides were using tough new types of wire, some of which had a sharpened prong every inch or two. Facing barriers like this, British soldiers were no longer in the mood to kick off any soccer balls. Among the new troops thrown into battle, "few there were whose demeanour expressed eagerness for the assault," wrote Graham Seton Hutchison, a company commander. "They were moving into position with good discipline, yet listless, as if facing [the] inevitable. . . . My eyes swept the valley—long lines of men, officers at their head in the half-crouching attitude which modern tactics dictate, resembling suppliants rather than the vanguard of a great offensive, were moving forward. . . . White bursts of shrapnel appeared among the trees and thinly across the ridge*. . . . An inferno of rifle and machine-gun fire broke. . . . The line staggered. Men fell forward limply and quietly. The hiss and crack of bullets filled the air and skimmed the long grasses."

Trapped with his men in no man's land, Hutchison saw, to his amazement, "a squadron of Indian Cavalry, dark faces under glistening helmets, galloping across the valley towards the slope. No troops could have presented a more inspiring sight than these natives of India with lance and sword, tearing in mad cavalcade on to the skyline. A few disappeared over it: they never came back. The remainder became the target of every gun and rifle."

---

*When a visitor goes to this spot today, or to many others referred to in Western Front memoirs as hills, valleys, or ridges, the slope is anything but steep, and sometimes barely perceptible. It is a reminder that the survivors were describing how the scene looked to them when peering cautiously out of a trench, or when pressed flat to the ground of no man's land to avoid bullets. If the position you were attacking had even the slightest bit of altitude, you could be trapped in a devastating field of fire.

Troops moving up to make such attacks saw their own future pass before them in the grisly traffic heading the other way. "The tide of wounded flowed back from the fields of the Somme in endless columns of ambulances," wrote the correspondent Philip Gibbs. ". . . Row on row, the badly wounded were laid on the grass outside the tents or on blood-stained stretchers waiting for their turn. . . . Whiffs of chloroform reeked across the roadways."

In his dispatches, Haig began to redefine success: "breakthrough" was gone; taking a toll on the Germans in a "wearing out fight" became the new catch phrase. He trumpeted the Somme as successful not because of the slivers of territory seized but because it was costing the Germans in dead and wounded—the first hint of a major shift in his rhetoric. Taking attrition as the standard of success turned out to be more realistic for this war than measuring land gained, but one problem with it was that the other side's losses were always unknown. The only thing you could know with certainty was your own staggering losses—and then hope that the enemy's were at least similar. After one battle in August Haig reported to London, based on little evidence, that German casualties "cannot have been less than our own."

This perverse logic sometimes led Haig to fly into a rage when he thought British losses—and so, by association, German ones—were too low. After a September attack on Delville Wood by the 49th Division, he was upset enough to deplore, in his diary, that "the total losses of this division are under a thousand!" The commander in chief's attitude set a powerful example for his subordinates. On September 30 of the following year, General Rawlinson wrote in *his* diary: "Lawford dined. In very good form. His Division 11,000 casualties since July 31st."

Some civilian archpatriots shared Haig's belief in high casualties as a measure of success. A month into the Somme battle, the general received a letter from an anonymous admirer: "The expectation of mankind is upon you—the 'Hungry Haig' as we call you here at home. You shall report 500,000 casualties, but the Soul of the empire will afford them. And you shall break through with the cavalry of England and France for the greatest victory that history has ever known. . . . Drive on, Illustrious General!"

What made it so easy for Haig to demand high casualties was that he chose not to see them. He "felt that it was his duty to refrain from visiting the casualty clearing stations," wrote his son, "because these visits made him physically ill."

What might Haig have seen if he had visited such a station? Here is a Royal Army Medical Corps officer's description of one near the Somme battlefield:

> Stretchers blocked the cellar floors, the passages, the battered shelter that remained above ground and the approaches outside. Often we worked for hours and hours on end without respite: at the crude dressing-tables, at men grounded on stretchers, at men squatting or sitting. . . . There was a constant movement of bearers shuffling and staggering with stretchers, negotiating the cellar stairs, seeking a way in or out and a bare space whereon to deposit their burdens. . . . Sometimes a man on a stretcher would vomit explosively, spewing over himself and his neighbors. I have seen mounted troops brought in with liquid faeces oozing from the unlaced legs of their breeches. Occasionally a man would gasp and die as he lay on his stretcher. All this was routine. . . . No one spoke much . . . we got on with our work.

This particular station was in the basement of a château. Many were worse: a foot deep in mud, with no running water, or under fire. Take the experience of any man passing through such a spot and multiply it by 21 million — the number of men wounded in the war.

Haig's diary says little about the wounded, except for notes such as one on July 25, 1916, in which he recorded a surgeon's informing him that "the spirit of the wounded was beyond all praise . . . all were now very confident, very cheery and full of pluck. Truly the British race is the finest on Earth!"

Reaching Haig's desk daily were the dependably optimistic reports of his intelligence chief, Brigadier General John Charteris, whom a fellow officer described as "a hale and hearty back-slapping fellow, as optimistic as Candide, who conjured forth resounding victories from each bloody hundred yards' advance like rabbits from a hat." A mere captain at the start of the war, Charteris was a member of the "Hindu gang" of Haig protégés in India whose careers had ascended rapidly with his own. Charteris's intelligence assessments were professional enough on such questions as where enemy troops were deployed, but when it came to the more nebulous matter of German morale and ability to fight on, he regularly offered Haig the rosiest possible view. On July 9, for instance, Charteris assured Haig that if the British kept up the offensive for another six weeks, the Germans would have no more reserves.

The flow of British dead soon grew so great that they were buried in mass graves. As an endless succession of hospital trains full of wounded men pulled into Charing Cross and Waterloo stations and the platforms thronged with frantic wives and mothers, the War Office began sending Haig polite but anxious messages questioning why so many men were dying—and for so little. Still the carnage continued: 30,000 British troops were killed or wounded on a single day in mid-September. "'*The powers that be*' are beginning to get a little uneasy in regard to the situation," Haig jotted on a note from the chief of the Imperial General Staff, but he replied only that "the maintenance of a steady offensive pressure will result eventually in [the Germans'] complete overthrow." No one challenged him: the King visited Montreuil and pronounced himself pleased; Asquith came too, and Haig found him "most charming," although noting disapprovingly how much brandy the prime minister drank. (Years later, after excerpts from Haig's diary had been published, Winston Churchill urged a luncheon guest, "Have another glass, my dear boy. I shan't write it down in my diary!")

As the fighting dragged on into the autumn rains, shortly before yet another British attack a private named Arthur Surfleet and a friend walked past a graveyard near their encampment. To their surprise, they found men at work digging graves—for troops who had not yet been killed. "If that is not callous, I don't know what is. The very fact that we turned away and sludged and squelched our way into the filthy huts, *merely disgusted,* makes me think a curious change must have come over us all since we got out here."

A curious change it was, and Surfleet was not the only one who felt it. After all the hype about the "Big Push," the terrible casualties of the Somme made the second half of 1916 a turning point for many British soldiers. It was not a turn toward rebellion but toward a kind of dogged cynicism, a disbelief that any battle could make a difference. The soldiers still marched dutifully to the front, but no longer sang. One enlisted man heading into the trenches carrying a roll of maps tied with a red ribbon heard a fellow soldier call out, "For God's sake let him pass, it's a bloke with the Peace Treaty."

The huge death toll led soldiers less to question the purpose of the war than to feel deeper solidarity with those who endured it with them. Surfleet, for instance, sensed an "esprit de corps or comradeship—I don't know what it was." He felt he could "look the rest of the lads in the face and claim to be one of them." Sometimes the satisfaction came from initiating others. Burgon Bickersteth, a former Anglican lay missionary, described the moment of turning over a position in the trenches to new troops:

> There is something highly exhilarating about "handing over." One feels superior in knowledge and experience, anxious not to "put the wind up" the newcomer unduly, yet not averse to impressing him with the "bloodiness" of the place. "Here they snipe during the day." "By that big coil of wire over there the Boches creep out at night"—and so on. The doings of the last few days, terrifying at the time, assume quite rosy colours. "But it's all right," one hastens to add, "it's quite cushy really, there is nothing to worry about." "Oh no," says the newcomer, rather uncertainly.

In such a voice we hear the force that ensures that soldiers seldom mutiny, and that makes the larger purpose of a war—or the lack of one—almost irrelevant to those who fight. The potential for human brotherhood that the socialists talked about was profoundly real, but the brotherhood men now felt most easily was of the shared baptism of combat. The more wrenching and painful that experience, the greater the sense of belonging to a fraternity that no mere civilian could penetrate. Although the poet Robert Graves felt the war was "wicked nonsense," and his memoir, *Good-bye to All That*, is a classic statement of disillusionment, he found conversation with his parents "all but impossible" when he came home wounded in the middle of the war. In the end—and Graves was not alone in this—he cut short the time he could have stayed in England in order to return to the front. "Once you have lain in her arms," another writer and Western Front veteran, Guy Chapman, said of war, "you can admit no other mistress. You may loathe, you may execrate, but you cannot deny her. . . . No wine gives fiercer intoxication, no drug more vivid exaltation. . . . Even those who hate her most are prisoners to her spell. They rise from her embraces, pillaged, soiled, it may be ashamed; but they are still hers."

What might break the murderous deadlock? As the hope of a breakthrough withered, exhausted troops yearned for a superweapon. Whatever it would be, it would have to be invulnerable to bullets and, above all, cut through barbed wire. The civilian public, too, was eager for a magical war-winning device, and repeated tantalizing rumors of one. Finally, in mid-September 1916, the British launched their new secret invention, the tank. Ironically, it took this technologically most complex weapon to conquer the simplest, against which much else had been tried, from grappling hooks to torpedoes on wheels. As the new tanks rumbled onto the ravaged landscape of the Somme, it appeared that the problem of barbed wire had at last been overcome.

The first models were giant steel rhomboids, their two caterpillar tracks running around the entire frame of the tank. Guns bristled from side turrets and sometimes the front and back as well. The whole thing, covered with armor plate, weighed 28 tons and was 32 feet long. Imagine the terror of the German soldier who saw this grinding toward him across no man's land, rolling over barbed wire as if it were grass. If appearance alone could bring victory, tanks would have won the war on the spot.

By the next world war, fast-moving tanks would be thought of as a substitute for the cavalry. But this first generation, compared to its descendants, was as a hippo to an antelope: its speed averaged only two miles per hour. In addition, on some models the radiator was *inside* the cramped crew compartment, which could quickly heat up to 125° F; entire crews sometimes passed out from the heat and engine fumes. The tank suffered, too, from the era's strange mismatch between firepower and communications: it carried no radio, only homing pigeons, which could be pushed out a small opening in hopes they would fly back to headquarters. Of the 49 machines that lumbered into this first engagement, all but 18 broke down before or during the fighting, or got stuck in deep shell craters, becoming sitting ducks for enemy artillery. The surprise effect of the tank's first appearance—which might have been far greater had Haig waited until more were available—was squandered, just as the Germans had failed to take full advantage of their first use of poison gas the year before.

While tank designers hurried to make improvements (and the Germans to make armor-piercing weapons), Haig was thrown back again on painfully familiar tactics: massive artillery bombardments followed by infantry attacks. The two sides fired 30 million shells at each other during four and a half months of battle. (Even today, every heavy spring rainfall in the region uncovers the metallic glint of shrapnel; in 2005 alone, nearly 90 years after the fighting, French explosives disposal teams would remove 50 tons of shells from the Somme battlefield.) Still, Haig doggedly ordered his men onward. On October 7, 1916, he assured the Imperial General Staff that "a very large number, if not yet all, of the German forces in our front feel that the task of stopping our advance is beyond their ability."

But the position of the German front line told a different story: when autumn rains and mud brought combat to a halt, troops under British command had suffered almost 500,000 casualties on the Somme front, including at least 125,000 deaths. French soldiers, who also took part in the battle, had lost 200,000 dead and wounded. The Allies had gained roughly seven square miles of ground.

It would be too easy, however, to see the Somme solely as a monument to the thickheadedness of Douglas Haig. The Germans brought their own kind of fatal stubbornness to the battle, principally through a disastrous order issued by Chief of Staff General Erich von Falkenhayn that "not one foot of ground should be lost." This meant that whenever a British attack did succeed in gaining a patch of pulverized earth, the Germans tried to retake it, often marching directly into lacerating machine-gun fire just like their foes. By one count there were more than 300 of these counterattacks during the months-long battle, and they, more than anything else, helped make the Somme almost as costly in lives for the Germans as it was for the Allies. The journalist Philip Gibbs watched one, where the German soldiers "advanced toward our men, shoulder to shoulder, like a solid bar. It was sheer suicide. I saw our men get their machine-guns into action, and the right side of the living bar frittered away, and then the whole line fell into the scorched grass. Another line followed. They were tall men, and did not falter as they came forward. . . . They walked like men conscious of going to death." Seldom, in this war, did one side have a monopoly of folly.

15

CASTING AWAY ARMS

AFTER TWO YEARS of fighting, the war's death toll already far exceeded that of the entire decade and a half of the Napoleonic Wars. And these were not just military deaths. Although Britain and France had regarded Germany's air raids on cities as shocking acts of barbarism, they themselves were now bombing Germany from the air, and the Royal Navy was indirectly killing a far larger number of civilians by its tight blockade. British naval control of the key chokepoints of the Strait of Gibraltar, the Suez Canal, the English Channel, and the North Sea threw a near-impenetrable barrier around the Central Powers. Germany was thereby cut off from major sources of a wide range of raw materials, from cotton to copper, as well as the 25 percent of its food it had imported before the war. Moreover, crops at home were stunted, for German farms had imported half their fertilizer.

Germany's high command had never planned for any of this, since they were so certain the war would be short. With the army and navy first in line for food, civilians increasingly went hungry, and by the war's end hundreds of thousands of them would starve to death. Bad weather in late 1916 killed nearly half the country's potato crop and brought to Germany and Austria-Hungary what became known as the "turnip winter." More than 50 food riots erupted. When a horse collapsed and died on a Berlin street one morning, a foreign visitor described the scene: "Women rushed towards the cadaver as if they had been poised for this moment, knives in their hands. Everyone was shouting, fighting for the best pieces. Blood spattered their faces and their clothes. . . . When nothing more was left of the horse beyond a bare skeleton, the people vanished, carefully guarding their pieces of bloody meat tight against their chests."

Europe had not seen war like this before: millions of civilians mobilized into factories making weapons, with the entire population targeted as each side tried to starve the other into submission. In response to the blockade, German U-boats roamed the North Atlantic, the Arctic Ocean, the Mediterranean, and the North Sea, their captains peering through spray-splattered periscopes, not mainly stalking enemy warships (which, being faster, could almost always evade them) but Allied merchant vessels. It did not matter whether these were carrying arms, industrial goods, or food; all were targets. By the end of the war, U-boat torpedoes would send 5,282 merchant ships to the bottom of the sea, and tens of thousands of sailors with them. So far, despite increasingly urgent attempts, the Allies had not found ways of detecting U-boats when they were submerged.

Total war brought something else unfamiliar to Europe's civilians. Hundreds of thousands—from Belgium, Eastern Europe, and the occupied parts of France and Russia—found themselves conscripted into labor battalions and put to work on tasks ranging from producing munitions in German factories to digging trenches at the front. Often these men and women lived in harsh barbed-wire-ringed camps. Nor were the hands of the Allies clean: like the Germans, they had for decades used forced labor in their African colonies, but now the number of such laborers swelled and their working conditions grew unbearably hard as both sides conscripted huge numbers of African porters to carry military supplies long distances through terrain that lacked roads for vehicles.

Massive civilian deaths and forced labor camps would become all too familiar across Europe only two and a half decades in the future, and one feature of 1914–1918 eerily foreshadowed a still later part of the twentieth century. To prevent civilians in occupied Belgium from fleeing into neutral Holland, in 1915 the Germans lined the border between the two countries with a barbed-wire fence, electrified at a lethal 2,000 volts. Some people succeeded in getting through, but at least 300 died trying.

Unlike other wars before and since, there were no behind-the-scenes peace negotiations while the battles raged. Both sides were committed to fight to the bitter end, and by now, two years into the war, if someone in a prominent position on either side so much as advocated peace talks, it was considered close to treason. When Reverend Edward Lyttelton, the headmaster of Eton, gave a sermon outlining some possible compromises that might end hostilities, the resulting uproar eventually forced him to resign.

For people not in such positions of authority there was, for the time being, a little more leeway. From the beginning, Bertrand Russell had proposed peace terms, such as promising Germany no loss of "genuinely German territory"—as opposed to disputed land like Alsace and Lorraine or an occupied country like Belgium. He suggested that for the future an "International Council" should be set up to resolve disputes before they turned into war. In 1916, he wrote to President Woodrow Wilson urging him to use his influence to start peace talks.

Although Russell had spent most of his life in the rarefied circles of Cambridge and literary London, he discovered, to his surprise, that he had the ability to talk to a far wider audience. In the summer of 1916, he toured industrial and mining towns in south Wales for three weeks speaking in favor of a negotiated peace. Although his steps were dogged by hecklers and by uniformed and plainclothes police, his audiences in this staunchly radical region sometimes reached 2,000 or more and cheered him enthusiastically. When the authorities closed meeting halls to him, he spoke in the open air. After the tour, two Scotland Yard detectives visited Russell at home to inform him that he was banned from giving more such lectures, scheduled in Scotland and the north of England. "It makes my blood boil," he wrote. A War Office official proposed withdrawing the lecture ban, but only if Russell would abandon politics and return to mathematics.

Russell and other war opponents continued to press for negotiations, but one activist did something bolder. In a quixotic effort to actually start them, she went to Germany.

After working with a Quaker relief organization in France early in the war, Emily Hobhouse had provoked the ire of Whitehall by spending several months in Holland doing follow-up work after the 1915 women's peace conference at The Hague. Correspondence and telegrams about denying her a passport and permits for future travel flew back and forth among alarmed British bureaucrats. Violet Cecil's brother-in-law, a high-ranking official at the Foreign Office, in one letter called Hobhouse "a woman known to have indulged in absurd and undesirable conduct."

Always a loner, in late April 1916 Hobhouse was the sole Briton to join socialists from both sides and several neutral countries who met in a hotel at the small Swiss village of Kiental. Mostly sectarian ideologues, few of whom, least of all Hobhouse, represented parties of any size, they spent a week arguing such questions as "The Attitude of the Proletariat to the Question of Peace"—which drew seven competing resolutions from a mere 43 delegates. The conference's final compromise manifesto proclaimed, "Down with the war!" and was issued to an uninterested world on May Day. The delegates could only have felt grim as they went their separate ways while workers did their best to kill each other on half a dozen fronts. May Day of 1916 was no advertisement for international proletarian solidarity. One sign of hope flickered briefly in Berlin, however, where the socialist Karl Liebknecht led a small peace demonstration. He was quickly jailed, as was his colleague Rosa Luxemburg. But 50,000 Berlin munitions workers put down their tools on the day of his trial—the first political protest strike in wartime Germany.

Hobhouse's one-woman crusade against Britain's Boer War concentration camps had sent reverberations around the globe; seldom had a single person done so much to put an issue on the international agenda. Now, in the teeth of an immeasurably larger conflict, she hoped to do so again. In June, to the dismay of British authorities, Hobhouse popped up in Berlin, where she met, among others, Foreign Minister Gottlieb von Jagow, whom she had known before the war. Her account of their conversation was colored by wishful thinking, for she came away believing he was prepared to use her as a channel to exchange possible peace terms with the British government. She was hearing no less wishfully, it seems, when she believed two other unnamed "high authorities" who suggested that Germany might be willing to cede Alsace and Lorraine to France in return for peace. Hobhouse also visited a Berlin internment camp for British civilians who had been living in

Germany at the outbreak of the war, and talked with von Jagow about an exchange of civilian prisoners.

The day of her return to the British capital, with typical confidence, she telegraphed the foreign secretary, Sir Edward Grey, assuming he would want to hear firsthand the messages she was bringing from Berlin: "Arrive London about midday await kind instructions Westminster Palace Hotel." She waited in vain. But in her determined fashion, she eventually managed to talk with at least one person in the Foreign Office, as well as various MPs, several newspaper editors, the Archbishop of Canterbury, and even her antagonist from South Africa days, Alfred Milner. "A bridge is needed," she wrote to her old friend the Boer leader Jan Smuts, now a trusted ally of the British. "Let me be that bridge. I have begun to build it—and am not afraid to cross it alone to begin with."

When officials seemed disbelieving about Alsace and Lorraine —given that Germany had sent no other such signals—Hobhouse lobbied them instead with a detailed plan for a prisoner swap. Why couldn't Britain and Germany at least exchange all civilian prisoners who were not men of military age? Even the Foreign Office had to acknowledge that this was "quite sensible." She also had ideas about how to partially lift the British naval blockade in a way that much-needed food could reach occupied Belgium. The government had little interest, however, and refused her a passport to leave the country again. Outraged MPs asked in Parliament how this British citizen had managed to spend several weeks in enemy territory. Surprisingly, it turned out that there was no explicit regulation against doing so; one was now hastily issued after the fact. As always, though, the government was wary of creating a martyr. "After a good deal of discussion," Asquith reported to the King, "the Cabinet agreed that it would be inexpedient either to prosecute or to intern her."

Visiting Berlin was not all that Hobhouse had done; she had also taken a two-week, tightly supervised tour of German-occupied Belgium. She reported in Sylvia Pankhurst's *Woman's Dreadnought* that the German occupation was nowhere near as cruel as the British burning of Boer farms in South Africa. That may have been true, but the Germans had been brutal, prefiguring the Nazis' even more ruthless occupation regimes of the Second World War. In addition to deliberately shooting more than 5,000 Belgian civilians and setting fire to thousands of buildings, they had poured gasoline into the famous university library at Louvain and burned it to the ground, along with its priceless collection of 230,000 books and 750 medieval manuscripts. Occupation authorities shipped back to Germany money from Belgian bank vaults, machinery from Belgian factories, more than half of the country's cattle, nearly half its pigs, and two-thirds of its horses. Hobhouse was aware of little of this, for she had not been allowed to speak to any Belgians. When, after interrogating her at Scotland Yard, Basil Thomson reported that she had come to "the sort of conclusions the Germans desired her to form," he was largely right.

Although the British government gave her no credit and insisted it had been planning something similar all along, one aspect of her vociferous lobbying paid off: the Foreign Office submitted to Parliament a proposal for a civilian prisoner exchange that seemed drawn from her blueprint. Some months later the British and German governments reached an agreement on the subject. More than that Hobhouse did not accomplish. But however hopeless her lone-wolf diplomacy, and however naive she was about what she saw in Belgium, in the entire course of the deadliest conflict the world had ever seen, she was the sole person from any of the warring countries who actually journeyed to the other side in search of peace.

Those in power dismissed Hobhouse out of hand, but on one man she made a lasting mark. Stephen Hobhouse, the son of a first cousin, was in his early thirties at the outbreak of the war and very much a child of privilege. His father was an MP and a wealthy landowner. Having grown up with a succession of governesses in a grand country house built in 1685, Stephen had been sent off to Eton, where he won a book prize (*Deeds that Won the Empire*) for his academic achievements, a silver cup for marksmanship, and another for commanding the best-performing section of his battalion of the Eton College Rifle Volunteers. In 1897, the Diamond Jubilee year, the Volunteers marched to nearby Windsor Castle and from its courtyard serenaded Queen Victoria by torchlight.

Then came Oxford, boating on the Thames, shooting parties, London dances during the social season. Once the Boer War began, however, Hobhouse found his "patriotic ardor for the British cause" challenged. "With Emily, in particular, a cousin whom I often saw . . . I remember arguing earnestly. . . . Thus, no doubt, it was that my mind was prepared for the awakening."

This awakening came at the age of 20, after he read a sixpenny pamphlet by Tolstoy he had bought at the Oxford railway station. From then on, Stephen Hobhouse would be an ardent pacifist. He also found himself appalled that, as the eldest son, he stood to inherit his family's "semi-feudal" 1,700-acre estate and would be expected, on his 21st birthday, to make the traditional speech of greeting to its assembled tenant farmers and their families. To an aunt, he wrote, "I cannot make up my mind just how far to compromise in accepting things as they are, and striving after them as they ought to be."

He made few compromises. After renouncing his inheritance, he became a Quaker and ran a boys' club for London slum children. He had suffered a variety of health problems, including two nervous breakdowns and a bout of scarlet fever, but none of this daunted him from moving into a modest cold-water flat in a working-class neighborhood, where he copied his fellow tenants by using a newspaper for a tablecloth. He worked for a Quaker relief mission in Greece and Turkey that aided refugees from the Balkan Wars of 1912–1913 and, just as his cousin Emily had in South Africa, saw firsthand the way war could turn farms and villages to rubble.

In 1914, two days before Britain entered the war, Hobhouse heard Keir Hardie make his desperate plea for peace at the foot of Nelson's Column in Trafalgar Square. The following year he met his future wife, Rosa, at a dinner party of Christian pacifists, where he was touched to see "the look of eager and affectionate curiosity on the face of my cousin Emily" as she noticed the first glimmer of a budding romance. They married a few months later, but, determined to live simply, took the bus home from their wedding. In early 1916, Rosa shared the speaker's platform with Charlotte Despard at an Independent Labour Party meeting and not long after spent three months in jail for distributing pacifist leaflets. Drafted later that same year, Stephen refused both military and alternative service, citing his convictions as an "International Socialist" and a Christian.

The prosecutor at Hobhouse's court-martial was a young second lieutenant, A. V. Nettell. Knowing the prisoner's health was fragile enough to disqualify him from the military, Nettell unsuccessfully urged him to take the army medical examination. Unlike a number of officers who roughed up COs in their custody, he treated Hobhouse and 11 other COs jailed with him respectfully. The dozen men were duly sentenced to hard labor, but before being taken away, Hobhouse presented Lieutenant Nettell with a copy of Wordsworth's poems, signed by all 12. The gift made a huge impression. "Few things moved me as much. . . . I thank God with all my heart for having known him," Nettell wrote to Hobhouse's widow, Rosa, a half century later.

Already worried that Stephen's health might break in prison, his wife and parents became even more alarmed when they heard that he had been placed in solitary confinement.

As ever more families received telegrams with news that a son or husband had been killed or was missing in action, Britain's clairvoyants did a lucrative business. For a fee, they would stage a séance to put grieving relatives in touch with the spirit of a missing soldier who was sending back through the ether clues as to where he was captive. The confirmed dead, of course, they could not bring back. From the most distant Scottish island to the heights of London society, the war was unceasingly taking its toll. On September 15, 1916, as he led his troops in yet another attack on the Somme front, a German bullet struck the chest of Raymond Asquith, son of the prime minister. Trying to keep up his men's spirits by a show of nonchalance, he lit a cigarette after falling to the ground. He died on his way to a first-aid station.

So many deaths for a sliver of earth so narrow it could barely be seen on a wall map of Europe. How was it all to be explained back home? No one was more aware of that problem than the apostle of high casualties himself. "A danger which the country has to face . . . is that of unreasoning impatience," Haig wrote in mid-1916. "Military history teems with instances where sound military principles have had to be abandoned owing to the pressure of ill-informed public opinion. The press is the best means to hand to prevent the danger in the present war."

And so the press was mobilized, more rigorously than ever. As John Buchan put it afterward, "So far as Britain is concerned, the war could not have been fought for one month without its newspapers." A blizzard of regulations shaped what could appear in print, the government periodically notifying editors of topics "which should not be mentioned" and, wielding the ominous power of vagueness, indicating "subjects to be avoided or treated with extreme caution." Mention of these instructions themselves was forbidden. Lloyd George even told Bertrand Russell he would not hesitate to prosecute someone for publishing the Sermon on the Mount if it interfered with the war effort. When it was all over, the drumbeaters would be duly honored: at least twelve knighthoods and half a dozen peerages were conferred on wartime newspaper correspondents, editors, or owners, the peerages usually going to the owners.

At the front, correspondents routinely sugarcoated British losses. Writing during the Somme bloodletting, William Beach Thomas of the *Daily Mail* had this to say of the dead British soldier: "Even as he lies on the field he looks more quietly faithful, more simply steadfast than others." Beach Thomas, who spent most of the war in France, later admitted, "I was thoroughly and deeply ashamed of what I had written." Haig regarded the half-dozen permanent Western Front correspondents as so many additional British troops. They were outfitted with captains' uniforms and provided with drivers, escorts, and comfortable accommodations. At one point, pleased with the patriotic tone of their dispatches, Haig invited the group to see him and gave them his highest compliment: "Gentlemen, you have played the game like men!"

The game worked more effectively on readers at home than on soldiers. The average war correspondent, recalled C. E. Montague, whose job was to shepherd and censor just such men, wrote "in a certain jauntiness of tone that roused the fighting troops to fury against the writer. Through his despatches there ran a brisk implication that regimental officers and men enjoyed nothing better than 'going over the top'; that a battle was just a rough, jovial picnic; that a fight never went on long enough for the men. . . . Most of the men had, all their lives, been accepting 'what it says 'ere in the paper' as being presumptively true." No more. Montague once found himself in a dugout with a sergeant who said, "Can't believe a word you read, sir, can you?"

Key to presenting the war to the public was the trusted John Buchan, now at the front in a bewildering variety of roles. While continuing to publish a patriotic spy novel nearly every year, he was also, in modern terms, an embedded correspondent, writing for the *Times* and the *Daily News*—and was simultaneously in uniform as an officer in Haig's Intelligence Corps, drafting the weekly communiqués that were sent to the press, British diplomatic posts, and elsewhere. In addition, his literary renown and genial personality made him the ideal guide for taking VIP visitors on tours of the front. Haig typically turned Lord Northcliffe, owner of the *Times* and other newspapers, over to Buchan for a weeklong red-carpet trip. Afterward, the satisfied general found Northcliffe "most anxious to help the Army in every possible way." (A subsequent visit led the commander in chief to triumphantly record Northcliffe's suggestion to "send him a line should anything appear in *The Times* which was not altogether to my liking.")

Buchan's novelist's eye did take in some of Haig's peculiarities, although he did not share them with readers until decades after the war. He noticed, for example, that once Haig became commander in chief, his speech sounded less Scottish; his accent seemed to move southward, as it were. And he observed that Haig did not have "Sir John French's gift of speaking to the chance-met soldier. Once, I remember, he tried it. There was a solitary private by the roadside, whom he forced himself to address.

"*Haig:* 'Well, my man, where did you start the war?'

"*Private* (pale to the teeth): 'I swear to God, sir, I never started no war.'

"It was his last attempt." Haig was similarly inept at the dinner table. "When eminent and cultivated guests came on a visit . . . to prevent the Commander-in-Chief sitting tongue-tied a kind of conversational menu had to be arranged. For example Walter Pater, who had been his tutor, had once said something to him about style which he remembered, and it was desirable to lead the talk up to that."

Meanwhile, Buchan, a fount of writerly energy, continued to spin out the successive best-selling installments of *Nelson's History of the War.* Several short volumes about the Somme appeared by the end of 1916, almost before the smoke had cleared. They succeeded as propaganda because Buchan's prose focused on comprehensible, human-scale events: a trench taken, a village overrun, a hillock triumphantly seized. The books' maps were of close-up scale as well, managing to magnify British advances so that they swept across an entire page. And how could the reader, who before the war had never heard of these tiny French villages, doubt that this hamlet or that ridge was as "important" or "strategic" as the famous writer claimed?

Buchan's Somme volumes are filled with short profiles of heroes, like Private McFadzean of the Royal Irish Rifles, who threw himself on two exploding grenades to protect his comrades; or Lord Lucas, a one-legged pilot who vanished over German lines. All of these men, "clerks and shopboys, ploughmen and shepherds, Saxon and Celt, college graduates and dock labourers, men who in the wild places of the earth had often faced danger, and men whose chief adventure had been a Sunday bicycle ride," had served their country gallantly, and every Briton, of course, should be proud of them. The photographs in the books are upbeat too: Scottish troops with bagpipers, or soldiers heading to the front cheering and raising their helmets in greeting.

That the first foray of the new tank had been an awkward failure in no way deterred Buchan from celebrating it; he presciently sensed the romance the public would soon have with the "strange machines, which, shaped like monstrous toads, crawled imperturbably over wire and parapets, butted down houses, shouldered trees aside, and humped themselves over the stoutest walls. . . . The crews of the tanks—which they called His Majesty's Landships—seemed to have acquired some of the light-heartedness of the British sailor. . . . With infinite humour they described how the enemy had surrounded them when they were stuck, and had tried in vain to crack their shell, while they themselves sat laughing inside."

Buchan did not mention the tank crews reduced to charred skeletons when shells ignited their vehicles' fuel tanks, or any such detail about how death or injury came to nearly half a million British soldiers at the Somme. Instead, following Haig and General Charteris, he insisted that "a shattering blow" had been struck against enemy morale, and concluded somewhat vaguely that "our major purpose was attained." That, of course, was what Britons wanted urgently to feel.

Did Buchan believe all this? Surely not. He had close friends in infantry regiments who knew just how mindless the slaughter had been; indeed, the historian of propaganda Peter Buitenhuis speculates that it was "the strain of duplicity" in what he wrote about the Somme that soon afterward gave Buchan an ulcer attack that required surgery. But we will never know more, for any anguish Buchan felt on this score he kept entirely to himself; there is no sign of it in his published work, diary or letters.

His fellow writer turned propagandist, Rudyard Kipling, shaken to the core by the loss of his son, continued to report from various fronts, but his work took a dark and bitter turn. "Whenever the German man or woman gets a suitable culture to thrive in," he wrote in mid-1916, "he or she means death and loss to civilised people, precisely as germs of any disease. . . . The German is typhoid or plague—*Pestio Teutonicus*." In one speech, he declared that the world was divided into "human beings and Germans," although his rage at some of those human beings—Jews, the Irish, and lazy trade unionists who had supposedly left the nation short of munitions—was growing as well.

He was consumed by not knowing John's fate. From letters or interviews with more than 20 survivors of the Battle of Loos, Kipling and his wife compiled a timeline of John's last known movements on the day he disappeared, marking these on a map. In desperation, he had leaflets printed in German asking for information, and arranged with the Royal Flying Corps to drop them over German trenches.

Confirmation that John had been wounded before vanishing came from the writer Rider Haggard, who had tracked down the last fellow Irish Guardsman to see him alive. John had been crying in pain, the soldier told Haggard, because a shell fragment had shattered his mouth. Haggard did not dare to pass that news on, and so the unknowing Kipling was able to imagine:

> My son was killed while laughing at some jest. I would I knew
> What it was, and it might serve me in a time when jests are few.

Visitors to his country house in Sussex found the writer looking older and grayer, with more lines in his face. When Julia Catlin Park, an American friend, came to see him, he mentioned his boy only as she was leaving; then he squeezed her hand hard and said, "Down on your knees, Julia, and thank God you haven't a son."

The unfathomable carnage of the Somme presented the military with its most difficult public relations problem yet, driving the new profession of propaganda beyond the printed word. More innovative in communications than on the battlefield, the authorities turned to the new medium of film and produced one of the earliest and most influential propaganda movies of all time. Two cameramen with their cumbersome hand-cranked cameras were given unprecedented access to the front lines, and the resulting 75-minute *Battle of the Somme* was rushed into cinemas in August 1916, when the battle was not yet at its midpoint. It opened in 34 theaters in London alone, and 100 copies were soon circulating around the country. Long lines formed outside theaters, and in West Ealing the police had to be called out to control the impatient crowds. In the first six weeks of its release more than 19 million people saw the film; eventually, it may have been seen by a majority of the British population. (Noticing this success, the Germans hurried out a copycat production of their own, *With Our Heroes at the Somme*.)

The film offered jerky, flickering, sometimes blurred footage interspersed with the printed titles of the silent-film era. The medium was still a novelty, and in scene after scene everybody looks curiously at the camera, including men who, you would think, had more urgent matters on their minds: British troops on their way into battle, captured Germans, the walking wounded, even one British soldier hurrying along a trench, bearing on his shoulders a comrade who would, a screen title informs us, die 30 minutes later.

For audiences accustomed only to short, set-piece newsreel clips of formal occasions like parades, the film was nothing short of electrifying. Its black-and-white images also provided a wealth of detail about the front-line lives of ordinary, working-class soldiers, for here were the army versions of daily routines people at home knew so well—feeding and watering horses, preparing a meal over a fire, opening mail, washing up in a roadside pond, attending a church service in a muddy field —plus the drudgery of unloading and carrying endless heavy boxes of artillery ammunition.

Many parts of the film were calculated to inspire awe, such as shots of huge mines exploding underneath the German lines or the firing of heavy howitzers. TERRIFIC BOMBARDMENT OF GERMAN TRENCHES, says the title. Some scenes, including a famous one showing men swarming out of a trench to attack, several dropping when shot, are now believed to have been faked, taken well behind the lines, but neither audiences nor critics appeared to notice at the time, so riveted were they at what seemed to be the authentic nitty-gritty of the real war.

Millions of people must have watched *The Battle of the Somme* yearning for a glimpse of a familiar face—or dreading it: what if a husband or son appeared on the screen wounded or dead? For although the battle's casualties were sometimes presented sentimentally—THE MANCHESTERS' PET DOG FELL WITH HIS MASTER CHARGING DANZIG ALLEY — or misleadingly—WOUNDED AWAITING ATTENTION AT MINDEN POST. SHOWING HOW QUICKLY THE WOUNDED ARE ATTENDED TO — the remarkable thing is that they were presented at all. Unlike almost all earlier propaganda in this war, the film did not shy away from showing the British dead and surprising numbers of British wounded: walking, hobbling, being carried or wheeled on stretchers.

The film's images, wrote the *Star*, "have stirred London more passionately than anything has stirred it since the war [began]. Everybody is talking about them. . . . It is evident that they have brought the war closer to us than it has ever been brought by the written word or by the photograph." Men in the audience cheered when attacks were shown; women wept at the sight of the wounded; people screamed at the staged sequence showing British soldiers falling as if hit by bullets.

Letters from the bereaved about the film (or "films," as a movie long enough to require several reels was sometimes called) filled the newspapers, many voicing the same theme. "I have lost a son in battle," ran a typical one to the *Times*, "and I have seen the Somme films twice. I am going to see them again. I want to know what was the life, and the life-in-death, that our dear ones endured, and to be with them again."

The government had taken a calculated risk in allowing these images into the nation's theaters. David Lloyd George, recently made secretary of state for war, argued that the film, however painful to watch, would reinforce civilian support for the war—and he was right. The more horrific the suffering, ran the chilling emotional logic of public opinion, the more noble the sacrifice the wounded and dead had made —and the more worthwhile the goals must be for which they had given their all.

What did the battlefield look like after four and a half months of fighting? One civilian had a rare opportunity to take a close look, and to a few select friends offered a vivid description of the Somme in mid-November 1916, just as the long, fruitless offensive was coming to a halt:

"All the villages . . . are absolutely flat—not one stone standing upon another. As you look over the vast expanse of desolation all you see is certain groups of stumps of trees, all absolutely stripped of leaves and branches. . . . There are not two square yards of ground anywhere, which have not been shattered by shells." All roads were "feet deep in sticky mud, through which innumerable vehicles of all kinds were struggling, riders plunging, troops marching, either pretty spick and span on their way to the advance trenches, or covered with mud from head to foot and intensely weary on their way back." At Delville Wood, bitterly fought over for months, "many dead bodies, decomposed almost to little heaps of dust and rags, helmets, German and British, rifles, entrenching tools, shells, grenades, machine gun belts, water bottles, and every conceivable fragment of weapons and shreds of clothing littered the whole ground between the blasted trees."

The observer, writing in the wake of an exclusive eight-day tour, was Alfred Milner. After crossing the Channel, "the only experience even faintly approaching discomfort" he met with was a night in a French farmer's house; otherwise he slept in commandeered châteaux. In one, "I had a capital bedroom and every comfort. . . . The Divisional Band played during dinner—not badly. Bands are very important out here and there are not enough of them." Each day was a busy round of meetings with generals, a horseback ride with an escort officer, a stop at a Royal Flying Corps base to see the latest-model fighter planes, a look at the new tanks. Milner watched German antiaircraft guns in action ("The bursting shells looked like so many little fleecy clouds"), heard the "tremendous gun-fire" of artillery, and was taken through several captured German dugouts, one of them "a perfect series of underground chambers, panelled, in some cases upholstered, and connected by galleries."

Again and again he met officers he had known in South Africa, including, of course, the commander in chief. For three nights he had dinner with Haig and his staff, and each time, Milner proudly noted, "I had [a] ½ or ¾ hour private talk with Haig in his own room after dinner, before he settled down to his work and I returned to the general sitting-room." However awkward a conversationalist he may have been in a group, the general was an expert in making influential people feel important; Milner did not know that these intimate after-dinner chats were Haig's standard routine with visiting VIPs. On Sunday, the general took him to hear his favorite preacher, Reverend Duncan. After breakfast on Milner's last morning at headquarters, "Haig took me into his room and went over with me, on a big raised map, the operations of yesterday, showing me exactly the positions we had gained and why he attached importance to them." That Haig would lavish such attention on a visitor with no government position might seem strange, but he had a keen eye for whose star was rising in London. It was he who had invited Milner to come to the front.

For more than two years, Milner had been growing increasingly restless, convinced that he was far more capable than the men surrounding the colorless, uninspiring Asquith, who seemed to have no clue about how to break the war's endless stalemate. Derisively nicknamed "Squiff," the prime minister drank too much, allowed no crisis to interfere with his two hours of bridge every evening, and, while hundreds of thousands died, spent leisurely nonworking weekends at friends' country houses. On one occasion he raised eyebrows by attending a Saturday morning meeting at 10 Downing Street in his golf clothes. His critics, including the stridently prowar newspaper of Milner's British Workers' League, grumbled about "Squiffery" infecting the entire government.

The success of conscription—which Milner had vigorously championed—in keeping the trenches filled with troops seemed to him and his admirers proof of his foresight. Now his mind brimmed with strong opinions on much else, sometimes shaped by back-channel information from friends high in the army. In the House of Lords in 1915, he had been one of the first to argue for withdrawing British troops from the disastrous beachhead at Gallipoli—rare outspokenness for a legislator in wartime. He had ideas for ramping up the propaganda campaign, and, among many other peeves, fumed that the Royal Navy had been "outwitted" by the Germans at Jutland.

Whenever he asked, his speeches were reported at length in the *Times*. Surprisingly, given that they had been fierce political opponents over the Boer War, one of Milner's allies was the new secretary for war, Lloyd George. Beginning in early 1916, when they first held a working dinner at Milner's house, a small group of influential political figures and journalists, sometimes including Lloyd George, met regularly for confidential talk. Dubbed the "Monday Night Cabal," the group had a common goal: maneuvering Asquith out of power. It was almost certainly word of these meetings that had led Haig to invite Milner to France.

Although it is the war's great battles that are most remembered, the air above the Western Front was also filled with bullets, mortar rounds, shrapnel bursts, and deadly clouds of poison gas (now delivered by artillery shells) even when no named battle was raging. The toll from these constant skirmishes was part of what British commanders chillingly referred to as the "normal wastage" of up to 5,000 men a week. For soldiers, minor engagements, never mentioned in a newspaper, could be every bit as fatal or terrifying as a major battle.

Take, for example, events during the frigid predawn hours of November 26, 1916, in a supposedly quiet sector of the front, north of where the Battle of the Somme had just drawn to a close. Holding the line here were several "Bantam Battalions." At the start of the war, a new recruit had to be at least five feet three inches tall; shorter volunteers were turned away. As the need for bodies increased, however, men above five feet were allowed to enlist in special units and issued rifles with smaller stocks. Since shortness is often due to childhood malnutrition, these battalions were filled with men who had grown up poor, often in Scotland or the industrial north of England. In civilian life many had been miners, a job where being short could be an advantage, for underground coal seams in some northern mines were only three feet high. Scorned by tradition-minded British generals who felt bigger was better, and mocked by the Germans, who made rooster calls across no man's land, the Bantams fought and died like everyone else. More than one out of three Bantams involved in the Somme fighting were killed, wounded, or declared missing during the first two months of battle. One unit made up a song:

> We are the Bantam sodgers,
> The short-ass companee.
> We have no height, we cannot fight.
> What bloody good are we?
> And when we get to Berlin, the Kaiser he will say
> Hoch, Hoch mein Gott, what a bloody fine lot
> is the Bantam companee.

On the sector the Bantams now held, the front line ran through a spot called King Crater, only 50 yards from the German trenches. Among the Bantams was Lance Sergeant Joseph "Willie" Stones. Twenty-five years old, with a wife and two small daughters at home, he had served in France for a year, winning the praise of his superiors and two promotions. At about 2:15 A.M. on November 26, Stones was accompanying a lieutenant on an inspection of the front-line trench when they ran into a group of some dozen German raiders who had slipped across no man's land undetected. The Germans shot and fatally wounded the lieutenant. Stones escaped. He ran along the trench and then toward the rear, shouting desperately: "The Huns are in King Crater!"

The Germans, meanwhile, rushed along the British trench in the other direction, shooting, tossing hand grenades into dugouts, and then slipping back across no man's land with a prisoner in tow. Theirs was one of several German raids on this sector of the front that night. Some British troops, thoroughly panicked, fled the front-line trench, shouting, "Run for your lives, the Germans are on you!" Among them were Lance Corporal John McDonald, who had been in charge of a sentry post near King Crater, and Lance Corporal Peter Goggins, who had been in a nearby dugout. Stones and another soldier were ordered to a halt some distance to the rear, and found to be without their rifles—a serious offense.

It is easy to imagine the complete terror the troops must have felt as the darkness suddenly rang with German voices, bursting grenades, and the screams of the wounded. After fleeing, Stones, by the testimony of one soldier who saw him, "seemed to have lost the use of his legs. He sat down for a good while and tried several times to get up." Even after being ordered back to the front line, he still "could not find the use of his legs." (Stones had twice before gone to the battalion medical officer complaining of rheumatic leg pain.) A sergeant described him as being "in a very exhausted condition and trembling. . . . He said that the Germans were chasing him down the trench. . . . He seemed thoroughly done up."

Panic, in the eyes of those in command, was no excuse for a soldier's "casting away his arms and running away from the front line," in the words of the formal charge against Stones, nor was his claim that he had run toward the rear to warn his comrades at the orders of his dying lieutenant. In December 1916, a string of courts-martial dealt with the traumatic night's events by sentencing 26 Bantams, including Stones, Goggins, and McDonald, to death.

Generals frequently recommended mercy after a court-martial decreed capital punishment, and Haig, whose decision this ultimately was, usually agreed, commuting 89 percent of the death sentences that crossed his desk during the war. Joseph Stones had good reason to hope that his own sentence would be commuted, for his company and brigade commanders both urged clemency. "I have personally been out with him in no-man's-land and I always found him keen and bold," wrote the first. ". . . I can safely say that he was the last man I would have thought capable of any cowardly action." But the division commander and two generals above him confirmed the sentences, and the fate of all the condemned Bantams now rested with Haig.

Casting away arms in the face of the enemy was not the only offense that revealed a draconian side to British military justice. That same December, a man in a nearby unit did something that in civilian life would be no crime at all: he wrote a letter to a newspaper.

At 32, Albert Rochester was older than the average soldier, and when he enlisted at the start of the war he had a pregnant wife and three children. An ardent socialist and a columnist for the newspaper of the National Union of Railwaymen, he had been a signalman for the Great Western Railway, operating the semaphores that showed locomotive engineers whether a track was clear. He sustained a wound at the Somme, and in December 1916 was at the front as a corporal. Although Keir Hardie had been devastated when hundreds of thousands of unionists like Rochester volunteered, enlisting did not mean that they abandoned all awareness of class.

The British military, like most armies, replicated its society, and every officer had a batman, or personal servant. This galled Rochester no end, and was the main subject of the angry letter he wrote from a rest billet behind the lines that he described as a "filthy, manure-soaked . . . mud-swamped, stinking, rat-ridden barn." He sent his missive to the London *Daily Mail,* because he was particularly exasperated with its correspondent William Beach Thomas, who had been sending home "ridiculous reports regarding the love and fellowship existing between officers and men." Rochester wrote:

In the infantry arm of the service, there are no less than 60,000 (or 3 complete divisions) of men employed as servants. Look next at the Infantry Brigade Headquarters staff—comprised of six Officers. Those half dozen men retain around them fifteen to eighteen servants, grooms, mess waiters etc. Infantry brigade headquarters therefore swallow up another 5000 men (5 battalions). . . . Each General, Colonel, Major, many Captains and Subalterns have their horse and groom. . . . It is generally recognised that those animals . . . are to Officers in France practically useless, excepting for a once-a-fortnight canter. . . . I leave my readers to guess what those horses and grooms are costing the nation in fodder, rations, saddlery etc. . . . Probably if a roll call was taken of the batmen, grooms, servants, waiters, commissioned and non-commissioned "cushy" jobs, it would be found that quite half a million men were performing tasks *not necessary to the winning of this war.*

In the peroration that ended his letter can be heard both Rochester's patriotism and his socialist beliefs: "I ask then, as a soldier, on behalf of Millions of Citizen-soldiers, that . . . the Officer be regarded as NOT of Royal blood; that he be expected to clean his own boots, get his own food and shaving water. It may generate within him more respect for his rank and file brethren. And certainly release men for more essential military work."

Rochester's letter never reached the *Daily Mail*. A censor stopped it, and the writer was hauled before a court-martial on charges of "conduct to the prejudice of good order and military discipline."

At his trial, Rochester defended himself with withering eloquence. If, he said, serving officers such as Winston Churchill could speak out publicly, surely "the private soldier" could as well. The reference to Churchill, someone no censor ever tamed, was brilliantly appropriate. Churchill had spent the first half of 1916 commanding an infantry battalion at the front, but in the middle of that period he had returned home on leave and given a speech in the House of Commons attacking the management of the navy.

Rochester would have made a formidable lawyer. "I appreciate," he said, "that one object of the Censorship regulations is to prevent documents coming into the hands of the enemy which might lead him to think that there was some dissatisfaction in the Army. . . . [But] I think the letter might add to the discouragement of the enemy in so far as I have merely tried to increase the fighting strength of our Army. . . . I think the letter would show the enemy a desire on the part of the rank and file to fight in every way to a knock-out blow." Furthermore, he pointed out, he had passed through London on leave two weeks earlier, and if he had wanted to evade censorship, why would he not have taken his letter directly to the *Daily Mail* then?

The only witness in his defense was the divisional chaplain, who offered a somewhat backhanded endorsement: "I have known the accused about three months. . . . I think he is a thoroughly sincere man and a genuine patriot; he has rather pronounced opinions on political questions; I believe he would call himself a socialist; he has been in the habit of speaking in public rather forcibly on political questions. . . . But I have nothing to suggest that his opinions would lessen his readiness to submit to discipline."

The court-martial found Rochester guilty. Friends who waited on tables at his brigade's officers' mess told him that they had overheard officers talking angrily about earlier letters he had sent home, which they had read as censors, so it is possible that they were waiting for an excuse to punish him. According to Rochester, when his letter was discovered, he was first hauled before his commanding general, an Indian-army veteran, who fumed, "I'll break you, my man: I'll break your very soul."

Stripped of his corporal's stripes, he was sentenced to 90 days of Field Punishment Number One, plus menial labor and an hour every morning and afternoon of "pack drill"—rapid marching while wearing a full load of equipment. The general was out to break him, and "frankly," Rochester wrote later, ". . . I felt afraid."

A burly sergeant took him to a small outbuilding, guarded by sentries, that served as the nearest military prison. It was a particularly harsh winter; rivers froze solid and soldiers in the trenches found ice forming on the edge of their plates before they had finished eating. A handful of men shared Rochester's cell on this piercingly cold night. "Only one blanket per prisoner was allowed, so that for warmth, we laid one blanket on the filthy straw, and anchored together under the remaining bedding. Live rats . . . kept us awake for hours, so that we began to confide in each other." As they talked through the night, Rochester realized that the others had troubles far worse than his.

His cellmates were Bantams, and included Stones, Goggins, and Mc-Donald.

The three were, Rochester discovered, working-class men like himself: Stones and Goggins were coal miners from Durham, in England's far north, known for its militant unionism, and McDonald was a steelworker from nearby Sunderland. "These men huddled up along side me," remembered Rochester, ". . . all spoke hopefully of acquittal. Poor devils!"

In the morning, after a meager breakfast, pistol-carrying military police took the three condemned Bantams away to a more isolated cell. Rochester, meanwhile, was led off between two sentries to a storage dump, where he was given three wooden posts, three ropes, and a spade. Then the sentries marched him up a hill "until we reached a secluded spot surrounded by trees." An officer and two sergeants arrived and marked three places in the snow, a few yards apart, ordering Rochester to dig a posthole at each. Suddenly he realized that this was where his cellmates were to be shot—unless Haig commuted their sentences.

In Britain, this winter was a depressing one for opponents of the war. Several thousand conscientious objectors were in prison, but there were few signs of the groundswell of antiwar feeling that they kept hoping for. Sometimes, however, encouragement came from unexpected sources. In December, Bertrand Russell received a letter that began, "To-night here on the Somme I have just finished your *Principles of Social Reconstruction*. . . . It is only on account of such thoughts as yours, on account of the existence of men and women like yourself that it seems worth while surviving the war. . . . You cannot mind knowing that you are understood and admired and that those exist who would be glad to work with you." The writer, Second Lieutenant Arthur Graeme West of the 6th Oxfordshire and Buckinghamshire Light Infantry, was killed three months later, at the age of 25.

As the year drew to a close, Herbert Asquith at last paid the price for his lackadaisical leadership. Under pressure, he capitulated to a proposal, put forward by Milner and other critics, for tight, decisive control over the war effort to be vested in a small committee—soon to be known as the War Cabinet—headed by Lloyd George. Soon after, his support in Parliament eroding further, Asquith went to Buckingham Palace to hand in his resignation to the King. Lloyd George became his successor. The new prime minister quickly decided on the other four members of his War Cabinet, an all-powerful body that would meet more than 500 times before the war was over.

On the evening of December 8, 1916, at his London lodgings, Milner received a message summoning him to 10 Downing Street. Before leaving the house, he sent a note to Violet Cecil with the news, adding, "My own disposition is strongly against being in the Govt. at all, most strongly against being in it unless I am part of the Supreme Direction." But part of the new inner-circle War Cabinet he was to be, as minister without portfolio, charged with supervising the war effort. At 64, after more than a decade in the political wilderness, Alfred Milner had suddenly become one of the most powerful men in the embattled empire he loved.

V

1917

16

BETWEEN THE LION'S JAWS

WHILE THE THREE condemned Bantams waited to hear if Haig would commute their sentences, they had good reason for hope. Haig had, after all, commuted nearly nine out of every ten death sentences. After his arrest, Joseph Stones had shown no foreboding in a letter to his sister: "I am sending out a few lines to say I am going on all right. I've had no time to write before. . . . It will soon be Christmas and I hope you all enjoy yourselves. I only wish I had been at home to make you all happy."

However, Haig made it clear that he felt there were times when the supreme penalty was fully justified. In the first weeks of the Battle of the Somme, for instance, a private named Arthur Earp was tried for leaving his post in a front-line trench. The court-martial sentenced him to death, the prescribed penalty, but recommended mercy. When the verdict reached the general commanding Earp's division, he concurred, as did the general at the next level up, the corps commander. But when the case reached Haig, at a time of soaring casualties, he was in no mood to be merciful. He confirmed the sentence. The report of the court-martial said, "The court recommend the accused for mercy owing to the intense bombardments which the accused had been subjected to & the account of his good character," but Haig underlined the phrase about bombardment and wrote, "How can we ever win if this plea is allowed?" He then ordered that this opinion "be communicated to the Corps and Divisional commanders." In army protocol, this was a stinging rebuke; each general subsequently felt obliged to write "noted" under Haig's comments.

An undercurrent of rumor drifted back to England. "Reports of large numbers of executions at the Front came to us constantly," wrote Sylvia Pankhurst, who visited the grief-stricken family of one executed soldier from London's East End. "Men often told us sadly that they had been in firing parties which had been ordered out to shoot six or seven poor fellows." As the bloody deadlock in the trenches continued, discipline became steadily tougher and each year of the war so far had seen an ominous, sharp increase in the number of British military executions, mostly for desertion: four in 1914, 55 in 1915, 95 in 1916. (The actual total is somewhat higher, for records of executions among the more than 100,000 Indian soldiers on the Western Front have disappeared.) The considerably larger German army, which we usually think of as more draconian in discipline, sent only 48 men to the firing squad during the entire war.

The army's stringent disciplinary code took no account of what was then called shell shock. Simply put, after even the most obedient soldier had had enough shells rain down on him, without any means of fighting back, he often lost all self-control. This could take many forms: panic, flight, inability to sleep or—as with Joseph Stones—to walk. "Apart from the number of people . . . blown to bits, the explosions were so terrific that anyone within a hundred yards' radius was liable to lose his reason after a few hours," wrote a British lieutenant after being under mortar fire at Ypres, "and the 7th battalion had to send down the line several men in a state of gibbering helplessness." So many officers and men suffered shell shock that, by the end of the war, the British had set up 19 military hospitals solely devoted to their treatment. Senior commanders like Haig, seldom under fire themselves, grasped little of this. They thought not in terms of mental illness but merely of soldiers doing or not doing their duty.

When the death sentences meted out to the Bantams worked their way up the chain of command to him, Haig commuted the great majority. But he held Stones, Goggins, and McDonald to a more severe standard, presumably because they were noncommissioned officers. "I confirmed the proceedings on three," he wrote in his diary, "namely 1 sergeant and 2 corporals."

On a freezing January night a few days later, heavy snow covered the ground, artillery boomed, and moonlight glinted off the bayonets of guards at the farm where the divisional military police had its headquarters. A staff car pulled into the barnyard and four officers stepped out. The three prisoners were brought outdoors in handcuffs. One officer unrolled a piece of paper and, by flashlight, read aloud Haig's confirmation of the death sentences. One prisoner gasped; the other two remained silent.

Just before dawn, an ambulance picked up the three men from the farm and took them to the execution site. Manacled and blindfolded, they were tied to the stakes for which Albert Rochester had dug holes. Rochester watched as an officer pinned a white envelope over each man's heart as a target. A separate 12-man firing squad aimed at each of the three; at an officer's command the crackle of 36 gunshots rang out. To be sure the job was done, the officer approached and fired a final revolver shot into each prisoner's body.

"As a military prisoner," wrote Rochester later, "I helped clear away the traces of that triple murder. I took the posts down—they were used to cook next morning's breakfast for the police; the ropes were used in the stables."

> The ambulance conveyed the dead bodies back to the barn. . . . I helped carry those bodies towards their last resting place; I collected all the blood-soaked straw and burnt it.
>
> Acting upon police instructions I took all their belongings from the dead men's tunics. . . . A few letters, a pipe, some fags, a photo.
>
> I could tell you of how the police guffawed at the loving terms of good cheer from the dead men's wives; of their silence after reading one letter from a little girl to "dear Daddy"; of the blood-stained snow that horrified the French peasants; of the chaplain's confession, that braver men he had never met than those three men he prayed with just before the fatal dawn; of the other cases of army "justice" I discovered. . . . But what's the use!

Back in Durham, Stones's wife, Lizzie, who had been supporting herself and their two young daughters on an army dependents' allowance of 17 shillings and sixpence a week, was told that Joseph's execution meant the end of that money, and that she would not be eligible for a widow's pension. A fellow miner had promised Stones he would look after Lizzie and the girls if Stones did not return from the war. He married her, but because of the stigma of the execution, they moved away from Durham.

Never one to keep quiet, Rochester, still serving his own jail term for his unpublished letter to the *Daily Mail,* angrily told the military policemen guarding him that as far as he was concerned, the three men had been punished beyond all reason. He soon began to fear for his own safety. Once his sentence was up, he wondered, what if officers angry with him for denouncing their privileges assigned him to the most dangerous work, such as night patrols to repair barbed wire in no man's land?

One day in prison, however, a smuggled message reached him. "Dear Rochester," it said. "I was sorry to hear of your predicament. Don't worry, I'm taking steps to put things right." It was from the leader of the National Union of Railwaymen. A soldier from Rochester's platoon, home on leave, had got word to him that a union member was in prison, and why. Before long, news reached Rochester that his conviction had been overturned and he was to be released. His union chief had been to see the secretary for war, who was willing to do a favor for a union so crucial to the war effort.

Rochester was assigned to a new post in the crews running British military trains in France. This was not without its dangers, for railways were key targets for what he wryly called "pleasant little periods of shelling and bombing." But it was surely preferable to night patrols in no man's land. Rochester talked politics with French railway unionists, and scoffed at the grandly luxurious train of the director general of transport for the British forces: "Bath-rooms, smoke-rooms, dining-rooms; from pins to pile carpets, and libraries to slippers and champagne, it was a moving club . . . of cooks, valets, sergeant-majors, and commissioned duds." He was grateful to be alive, but vowed that once he was free to do so, he would tell the story of his three fellow prisoners who had not been so lucky.

• • •

Befitting the unprecedented scope of the war, Lloyd George's War Cabinet was something new in British politics. It was not a subcommittee of the full cabinet, but five men entrusted with total responsibility for waging the war. Central to it was the working relationship that developed between Lloyd George and Milner, as strong as it was unlikely. The prime minister was a Liberal and his new minister without portfolio a Conservative; Lloyd George, whose impoverished father died young, had been brought up partly by his uncle, a shoemaker, while the Oxford-educated Milner moved easily among the country's elite; Lloyd George had one of the golden tongues of his era—in English and his native Welsh—while Milner was a poor public speaker, with a voice people found squeaky or reedy. A decade and a half earlier, the Boer War had bitterly divided them, but with Britain now in the battle of its life, the two men turned out to be superbly compatible. The somewhat eccentric prime minister began each morning by drinking a strange concoction of eggs, honey, cream, and port; then he, the chief of the Imperial General Staff, and Milner would meet at 11 A.M. with an aide taking notes; only at noon would the other members of the War Cabinet join them. Milner was in the inner circle within the inner circle.

Because Milner so lacked any common touch, Lloyd George knew that he could never become a political rival. Instead, the prime minister recognized in him a world-class administrator with an eye for talent and for cutting red tape. He gave him plenty of leeway, and Milner in short order became the second most powerful civilian in Britain. A photograph from this time shows him in a bowler hat, gloves in one hand, umbrella in the other, taking a long, purposeful stride along Downing Street, restored to power at last. As 1917 began, he drew members of his old South African Kindergarten of bright young Oxford graduates into government positions: an undersecretaryship here, a head of a bureau there; one Kindergarten member was even installed as a private secretary to the prime minister. "Milner men," as the press called them, soon filled many of the temporary huts built for an overflow of wartime office space in the backyard of 10 Downing Street, known as the Garden Suburb. The president of Milner's British Workers' League was promptly made minister of labor. Wanting to put a higher priority on propaganda, Milner promoted his longtime protégé John Buchan to a powerful new post, director of information, reporting to Lloyd George. Buchan was surely pleased, for, beneath his affable public exterior, his letters show him to have been a man of keen ambition for high office. As prodigious a worker as ever, he continued to write installments of his multivolume history of the war and his novels, giving a villain in one of them the name von Stumm, that of a German contemporary of Buchan's at Oxford.

As the staggering scale of British losses at the Somme sank in, the new War Cabinet began questioning Haig's costly battering-ram strategy. Lloyd George suggested sending British arms and men elsewhere, anywhere they wouldn't run up against a solid wall of German barbed wire and machine guns—to Egypt, for instance, for a drive against the Turks. Or why not to Italy, for use against ramshackle Austria-Hungary? But Haig, a shrewd infighter, proved more powerful than his nominal superiors, and saw to it that little strength was diverted to other fronts from his armies in France and Belgium.

In this sub-rosa battle, Haig's cultivation of Lord Northcliffe was crucial, for Lloyd George partly owed his position to the press baron, whose papers had praised him and kept up a drumbeat of criticism that had helped force Asquith to step down. When Lloyd George and the War Cabinet began trying to intervene in military strategy in a way that the mild Asquith had never dared, Haig turned to Northcliffe and confided to his diary that the magnate was "fully alive to his responsibility for putting Lloyd George into power," as well as "determined to keep him in the right lines or force him to resign." Nor did Haig's widely known relationship with the royal family do him any harm. "It gives me great pleasure and satisfaction," King George V wrote to him, "to tell you that I have decided to appoint you a Field Marshal in my Army. . . . I hope you will look upon it as a New Year's gift from myself and the country."

Haig was safe, but the first major military development of 1917 would not take place on the Western Front—or even on land.

In the previous two years, despite the millions of soldiers killed and wounded, nowhere along its entire length of nearly 500 miles had the front line moved in either direction by more than a few hours' walk. Military history had not seen the likes of this before, and the Germans were no less frustrated than the Allies.

Furthermore, the German government was battling against opponents, east and west, whose combined armies were significantly larger, and on the home front the situation remained dire. In a country already desperately short of food, abnormally severe temperatures froze rivers and canals that usually delivered coal, and millions of city dwellers, as the historian David Stevenson has put it, "endured cold and hunger unknown since pre-industrial times."

Austria-Hungary was in even worse condition, and militarily was more of a burden to Germany than the ally it was supposed to be. Its comic-opera army, rich in splendid uniforms, was weak in everything else, and its government was so inept that for the first eight months of war it had not bothered to stop a Vienna trading firm from doing a booming business selling food and medicine—through neutral countries—to the Russian army. The failure to take Verdun dashed any hopes Germany had for new frontal assaults against either the French or the British. So what was to be done? Like Lloyd George, the Germans were looking for ways around the impasse of the Western Front. And this led them to take one of the great gambles of the war.

Since the conflict began, German submarines had been sinking Allied ships by the hundreds, notoriously torpedoing the British passenger liner *Lusitania* in 1915. The prime targets were ships crossing the Atlantic, delivering essential food and a wide array of arms and manufactured goods Britain and France were buying from American suppliers. The Germans were wary, however, of sinking American ships, which could provoke the neutral United States into joining the Allies.

Germany's gamble of early 1917 was to declare unlimited submarine warfare, making fair game almost any vessel headed for Allied ports—including those from a neutral country. Cutting off the Atlantic supply lines so crucial to the British and French war effort, the Germans hoped, would force the Allies to sue for peace. The danger of unlimited submarine warfare, of course, was that it was certain to sink American ships and kill American sailors, therefore sooner or later drawing the United States, the world's largest economy, into the war. As reckless as this might seem, the German high command calculated that, even if the United States declared war, severing the Atlantic lifeline would strangle Britain and France into surrender in less than six months, long before a substantial number of American troops could be trained and sent to Europe. Despite its size the United States had a standing army that ranked only seventeenth in the world. In any case, how would American soldiers cross the ocean? German naval commanders were confident that U.S. troopships and merchant vessels alike would fall victim to U-boats, because Allied technology for locating submarines underwater was still so primitive as to be almost useless.

In January 1917 the Germans sank 171 Allied and neutral ships; in February, after the new declaration, 234; in March, 281; and in April, 373. Measured in tonnage, the losses were even more catastrophic: the Germans sank more than 880,000 tons of merchant shipping in the month of April alone, a pace of destruction high enough to polish off every single cargo ship on the world's oceans in less than three years. And they were managing to inflict this deadly toll with, on average, only 30 submarines on station in the shipping lanes at any given time. One out of four ships leaving Britain to go overseas, the authorities calculated, would not survive to return. Faced with these odds, the captains of hundreds of neutral vessels in British ports refused to sail.

The Germans had finally found a way to hit Britain in its stomach. In the first six months of unlimited submarine warfare, 47,000 tons of meat ended up at the bottom of the ocean, and much larger quantities of other food. Gloom over these losses dominated meetings of the War Cabinet. The U-boats, it seemed, might starve Britain more quickly than the Royal Navy blockade could starve Germany. "In five months at this rate Britain would be forced to her knees," wrote Churchill, adding, "It seemed that Time, hitherto counted as an incorruptible Ally, was about to change sides."

Nothing breeds spy hysteria like a war that is not going well. If food is short and newspapers are filled with reports of ships lost at sea, if soldiers are dying by the thousands but the front line does not move, it is tempting to believe that all this is not just the fault of the enemy but also of unseen traitors at home. British paranoia was fed by many springs, from John Buchan's fast-paced espionage novels to Christabel Pankhurst's *Britannia* and its shrill denunciations of treacherous Germanophiles in high positions to the aptly named Horatio Bottomley, a demagogic orator and editor who called for conscientious objectors to be taken to the Tower of London and shot.

When panic fills the air, of course, there are careers to be made, high and low, by discovering hidden enemies. England did not lack for people eager to do so, among them Scotland Yard's debonair self-promoter Basil Thomson. Unfortunately for him, bona fide German agents were depressingly rare. Despite efforts to blame factory fires or accidents on them, not a single known act of enemy sabotage took place in Britain during the entire war. And so for the ambitious spycatcher, promotions and publicity meant ferreting out homegrown subversives: typically, at one trade union meeting in Southampton in the middle of the war, two embarrassed detectives were found hiding under a grand piano.

Various government departments rushed to create intelligence units. One such bureau had been set up in 1916 by officials at the new Ministry of Munitions, on edge about a wave of strikes that rippled through factories turning out guns, shells, and other crucial war equipment in the Midlands and along Scotland's River Clyde. There were also rent strikes by Scottish women munitions workers angry over rising prices and inadequate housing.

Unlike many in ruling circles, Alfred Milner acknowledged that workers had genuine problems, including "the bullying and unscrupulousness of some employers . . . and profiteering." But once these were dealt with, he believed that the government should "go for the agitators. The removal of grievances alone will not disarm them. They are out for mischief." Soon after he joined the War Cabinet, a flurry of alarmist reports from the Ministry of Munitions intelligence unit landed on his desk. "It is impossible for anybody to say at present to what lengths the coming industrial troubles may be carried," read one. "The general strike may occur." Subversives in the workforce were more prominent than ever — "30 per cent are disloyal and confirmed slackers" — because "Army enlistments have depleted the patriotic element." Worse yet, the report warned, the flood of policemen entering the army had shrunk the forces that normally could keep labor under control at home.

As the historian Sheila Rowbotham points out, the agents who penned these reports were often ex–military men who viewed those they were spying on through the lens of their own experience. Accustomed to clear hierarchies of power and orders promptly obeyed, they saw any strike as provoked by a ringleader and not by high rents or low wages. When they looked at bedraggled, anarchic groups of pacifists they imagined a strict chain of command. FBI surveillance reports on the American antiwar movement of the Vietnam era reflect the same mindset.

The militants, the Ministry of Munitions agents claimed, had devised multiple ways of spreading the signal for a strike to start: "a quadruple line of communication was used, one man going by train, a second by motor car and a third by motor cycle," while a telegram was dispatched with the coded message "Come in Chambermaids." The situation, as the agents saw it, was dire: "We are undoubtedly up against a very dangerous and mischievous organisation . . . which is, in reality, an industrial revolution."

The reports that flowed to Milner and a few other officials were studded with cryptic mentions of undercover men: "F" and "B" were supplying useful information, and "V" had managed to befriend a particularly dangerous agitator. An agent code-named "George" reported on a meeting in Sheffield where one speaker said, "What the working classes will have to do, is to refuse to go on making tools for the prosecution of the war."

There were indeed many strikes in Britain at this time, but despite what Keir Hardie had hoped for, they were not directed at the war itself. Inflation was taking a toll on wages, and workers were angry at other ways employers were using the excuse of wartime to undo some of labor's hard-won gains. Still, Hardie's spirit was not dead. Even though many opponents of the war were writers and intellectuals, plenty of them came from the working class.

No Oxford or Cambridge or Bloomsbury lay in the background of John S. Clarke, for example, one man the agents were doing their best to keep an eye on. Born in poverty-stricken County Durham, home to the three executed Bantam soldiers in France, he was the thirteenth of fourteen children, only half of whom survived to adulthood. Clarke's family was in the circus. By the age of 10 he was in the ring, doing tricks while riding a horse bareback with no bridle. At 12 he went to sea, witnessing a murder on board a tramp steamer and getting knifed in a pub on the Antwerp waterfront. He jumped ship in South Africa and lived with Zulu villagers for two months before working his way home. Whenever there was no ship he felt like sailing on, he returned to the family trade. One evening, he had to fill in when a drunken fellow performer tripped over a rope and knocked himself out. That was how, at 17, he found himself in the circus ring as the youngest lion tamer in Britain.

The most dangerous thing about a lion, Clarke later wrote, was not its teeth but its claws. One ill-tempered lion seems not to have realized this, and early in Clarke's career it seized his thigh in its mouth. "I never moved, but talked gently until his jaws relaxed, and still talking, I edged away." Clarke's work with a variety of animals left many a scar on his body. Soon he was caught up in the radical movements of the day, getting arrested in 1906, at the age of 21, for taking part in a conspiracy to smuggle arms from Scotland to revolutionaries in Russia. He had little formal schooling, and essentially educated himself, giving fulsome voice to his politics in articles, pamphlets, and doggerel:

> The landlord calls it rent and he winks the other eye,
> The merchant calls it profit and he sighs a heavy sigh,
> The banker calls it interest and puts it in the bag,
> But our honest friend the burglar simply calls it swag.

After various adventures, including running a zoo, Clarke joined the small, militantly left-wing Socialist Labour Party and became an editor and writer for its newspaper, the *Socialist*. He and his party comrades were fiercely, uncompromisingly against the war. "You gave us war," the paper combatively declared. "We in return give you revolution." By the war's end, despite repeated raids and harassment of its printers, the paper would have a circulation of 20,000. It regularly published Clarke's attacks on the war and on industry profiteers, and also celebrated resistance in other countries, printing, for instance, the defiant speech the socialist Karl Liebknecht gave before a German army court-martial in 1916.

The newspaper's readers were concentrated in Scotland and the north of England, where party activists had led some of the strikes that left government intelligence agents so alarmed. After a friendly policeman tipped off Clarke that he was soon to be arrested, he fled Scotland and settled out of sight on a sympathizer's farm near Derby, earning his keep as a laborer while he and several others continued to edit the *Socialist* underground.

Derby was a center of labor militance, a city of railroad yards, coal smoke, and aging red-brick factories, with plants that made fuses and aircraft engines for the military, as well as parts for rifles and artillery pieces. Whether the spy hunters from the Ministry of Munitions were aware that the area was a clandestine base for Clarke and the *Socialist* we do not know. But in their hunt for subversives, they put under surveillance the very friend who almost certainly had helped arrange Clarke's hiding place. For undercover operatives looking for glory and advancement, she seemed the perfect target, combining several strands of left-wing activity in a single household.

Matronly and determined-looking, 52-year-old Alice Wheeldon supported herself by selling secondhand clothes out of the front room of a house on Derby's Pear Tree Road. She was known as a woman who brooked no nonsense: when someone once heckled her as she gave a political speech, she tapped him on the head with her umbrella. A railway locomotive driver's daughter, she had worked as a house servant when young and was now estranged from her alcoholic husband, a mechanic. One daughter, Nellie, helped Alice in the old-clothes shop; two others, Hettie and Winnie, in their twenties, were schoolteachers, as was Alice's son, Willie, until he was drafted in 1916. Refused status as a conscientious objector, he was now in hiding, hoping to flee the country. The whole family were longtime leftists: Alice and her two teacher daughters had belonged to the Pankhursts' WSPU until it backed the war, and, along with their friend John S. Clarke, they were members of the Socialist Labour Party. Hettie Wheeldon was also secretary of the Derby branch of the No-Conscription Fellowship. Although Winnie was married, she was, the Ministry of Munitions agents eagerly reported, a believer in free love and at one point had been an atheist.

The crucial thing, in the eyes of the agents, was that the Wheeldon family had been sheltering young men fleeing the call-up — the "flying corps," as they were known. Some draft evaders were principled left-wingers, others simply very young and very scared. "Many comrades kept an open door for men on the run," remembered one radical who knew the family well. "In Derby, the house of Mrs. Wheeldon was a haven for anyone who was opposed to the war." At the start of 1917, the Wheeldons were keeping a young socialist in the house, who, Hettie wrote to her sister, "is terrified. Sticks in all day and only emerges at night." A frequent visitor who put a gleam in the secret agents' eyes was a suitor of Hettie's, a labor agitator working as a mechanic for the Cunard shipping line in Liverpool and using contacts with radical seamen and Irish nationalists to smuggle deserters and war resisters out of England.

To a spycatcher's mind, finding a pretext to arrest the entire household would be a coup indeed. The agents began monitoring the Wheeldon family's mail. The contents of one package that Alice sent to Winnie, who lived with her husband in Southampton, included, they carefully noted, four mince pies, two pairs of socks, and a stuffed chicken. Thanks to the closely watched correspondence, we have a touchingly detailed portrait of life inside this beleaguered family, ranging from everyday human concerns (Winnie wrote to her mother fretting that her menstrual period was late) to what they read, which included socialist newspapers, the NCF's *Tribunal,* and George Bernard Shaw's play *Mrs. Warren's Profession.* Even in wartime, life for committed socialists was a life of constant reading.*

One day a Ministry of Munitions secret agent using the name of Alex Gordon turned up at the Wheeldon house claiming to be a "conchie," or conscientious objector, on the run. Ever trusting, Alice put him up for the night and confided in him her worries about the dangers facing her fugitive son. She was trying to arrange covert passage out of the country, she said, for Willie, another draft evader, and Winnie's husband, who also feared being called up. Delighted, Gordon swiftly brought in his immediate superior, Herbert Booth, introducing him as "Comrade Bert," supposedly an army deserter. Although Hettie was suspicious, Alice seems to have believed both men, who then sprang their trap.

On January 30, 1917, Alice, her daughters Hettie and Winnie, and Winnie's husband, Alf Mason, were all arrested, Winnie and Hettie at the schools where they taught. Hettie's astonished pupils watched from a classroom window as plainclothesmen in bowler hats took their teacher away. The family had always known they ran a risk for helping antiwar fugitives, but the charge now made against them left them astounded. It was that all four "did amongst themselves unlawfully and wickedly conspire, confederate and agree together . . . willfully and of their malice aforethought to kill and murder." And whom were they accused of conspiring to murder? Headlines on both sides of the Atlantic screamed the shocking news: their targets were Arthur Henderson, a member of the War Cabinet, and Prime Minister David Lloyd George.

---

*On his antiwar speaking tour of Wales some six months earlier, Bertrand Russell wrote to a lover about "all the working-men who are hungry for intellectual food. . . . I am amazed at the number of them at my meetings who have read my 'Problems of Philosophy.'"

For a government eager to disgrace the antiwar movement, there could be no more dramatic charge. The country's attorney general himself went all the way to Derby to lay out the case against the accused at a preliminary hearing. Stunned, the four family members waited in jail for their trial to begin.

The same month the Wheeldons were arrested, the passenger liner *Kildonan Castle,* in better days a luxury steamer on the run to Cape Town, quietly slipped out of the Scottish port of Oban, escorted by a Royal Navy destroyer. No announcement was made in the press. On board the ship was a high-ranking delegation of British, French, and Italian military and civilian officials, 51 strong. Heading the British contingent, on his first overseas assignment since joining the War Cabinet, was Alfred Milner.

The delegation was on its way to Russia. That country had so far suffered a staggering six million war casualties, Milner estimated. Its huge, clumsy army had been repeatedly and embarrassingly beaten by far smaller numbers of German troops, who now held a wide swath of Russian territory, its grain, coal, iron, and other riches feeding the German war effort. British and French leaders were increasingly exasperated by the sluggishness of their ally. What could be done?

Running a gauntlet of German submarines, Allied ships had been delivering large amounts of equipment and supplies to Russia's Arctic Ocean ports. In two years, for instance, Britain had sold Russia 2.5 million rounds of ammunition, a million rifles, 27,000 machine guns, 8 million hand grenades, and almost 1,000 fighter planes or aircraft engines. But British military attachés saw few signs of any of these actually reaching Russia's armies in the field. Why? It was difficult to get information out of the secretive authorities, yet Russian envoys kept asking for more supplies, as well as huge loans to cover their cost. What could really be expected from Russia as a partner in the war? This group of notables was on a mission to find out.

As the ship and its escort skirted the northern edge of the European continent, lookouts watched constantly for German U-boats. All on board knew that no one could survive more than a few minutes in these icy waters. The first shock for the Allied delegation only came, however, when the *Kildonan Castle* arrived at Port Romanov, today's Murmansk, the single ice-free port in the Russian Arctic. Thousands of boxes of British and French munitions lay piled up on the town's docks and in vacant lots. Crates of dismantled Sopwith and Nieuport fighter planes, awaiting reassembly, sat covered with snow. While ships were delivering a daily average of 1,500 tons of supplies, it turned out that the rail line leaving the port, hobbled by equipment shortages and official corruption, could carry away only 200 tons a day.

The delegation had to take that same line to the imperial capital. Traffic crept so slowly that even this VIP train of cabinet ministers and generals, met midway by special emissaries from Tsar Nicholas II, took three days and nights to huff and wheeze the 700 miles to the city now called Petrograd. (In a fit of patriotism, Russia had rid itself of the German-sounding "St. Petersburg.") At the royal palace in Tsarskoe Selo, outside the city, escorted by court officers in full dress uniforms, the Allied delegation was presented to the Tsar. Milner delivered several letters from the Tsar's cousin King George V and two days later talked with him privately for nearly two hours. After a lunch that included the Tsarina and several of their children, Milner told his friend General Henry Wilson, the senior British military official in the delegation, that the imperial couple, "although very pleasant," had "made it quite clear that they would not tolerate any discussion of Russian internal politics."

An endless succession of silver-plate banquets, gala receptions, opera performances, and medal-awarding ceremonies exasperated the always efficient Milner. At one event, an observer noticed that he "kept throwing himself back in his chair and groaned audibly," muttering "We are wasting time!" To his dismay, toasts and long-winded speeches about friendship between the two great allies stretched one Anglo-Russian luncheon into an agonizing five hours. Some of the other delegates, however, thoroughly enjoyed themselves.*

Milner felt he got straight talk only when he met some reform-minded officials in Moscow, who spoke frankly of Russia's precarious state. Wilson, meanwhile, made a quick visit to the front lines, where he learned that, after two and a half years of war, Russian soldiers still

---

*"I wore the Grand Officer of the Legion of Honour and the Star and Necklace of the Bath, and my medals," wrote General Wilson in his diary. ". . . And altogether I was a fine figure of a man! I created quite a sensation at the Foreign Office dinner and the reception afterwards. . . . Lunched with the Grand Duchess. . . . Lovely palace overlooking the Neva."

did not have wire cutters. Expected to tear down German barbed wire entanglements by hand, some asked him whether British troops did the same. While the delegation was in Moscow, bread riots broke out in the streets. Inflation was out of control, and the government was printing new banknotes so fast they did not even have serial numbers.

So great was their fear of German spies gathering information from Russia's eminently bribable officialdom that, on their departure for home, the Allied delegates left Petrograd in the middle of the night, each person sacrificing a pair of shoes. These were left outside their hotel room doors to be polished, as if they expected to be in their rooms the next morning, rather than heading for their ship. After another slow-motion train journey, Milner sailed for England plunged into gloom. On the streets of the Petrograd he had left behind, there was an antiwar demonstration, and the British military attaché estimated that a full million Russian soldiers had deserted the army, most slipping quietly back to their villages.

Once home, however, in a most uncharacteristic burst of wishful thinking, Milner told the War Cabinet that "there is a great deal of exaggeration in the talk of revolution and especially about the alleged disloyalty of the army." Despite the railway bottleneck he had seen, he urged his colleagues to do all they could to bolster Russia with more military aid, perhaps accompanied by Allied technicians who could make sure the supplies reached the front and were used. He saw no alternative. An inept ally in the east was better than none, and if the Tsar's army did not have the weapons to keep on fighting the Germans, he reasoned, the danger of revolution would be far greater. "If an upheaval were to take place," he wrote, "its effect on the course of the war might be disastrous."

17

THE WORLD IS MY COUNTRY

B
Y NOW THE WAR had become the most deadly catastrophe
to strike Europe since the pandemic of the fourteenth century,
the Black Death. "I did not write the truth to you before,"
an Indian soldier named Bhagail Singh told his family from the Western Front in January 1917, his words copied by censors monitoring the
troops' morale. "Now I write the truth. . . . Consider us as having died
today or tomorrow. There is absolutely no hope of our ever returning. . . . None will survive. I pass both day and night in lamentation."
The next month another Indian wrote: "We are like goats tied to the
butcher's stake. . . . There is no hope of escape."

Unlike the bubonic plague, of course, the cataclysm ravaging the
continent was entirely man-made—and the organized opposition remained small. Although deserting soldiers in Russia were voting against
the war with their feet, more open protest there was dangerous, and
dissenters in most other countries were dealt with no less harshly. Even
had there been more freedom for protesters, however, there might not
have been many more protests. The war had everywhere unleashed
powerful national chauvinism, witch-hunts for traitors, and public fury
at any apparent lack of resolve to fight.

Only in Britain was there the political space for a substantial antiwar movement, and yet in early March 1917, just after Milner returned

from Russia, several of its members were about to become the subjects of the war's first big show trial. The attorney general, F. E. Smith, had already announced that he would prosecute the Wheeldon case personally. A blood-and-thunder right-winger, Smith was known for his love of brandy and cigars, his wit and his snobbery. A trade union leader newly elected to the House of Commons, who had not learned his way around, once asked him the way to the men's room. "Down the corridor, first right, first left and down the stairs," Smith told him. "You'll see a door marked 'Gentlemen,' but don't let that deter you."

Smith used his influence to get the trial moved from Derby to London, a better place for a public shaming designed to intimidate antiwar forces. "The persons in this case," he declared, "are a very desperate and dangerous body of people . . . bitterly hostile to this country, shelterers of fugitives from the Army, and persons who do their best to injure Great Britain in the crisis in which this country finds itself to-day."

Meanwhile, young Willie Wheeldon, on the run as a draft dodger, was captured at Southampton. The public was riveted, making the case a boon for tabloid newspaper sales: eight photographs and a banner headline, "The Lloyd George Murder Plot," filled the front page of the *Daily Sketch.* In other newspapers, Alice Wheeldon and her two daughters were shown in their long prison dresses, under the eye of a warder in the jail where they were awaiting trial. From their cells, the three women could hear regular reminders of the war: the firing of guns at a nearby artillery officers' academy. "I think this is only one of the convulsive death rattles of Capitalism," Hettie Wheeldon wrote to a friend about the ordeal they were going through. Her mother also wrote from jail, ending one letter: "Yes, we will keep agoing as you said and will break before we bend. So long, comrade, keep the flag flying . . . we will meet again." Then, beneath her signature, she added her defiance of the patriotic mania in the air: "The world is my country."

The trial took place at the Old Bailey, the columned stone courthouse topped with a no less imposing tower and dome. In the packed courtroom, reporters rubbed elbows with society figures and antiwar activists. The gist of the government's case against the Wheeldons was summed up by the attorney general: from Winnie's husband, Alf Mason, an assistant in a chemistry lab, Alice had obtained two vials of strychnine and two of curare, wrapped in cotton wool and packed in a tin box. Secret agent Herbert Booth then took the stand, testifying that

Alice had told him and his colleague Alex Gordon that Lloyd George played golf on Saturday afternoons, so it would be easy for someone to hide behind a bush on the golf course and, like South American Indian hunters, to use a blowpipe to shoot him with a poison-tipped dart.

The evidence for this unlikely assassination plot was, to say the least, thin. Aside from displaying the package of poison, the prosecution relied mainly on Booth's word, even though he had spent much less time in the Wheeldon household than his subordinate Gordon. Attempting to shock the jury, the prosecution pointed out that in one letter Winnie had called Lloyd George "that damned buggering Welsh sod." F. E. Smith was a dazzling courtroom orator, and the denunciations, sinister hints, and references to Britain's hour of danger offered up by him and three assistant prosecutors overwhelmed jury and judge. Several times, the judge praised the prosecutors, and joined them in questioning witnesses. Alice proudly affirmed that the family had indeed helped men fleeing the draft. From her defiant denials and her unwillingness to plead for mercy, it was clear that she and her "co-conspirators" knew they had little chance of persuading the jury of their innocence. During a preliminary hearing, Hettie Wheeldon had conspicuously read a newspaper, as if to indicate that there was no point in paying attention to such a farce. During the trial itself the judge admonished the prisoners for showing "levity." But when responding on the witness stand to a question about her son, who had been sentenced to 18 months in prison for evading the call-up, Alice, whom one newspaper described as "haggard and pale," acted with anything but levity. She wept.

Although what little incriminating evidence there was appeared to come mainly from the first agent to worm his way into the Wheeldon house, Alex Gordon, Smith announced "that for reasons which seem to me good I shall not call this witness before the Court." In vain did the Wheeldons insist that it was the mysterious Gordon who had requested poisons they had obtained for him. He had, they declared, promised help in getting Alice's son and other draft evaders out of the country—but he claimed that to do so he needed to poison some dogs guarding an internment camp where COs were being held. In vain did the Wheeldons' otherwise inept lawyer ask, Why did the prosecution choose not to call its key witness? He himself wanted to question Gordon, he said later, but prosecutors would not reveal the man's whereabouts.

The trial lasted less than a week. At the end, the judge made clear what verdict he expected, calling poisoning "the most dangerous and dastardly of all conspiracies." After a grueling ten-hour Saturday session of testimony and concluding arguments, he asked the jury to start deliberating immediately. They conferred for a mere half hour. Hettie Wheeldon was declared not guilty, but her mother was found guilty of conspiracy, soliciting and proposing to murder. For their role in supplying the poison, Winnie and Alf Mason were found guilty of conspiracy. Because of their youth—Alf was 24 and Winnie 23—the jury recommended mercy.

But the judge had no interest in mercy, and without delay he sentenced Alice Wheeldon to ten years' hard labor, Alf Mason to seven years, and Winnie, whom he declared under the "bad and wicked influence of your mother," to five. Alice took her sentence stoically. Guards led the prisoners away. In a final statement to the courtroom, the judge virtually condemned universal education. He was shocked, he said, that the two Wheeldon daughters were schoolteachers, yet had spoken of the prime minister in "language which would be foul indeed in the mouth of the lowest hooligan. . . . It is difficult to imagine that education is the blessing we had hoped."

As the proceedings were about to end, something occurred that would have been unheard of in any normal criminal trial. A person with no relation to the case entered the witness box and spoke to the courtroom. The judge not only gave his approval, but asked newspaper reporters present to "take note." The speaker, as elegantly dressed and well spoken as ever, was Emmeline Pankhurst.

She was there because the Wheeldon women had once been members of her Women's Social and Political Union, and now, as a loyal patriot, she was eager to dissociate herself and the WSPU from them. "My Lord," she said to the judge, "since the name of Mr. Lloyd George has been mentioned in connection with us, I want to say that at this present moment, in this crisis of our country's fortunes there is no life which we think more essential to the safety of our country than that of the Prime Minister. We feel that so strongly, that we would even endanger our own, if it were necessary, to safeguard his. And I want too, for the honour of women . . . to say the opinions of the prisoners, their actions, their mode of expressing themselves, are abhorrent to us that have devoted ourselves since the commencement of this War to patriotic work."

A mere four years before, Lloyd George had so enraged WSPU suffragettes by his opposition to votes for women that they planted a bomb in the house he was having built. "We have tried blowing him up to wake his conscience," Emmeline Pankhurst said proudly at the time. For endorsing that crime, Pankhurst had been awarded a three-year prison sentence in this very courthouse. Now the past was conveniently forgotten. And she would do a far greater favor for the prime minister, on a mission abroad, in the months to come.

After the Wheeldon trial, those on the right spoke in horror of a murder plot emanating from a sinister nexus of socialists and draft dodgers. Many on the left, however, were convinced that Booth and Gordon had framed the Wheeldons. To some war supporters, too, the conspiracy sounded less plausible than the plot of the latest John Buchan novel, and several MPs asked embarrassingly pointed questions in Parliament. Like the Sacco-Vanzetti case in the United States, the Wheeldon affair has continued to stir strong emotions ever since.[*] And it raises a question: Why, in the midst of a terrible war, did the British government devote so much effort to prosecuting this unlucky family on such far-fetched charges?

Intimidating the antiwar movement was, of course, the main motive, but a wide array of personal ambitions were also involved. Attorney General Smith, a holdover from the Asquith government, leapt at the chance to prove his loyalty by personally prosecuting the case against the new prime minister's alleged would-be murderers. Intense rivalry among proliferating counterintelligence agencies further inflamed matters. The military, Basil Thomson at Scotland Yard, and the Ministry of Munitions spy unit were all engaged in a fierce turf war —and an investigation that won a dramatic conviction in court would be a boon. Within the Ministry of Munitions unit itself, in the weeks before he ingratiated himself with the Wheeldons, Alex Gordon felt his job was at risk, for he had slipped up badly on a previous assignment. From Manchester, he had reported that all was calm, only to see the

---

[*] In recent decades alone, it has inspired Pat Barker's novel *The Eye in the Door,* two plays, two nonfiction books, a BBC television drama, and a volume of poems.

city's trolley car drivers promptly go out on strike. The Wheeldon case offered a chance for him to make up for his mistake and regain favor.

Meanwhile, the ambitious Thomson found himself in an ambiguous position. If there *was* a murder plot against the prime minister, he wanted credit for foiling it. But he was equally eager to show that the Ministry of Munitions spycatchers who nabbed the culprits were an unreliable bunch, no match for his Scotland Yard professionals who deserved to take over their work. (Soon after the Wheeldon trial, they did.) In one of several self-aggrandizing memoirs he wrote after the war, Thomson managed to make both claims, while hinting that the idea of the "poison plot" originated with Alex Gordon. Describing the agent as "a thin, cunning-looking man of about thirty, with long, greasy black hair," he added, "I had an uneasy feeling that he himself might have acted as what the French call an *agent provocateur.*"

Thomson was right. If not for wartime paranoia, the prosecution's story of a plan to kill the prime minister with a blowpipe and dart would have been quickly discredited because the key witness who claimed to have first heard it, Gordon, never testified. Little wonder, because he was a prosecutor's nightmare. Only after the arrest of the Wheeldons, it appears, did the prosecution team learn that Gordon was not his real name, that he had a police record, and that he had once been found criminally insane.

His subsequent short career as a spy revealed him as an unabashed *agent provocateur* who relished the role. The very day Mason and the Wheeldons were sentenced, an alarmed intelligence operative informed Milner and other top officials that "Gordon went to Leicester and Coventry and offered poison and bombs to the A.S.E. [a labor union] man there." More reports of this sort kept coming in. Clearly, if Gordon continued traveling around Britain offering people poison, sooner or later he would be exposed, humiliatingly unraveling the case against the Wheeldons. The authorities swiftly found a solution: Gordon was put on board a ship at Plymouth with £100 and a one-way ticket to Cape Town.

The Wheeldons' friend and political comrade, the former lion tamer John S. Clarke, liked to write inscriptions for the tombstones of his political enemies even while they were still alive. His "Epitaph on Alex Gordon," published in the newspaper he continued to edit in hiding, the *Socialist,* became a favorite recital piece at labor gatherings:

Stop! stranger, thou art near the spot
Marked by this cross metallic,
Where buried deep doth lie and rot,
The corpse of filthy Alex.

And maggot-worms in swarms below,
Compete with one another,
In shedding tears of bitter woe,
To mourn — not eat — a brother.

Less than a week after the Wheeldons were sentenced, the known world turned upside down.

"During the afternoon of March 13, 1917," Winston Churchill would later remember, "the Russian Embassy in London informed us that they were no longer in contact with Petrograd. For some days the capital had been a prey to disorders. . . . Now suddenly . . . there was a silence. . . . The great Power with whom we had been in such intimate comradeship, without whom all plans were meaningless, was stricken dumb. With Russian effective aid, all the Allied fronts could attack together. Without that aid it might well be that the War was lost."

Within days of Milner and his delegation's leaving the Russian capital, demonstrators began marching in the snowy streets, protesting against the endless war and shortages of food and fuel. They shouted revolutionary slogans, broke shop windows, and sang "The Internationale." And that was only the beginning. The marchers' ranks were soon strengthened by some of the 200,000 munitions workers who now went out on strike. Bitter fighting broke out on barricaded, freezing boulevards, and the Tsar's government lost control of the city. A unit of troops mutinied, killing their commanding officer, and put themselves and their rifles at the service of the rebels. The rest of the capital garrison, ordered to suppress the mutineers, instead joined them, rampaging into government buildings and camping defiantly in palace ballrooms. An armored car rolled through the city with FREEDOM! chalked on its side. Crews of Russian naval vessels in the harbor mutinied as well.

It was the kind of upheaval in the ranks that every general in this war had always dreaded. By March 17 the Tsar had been forced to abdicate, a new Provisional Government was in power, and a few days later, at the palace where Milner had visited them the previous month, Tsar Nicholas II and his family were placed under house arrest. Petrograd's main prison and the secret police archive were set ablaze. Across the vast country, jubilant soldiers and civilians began ripping down flags and smashing statues and plaques with the double-headed eagle emblem of the Romanov dynasty. More than 300 years of Romanov rule were suddenly history.

The Germans were delighted, while the dismayed Allies took cold comfort when Russia's Provisional Government, under strong pressure from them, announced it would remain in the war. That promise meant little, however, for the very municipal government of Petrograd —in a process repeated in some other cities—came under the control of a much more radical soviet, or council, which began issuing its own orders to the army. Among them, men in all military units were to elect their own soviets, a dramatic break in the centuries-old chain of command. The already high rate of desertion only increased, sailors lynched dozens of naval officers, and on March 27, 1917, the Petrograd Soviet declared that the peoples of Europe should "take into their own hands the decision of the question of war and peace." It urged the workers of Germany and Austria-Hungary to join their Russian comrades in refusing to fight in the war of "kings, landowners, and bankers." A Russian War Ministry official confessed to the British military attaché that army discipline was collapsing: when replacement troops were sent forward, so many deserted that less than one man in four reached the front. The army was still fighting, but at this rate, how long would that last?

Radical opponents of the war across the continent were thrilled with the news from Petrograd. "The wonderful events in Russia," wrote Rosa Luxemburg from the German prison cell where her antiwar protests had landed her, "affect me like an elixir. . . . I am absolutely certain that a new epoch is starting now and that the war cannot last much longer." The conscientious objectors serving time in London's Wormwood Scrubs were delighted that as one of its first acts, the Provisional Government had granted amnesty to all political prisoners—including more than 800 war resisters in Russian jails.

Emrys Hughes, the future husband of Keir Hardie's daughter, was in prison in Wales when another CO furtively handed him a newspaper page wrapped in a handkerchief; he turned his back to the peep-hole in his cell door and read the electrifying news: "The old order was dead, a new society was being born . . . the end of the war was in sight." Bertrand Russell hailed the upheaval in Russia as "a stupendous event . . . more cheering than anything that has happened since the war be-gan." As March ended, nearly 12,000 Londoners packed a rally in the Royal Albert Hall to show their support for the Russians who had over-thrown the Tsar; 5,000 more were turned away at the door. It was the first time in over a year that a dissident public meeting in the city had not been broken up by patriot gangs. "I longed to shout at them at the end to come with me and pull down Wormwood Scrubs," wrote Rus-sell. "They would have done it. . . . A meeting of the kind would have been utterly impossible a month ago."

"I remember the miners," the Labour politician Aneurin Bevan re-called years later, "when they heard that the Tsarist tyranny had been overthrown, rushing to meet each other in the streets with tears stream-ing down their cheeks, shaking hands." May Day gatherings brought more celebrations: a crowd one left-wing newspaper claimed at 70,000 in Glasgow, a big peace march in London, and a rally in Liverpool that featured actual Russians: 150 bewildered sailors who happened to be in port and found themselves greeted as heroes. In Manchester, the head of the transport workers' union declared, "Revolutions like charity be-gin at home."

France saw strikes and the largest May Day demonstrations of the war years, with red flags flying and speakers calling for peace. An Amer-ican correspondent on the Eastern Front watched through his field glasses as Russian and German enlisted men met in no man's land to communicate in sign language: the Russians blowing across their open palms to show that the Tsar had been blown away, the Germans thrust-ing their bayonets into the earth. Could this finally be the moment that Hardie had hoped for so fervently, when soldiers on both sides re-fused to continue killing each other? Sylvia Pankhurst jubilantly called the change in Russia "the first ray of dawn, after a long and painful night."

At sea, as on land, nothing was going well for the Allies. Germany's ramped-up U-boat war had severely disrupted the vital transatlantic lifeline and sowed fear among sailors and passengers. For them, the danger of being sunk by a torpedo was magnified by the fact that the explosion could crack a ship's engine room boilers, releasing below decks a high-pressure blast of scalding steam. An officer on a merchant ship taking supplies to Russia reported that some officials he was carrying stayed on deck, near the lifeboats, for most of the voyage. The area just southwest of Ireland, crossed by ships approaching most major English and Irish ports, became what Churchill called "a veritable cemetery of British shipping."

Once a submarine had shown its location by firing a torpedo, a Royal Navy ship could attack it by dropping depth charges—explosives set to go off underwater, at the level the submarine was thought to be. But seldom was a warship close by, for it was impossible for them to escort each of the thousands of cargo vessels crossing the Atlantic. Few U-boats were sunk and, ominously, the Germans were increasing the size of their submarine fleet. Senior Admiralty officers had long resisted one possible solution: sending merchant ships in convoys, guarded by a screen of destroyers or other small warships. Convoys were cumbersome, limited to the speed of the slowest ship, and ports became clogged when dozens of ships arrived together. The navy chiefs, writes war historian Trevor Wilson, "were imbued with a proud tradition, according to which going hunting for the enemy seemed a proper course and chugging along in support of merchantmen did not." The navy preferred to be, as it were, cavalrymen of the sea. But wiser heads eventually prevailed. Milner, now wielding unprecedented powers supervising Britain's entire war economy, was acutely aware of its dependence on shipping and helped persuade Lloyd George to adopt the convoy system. On May 10, 1917, 17 merchant vessels and their naval escorts set off for England from Gibraltar, and, at a time when more than 300 ships a month were being torpedoed, not a single ship in the convoy was sunk.

Convoys made life far more difficult for U-boats, for if one did torpedo a cargo ship, fast destroyers with the convoy could rush to the scene to drop depth charges. And with electric engines limiting their underwater travel to a mere eight knots, less than a quarter of a destroyer's speed, submarines had trouble getting away. Before the year was over, more than half of Britain's overseas trade would be carried by ships in convoy. U-boat "kills" dropped dramatically. The submarine, though still much feared, was not going to win the war. Germany's great gamble at sea had failed.

The German high command had long known that unrestricted U-boat warfare would risk bringing the United States into the war. And so it did—but far sooner than the Germans had planned for. In March, the American press trumpeted news of the notorious "Zimmermann Telegram," gleefully decoded and given to Washington by British intelligence, in which Arthur Zimmermann, the German foreign minister, foolishly tried to induce Mexico to join the war on the German side by promising it Texas, New Mexico, and Arizona. Soon after, U-boats sank three American merchant ships, drowning many sailors and prompting an outcry in Congress and the press. On April 7, 1917, the United States declared war on Germany. Even though everyone knew it would take nearly a year before significant numbers of American troops could be trained and reach Europe's battlefields, the boost in morale to Britain, France, and Italy was incalculable. In addition, the large fleet of American destroyers quickly joined British warships in escorting convoys. For the first time in its history, the United States was committing itself to waging large-scale land warfare on the continent of Europe. The world's balance of power would never be the same again.

On the heels of its failed U-boat warfare bet, the Germans made an even riskier gamble. Although Russia's armies were in a state of near collapse, the Central Powers still had to keep more than a million soldiers on the long Eastern Front. If, however, Russia fully imploded in revolution and ceased to fight, the German high command could move most of those troops to France and Belgium, launch a decisive offensive to capture Paris, and send the Allied armies reeling before the Americans could arrive in force. The Germans needed, therefore, to ignite further upheaval in Russia.

From the beginning of the war, German agents had been in touch with the most extreme group of dedicated Russian revolutionaries, the Bolsheviks, many of whose leaders were in exile in Switzerland. The Bolsheviks wanted to overthrow capitalism and militarism everywhere, including Germany. But what mattered more to Berlin was that these Russians were determined to take their country out of the war. The Bolsheviks were hamstrung, however, because their exiled leadership was cut off from sympathizers at home. The faction's dominant figure, Vladimir Ilyich Lenin, was living with his wife in a single rented room in a shabby working-class apartment in Zurich, next to a sausage factory. He spent part of each day at the public library, researching and writing acerbic articles and pamphlets attacking rivals on the left and predicting the imminent demise of capitalism, but, more than a thousand miles away from his followers, was in no position to seize power.

In early April 1917 the German government provided what later became famous as the "sealed train" to the Bolshevik leadership. It carried them across Germany, from the Swiss border to the Baltic Sea, where they could embark for Petrograd and make their revolution. The 32 Russians in threadbare clothes who took the journey would, within a mere six months, leapfrog from penniless exile to the very pinnacle of political power in a vast realm that stretched from the Baltic to the Pacific.

As the train steamed through the night, it carried, as escorts to the revolutionaries, two German officers—one of whom spoke fluent Russian but was under orders to conceal it, all the better to report overheard conversations back to Berlin. The exuberant passengers sang leftist songs, but when the train pulled into Mannheim, one of the German officers angrily demanded that they be quiet. At Frankfurt, some German soldiers on the station platform heard that the train was full of Russian revolutionaries and rushed up to talk. Although their commanders ordered them away, the encounter left the Russians optimistic that Germany, the industrial titan of the continent, was as ripe for revolution as their own backward peasant land.

For most of the journey Lenin stood by a train window, thumbs in the armholes of his vest. One thing above all struck him about the fields and villages the train rolled through: there were no young men. They were all at the front.

The escort officers handed out sandwiches and beer; Lenin's wife brewed tea for all on a portable kerosene burner. Finally the train reached the Baltic, where the Bolsheviks boarded a ferry and then traveled on through Sweden and Finland to Russia, where party organizers assembled a huge crowd to greet them at Petrograd's Finland Station. In a country ravaged by war and now throwing off centuries of autocracy, the party's message of "peace, land, and bread" had immediate, powerful resonance. And on a war-weary continent it could be highly contagious. In Churchill's words, Germany had sent Lenin on his way to Russia "like a plague bacillus." It remained to be seen how fast the bacillus would multiply.

What Churchill saw as a bacillus, Britain's war resisters saw as their deliverance. Few of them cared about the differences among various left-wing factions in Russia; they simply hoped, above all, that if popular pressure would at last force one country to completely stop fighting, others would follow.

In the meantime, the war was putting ever more COs into the gray uniforms covered with arrows worn by British prisoners. Among them was Stephen Hobhouse. In each of the prisons he was in, he found long rows of cells, four or five stories of them, facing each other across an open area. "Across the central space at first-floor level is stretched a wire netting to catch any unhappy man trying to commit suicide from above." Every cell had a peephole in the door "through which at times could be seen the sinister eye of the warder spying on the inmate." The warders sometimes padded silently along the corridors in felt slippers, to catch the prisoners unawares. Two of the day's meals consisted only of porridge, dry bread, and salt; the third was mostly potatoes. Each day began with emptying your cell's latrine bucket. You were allowed to send and receive one letter a month—but none at all for the first two months. There were regular chapel services, but once "while I was singing the *Te Deum* and looking round about me to get a sense of fellowship with the other faces, the warder's harsh voice broke in with 'Number B.27, look to your front.'"

Hobhouse had encouragement from an unexpected source. "Every soldier realises that mental suffering—such as is caused by solitary confinement etc.—requires infinitely more courage to bear than does physical suffering," wrote his brother Paul, who had twice been wounded at the front and was on his way back to the trenches. "However much we may disagree as to methods, I pray you may have some alleviation from your present lot and keep in good health for all the reconstruction after the war. Good luck to you."

Stephen had been thrown into solitary because he refused to obey the "rule of silence," by which prisoners were forbidden to speak to each other. Almost all COs worked out subterfuges to communicate anyway: muttering under their breath or tapping the water pipes that ran through each cell block, turning them into a Morse-code party-line telephone. But Hobhouse would have none of this. "Stephen had a very . . . *awkward* kind of conscience," recalled a fellow prisoner. "The spirit of love requires that I should speak to my fellow-prisoners," he wrote to his wife, Rosa, "the spirit of truth that I should speak to them openly." And so, he told the warders, he planned to talk to his comrades whenever he felt like it.

From then on, the materials for the mailbags he sewed as required prison labor were brought to his cell. And when the men were allowed out for daily exercise, Hobhouse was kept separated from the others. From the front in France, his brother Paul sent a message to the family: "Tell Stephen not to lose heart."

Hobhouse's integrity evidently touched even his keepers. On one of the monthly visits he was allowed, he was talking to Rosa under a guard's supervision, with just a table between them instead of the usual double set of bars or wire screens. As the visit ended, she asked if she could kiss her husband goodbye. "The warder bluntly refused." Stephen was marched back to his cell. Soon afterward, he recalled, "I heard a key in the lock, and the tyrant of our visit came in, and, in a way that indicated how deeply moved he was, begged me to believe that he felt as unhappy over the incident as we must be feeling. . . . My faith in humanity was renewed."

When his mother paid her first visit, she was driven to the prison by the family chauffeur, a former coachman, who entered with her. "Sorry to see you like this, Mr. Stephen," he said.

The immensely energetic Margaret Hobhouse was accustomed to getting her way in the world. Though no pacifist, she loved her son and was deeply worried about what prison conditions might do to someone with a history of nervous breakdowns before the war who was now experiencing nausea and digestive problems. So she turned to someone she thought could help. When as a baby Stephen Hobhouse had been baptized at a small country church near his family's Somerset estate, his godfather had been unable to attend, and so, following an old custom, a close family friend stood in as proxy godfather. The friend was Alfred Milner.

Milner listened carefully to Margaret Hobhouse and did his best. Files in the British National Archives are filled with memos and letters about Hobhouse's case, to Milner and functionaries below him, from bureaucrats scrambling to show they were taking the minister's concern seriously. From the prison at Wormwood Scrubs came typed excerpts copied from a letter Hobhouse had written to Rosa. From an official with an indecipherable signature came this shrewd evaluation: "If it were possible to discharge him from the Army on medical grounds I do not think he would be likely to become a dangerous peace agitator. He is a pure visionary. . . . He has a certain following who admire him for his sufferings for the cause. But his consequence would probably be diminished rather than increased if it were found possible to put an end to his 'martyrdom.'" Finally, from Lord Derby, now secretary for war, came a stubborn letter to Milner commenting acidly on conscientious objectors ("the majority of them are neurotics") and insisting that he could not release Hobhouse because "he absolutely declines to be examined by the Doctors."

Had he known that his mother had intervened on his behalf, Stephen Hobhouse would certainly have been appalled. She did something else as well, although neither he nor the public was aware of the full story. As Stephen described it, "Though she thought her eldest son wrong-headed and foolish in his extreme form of conscientious objection, she became more and more convinced of the cruel injustice of the hardships which he and the roughly 1,350 war resisters now in prison were enduring. She conceived the idea of collecting the facts and of publishing them with a reasoned appeal in a book."

I Appeal unto Caesar appeared in mid-1917, written, the cover said, "by Mrs. Henry Hobhouse." It rapidly sold 18,000 copies, and hundreds of trade union branches and other civic groups supported her appeal for the release of imprisoned COs. The book was taken seriously in large part because Margaret Hobhouse supported the war — she was a Conservative, the mother of two sons at the front, and the wife of a prominent and wealthy man active in Church of England affairs. To give it even more respectability, *I Appeal unto Caesar* had an introduction by the renowned Oxford classicist Gilbert Murray and endorsements by four eminent peers. None of them were opponents of the war, nor were many of those who reviewed it favorably. "This little book has stirred me deeply," wrote the novelist John Galsworthy in the *Observer.* "I urge one and all to read it."

Only more than half a century later did a Canadian scholar, Jo Vellacott, discover who secretly ghostwrote the book: Bertrand Russell. Margaret Hobhouse, after all, was not a writer, and Russell was a brilliant one; correspondence between them (which she asked him to destroy, although he did not do so) shows that both understood the book would have far more credibility if she were thought to be the author.

Russell was not only a socialist and the acting chairman of the No-Conscription Fellowship, he was also an ardent freethinker. Was he amused as he put his supple pen to writing a text that ostensibly came from a pillar of the ruling class and a supporter of the war and organized religion? It appears he was, for he could not resist slipping in a few sly tongue-in-cheek passages. While supposedly commenting on the misguided beliefs of the imprisoned COs, *I Appeal unto Caesar* says:

> They maintain, paradoxical as it may appear, that victory in war is not so important to the nation's welfare as many other things. It must be confessed that in this contention they are supported by certain sayings of our Lord, such as, "What shall it profit a man if he gain the whole world and lose his own soul?" Doubtless such statements are to be understood figuratively, but the history of religion shows that founders of religions are always apt to be understood literally by some of their more slavish followers. . . . They believe . . . that hatred can be overcome by love, a view which appears to derive support from a somewhat hasty reading of the Sermon on the Mount.

No one detected Russell as the ghostwriter of these double entendres. Milner even gave a copy of the book to the King. In gratitude to Russell, Margaret Hobhouse made an anonymous contribution to the No-Conscription Fellowship. Russell himself, lips sealed, offered this comment in an article under his own name in the NCF's journal: "As a result largely of Mrs. Hobhouse's 'I Appeal Unto Caesar,' many influential people who formerly had only contempt and derision for the C.O. have now come to believe that the policy of indefinitely prolonged imprisonment is not the wisest." Stephen Hobhouse and his like-minded comrades, however, remained in prison.

Under Haig's command, the roughly one and a half million British soldiers on the Western Front continued to wage war to little visible effect. Other than tens of thousands of deaths, the spring and early summer of 1917 included a hapless cavalry attack, in which doomed British horsemen rode off into a blizzard singing "The Eton Boating

Song," and the simultaneous detonation of 19 mines containing nearly a million pounds of explosives beneath German trenches in Belgium, producing what is believed to have been the loudest single man-made sound in history up to that moment.

Hoping for a path out of the endless bloodshed, millions around the world read the papers each day for news about Russia. Although the Provisional Government had not withdrawn from the war, it had proclaimed something that didn't yet exist in Britain: universal suffrage. The more radical Petrograd Soviet had gone further, issuing a call, after Lenin's return to Russia, for "peace without annexations or indemnities [reparations], on the basis of the self determination of peoples." Antiwar forces took encouragement as this spirit seemed to be echoed elsewhere. Although scoffed at, ironically, by both the British government and the Kaiser, the German parliament in mid-1917 passed a resolution, by an almost two-to-one margin, calling for a peace agreement without annexations or indemnities. Pope Benedict XV put forth a somewhat foggy peace plan echoing the idea and suggesting that all occupied territories be evacuated. In addition, there were occasional ambiguous peace overtures to the Allies—always rebuffed or ignored —from Germany's less enthusiastic junior partners, Austria-Hungary and Ottoman Turkey. All this kept hope in the air.

Addressing them as "my sisters," Charlotte Despard wrote an open letter to Russian women, embracing them with the same exuberance she had shown for so many other causes: "I am with you—we are one." If the Russian people could overthrow an autocracy, enfranchise everyone, and set up local councils of workers and soldiers, why could Britain not do the same? She and many others made plans to meet in the northern industrial city of Leeds in early June 1917 for the Great Labour, Socialist and Democratic Convention.

Milner, who kept a close eye on such matters, was dismayed at news of the conference, trumpeted in a leaflet titled "Follow Russia." He sent Lloyd George two clippings from a labor newspaper, underlining passages that particularly alarmed him, one calling for the people "of this and all the other belligerent countries to take matters into their own hands as the people of Russia have already done."

"My dear Prime Minister. . . . I think there is still time to instruct the Press . . . not to 'boom' the Leeds proceedings too much," he wrote. "And I fear the time is very near at hand, when we shall have to take some strong steps to stop the 'rot' in this country, unless we wish to 'follow Russia' into impotence and dissolution."

In Leeds, meanwhile, some 3,000 would-be revolutionaries, meeting in an enormous brick movie theater with an ornate Gothic façade and organ, kicked off the proceedings with a rousing rendition of "The Red Flag" and a moment of silence in memory of Keir Hardie. All the major figures on the British left were there. Many delegates were still outraged about the Wheeldon frame-up, and one speaker railed against the "thousands of 'Alex Gordons' in the country." And, indeed, undercover operatives from the various competing intelligence agencies were in the audience. In a report to the War Cabinet, one noted, with satisfaction, that some Leeds hotels had canceled bookings for those coming to the conference, who had to stay in the homes of local socialists instead. "There can be no doubt on the part of any one who is familiar with . . . the Leeds Conference," the agent wrote, "that it is intended to lead, *if possible, to a revolution in this country.*" The resolution adopted by the delegates that most shocked him, so much so that he underlined its key phrase, called for "the complete *independence of Ireland, India and Egypt.*"

The example of Russia, repeatedly invoked, raised everyone's hopes. Despard, in her trademark black mantilla, black robe, and sandals, gave a militant speech and was elected to a 13-member "provisional committee" charged with setting up "Councils of Workmen's and Soldiers' Delegates" throughout Britain; she herself undertook to organize such a soviet in Newcastle. The delegates voted to send representatives to Russia in a show of solidarity. And Sylvia Pankhurst suggested to the crowd that the provisional committee to which she, too, was elected might someday be a Provisional Government of Great Britain.

Bertrand Russell received a huge ovation when he spoke about "the thousand men now in prison in this country because they believe in the brotherhood of men. . . . They who had to begin their battle when the world was very dark, now have the knowledge that the world looks no longer so dark as it did, and the hope and new happiness which has come into the lives of all of us, that also is with them in prison." He was more optimistic than he had been since the war began: "The control of events is rapidly passing out of the hands of the militarists of all countries . . . ," he wrote a few days later. "A new spirit is abroad."

18

DROWNING ON LAND

I F THERE WERE ever a war that should have had an early, negotiated peace, it was this one. Before the conflict began, the major powers may have been in rival alliances, but they had all been getting along reasonably well, exchanging royal visits, not squabbling over borders, and trading heavily with one another, and their corporations were investing in joint business ventures together. Could there ever have been a more improbable chain of events than the one from the assassinations at Sarajevo to an entire continent in flames a mere six weeks later? And why, in that case, could it not be undone?

The tragedy was that no one could come up with a peace formula that satisfied both sides. "No indemnities" attracted the Germans — but not France or Belgium, which had seen thousands of square miles of their territory reduced to charred rubble and tens of thousands of their citizens rudely conscripted to work in German war factories. Withdrawal of troops from occupied land appealed to France, Russia, Italy, Serbia, and Belgium, all of which were partly, wholly (Serbia), or almost wholly (Belgium) occupied, but not to Germany or Austria-Hungary, whose troops were fighting almost exclusively on enemy territory, much of which German expansionists yearned to acquire permanently. Restoration of colonies to their prewar owners — another ingredient of some peace plans — appealed to Germany but not to

Britain, France, Belgium, and South Africa, battling their way to control of Germany's potentially lucrative African possessions. On top of this, for the Allies the humiliation and suffering of being occupied, for the Central Powers the experience of being half starved by the blockade, and for both sides the unrelenting high-pitched propaganda that portrayed the enemy as unparalleled monsters, left the general public in all the warring countries—save Russia, now deep in revolutionary turmoil—so filled with rage at the other side that negotiations seemed politically unthinkable.

A further obstacle, one that accompanies many wars, also loomed. Men had been maimed and killed in such unimaginable numbers that any talk of a compromise peace risked seeming to dishonor them and render their sacrifices meaningless. Or this, at least, was the feeling when there still seemed hope of victory. But could that change if the Western Front deadlock continued and victory—for either side—came to seem impossible? Then, at last, might public opinion see the madness of the war? Especially in Britain, where they were most numerous, this was the hope that peace activists clung to.

The next attempt to break the stalemate on the Western Front came from France, which in April 1917 launched a major attack. It failed spectacularly: in the space of a few days, 30,000 French soldiers were killed and 100,000 wounded, gaining a few miles in one spot and in some places nothing at all. It was the Battle of the Somme all over again; the only thing different was the nationality of the troops being mowed down.

What followed, however, was something new: a rash of mutinies—the high command preferred the term "collective indiscipline"—that swept through the French army. Troops resting in reserve areas refused orders to return to the front, sang "The Internationale," and flaunted the red flag. One group of soldiers hijacked a train and tried to drive it to Paris. An infantry regiment took over a town and refused to move. Troops in a few units even elected soviets. Rebellions broke out in more than 30 divisions. It was not that troops deserted entirely, as in Russia; indeed, many of the mutineers stayed at their posts in the trenches, simply refusing to take part in suicidal new attacks. Clearly, though, the French army was almost paralyzed. The high command had to tell its British allies what was happening, in strictest confidence. Haig went to Paris, met with French leaders, and in his obdurate way insisted that attacks must continue. But he was worried: "Revolution is never very deep under the surface in France," he wrote to the secretary for war in London. "The crust is very thin just now."

The French general who ordered the ill-fated offensive lost his job, and a new commander, General Philippe Pétain, immediately set to work. He improved the rest billets behind the lines, upgraded the army's food, and increased leaves. Touring his front line, he spoke to every mutinous regiment, promising an end to attacks that needlessly wasted lives. And he was, by military standards of the time, very sparing in meting out punishment: although 3,427 men were convicted of mutiny, normally a capital offense, only 49 were shot. Despite hints of problems, the Germans never realized the extent of disarray in the army facing them—nor did readers of censored British and French newspapers. But Pétain's success at containing the upheaval came at a price: his still-restive army simply could not be ordered to undertake any major new attack. While he began the long work of rebuilding French military discipline and morale, he pressed his British allies hard to distract the Germans with a major assault of their own.

Should there be another offensive at all? Of course! Haig had no doubts, believing that the Germans' "breaking point may be reached this year," as he told his generals, his confidence fueled by a new stream of reports from his relentlessly optimistic intelligence chief, General Charteris. Germany was riddled with strikes and unrest, Charteris assured him, troop morale was falling, the army was on its last legs. To be sure that both his boss and the British cabinet would share this impression, before Haig and Lloyd George paid visits to a compound of German POWs, Charteris ordered all able-bodied prisoners removed, so that only the wounded or sickly-looking remained.

The small Belgian city of Ypres was by now the most ravaged in Western Europe. It lay at the center of a bulge of British-held territory that for several years had been shelled by the Germans from three sides. Its famous Cloth Hall was a jagged shell; its brick and stone buildings and cobblestone streets were in ruins. Tens of thousands of troops from all corners of the British Empire found shelter where they could, often in cellars. The entire salient was honeycombed with narrow-gauge trolley tracks on which carts of bullets, shells, food, and bandages made their way to the front. It was from this battered wasteland that Haig planned to launch his next big assault.

The War Cabinet was uneasy. The Russian army, which the new Provisional Government could barely manage to supply with food, was so depleted, British planners calculated, that Germany could afford to move up to 30 divisions to the west. When Haig predicted success for his offensive, Milner wrote, in an acid memo to his colleagues, "The argument seems to be that, since we can't overcome the unreinforced Germans, *ergo* we can reasonably hope to overcome them when [they are] strengthened by 30 divisions. Really lunatic." Lloyd George was equally dubious, but Haig was so well entrenched politically that the prime minister was never really able to assert control over the army high command. He would rail at the generals in his memoirs, published long after the war: "Their brains were cluttered with useless lumber, packed in every niche and corner."

In the end, no matter how lunatic Haig's strategy, the War Cabinet could offer no realistic alternative. In mid-June the field marshal laid out his plans in London. "He spread on a table or desk a large map," Lloyd George remembered, "and made a dramatic use of both his hands to demonstrate how he proposed to sweep up the enemy — first the right hand brushing along the surface irresistibly, and then came the left, his outer finger ultimately touching the German frontier with the nail across." Vanished was last year's talk about attrition as success; Haig was once again dreaming of a breakthrough. After smashing open the German line, the long-waiting cavalry would stream through the gap, and British troops would swing to the left to seize the medieval Belgian city of Bruges. When cabinet members visited the front, Haig's officers took them up a specially built observation tower that looked out over the land he expected to capture.

Given the number of men being moved into position, there would be no surprise. "Everybody in my hotel knows the date of the offensive down to the lift boy," observed the chief of the Imperial General Staff on a visit to Paris. As the launch date grew near, Haig seemed to interpret everything around him in military terms of obedience and duty. When Lady Haig told him that she was expecting their third child, he wrote back, without any trace of jest or irony, "How proud you must feel that you are *doing your duty* at this time by having a baby and

thereby setting a good example to all other females!" Convinced that
the forthcoming battle would cement his place in history, he suggested
to his wife that she write his biography.

In England, where German bombing raids and the sense that a great
battle was in the offing kept chauvinist fervor boiling, many people
with German names found it politic to change them—including the
royal family. Because Queen Victoria had married a German prince,
the British monarchy was officially the House of Saxe-Coburg-Gotha.
On July 17, 1917, two weeks before Haig's new offensive, a proclamation from Buckingham Palace announced that henceforth the family
would be known as the House of Windsor.

When he heard the news, Kaiser Wilhelm II is said to have remarked
that he was going to the theater to see a performance of *The Merry
Wives of Saxe-Coburg-Gotha*.

As 1917 wore on, antiwar rallies drew larger crowds. Charlotte Despard
and several other women formed a new organization, the Women's
Peace Crusade. "I should like the words 'alien' and 'foreigner' to be
banished from the language," she said in one speech. "We are all members of the same family." Despard traveled the country speaking and
visiting the families of COs to keep their spirits up. One hundred thousand readers bought copies of a peace pamphlet she wrote.

Christabel Pankhurst was horrified. "I consider the Pacifists a disease . . . a very deadly disease," she declared in *Britannia* this summer,
"which you will find has afflicted every dead nation of the past." The
spectacle of British labor unions daring to strike in wartime laid bare
her authoritarianism: "Could you listen to an orchestra in which each
person played according to his own ideas or the ideas of a committee
instead of answering to the beat of the conductor?" she thundered in a
speech. "Well, it is just the same in industry. There must be authority,
control, discipline."

Where Pankhurst could only bluster about control, Milner made
sure action was taken. Every working-class gathering should be monitored, he wrote in August to the home secretary, who was in charge of
police and prisons, lest it "turn into a pacifist and revolutionary meeting." Within the next several months, the police staged some 30 raids
on pacifist and socialist groups, seizing files, printing equipment, and
crates of pamphlets, and sabotaging those printing presses they left be-

hind. The government opened the mail of antiwar dissidents and quietly made sure that prowar publications and the printers of officially approved propaganda received almost all of the tightening supply of newsprint.

With some exceptions, however, the authorities did not jail people speaking out against the war or ban meetings. Seldom, points out the historian Brock Millman, "did the government prohibit, where it could discourage, or discourage where it was safe or politic to ignore." When some officials were considering prosecuting George Bernard Shaw for an antiwar article he had written, the home secretary successfully argued against it: "Shaw will make the most [of it] both here and in America. . . . But the very fact that we allow such matter to emanate from England would be proof of the lightness of our censorship and an indication of . . . strength."

And strength, in the end, was what the prowar forces had. Despite the heady resolutions at Leeds, efforts to organize workers' and soldiers' soviets came to naught. When Bertrand Russell led a meeting to form a soviet in London, Basil Thomson asked the jingoistic *Daily Express* to print the address. Several hundred hostile demonstrators, singing "Rule Britannia," stormed into the Congregational church where the "soviet" was meeting. The crowd broke down a door, shattered windows, ripped out the church's gas and water pipes, and left several delegates injured. It was only when someone told the police that Russell was the brother of an earl that they rushed to protect him from women waving boards studded with rusty nails. "The mob is a terrible thing when it wants blood," Russell wrote that day. Despard had no better luck with the workers' and soldiers' soviet she tried to convene at Newcastle. The only visible soldiers were rowdy off-duty ones who broke up the gathering with their fists.

Critics could point out, of course, that Despard and Russell were quite far from being either workers or soldiers. But the real cause of their failure was that Britain was a democracy, however imperfect a one. Unlike Russia, there was little pent-up popular hunger for revolution, and the government waging the war had been elected. The radical Leeds conference made the headlines, but a more accurate gauge of British working-class feeling was to be found at a meeting in Manchester this same year where delegates representing nearly two million union members voted by a margin of more than five to one that Britain should carry on the war until Germany was fully defeated.

Some of those prowar trade unionists flexed their muscles in a small but telling confrontation at the Scottish port of Aberdeen at the beginning of the summer of 1917. The Leeds conference had picked representatives to go to Russia as a show of solidarity, but when the delegates boarded a ship for the journey, they found an unexpected complication. On hand were two leaders of the right-leaning National Sailors' and Firemen's Union—one, its president, was a stalwart of Milner's British Workers' League—who informed them that the ship's crew would not sail unless they disembarked. With several thousand of its members dead from German U-boat attacks, the union was not in the antiwar camp. After a brief standoff, the delegates were escorted down the gangplank.

On the dock, however, these same union leaders warmly welcomed two passengers also heading for Russia: Jessie Kenney, a longtime suffragette, and Emmeline Pankhurst. Pankhurst had asked Lloyd George for permission to "explain to the Russian people the opinions as to the war and the conditions of peace held by us as patriotic British women," and the prime minister enthusiastically agreed. The Russian army might be faltering, but it was still tying down hundreds of thousands of German troops who would otherwise be in France and Belgium. Pankhurst, he hoped, could buck up the spirits of war-minded Russians and woo some of those tempted by revolution, for she had indisputable credentials as a rebel and troublemaker and was well known in Russia, where her autobiography had been translated and widely read.

When Pankhurst arrived in Petrograd, the moderate Provisional Government was still in precarious control, but the Bolsheviks, bolstered by the arrival of their leaders from Switzerland after the trip in the sealed train, were gaining strength. Red flags flew everywhere, and even the staff of the deluxe hotel where she was staying, the Astoria, went on strike while she was there. "I came to Petrograd with a prayer from the English nation to the Russian nation," she told local journalists between speeches to patriotic women's groups, "that you may continue the war on which depends the fate of civilisation and freedom."

One Russian especially caught her attention—and was quickly given star treatment in Christabel's newspaper back in England:

25-year-old Maria Bochkareva. The Tsar had given her special permission to enlist in the army, where Bochkareva had fought in a combat unit, bayoneted a German soldier to death, and been wounded several times. She smoked, drank, and swore, punched back at anyone who harassed her, and in a language where many words change with the speaker's gender, used the male forms. One observer described her as "a big peasant woman, strong as a horse, rough of manner, eating with her fingers by choice, unlettered, but of much native intelligence."

A staunch proponent of fighting the Germans, Bochkareva had recently formed a "Women's Battalion of Death." Its recruits shaved their heads, slept on bare boards during training, endured the same corporal punishment as male Russian soldiers, and sported a skull-and-crossbones insignia. She enforced strict discipline and succeeded in inspiring the battalion to overrun some German trenches, a rare act in this year of Russian military collapse. For Russians determined to stay in the war she was—like Emmeline Pankhurst in England—an unexpected poster girl, for her patriotism trumped her role as a militantly assertive woman. To right-wingers in a country riven by class conflict, she was that always treasured rarity: a working-class hero who was on their side.

As Bochkareva led her troops on parade in Petrograd's St. Isaac's Square, supporters threw flowers, an army band played, and a Russian Orthodox bishop blessed the skull-and-crossbones flag. The battalion marched in review, cheering robustly, past Pankhurst, who was dressed in an immaculate white linen suit, black bonnet, and gloves. "The creation of the Women's Battalion of Death is the greatest page written in the history of women," she told the unit's soldiers, "since the time of Joan of Arc."

Word came from the suburban palace where they were under house arrest that the Tsar and Tsarina would like to meet the famous visiting women's suffrage leader. The message was surprising, for the imperial couple had never been known as fans of suffrage for anyone, male or female. Pankhurst had to decline, since Britain was anxious for her not to hold any meetings that might unnecessarily antagonize the Provisional Government.

The summer of 1917 was a chaotic one. Russian troops were killing their officers or replacing them with soldiers' soviets, and by the hundreds of thousands they kept on leaving the front; history had never before seen an army dissolve on such a scale. There were more strikes and stormy meetings as the Provisional Government tried to corral the Bolsheviks and other radical sects into continuing the war. Pankhurst ignored suggestions that she and Jessie Kenney wear less stylish clothes, so as not to attract attention as members of the bourgeoisie, and also turned down an offer of bodyguards from a group of sympathetic army officers. From her hotel window in Petrograd she watched radical soldiers on parade, shouting "Down with capitalism!" and "Stop the war!" After Bolsheviks barged into the hotel itself and arrested 40 officers, she yielded to advice that it was best to leave for England, and quickly. By then it was obvious: a Bolshevik takeover was on the way.

And that was exactly what her daughter Sylvia fervently hoped for. She changed her newspaper's name from *Woman's Dreadnought* to *Workers' Dreadnought* as she awaited the class war that would end the war of nations. Testing the limits of censorship, she openly began to urge British troops to lay down their weapons, and published critical letters from soldiers at the front. In midsummer, while her mother was still in Russia, Sylvia scored an editorial coup. Her newspaper was the first to publish a statement unlike any the war had yet seen—an eloquent avowal from a front-line officer, and a highly decorated one at that, declaring his intention to stop fighting:

> I am making this statement as an act of willful defiance of military authority, because I believe that the War is being deliberately prolonged by those who have the power to end it.
>
> I am a soldier, convinced that I am acting on behalf of soldiers. I believe that this War, upon which I entered as a War of defence, has now become a War of aggression and conquest.

The letter writer, Second Lieutenant Siegfried Sassoon, had just published a much-praised book of war poems. Nicknamed Mad Jack, he had been awarded the Military Cross in France for carrying a wounded soldier to safety under heavy fire. Later, he was recommended for the Victoria Cross, though he did not receive it, for single-handedly capturing a German trench. Not only did Sassoon have impeccable military credentials, but he came from an eminent family: his cousin Sir Philip Sassoon, a baronet and a member of Parliament, was Haig's private secretary.

Sent back to England after being shot through the throat, and convalescing in a London hospital, he read a volume of Bertrand Russell's collected writings against the war, *Justice in Wartime*, and was inspired to act. Russell, whom he met, encouraged him to speak out, helped him draft his statement, and passed it on to a sympathetic MP. Two days after Sylvia Pankhurst published it, Sassoon's letter of defiance was read aloud in the House of Commons. Basil Thomson's agents raided the offices of both the *Workers' Dreadnought* and the No-Conscription Fellowship, where they seized 100 copies of the letter. Sassoon expected that he would be sent before a court-martial, where he could denounce the war in a forum that would gain wide attention. For peace activists, this promised an unparalleled opportunity to reach the public: a high-profile trial of a decorated officer who had seen his men die.

Surprisingly, in between haranguing antiwar crowds on Glasgow Green and attempting to start soviets, Charlotte Despard still treasured her infrequent meetings with her brother. "He is, I think, dearer to me than anyone else," she wrote, and every time they met was "a day to be written in red letters." John French's diary for 1917 records a drop-in visit to the Despard Arms, her teetotal pub for soldiers, perhaps the only one of her manifold activities uncontroversial enough for him, as commander in chief of the Home Forces, to be seen visiting. As always, money flowed through French's hands too easily, so Charlotte once again gave him a loan. The two shared a loss this year when one of their sisters, a volunteer nurse on the Balkan front, was killed by a piece of shrapnel.

The field marshal was still frustrated, as he later put it to a friend, that "I was driven out of France . . . at the instigation of Haig. . . . Nothing that can ever happen to me could compensate for the loss of 1916 and 1917 and half of 1918 *in the field.*" Instead, he had to content himself with traveling up and down Britain inspecting troops, training bases, coastal defenses, and antiaircraft batteries, pinning medals on chests and visiting wounded soldiers in their bright blue hospital garb. Gradually he managed to insinuate himself as a confidential military adviser to Lloyd George — a position that allowed him to spread any anti-Haig gossip that came his way. This he did so energetically that the King summoned him to Buckingham Palace for a dressing-down. When French made a visit to the Western Front, Haig refused to receive him, and when the secretary for war invited both men to dinner in London, French refused to come. To his mistress, Winifred Bennett, he wrote plaintively, "I do so want to hear the guns again!"

There were plenty of guns to be heard, more than 3,000 of them firing off more than four million shells, as Haig's artillery began the customary bombardment before the battle that today is usually known by the name of the tiny village that was one of its first objectives, Passchendaele. At each major British attack on the Western Front, some new element had fed the perennial hope of a breakthrough. At Loos it was the unprecedented size of the attacking force and the first British use of poison gas. At the Somme it was the weeklong artillery bombardment that was supposed to pulverize the German trenches. At Passchendaele? No new strategy or weapon of any sort distinguished this attack. In the end, what separated Passchendaele from the great paroxysms of bloodshed that preceded it was one gruesome fact no one had planned for: in addition to falling victim to German fire, thousands of British soldiers, nowhere near the sea, drowned.

It was for good reason that this corner of Europe had long been known as the Low Countries; the water table is less than two feet below ground in much of Belgium. Haig seems to have given no thought to the way his bombardment would wreck canals and drainage ditches and leave tens of thousands of craters that soon filled with water. "Haig's plans required a drought of Ethiopian proportions to ensure success," comments his biographer Gerard De Groot. The landscape in which the battle unfolded bore no resemblance to the dry, neatly sandbagged replica of a trench that had been constructed in London's Kensington Gardens. (A similar trench, no less unrealistic, drew many visitors to a park in Berlin.)

The area around Ypres was covered by mist when the British infantry assault began in the early morning of July 31, 1917. The mist soon turned into almost nonstop rain, the heaviest in some 30 years. Observation aircraft could not take to the sky, weapons jammed, and the clay soil of the watery moonscape of craters became sticky; one officer likened its consistency to cheesecake, another to porridge. Guns could barely be moved, and mules and horses pulling ammunition wagons sank up to their stomachs and had to be dug out. Ambulances carrying wounded soldiers skidded off slippery roads. As summer turned to autumn, the men were reminded that the British soldier's cold-weather greatcoat was not waterproof. It absorbed mud and water like a relentless sponge, adding up to 34 pounds to its weight. As the battle continued, one single day saw 26,000 British casualties. Still Haig pushed on.

"I cannot attempt to describe the conditions under which we are fighting," wrote John Mortimer Wheeler, later a well-known archaeologist. "Anything I could write about them would seem an exaggeration but would, in reality, be miles below the truth. . . . The mud is not so much mud as a fathomless, sticky morass. The shell holes, where they do not actually merge into one another, are divided only by a few inches of this glutinous mud. . . . The gunners work thigh-deep in water." Some British artillery pieces dug themselves so deeply into the mud with their recoils that they dropped below the surface; the crew would then put up a flag to mark the spot.

Private Charlie Miles of the Royal Fusiliers carried messages as a runner—a misnomer in this season: "The moment you set off you felt that dreadful suction. . . . In a way, it was worse when the mud didn't suck you down . . . [then] you knew that it was a body you were treading on. It was terrifying. You'd tread on one on the stomach, perhaps, and it would grunt all the air out. . . . The smell could make you vomit." And when shells landed, they blasted waterlogged, putrefying corpses into the air, showering pieces of them down on the soldiers who were still alive.

British, Australian, and Canadian troops inched ever closer to the little village of Passchendaele as newspaper headlines triumphally announced, "Our Position Improved; Heroism in the New Advance" (the *Times*); "Complete Success in Battle of the Pill Boxes; Haig's Smashing Blow" (the *Daily Mirror*). But water had filled some shell holes to a depth of over a man's head, and troops joked that it was time to call in the Royal Navy. If a soldier with a heavy pack trudging around a crater slipped or stumbled, or jumped to avoid an incoming artillery round, the muddy water, often already fouled with the rotting bodies of men or horses, might claim him for good.

"From the darkness on all sides came the groans and wails of wounded men," recorded Edwin Vaughn, a 19-year-old lieutenant, in his diary on a rainy night, "faint, long, sobbing moans of agony, and despairing shrieks. . . . Dozens of men with serious wounds must have crawled for safety into new shell-holes, and now the water was rising about them. . . . We could do nothing to help them; Dunham was crying quietly beside me, and all the men were affected by the piteous cries." After hours of rain, "the cries of the wounded had much diminished . . . the reason was only too apparent, for the water was right over the tops of the shell-holes." Of the more than 88,000 British Empire casualties in the Ypres sector listed on memorials as "missing," no one knows how many drowned. Belgian farmers' plows still uncover their skeletons today.

To the fear of drowning was added a new horror. The Germans had begun using mustard gas. Aside from its faint smell and the yellow color of the blisters it raised on a man's skin, this powerful toxin had nothing to do with mustard. Extremely concentrated, it did not require cumbersome canisters; a small amount was merely added to a high-explosive shell. Moreover, soldiers could fall victim without breathing it, for the chemical easily penetrated clothing, producing bloody blisters up to a foot wide. Troops who unknowingly sat on contaminated ground later found the huge blisters all over their buttocks and genitals. Since the compound was slow-acting, it might be six or eight hours before a man realized he had been stricken. The worst off were soldiers who had breathed droplets in the air, for their blisters were internal, gradually swelling to seal throats and bronchial tubes fatally shut, a process that might take as long as four or five weeks. Writhing, gagging patients sometimes had to be strapped to their beds. Horses and mules also succumbed to mustard gas by the thousands, but for them at least, death, by a handler's bullet, was mercifully quick.

Haig finally called a halt to the fighting in November 1917 after his soldiers seized a last piece of ground less than five miles from where they had started in July. More than 15,000 Canadians were killed or wounded in the concluding spasm of combat to capture the village of Passchendaele—which had been scheduled to be taken on the fourth day of the offensive, months before. It was such a patently meaningless sacrifice that, raging about it afterward at a meeting in London, Canadian Prime Minister Sir Robert Borden strode up to Lloyd George, seized his lapels, and shook him.

In the sanitizing language of newspapers and memorial services, these Canadians, and all the British Empire troops who lost their lives in the three-and-a-half-month battle, were referred to as the "fallen." But in the mud of Passchendaele, falling dead from a bullet wound was only for the lucky: "A party of 'A' Company men passing up to the front line found . . . a man bogged to above the knees," remembered Major C. A. Bill of the Royal Warwickshire Regiment. "The united efforts of four of them, with rifles beneath his armpits, made not the slightest impression, and to dig, even if shovels had been available, would be impossible, for there was no foothold. Duty compelled them to move on up to the line, and when two days later they passed down that way the wretched fellow was still there; but only his head was now visible and he was raving mad."

19

PLEASE DON'T DIE

A S DIRECTOR OF INFORMATION, John Buchan oversaw the expansion of the most sophisticated propaganda operation the world had yet seen. It produced a torrent of patriotic materials, including paintings and drawings by special war artists sent to the front, pictorial magazines, boys' adventure stories portraying the Germans as bloodthirsty barbarians, cards for cigarette packs, and a "German Crimes Calendar" with a new atrocity for each month. Telegrams put an upbeat twist on the latest war news for the press at home and abroad. One bureau turned out leaflets dropped from balloons over the German trenches. Lecturers were dispatched everywhere, from industrial districts in England threatened by the influence of antiwar radicals to the United States—where speakers were instructed to avoid the touchy subject of Ireland. Every American Catholic priest found himself receiving a monthly letter of war news from a supposedly independent committee of Catholics in Britain. American editors, reporters, and congressmen were welcomed on their arrival in London by a new Anglo-American Society Buchan started, and could enjoy VIP tours of the front in France while housed in a nearby château. Like his patron Milner, Buchan welcomed the colonies and dominions to the great struggle, and saw to it that films poured out with titles like *Canadians on the Western Front* and *New Zealand Troops in France*. One short film in 1917 even celebrated the black work battalions sent from South Africa; it showed Africans doing traditional dances and madly scrambling for a coin tossed to them by a laughing white officer. To reinvigorate popular support for the war, a fleet of 20 movie projector trucks, called "cinemotors," toured Britain showing films on the sides of buildings. Brass bands, celebrity speakers, and the occasional large artillery piece were all available to serve as attractions for rallies, while an airplane might swoop down and drop leaflets onto the crowd.

Buchan and his staff soon saw that despite the tank's embarrassingly ineffective battlefield debut the previous year, the public was hungry for a high-tech wonder weapon. The tracked behemoth was a huge success on the movie screen, attracting a total audience estimated at 20 million to a mid-1917 documentary on tank warfare. Paradoxically, it was only later that year that Britain fought the first real tank battle, at Cambrai, France, where the lumbering machines advanced several miles before the usual bungling set in and a German counterattack regained most of the captured ground.

The tank's greatest victory so far, however, was not on the battlefield but at home. While Cambrai was still raging, a "Trafalgar Square Tank Bank" began doing a booming business selling war bonds. The Coldstream Guards band played as celebrities addressed the crowd from atop the tank, and hundreds of people lined up to buy bonds through an opening in a side turret. Ninety percent of the visitors, it was claimed, had never bought a war bond before, so tanks were dispatched by train to 168 towns and cities throughout England, Scotland, and Wales. "Tank Banks" altogether sold £300,000,000 (some $17 billion in today's dollars) worth of war bonds, the authorities declared. In impressive testimony to the importance of the new weapon on the home front, some tanks were even recalled from France for this mission.

Although no one could have told it from his work or his public persona, 1917 was a bad year for Buchan, for his younger brother and two close friends were killed in combat within days of one another. Yet his immense productivity never slackened; he seemed to write books with as little effort as other people make dinner-table conversation. His wide circle of readers, he learned, included Grand Duchess Olga of Russia, the oldest daughter of the recently deposed Tsar. The family was now imprisoned in a house in the remote Siberian city of Tobolsk, and from there she wrote to Buchan that she, her sisters, and their father had greatly enjoyed his latest spy novel.

A novel he began writing in mid-1917, *Mr. Standfast,* was full of the usual secret agents athletically foiling mysterious German plots. But, reflecting a year that had seen strikes, the upheaval in Russia, and a stronger antiwar movement, Buchan had his familiar hero Richard Hannay infiltrate radical trade union circles in Glasgow, where he finds most Scottish workingmen to be loyal imperial patriots. One character in the book is a conscientious objector who, in the end, takes a non-combatant role in the army, and swims a river under heavy fire to deliver a vital message before dying of his wounds.

The same year, another well-known literary protagonist returned to action: Sir Arthur Conan Doyle, capitalizing on all the spy paranoia, brought Sherlock Holmes out of retirement. In "His Last Bow," Holmes skillfully infiltrates the spy ring of the sinister Von Bork, Germany's top clandestine agent in England on the eve of the war. Conan Doyle was another of those convinced that, for all its horrors, the conflict was a healthy purgative, a purification by fire. Looking ahead, Holmes says, "There's an east wind coming, Watson. . . . Some such wind as never blew in England yet. It will be cold and bitter, Watson, and a good many of us may wither before its blast. But it's God's own wind, none the less, and a cleaner, better, stronger land will lie in the sunshine when the storm has cleared."

In Belgium, the wind was cold and bitter indeed. The total of British dead and wounded at Passchendaele, officially the Third Battle of Ypres, is in dispute, but a low estimate puts the number at 260,000; most reckonings are far higher. Haig ceaselessly trumpeted Passchendaele as a triumph, but few agreed. "We have won great victories," Lloyd George said as the battle ended, in a remarkably frank speech that hinted at his impotent frustration with Haig. "When I look at the appalling casualty lists I sometimes wish it had not been necessary to win so many."

On other fronts, the war was going even worse. In late October came disastrous news from northern Italy: German and Austrian troops had broken through at Caporetto, sweeping forward some 80 miles after a surprise attack in fog and rain. The demoralized Italians, choking in inadequate gas masks, lost more than half a million men killed, wounded, or taken prisoner.

Against all this, the capture of a muddy, ruined village or two in Flanders seemed little to brag about. "For the first time," the war correspondent and novelist Philip Gibbs later wrote, "the British Army lost its spirit of optimism, and there was a sense of deadly depression among many officers and men with whom I came in touch. They saw no ending of the war, and nothing except continuous slaughter." Men joked bitterly about where the front line would be in 1950. One officer calculated that if the British continued to gain ground at the pace so far, they would reach the Rhine in 180 years.

It was during the autumn of 1917 that the British army experienced the nearest thing to a mutiny on the Western Front: six days of intermittent rioting by several thousand troops at the big supply and training base in Étaples, France, in which a military policeman killed one soldier. Amid protest meetings the red flag briefly flew, and one rebel was later tried and executed. Rates of desertion and drunkenness rose, and the army increased the ratio of military police to other soldiers. "Reinforcements . . . shambled up past the guns with dragging steps and the expressions of men who knew they were going to certain death," wrote one veteran about the mood around Ypres in October. "No words of greeting passed as they slouched along; in sullen silence they filed past one by one to the sacrifice." Haig, as usual, tolerated no dissent. When a brave colonel told him that further fruitless attacks would leave no resources for an offensive the next spring, Haig turned white with anger and said, "Col. Rawlins, leave the room."

As more rain fell in November, Haig's thoroughly undistinguished chief of staff, Lieutenant General Sir Launcelot Kiggell, made a rare trip forward. Approaching the battlefield at Passchendaele, he saw from his staff car for the first time the terrible expanse of mud, dotted with water-filled shell holes. Reportedly—although his defenders deny this—he said, "Good God, did we really send men to fight in that?" and then burst into tears. Shortly afterward military doctors judged him to be suffering from nervous exhaustion. He was bundled off to a low-stress but dignified post as troop commander and lieutenant governor on the Isle of Guernsey.

• • •

In Russia, over the night of November 6–7, 1917, the moment that the Allied governments had been dreading for months finally arrived. The Bolsheviks seized power in Petrograd, occupying telegraph stations and key official buildings and storming the Provisional Government's head-quarters—the Winter Palace, on whose balcony the Tsar and Tsarina had received the ecstatic cheers of patriotic crowds on the outbreak of war some three years before. Now the city's streets were filled with workers marching under triumphant red banners and jubilant revolutionary soldiers whose long greatcoats were crisscrossed with bandoliers.

Within days, to underline its commitment to peace instead of diplomatic business as usual, the new regime made public the secret treaties Russia had signed with the other Allied countries that it found in government files. These revealed the territorial gains all were hoping for. There were, for instance, detailed plans for dismembering the Ottoman Empire and parceling it out—either outright or as nominally independent states—among Russia, Italy, France, and Britain. As the Allied powers claimed they were fighting a war for freedom, these documents produced shock around the world—and, in some quarters, lasting fury. The Arabs Britain had urged to rebel against their Turkish masters had expected to rule themselves after the war, not to be the puppets of anyone.

An informal truce quickly made its way across much of the Eastern Front: photographs show German and Russian troops fraternizing in no man's land in their heavy winter coats, the Germans in brimmed army caps, the Russians in fur-lined *shapkas,* and larger groups of men from both sides together in rows, standing and kneeling as if members of a single sports team posing for a portrait. In a Europe exhausted by the war, who knew how easily the revolutionary example might spread?

Without Russia, Alfred Milner feared, the Allies might not be able to defeat Germany. And the spread of revolution could prove a more dangerous enemy to the established order than the Germans. Why, he wondered, should Britain and France not settle their differences with Germany—and then partition Russia among themselves? Britain's share, it hardly need be said, would include the central Asian parts of the Russian Empire that adjoined Persia and Afghanistan, strategic borderlands to India. If Germany was willing—and also willing, of course, to withdraw from France and Belgium—there were many interesting ways in which Russia could be divided. For a full year to come, Milner quietly but doggedly promoted this idea. There is no clear evidence that he or anyone else ever approached the Germans, and his proposal apparently never moved beyond the realm of confidential talk within the British government, but it bears a strange resemblance to the world of abruptly shifting superpower alliances that George Orwell would later imagine in *1984*.

Meanwhile, socialists and pacifists everywhere rejoiced at the Bolshevik coup. For the first time, a major power had a regime committed to overthrowing capitalism—and to swiftly withdrawing from the war that for more than three years had been killing off Europe's young men by the millions. "Glorious News from Russia!" read the headline in lion tamer John S. Clarke's *Socialist*. "May they open the door," Sylvia Pankhurst wrote in her *Workers' Dreadnought*, "which leads to freedom for the people of all lands!"

No group in Britain received the news of the latest phase of the Russian Revolution with greater joy than the war resisters in prison. Serving his hard-labor sentence at Walton Gaol in Liverpool, the 29-year-old Fenner Brockway was an editor still. Despite the rule of silence, he passed on news of the momentous events in Petrograd to his fellow prisoners in the *Walton Leader,* one of at least nine clandestine CO prison newspapers. It was written with pencil lead that Brockway and other convicts had smuggled into prison attached to the bottoms of their feet with adhesive tape; each issue was published on forty squares of brown toilet paper. The subscription price was extra sheets of toilet paper from each prisoner's supply. Twice a week, until guards finally discovered it after a year, a new issue of the paper—only one copy, of course, could be "published"—was left in a toilet cubicle the CO prisoners shared. Thanks to information from an imprisoned army deserter, the *Walton Leader* published one of the few uncensored accounts in Britain of the slaughter at Passchendaele. By contrast, the coup in Russia, Brockway wrote later, made the COs imagine "our prison doors being opened by comrade workers and soldiers."

One event that might bring that great day a step closer, British peace activists hoped, was Siegfried Sassoon's imminent court-martial. But they waited in vain, for the last thing the government wanted was an upper-class war hero turned public martyr. "A breach of discipline has

Early gas masks, here worn by Russian officers.

Practicing for the
great cavalry charge
that never came.

The propaganda campaign waged by both sides from 1914 to 1918 was the largest and most sophisticated the world had yet seen. Much British propaganda was secretly government-financed but presented as the work of independent civic groups.

A still from the documentary film *The Battle of the Somme:* a soldier carries a dying comrade.

Passchendaele, the battle that cost British forces more than 260,000 dead and wounded: the first day, July 31, 1917 (*below*), September (*opposite top*), October (*opposite bottom*).

Stephen Hobhouse: from Eton and Oxford to solitary confinement.

Joseph Stones: shot at dawn.

Albert Rochester, radical in uniform: Why should each officer have a personal servant?

A family of show-trial martyrs. From right: Alice Wheeldon,
her daughters Winnie and Hettie, a prison wardress.

John S. Clark: from circus animal tamer
to underground antiwar activist.

What generals on both sides feared: pacifists (at Dartmoor, Devon, *above*) and fraternizing soldiers (Russians and Germans on the Eastern Front, *below*).

been committed," said a War Office spokesman about Sassoon's defiant open letter, "but no disciplinary action has been taken, since Second Lieutenant Sassoon has been reported by the medical board as not being responsible for his action, as he was suffering from nervous breakdown."

Far from being thrown in jail, Sassoon was ordered to wait in a hotel in Liverpool. While there, he angrily threw his Military Cross ribbon into the River Mersey—but with no audience, the gesture went unreported. Instead of the public stage he had hoped for, Sassoon was sent off to the comfortable surroundings of a rehabilitation hospital for shell-shocked officers in Scotland. His protest soon dropped out of the newspapers. His time in the hospital produced no dividend for the peace movement, but an enormous one for English literature. A fellow patient was the 24-year-old aspiring writer Wilfred Owen, recovering from wounds and shell shock, to whom the older Sassoon offered crucial encouragement. Owen became the greatest poet of the war.

The War Office had been extremely shrewd. After three months in the hospital whose services he did not need, Sassoon found himself increasingly restless. Finally he accepted a promotion to first lieutenant and returned to the front. He did so not because he had abandoned his former views, but because, as he put it in his diary when he was back with his regiment in France, "I am only here *to look after* some men." It was a haunting reminder of the fierce power of group loyalty over that of political conviction—and all the more so because it came from someone who had not in the slightest changed, nor ever in his life would change, his belief that his country's supposed war aims were fraudulent.

Late 1917 was a time of great nervousness for British ruling circles. The *Times* ran a series of articles on "The Ferment of Revolution," and government control of the press tightened, as a new regulation subjected all books and pamphlets about the war—or the prospects of peace—to censorship. More than 4,000 censors were at work monitoring both the press and the mail. For the first time, police suppressed two issues of the *Workers' Dreadnought*. Rumors flew that German money was somehow financing antiwar organizing, and Basil Thomson was asked to step up his surveillance operations. Knowing that stoking official paranoia would help him gain more influence, he half insinuated, in a report to the War Cabinet, that one of the leading antiwar voices, the intrepid investigative journalist E. D. Morel, might have German backing: "The probabilities are certainly strong that Mr Morel did not work out of pure altruism. . . . As his activities have certainly been in the German interest . . . the public cannot be blamed for believing that Mr Morel has been financed by Germany in the past and may possibly be expecting financial reward for his peace activities in the future." In his diary, however, Thomson wrote the opposite, admitting that "I feel certain that there is no German money" going to the peace movement.

The government had long been wanting, as one Foreign Office official put it, to silence Morel and get him "safely lodged in gaol." Milner, in particular, pressed for action. "In no country but this," he complained in a note to Lloyd George, "would it be possible for him to carry on." Being beyond military age, Morel could not be prosecuted for refusing the draft, so in the end he was charged with violating an obscure regulation against sending pacifist materials out of the country and was sentenced to six months at hard labor.

He served his time at London's Pentonville Prison. In Morel's cellblock there were no other war opponents; in the cell next to him was a man who had raped a child; on the other side was someone who had stolen three bottles of whiskey. Even behind bars British attitudes toward class prevailed, and another prisoner, speaking to Morel in a whisper because of the rule of silence, called him "sir." Morel was able to exchange quick smiles with conscientious objectors from other parts of the prison only in chapel on Sundays. While a pastor preached on the righteousness of the war and officials announced battlefield "victories," warders sat on raised seats at the end of each row to ensure that prisoners did not talk.

Morel sewed canvas mailbags in a dust-filled room and wove rope into hammocks and mats for the navy. Sometimes he had to carry 100-pound slabs of jute to the workshop. The U-boat toll on Britain's food imports led to a cutback in prison rations, which, for hard-labor convicts, were minimal to begin with. With coal in short supply, little was diverted to heat prisons. Supper at Pentonville, eaten alone in one's cell, was, Morel wrote, "a piece of bread, half-a-pint of coldish porridge at the bottom of a tin which earlier in the day may have contained redherrings and still bears traces of them, and a pint of hot, greasy cocoa which one learns to regard as a veritable nectar of the gods, especially in cold weather." At night you could expect only "the cold of a cold cell—like nothing on earth. Nothing seems proof against it."

Morel was a powerfully built man of 44, but prison broke his health. "I saw E. D. Morel yesterday for the first time since he came out," Bertrand Russell wrote to a friend the following year, "and was impressed by the seriousness of a six months sentence. . . . He collapsed completely, physically and mentally, largely as the result of insufficient food. He says one only gets three quarters of an hour for reading in the whole day—the rest of the time is spent on prison work."

Although the food and working conditions were no better for COs, they at least were imprisoned together and could furtively communicate. (The underground newspaper that circulated in Winchester Prison was called the *Whisperer*.) "My first experience of the prison technique for overcoming the silence rule was in chapel," Fenner Brockway wrote. "We were singing one of the chants. Instead of the words of the Prayer Book, I heard these:—

> "Welcome, Fenner boy,
> When did you get here?
> How did you like the skilly [gruel] this morn?
> Lord have mercy upon us!"

The key during chapel, Brockway learned, was to sing or chant a message to the person next to you without turning your head or giving any sign of recognition that could draw the guards' attention. Prisoners smuggled books to each other in the mailbags they sewed, and even played chess; at one point more than half the COs in Maidstone Prison took part in a chess tournament. When a move might be whispered to your opponent only once a day, games could last a month or more. But punishment for infractions was severe: Brockway was put on bread and water for six days when the authorities discovered his toilet-paper newspaper. (He had by then managed to publish more than 100 issues, including a special memorial number on the second anniversary of the death of his mentor, Keir Hardie.) In one prison he was in, there were periodic executions of common criminals. "The place was deadly silent, each man listening for the opening of the door of the condemned cell, for the sound of the steps to the gallows, and then for the striking of the fatal hour on neighbouring clocks and the sound of the tolling bell which told that it was all over."

Also behind bars this grim autumn were Alice Wheeldon and her daughter and son-in-law. Alice was doing her hard-labor sentence in the Aylesbury Gaol, where the peephole on every cell door was at the center of a painted eye, complete with lash, brow, and pupil, eternally staring at the prisoner. The prospect of ten years in such conditions made her furious; she swore at the guards and disobeyed orders not to talk to other prisoners. She was also indignant at being strip-searched, and at the way Winnie's prison work assignment, as well as her own, was changed from the garden to the laundry, to avoid what officials called "undesirable association" with other prisoners. She called the prison governor, a guard dutifully noted, a "flaming vampire." Several times she went on hunger strikes, as did Winnie and Alf Mason; Alice knocked a cup out of a doctor's hand and broke it when he tried to feed her. But beneath the anger and defiance was despair: warders heard her weeping at night.

On December 21, 1917, she embarked on yet another hunger strike. Weakening, she was moved to the prison hospital four days later. "Christmas morning," a matron heard her say, "how the devil must laugh." Prison staff had been told from the beginning to watch her behavior closely, and a stream of messages from them flowed to the Home Office. "She says," reported one jailer, "she is determined to get out of prison 'in a box or otherwise.'"

Of course all correspondence was monitored. But only 80 years later, when these letters were finally opened for public view, could the desperate voice of Winnie Mason be heard, frantic that her mother was doomed to die in the hands of the state.

Having failed to talk Alice out of her hunger strike, Winnie grew alarmed when the authorities moved her steadily fading mother to another prison. At Aylesbury they had at least had some chance to "associate" with each other. "Oh Mam I don't know what to write to you," Winnie scrawled, "—when I think of all the opportunities Ive had of giving you a kiss or saying something to you & I've restrained myself rather than imperil our chance of association. . . . This last fortnight's been like a year every day . . . Ive been sending you thought waves every minute of the time. I *knew* you were ill . . . I simply cant bear to think of what you are going through. . . . You were always a fighter but this fight isn't worth your death. . . . I cant write it hardly. . . . Live for us all again.

"Oh Mam," Winnie's letter pleaded, "—*please* don't die."

Could the radicalism of people like the Wheeldons spread to the troops? Haig was concerned and had intelligence officers and mail censors keep him abreast of the soldiers' mood. "Sometimes advanced socialistic and even anarchical views are expressed" by the men, he noted. He also worried that British troops would be infected with subversive ideas by, of all people, Australians. Their army was far more egalitarian than Britain's, soldiers' pay was higher, and many officers had served in the ranks before being commissioned, since the country lacked a class of landowners who had been officers for generations. ("Look smart," one Australian officer is said to have told his men before an inspection by British commanders. ". . . And look here, for the love of Heaven, don't call me Alf.") British and Australian soldiers already served in separate units, but Haig ordered them kept apart in hospitals and base camps as well. "They were giving so much trouble when along with our men," he wrote, "and put such revolutionary ideas into their heads."

Haig enthusiasts were fewer now. The newspaper magnate Lord Northcliffe, too, had lost patience with him. Following the chain of command, Lloyd George asked the secretary for war, Lord Derby, to fire Haig; the influential Derby, a Haig loyalist who had protected the field marshal's back on other occasions, refused, on threat of resignation, and the prime minister backed down. The problem was that earlier efforts of Northcliffe's own newspapers plus John Buchan's skillful propaganda apparatus had helped put Haig on a pedestal from which it was politically impossible to remove him. Lloyd George, Milner, and their colleagues feared the reaction from the army and the public if they tried.

Should it be possible to replace Haig, they favored the apple-cheeked, potbellied Sir Herbert Plumer, several inches shorter than his fellow generals but a cut above them in intelligence, perhaps the best British general of the war. Compared with other commanders, he was known for using careful planning and shrewdly positioned artillery and underground mines to capture ground without extravagantly spending soldiers' lives. He was definitely not one of those who gauged success by the number of his own casualties. But the senior generals against whom Plumer could be measured were not exactly a brilliant array, and, comments one military historian, "during the war the main point in his favour was often that he was not someone else."

All that Haig's enemies at home were able to do was to leak damaging information about a few of his subordinates to the newspapers — with the prime minister himself accused of doing some of the leaking. Although it was only small potatoes, with these tactics they were able to claim the head of Haig's intelligence chief General Charteris, who was kicked upstairs to a face-saving new position. Always well informed by his London supporters, Haig knew that his own job was safe and confidently soldiered on. And not only did his critics lack the political clout to put another general in his place, they had no better ideas for how to win the war. Even today, with all the power of hindsight, it is hard to see what military strategy could have led to a swift Allied victory. The very nature of trench warfare doomed it to continue until one side or the other was so exhausted, bloodied, and depleted that it could simply fight no more. For all his blind spots, Haig understood this in a way that politicians hoping for a shortcut to victory did not.

The public began to sense that this would be a war of attrition, and the mood in England turned bleaker than at any moment since Napoleon had threatened to invade more than a century before. Hundreds of thousands of people were wearing black armbands. Flower-strewn homemade shrines to men who had died appeared on the streets. Efforts by Buchan's propaganda staff to buck up morale by repeating the great success of the films on the Somme and the tank fell flat: new documentaries drew only small audiences.

Word of the enormous bloodletting at Passchendaele came back to England with the legions of wounded soldiers, a macabre counterpoint to the parade of triumphal headlines. Some of the survivors were in wheelchairs or hobbled along with crutches or on wooden legs. Here and there groups of them took to the cricket field as an "arms and legs side," with the other team agreeing to bowl gently. One spectator wrote of watching such a match at Piltdown, near the south coast, where the artillery barrages were often audible: "All the time the big guns were roaring in Flanders so we could hear the War & see the sad results of it."

Air raids increased and ever more deaths occurred in the munitions factories where millions of women now worked. Artillery shell plants were particularly prone to explosions: 26 women died in one in 1916; 134 workers would be killed in one in Nottingham in 1918. And women who loaded explosives into shells found the chemicals turned their skin yellow — they called themselves canaries — contamination that proved not only disfiguring but sometimes led to early death.

The war sapped daily life in countless ways. With enormous quantities of coal and 370 locomotives diverted to France, some 400 smaller British railway stations closed. Buses, trolleys, and trains were always overcrowded. As another unusually cold winter set in, coal rationing was imposed in London, and people lined up with everything from baskets to baby carriages to buy it. With paper scarce, newspapers shrank and raised their prices. Bacon, butter, margarine, matches, and tea were in short supply and long food lines appeared, filled with women, children, and the elderly. Wheat husks and potatoes were used as filler in bread, and throwing rice at weddings was made a criminal offense. By late 1917, one city after another began rationing food. Here and there workers staged one-day strikes to protest the shortages. In November, COs in prison saw their bread ration cut in half, to 11 ounces a day.

Could the war ever be won? Flashes of cynicism and helplessness could be heard even among the country's elite. "We're telling lies," the newspaper proprietor Lord Rothermere (who had already lost one son to the war and would soon lose another) said in a spontaneous outburst to a journalist in November 1917. "We daren't tell the public the truth, that we're losing more officers than the Germans, and that it's impossible to get through on the Western Front. You've seen the correspondents . . . they don't speak the truth and we know they don't."

Officers continued to die at a higher rate than enlisted men, junior officers especially. Although after the first six months of the war they ceased to carry swords, British infantry officers were still easily identified by German snipers from their Sam Browne belts of polished leather and swagger sticks or pistols. It was also young officers who flew the rickety fighter aircraft that were lost to crashes as well as German fire. By 1917, a British fighter pilot arriving at the front had an average life expectancy of less than three months.

Up until now, those who questioned whether the war was worth the human cost had almost all come from the left end of the political spectrum. But as 1917 approached its close, such a voice unexpectedly rang out from the highest reaches of the country's hierarchy. Lord Lansdowne, a great landowner, former viceroy of India and secretary for war, had as foreign secretary years earlier forged the understanding with France that virtually ensured Britain's participation in the war. Early in the fighting he had lost a son. His doubts about battling to an unconditional victory began after the Somme. Very much a man of his class, he was particularly appalled by the number of British officers slain. "We are slowly but surely killing off the best of the male population of these islands . . . ," he had written to Asquith, then prime minister. "Generations will have to come and go before the country recovers from the loss."

His misgivings only grew, and Passchendaele made him decide to go public. After the shocked *Times* refused to publish it, an open letter from him appeared in the *Daily Telegraph* on November 29, 1917. "We are not going to lose this War," Lansdowne wrote, "but its prolongation will spell ruin for the civilised world, and an infinite addition to the load of human suffering which already weighs upon it." He prophetically sensed something about the future the great conflict was leading to: "Just as this war has been more dreadful than any war in history, so, we may be sure, would the next war be even more dreadful than this. The prostitution of science for purposes of pure destruction is not likely to stop short." He then laid out some proposals for a negotiated peace, including future compulsory arbitration of international disputes. Lansdowne was privy to government intelligence reports that many influential Germans and Austrians favored negotiations. He believed that Lloyd George's rhetoric about a "knock-out blow" only provided ammunition to German die-hards determined to fight to the bitter end. The Allies should strengthen the hand of "the peace party in Germany," he wrote, by offering assurances that they "do not desire the annihilation of Germany as a Great Power."

Attacked by many former colleagues and by right-wing patriots, Lansdowne was, to his bewilderment, greeted with great warmth by the socialists whom he had always found an anathema. Bertrand Russell praised his courage and, noting the fury toward Lansdowne in the mainstream press, wryly remarked, "Before long, it will probably be discovered that his great aunt was born in Kiel, or that his grandfather was an admirer of Goethe." Kipling thought Lansdowne an "old imbecile" who had taken such a cowardly position only because some woman must have "worked upon" him.

In their confidential reports on the public mood, undercover intelligence agents began speaking darkly of "Lansdownism." Many soldiers, however, wrote to Lansdowne congratulating him on his bravery. But he represented no mass of followers and sparked no new peace movement. Indeed, not long after his letter appeared, Britain and France issued a hard-line declaration explicitly shutting the door on any negotiations, something that decisively undermined moderates hoping to gain influence in Germany. And by now there was another barrier to any chance of a compromise peace: the British and French governments were counting on the millions of fresh troops promised by the United States to at last bring about an Allied victory.

Margaret Hobhouse, still campaigning for the release of her son, managed to get 26 bishops and more than 200 other clergymen to sign a statement arguing for more lenient treatment of COs. With Milner pulling strings behind the scenes, in December 1917 some 300 of the more than 1,300 COs in prison were ordered released on grounds of ill health. Stephen Hobhouse accepted his freedom, knowing it was not for him alone. Opposition to the mass release was quelled when it was agreed that Parliament would be asked to disenfranchise, for five years, conscientious objectors who had gone to jail. Milner seems to have deftly engineered this particular bargain, getting his former Kindergarten member who was editor of the *Times* to produce an editorial on the subject at the right moment.

The Hobhouses were a family in which, Stephen wrote, "differences of outlook were put aside." (And yet, he added, "my father could never quite forget the disgrace that his eldest son had brought upon himself.") His two brothers in the army were both home on leave, and they, Stephen, and his wife spent Christmas together in their parents' house. Paul Hobhouse, although recovered from his wounds, seemed to feel some foreboding. "I thought P. changed in tone—had lost his buoyancy," wrote a relative who saw him just before he departed for the front, ". . . and was more grave and silent."

Meanwhile, on the other side of Europe, the Christmas season of 1917 saw a landmark in the war. To negotiate an end to hostilities between Russia and the Central Powers, a Bolshevik delegation passed through the Eastern Front under a white flag, near the ancient riverside city of Brest-Litovsk, in Russian territory now occupied by the Germans. Awaiting them in the city's sprawling red-brick fortress was a group of generals in dress-uniform spiked helmets and other officials prepared to negotiate for Germany and its allies. The Bolsheviks ushered into the fortress were unlike any other group of diplomats and negotiators in European history. The Germans and Austrians, the upper reaches of whose diplomatic services were the almost exclusive preserve of the aristocracy, were hard put to contain their astonishment.

Facing the foreign ministers of the two countries across the long negotiating table was a Bolshevik delegation headed by a bearded Jewish intellectual. Educated as a doctor, Adolph Joffe had spent part of his life in exile and, in Vienna, had undergone Freudian psychoanalysis. Another Jew high in the revolutionary movement, Lev Kamenev, was his chief associate. And to even more dramatically show the world that this was not diplomacy as usual, the remainder of the Bolshevik delegation included a worker, a soldier, a sailor, a peasant, and a woman, Anastasia Bitsenko, who had spent 17 years in Siberia for assassinating the Tsar's former minister of war. The elderly peasant, Roman Stashkov, had been included at the very last minute. Joffe and Kamenev, driving to the Petrograd railway station, had suddenly realized that, for political reasons, their delegation had to include a representative of the class that constituted the vast majority of Russia's people. They noticed the unmistakably peasant-like Stashkov walking along the street, stopped their car, found that he belonged to a left-wing party, and invited him along. The bewildered Stashkov, his enormous gray beard untrimmed, sat through the meetings at Brest-Litovsk beneath glittering chandeliers, but could not rid himself of the habit of addressing his fellow delegates, in the prerevolutionary manner, as *barin,* or master.

On December 15, 1917, the two delegations announced an armistice. The war between the Central Powers and Russia, which had left millions of dead and wounded and tens of thousands of square miles of devastated land, was over. The news reverberated around the world.

Russia and its former enemies immediately began protracted negotiations toward a permanent peace treaty. Hoping to speed the process along, the Germans gave a banquet, one of the more unusual on record. While the diplomats wore their high-collared formal attire and the chests of the German and Austrian generals glittered with medals, the Russian worker delegate, in everyday clothes, used his fork as a toothpick. The bearded old peasant Stashkov, unfamiliar with wine, asked which was stronger, the red or the white—and then proceeded to get cheerfully drunk. The Austro-Hungarian foreign minister, Count Ottokar Czernin, kept a close eye on Bitsenko, the assassin. "All that is taking place around her here she seems to regard with indifference," he observed. "Only when mention is made of the great principle of the International Revolution does she suddenly awake, her whole expression alters; she reminds one of a beast of prey seeing its victim at hand and preparing to fall upon it and rend it."

The Germans and Austrians had no doubt they were the prey, but were polite conversationalists nonetheless. The mild-mannered Joffe sat between Field Marshal Prince Leopold of Bavaria, the German commander in chief on the Eastern Front, and Count Czernin, who found his tone "kindly." To Czernin, Joffe said, "I hope we may be able to raise the revolution in your country too." If the entire war did not end soon, Czernin noted wryly in his diary that night, "we shall hardly need any assistance from the good Joffe, I fancy, in bringing about a revolution among ourselves; the people will manage that."

VI

1918

20

BACKS TO THE WALL

IF OBSERVERS ON another planet had been able to look closely at the Earth at the start of 1918, they might have been struck not only by the unusual propensity of its inhabitants to kill one another, but by their willingness to travel huge distances to do so. Never had so many people gone so far to make war. Under British command on the Western Front were troops from Canada, South Africa, the West Indies, Australia, New Zealand, and India—which alone would send nearly a million soldiers overseas to various fronts by the end of the war. Canadian Private John Kerr, who would later win the Victoria Cross, had walked 50 miles from his Alberta farm to enlist; to join a unit fighting in Africa, Arthur Darville Dudley, a British settler in Northern Rhodesia, rode 200 miles by bicycle on dirt roads and paths through the bush. Soldiers from Jamaica and other Caribbean islands found themselves fighting in both East and West Africa as well as in towns in Palestine whose names they knew from the Bible. To help protect Allied shipping in the Mediterranean came a naval squadron from Japan. British troops from Wiltshire and Devon were fighting soldiers from Bulgaria—an ally of Germany—in Greece. Later in the year, Africans from the French colony of Senegal would fight alongside soldiers from Serbia. From Egypt, the British brought some 80,000 men to work on the docks at Marseille and elsewhere in Europe. More than 90,000

Chinese did construction work for British forces in France or unloaded supplies at the ports. Other military laborers came from Fiji in the Pacific, Mauritius in the Indian Ocean, the mountains of Basutoland in southern Africa, and the French colonies of Vietnam and Laos. Living quarters for African and Asian laborers behind the Western Front were almost always in fenced-off compounds, an attempt—not entirely successful—to prevent any mixing that might give rise to ideas about equality.

The troops on three continents fought not just in steel helmets but in fezzes, turbans, kepis, and tropical pith helmets. Guns and supplies were hauled into battle by oxen, horses, mules, and trucks in France, by camels in the Middle East, and everywhere by exhausted men. Soldiers succumbed to malaria and sleeping sickness in Africa and to frostbite in the Alps, where the Italians fought from fortifications hacked out of snow and ice. On both sides, the colossal cost of the war was measured not only in human life: British war-related spending had by 1918 reached 70 percent of the gross national product—triple what it had been at the height of battling Napoleon, and higher than it would be in the Second World War. Only huge loans made this possible, and taxpayers in the warring countries would bear the burden for years to come as these were repaid; Britain's national debt, for example, increased more than tenfold during the conflict. And no end was in sight: Lloyd George and other officials would soon be making plans for a war continuing into 1920 and beyond.

For the Allies, the signs were not good. A year before there had been roughly three British Empire, French, or Belgian soldiers for every two Germans in the west. Now, every week, trains were racing across Germany bringing troops no longer needed against Russia—just as tens of thousands of British and French soldiers were being urgently diverted from the Western Front to prop up the collapsing Italian army. By January 1918, therefore, there were some four Germans for every three Allied soldiers in the west. The U.S. Army was not yet much help: although millions of men were being drafted and trained, barely more than 100,000 of them, almost all inexperienced, had made it to Europe. And if casualties continued at the current rate, British forces would need to find more than 600,000 men in the coming year just to replace their losses—far more than conscription could supply. As Churchill put it, "Lads of eighteen and nineteen, elderly men up to forty-five, the last surviving brother, the only son of his mother (and she a widow), the father the sole support of the family, the weak, the consumptive, the thrice wounded—all must now prepare themselves for the scythe." Nonetheless, Haig wanted to launch new attacks in Belgium once the weather allowed. The War Cabinet was dismayed.

Behind the scenes, Milner continued to promote his belief that the real enemy was not Germany but revolutionary Russia, an idea so inflammatory that almost all mentions of it are only in diaries. Writing after a dinner with Milner, a member of the War Cabinet staff predicted that the remainder of the war would be "to decide where the Anglo-German boundary shall run across Asia." A similar note was sounded in the diary of the well-connected writer Beatrice Webb in early 1918, just after she met with Lloyd George: "The P.M. and Milner are thinking of a peace at the expense of Russia. . . . With Russia to cut up, the map of the world is capable of all sorts of rearrangements."

The Germans, however, showed no signs of being interested: they had already beaten Russia and, following the end of the fighting, had helped themselves to a colossal additional expanse of its territory. Why should they share the spoils? They were determined to next achieve a similar victory over Britain and France and dictate a Europe-wide peace. While Milner's imagined rearrangement of the globe languished, the Germans prepared a new offensive.

Although the balance of troops on the Western Front favored Germany, the army high command, which by now was largely running the government, could hear two clocks ticking. They knew that the great battle to decide the war had to be won before summer; otherwise hundreds of thousands, and soon millions, of American troops would join the fight. And in Germany itself there were signs that the country might not be able to hold out long.

Civilians were suffering more painfully than ever. With imports kept out by the British naval blockade, metal was so scarce that everything possible—kettles and cooking pots, doorknobs, brass ornaments, telephone wire, and well over 10,000 church bells—was being confiscated and melted down for munitions. Buried pipes were ripped from beneath the streets. Coal was in short supply, and those waiting in line for it were often shod in cardboard shoes with wooden soles, since scarce leather was saved for soldiers' boots. So many horses had been sent to the front that the Berlin Zoo's elephants were put to work hauling wagons through the streets. Real wages in nonmilitary industries had dropped to almost half of prewar levels. Nitrates once used in fertilizers went into explosives, making food even scarcer. Bread was made from potato peels and sawdust, coffee from bark, and with horsemeat a rare luxury, often the only meat on sale was that of dogs and cats. The rich turned to a thriving black market, while the poor were left to forage in harvested fields and urban trash dumps for whatever scraps of grain or food they could find. Daily calorie consumption was more than halved, which meant that, on average, German adults lost 20 percent of their body weight during the war. In Austria-Hungary, conditions were even worse.

The brilliant radical theorist Rosa Luxemburg was in a prison in Breslau, cold, ill, and hungry, her hair turning white. She watched grimly as horses drew carts into the prison yard filled with uniforms scavenged from wounded or dead soldiers, sometimes torn by bullets or shrapnel and spotted with blood. The prisoners were put to work cleaning and mending them, so that they could clothe fresh bodies being sent into battle. One day she saw a cart arrive pulled by water buffaloes, war booty from Eastern Europe. "The cargo was piled so high that the buffaloes could not make it over the threshold of the gateway. The attending soldier . . . began to beat away at the animals with the heavy end of his whip so savagely that the overseer indignantly called him to account. 'Don't you have any pity for the animals?' 'No one has any pity for us people either!' he answered." Millions more felt the same.

Wartime privations inflamed an angry nationalism in Germany, producing a foretaste of the hysteria that, a quarter century later, would reach a climax of unimaginable proportions. Ominously, making the fraudulent claim that Jews were shirking military duty, right-wing forces demanded and won a special census of Jews in the army. Anti-Semitic books, pamphlets, and oratory proliferated. By 1918, the head of the Pan-German League was calling for a "ruthless struggle against Jews."

The generals, however, worried not about anti-Semitism but about revolution. Emboldened by the Bolshevik takeover in Russia, and tired of endless war and shortages, some 400,000 workers went on strike in Berlin at the end of January 1918, demanding peace, new rights for labor, and a "people's republic." The strikes spread to other cities, and to the German navy, less disciplined than the army, which experienced a series of hushed-up mutinies and protests. In shaky Austria-Hungary the strikes grew far larger, and fractures along ethnic lines began to show: Polish, Serbian, Croatian, and Slovene deputies in the imperial parliament were loudly demanding autonomy or independence. Eight hundred sailors in the Austro-Hungarian navy in the Adriatic mutinied and raised the red flag; the naval command had to dispatch three battleships manned by loyalists to suppress them. The entire precarious empire threatened to dissolve if the war went on much longer. The inhabitants of Germany's other major ally, Ottoman Turkey, were suffering near famine. As the economy spiraled downward, the government recklessly printed huge quantities of paper currency for its war expenses. Hundreds of thousands of Turkish soldiers began to desert, many still armed, to live off the countryside as brigands.

The example of Russia made one thing dramatically clear: whatever happened at the front, a country could also collapse from within. The German authorities declared martial law in Berlin and Hamburg, and conscripted tens of thousands of strikers into uniform. That stopped the unrest for the moment, although at the cost of scattering militant leftists throughout the army. To fend off further strikes, the German military needed a swift, decisive victory. In early March 1918 Haig received an intelligence report that "an offensive on a big scale will take place during the present month."

Inside the fortress-like Holloway Prison in London, Alice Wheeldon's hunger strike finally brought results: she faced down Lloyd George and won. The prime minister's private secretary called the Home Office, an official there recorded, to say that Lloyd George "thought she should on no account be allowed to die in prison." After less than ten months of her ten-year sentence, the heavy doors of the jail swung open and she walked free. Her early release was again proof of the care the British government took to avoid creating martyrs.

Official wariness of antiwar forces remained as intense as ever. The 1918 New Year's card sent out by the War Office counterintelligence unit bore the legend "The Hidden Hand" and showed a helmeted, flag-swathed Britannia wielding a trident against the hairy, bearded beast Subversion. Smoke and fire issuing from its mouth, the beast is creeping toward a British fighting man, preparing to stab him in the back. In late January, Basil Thomson warned the War Cabinet of "a rather sudden growth of pacifism."

More than 1,000 COs were still behind bars, attendance at peace rallies was on the rise, and, to the government's dismay, the envoy to Britain of what was now known as Soviet Russia, Maxim Litvinov, was eagerly sought after as a speaker by groups on the left. Britons in such organizations could also take some encouragement from comrades in the United States. American radicals scoffed at President Woodrow Wilson's high-flown rhetoric about democracy and self-determination, insisting that the real reason the U.S. was fighting for an Allied victory was to ensure that massive American war loans to Britain and France would be paid back. The U.S. quickly began conscription, and although American war resisters were never as numerous as their British counterparts, more than 500 draftees refused any sort of alternative service and went to prison. The labor leader Eugene V. Debs, for whom Hardie had campaigned years before, left a sickbed in 1918 to give a series of antiwar speeches, for which he, too, was thrown behind bars. The judge told him he might get a lesser sentence if he repented. "Repent?" asked Debs. "Repent? Repent for standing like a man?" Still in his cell in the Atlanta Federal Penitentiary, in 1920, he would receive nearly a million votes for president on the Socialist ticket.

British officials feared that another "victory" as costly as Passchendaele could put their country, like Russia, at risk of upheaval. As surveillance intensified, the number of agents under Thomson's command grew to 700, though now he had competition from the army. Its own busy operatives produced a voluminous Weekly Intelligence Summary for John French's Home Forces headquarters, with eight categories including "General Public Opinion" and "Acts of Disloyalty." Reports under each heading were contributed by regional army commands around the country, one of which added a ninth category, "Movements of Irishmen." Agents dutifully recorded the graffiti in army latrines; scrawled on the wall of one in Yorkshire was "What the hell are we fighting for, only the capitalists."

At times the writers of these confidential Weekly Intelligence Summaries sounded as if they, like the Bolsheviks, expected revolution to sweep across Europe. "There is scarcely a community or group of people in England now," reported a gloomy officer of the London District Command in early 1918, "among whom the principles of Socialism and extreme democratic control are now beginning to be listened to with ever increasing eagerness. . . . There is no gathering of working people in the country which is not disposed to regard Capitalism as a proven failure." Accounts of speeches by Sylvia Pankhurst, Emily Hobhouse, and Charlotte Despard appeared in these files: "The whole tone of Mrs. Despard's speech was that of resistance to authority," reported one agent. Those with "sound views" were also duly noted: "Mrs. Pankhurst and Miss Christabel Pankhurst are conducting a patriotic campaign in all the major industrial centres, of which favourable reports have come to hand." With Lloyd George's approval, a group of business magnates had given Christabel £15,000 (more than $850,000 in today's money) for her anti-socialist campaigning.

Sylvia's *Workers' Dreadnought* was probably the most widely read of the handful of newspapers opposed to the war, and army intelligence agents busily clipped articles from it for their files. She was also involved in a new group, the People's Russian Information Bureau. In contrast to the anti-Bolshevik mainstream press, it promised to put before the public the glorious truth about the Russian Revolution.

But what was that truth? Some of it, despite her rosy vision, was not so glorious. Shortly after the Bolshevik coup, the country had chosen a new legislature in the first real election Russia had ever had. The Bolsheviks won just under a quarter of the vote. But when the legislature met at the Tauride Palace in Petrograd in January 1918, the Bolsheviks and some allies walked out. Troops loyal to them then surged into the meeting hall, turned out the lights, and broke up the gathering. The lights remained out: it would be some 70 years before Russia had another democratically elected legislature. Some radicals in other countries, impatient with the elected parliaments that had embroiled Europe in war, thought little of it, but for many, the euphoria with which they had greeted the Russian Revolution evaporated. In her prison cell in Germany, Rosa Luxemburg was outraged, and railed against Lenin's "rule by terror. . . . Freedom only for the supporters of the government . . . is no freedom," she wrote. "Freedom is always for the one who thinks differently."

Meanwhile, with a surprising absence of fanfare, another legislative body took a step that, if it had occurred before the war, would have been the news story of the year. Britain gave women the vote.

Emmeline Pankhurst was delighted, although she had little to do with getting this particular bill through Parliament. The great step forward, which so many women had worked for, gone to jail for, and in a few cases died for, was part of a comprehensive electoral reform. Among other things, the new law enfranchised almost all men over 21 —over 19 if they were in the armed forces. However, given that some half-million British soldiers had so far been killed, many MPs worried that enfranchising all women would make them a majority of voters— something clearly unthinkable. How could that be avoided? Very simply: the new bill enfranchised only women over 30. Nor was even that unconditional: property and other qualifications excluded about 22 percent of these older women.

The women's franchise clause of the bill passed the House of Commons by an astonishing seven-to-one margin. In a Parliament that had long resisted women's suffrage, how could this be? For one thing, giving the vote to almost all men taking part in the war effort made it hard to deny it to women, for so many were making munitions for the front or filling the jobs of men gone off to war, even serving as members of the Ladies' Fire Brigade (albeit discreetly clothed in dresses). And hadn't so many suffragettes, like Mrs. Pankhurst, proved their loyalty to their country in its hour of need? Finally, there was the ominous example of the Russian Revolution. Who knew what pent-up discontents might burst forth violently in Britain after the war? Giving most women the vote would eliminate one of them.

For the people of Russia, the chain of events ignited by their revolution would bring a far bloodier future than the sunlit one its supporters had first imagined. But for the dispossessed in Western countries, wringing concessions from reluctant elites, the specter of that revolution, as an example of what could happen if justice was too long denied, would prove an enormous boon. The women of Britain were among its first beneficiaries.

Ever since the Battle of Omdurman twenty years earlier, Winston Churchill had had a knack for being present at moments that would find their way into the history books. On March 21, 1918, he was using his role as minister of munitions as an excuse to visit the front, and was spending the night at a divisional headquarters in northern France when the long-expected German attack came at last. On high ground, the headquarters overlooked many miles of the front line. "Exactly as a pianist runs his hands across the keyboard from treble to bass, there rose in less than one minute the most tremendous cannonade I shall ever hear," he wrote. The German barrage "swept around us in a wide curve of red leaping flame . . . quite unending in either direction."

This was the heaviest bombardment the British army had ever experienced; the writers Leonard and Virginia Woolf could hear it at their Sussex home across the English Channel. An unprecedented concentration of heavy German artillery poured out more than a million shells in a mere five hours—compared to the British taking nearly a week to fire one and a half million before the attack on the Somme. "At half-past four in the morning," recalled one British officer, "I thought the world was coming to an end." The intensity of the barrage rendered some soldiers helpless. "The first to be affected were the young ones who'd just come out," remembered a veteran of this night. "They would go to one of the older ones—older in service that is—and maybe even cuddle up to him and start crying."

The attack came at a bad time, for Haig's troops were in the midst of a complicated reorganization that involved reducing the number of battalions in each division. The German blow also struck at a vulnerable point: spreading their forces thinner, the British had just extended their sector of the front, taking over from the French about 25 miles of trenches, some of them poorly constructed—and with supply roads leading to Paris, not to British bases. Finally, most of the terrible loss of British blood in 1915, 1916, and 1917 had been during British offensives, and after three years without experiencing a major German assault, Haig was overconfident and his defensive positions not as strong as they could have been. Despite information that some kind of attack was coming, he had just granted leave to 88,000 troops.

On the German side, four factors made the attack formidable, only three of which the generals themselves had planned on. The first was surprise: the Germans kept their ammunition dumps covered so they couldn't be seen from the air; assault troops were moved up to the front at night; and, unlike the British offensive at Passchendaele, this one was not preceded by a two-week bombardment that gave ample advance notice. All the artillery fire was packed into those five hours. Second, that fire was staggering: the Germans had quietly maneuvered into position more than 6,400 guns and 3,500 mortars, whose barrage combined high explosives with shells containing poison gas. Mixed with the latter was quick-acting tear gas, which tempted many an unwary British soldier to take off his gas mask and rub his streaming eyes, only to then breathe in the gas that would hours later kill or disable him. Third, the Germans were fighting differently, having put 56 divisions through a rigorous three-week retraining program. Instead of tens of thousands of troops forming an easy target by advancing in plain view in a line abreast across miles of front, men were divided into groups of seven to ten "storm troopers," under officers making decisions on the spot, not following a schedule laid down by generals in the rear. The groups darted forward, using gullies or other natural cover, aiming to slip between British machine-gun posts and overwhelm artillerymen in the rear, who thought themselves out of range of any infantry attack.

That they could succeed so well in this task was due to a fourth factor, the fortuitous assistance of nature. Dense, low-lying fog cloaked the battlefield until midday, allowing the storm trooper teams to reach and cross British front-line trenches while largely unseen by machine-gunners who otherwise would have decimated them. Already dazed by the artillery barrage, most British troops didn't see the Germans until they were close enough to throw hand grenades into British trenches. The Germans had found the most imaginative new tactics yet seen in trench warfare, and they worked. The British trenches rang with panicked cries of "Jerry's through!" By the day's end the Germans had captured more than 98 square miles of ground, and the British were evacuating another 40. Losses of position on this scale had not happened since the rival armies had dug in more than three years earlier.

The Germans knew they had to break one army, the French or the British, and had decided on the latter. The aim was to drive a spearhead deep into British lines and then veer westward, toward the French coast, trapping hundreds of thousands of soldiers with only the English Channel at their backs. Germany's last great gamble had begun, and after this it had no more cards to play. Its cities short of food, its farms and factories stripped of young men, the country was like a bloodied boxer in the final round, risking all his remaining strength on a knock-out punch. General Erich Ludendorff, directing the assault, declared that if victory required it, he was willing to lose a million men. If the offensive failed, he said, "Germany must go under."

At the end of the first day, German losses of 40,000 were—startling for an offensive in this war—almost even with Britain's 38,500. And yet the balance was in Germany's favor, because some two-thirds of its casualties were wounded, many of whom would recover to fight again, whereas a humiliating 21,000 of the British total never would: they had been taken prisoner. The new storm trooper tactics had caught them by surprise. "I thought we had stopped them," said one private, who had been aiming his machine gun forward through the fog, "when I felt a bump in the back. I turned round and there was a German officer with a revolver in my back. 'Come along, Tommy. You've done enough.' I turned round then and said 'Thank you very much, Sir.'"

As British troops retreated, they were forced to give up even the graveyards of men killed in earlier battles. Wounded men filled the hospitals and fleeing French civilians carrying their belongings clogged the roads. "Old women in black dresses there were," remembered one British officer; "bent old men trundling wheelbarrows; girls in their Sunday best—to wear it the best way to save it; farm carts loaded with the miscellany of hens, pigs, furniture, children, mattresses, bolsters; moody cows being whacked and led by little boys." Behind them columns of smoke rose from their farms and villages, torched by Allied soldiers who wanted to leave nothing of use to the Germans.

The Kaiser was delighted. "The battle is won," he shouted jubilantly to a soldier on guard at a railway platform as he boarded his private train. "The English have been utterly defeated!" He gave German schoolchildren a holiday, and presented Field Marshal Paul von Hindenburg, the supreme military commander, with the Grand Cross of the Iron Cross with Golden Rays, a medal last awarded to Marshal Gebhard von Blücher for defeating Napoleon. To General Ludendorff, the actual architect of the attack, he presented an iron statuette of himself. Once again, he could imagine himself as master of all Europe. In Berlin, flags were broken out and church bells rang.

In London, John French used the occasion to urge Lloyd George to fire Haig. From the capital, Alfred Milner traveled through the night to France to survey the damage and report back. Before he left, he dashed off a pessimistic note to Violet Cecil: "The force of the blow was beyond all precedent, even in this war, and beyond expectation." After conferring with British commanders, he joined Haig, French Prime Minister Georges Clemenceau, and French military leaders for an emergency conference at the town of Doullens, which had seen wars ever since the Middle Ages. As the shaken dignitaries gathered around an oval table beneath a chandelier in the mansard-roofed town hall—Milner with his stern, drawn face, an unsmiling Haig in uniform and boots, and the balding, stocky Clemenceau fearing his entire country might be overrun—it was a desperate scene. The leaders could hear the constant pounding of artillery and the gravelly rattle of British tanks maneuvering into position to guard the town's perimeter against a German breakthrough. Haggard, dust-covered troops were retreating through the streets.

The Germans continued to press forward, although, without the element of surprise, not as swiftly and dramatically as on the first day. Particularly heartbreaking for British soldiers was their retreat over ground they had gained at such terrible cost during the great battles at the Somme and Passchendaele. By early April, German forces had advanced 40 miles, overrunning 1,200 square miles of France—yet still not enough to veer toward the coast as planned—and a shockingly high percentage of British losses continued to be men taken prisoner: 90,000 in just the first two weeks of the offensive. German newsreel cameramen eagerly filmed them, along with newly captured French and Belgian towns. Canisters of film were rushed back to Berlin, and soon evidence of the seemingly unstoppable drive toward Paris was on screens throughout Germany.

The German advance brought another new and terrifying weapon into the war, the first sign of which came two days after the offensive began, when Parisians were startled by a succession of massive explosions, each 20 minutes apart—in front of the Gare de l'Est, by the Quai de la Seine, in the Jardins des Tuileries, in the suburb of Châtillon, and at other widely scattered spots. As buildings collapsed, crushing those inside, people on the street rushed for shelter—but it was unclear what they were sheltering from, for the Germans were some 70 miles away, and there were no airplanes in the clear blue sky. It took several hours and a sharp-eyed French military aviator to discover that Paris was being bombarded by specially manufactured guns mounted on railway cars, their barrels more than 100 feet long. It took about three minutes for each giant shell to cover the distance to the city, climbing to an altitude of 25 miles at the top of its trajectory. This was by far the highest point ever reached by a man-made object, so high that gunners, in calculating where their shells would land, had to take into account the rotation of the Earth. For the first time in warfare, deadly projectiles rained down on civilians from the stratosphere.

When he returned to London, friends found Milner looking pale. He and the rest of the War Cabinet found new troops for Haig, but only by desperate measures: two divisions were recalled from Palestine and one from Italy, and the army lowered the minimum age for the draft to 17½. The government also took a momentous, long-delayed step: it announced it would extend conscription to Ireland. For fear of the response — both in Ireland and among Irish Americans — this had never been done before, but how, people in England now complained, could the army call up even 17-year-olds and let the Irish be exempt?

Over several months, as the British and French held many urgent high-level strategy meetings, Milner spent about half his time in France, ironing out disputes. Few of the two countries' generals spoke each other's language well, and Milner's fluency in French helped; he sometimes interpreted for Lloyd George. Between trips he reported to the King, who at one point invited him to Windsor Castle for the weekend — although of course Violet could not go with him.

In purely military terms, the spring of 1918 was Haig's finest hour. Paradoxically, when the mere appearance of weakness or indecision at the top might have been fatal, the same qualities that had led him to uselessly sacrifice so many British lives at the Somme and Passchendaele — his stubbornness, his unshakable faith in the rightness of Britain's cause, his almost mindless optimism in the face of bad news — proved essential. They made him into the calm, unyielding defensive commander that British troops needed.

The Germans still had many more troops on hand than the Allies, for the collapse of Russia had enabled them to add a stunning 44 divisions — more than half a million men — to their army in the west. In early April, after German forces launched another storm-trooper-led attack near Ypres, Haig issued a dispatch to all his soldiers, drafted with few changes in his own steady, confident handwriting: "Many amongst us are now tired. To those I would say that victory belongs to those who hold out the longest. . . . Every position must be held to the last man: there must be no retirement. With our backs to the wall, and believing in the justice of our cause, each one of us must fight on to the end."

British troops did indeed feel they had their backs to the wall. Haig's words embodied something else as well, absent from years of earlier exhortations: honesty. To say that "victory belongs to those who hold out the longest" was acknowledging at last that the war would be won not by dramatic cavalry charges, but by attrition. Which army would exhaust itself first? Moving over an already ravaged landscape now freshly gouged by new shell holes, the German advance continued.

In mid-April, as Britain's retreating armies continued to stagger backward under the worst German blows in nearly four years of fighting, Milner became secretary of state for war. His signature now appeared on the condolence cards sent to soldiers' families, below a standard message: "The King commands me to assure you of the true sympathy of His Majesty and the Queen in Your Sorrow. He whose loss you mourn died in the noblest of causes."

The cards flowed out in a ceaseless stream. (Families of officers were notified sooner, by black-bordered telegrams.) But when it came to Stephen Hobhouse's youngest brother, his parents, like so many others, simply received word that in the new German offensive the 23-year-old Paul was "missing, presumed killed." He had been seen fighting, then falling, when his unit's position was overrun. Several months later, the family's hopes were raised when a fellow officer passed on a rumor that Paul was wounded and a prisoner in Germany. With mail going through contacts in neutral countries, Stephen got in touch with a pacifist committee in Berlin. "I was very glad to be able to set on foot by this means a search for my brother Paul. Alas, no trace of him could be found. My poor mother for over six months . . . persisted in the fond belief that Paul would return." During that time Margaret Hobhouse never ceased to write letters to her son, although they eventually came back marked "Undeliverable. Return to Sender." Paul's body was never found.

The German attacks of March and April 1918 were a severe setback to the British army but by no means a boost to antiwar feeling. When troops had their backs to the wall, the public showed little desire to question the war's aims. The number of workdays lost to strikes

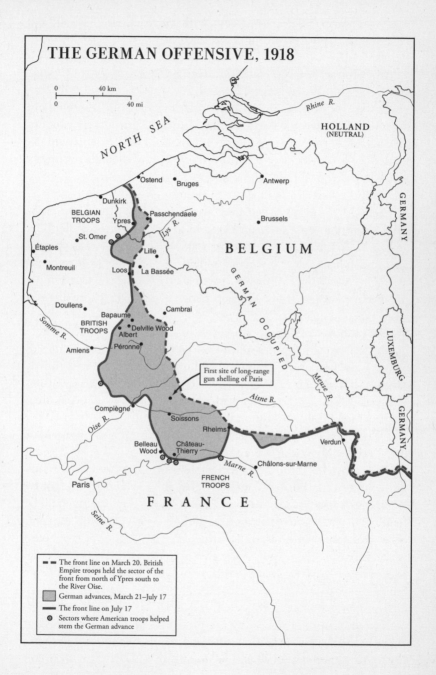

THE GERMAN OFFENSIVE, 1918

0 ____ 40 km
0 ____ 40 mi

Rhine R.

HOLLAND
(NEUTRAL)

NORTH SEA

Ostend • Bruges • • Antwerp

Dunkirk

BELGIAN TROOPS
Ypres • Passchendaele

St. Omer

Étaples •

Montreuil •

Lille •

Loos • La Bassée

Lys R.

B E L G I U M

• Brussels

GERMANY

Doullens •

Bapaume •

BRITISH TROOPS
Albert • • Delville Wood

Somme R.

Amiens •

Péronne •

Cambrai •

GERMAN OCCUPIED

Meuse R.

LUXEMBURG

First site of long-range
gun shelling of Paris

Compiègne •

Oise R.

Soissons •

Aisne R.

Rheims •

Verdun •

GERMANY

Belleau
Wood • Château-
Thierry •

Marne R.

Châlons-sur-Marne •

Paris •

FRENCH TROOPS

F R A N C E

Seine R.

- - - The front line on March 20. British
Empire troops held the sector of the
front from north of Ypres south to
the River Oise.

⬛ German advances, March 21–July 17

――― The front line on July 17

⊚ Sectors where American troops helped
stem the German advance

dropped. "The recent severe fighting on the Western front appears to have had a most salutary effect on public opinion," the Scottish Command told army headquarters in a Weekly Intelligence Summary; in Aberdeen, overage men were volunteering, and a deserter surrendered himself "on account of the gravity of the situation." Another agent reported that "at Liverpool recent events have had a steadying influence on the working man." The intensified fighting produced the same result in Germany, where threats of labor militance temporarily evaporated.

Redoubling his efforts to keep up civilian morale, Rudyard Kipling spoke at munitions factories and barraged high officials with long, detailed memos about everything from mobilizing "parsons and priests" for the war effort to bringing documentary films—he sketched out scenarios for half a dozen—to factories so workers could see the splendid effect of the weapons they produced. The British workman "has a great respect for the gift of the gab," he declared. ". . . Almost as important as the cinema is the lecturer who accompanies [it]. . . . The munitions workers listen best to a person they consider of their own class." John Buchan's propaganda offensive also aimed at the working class, taking labor unionists on tours of the front line; by mid-1918, more than 1,000 union leaders and rank-and-file members had been on these trips. Union men serving at the front were encouraged to write to their branches back home, especially when strikes loomed; military censors made sure it was the patriotic letters that got through. The jingoistic newspaper *John Bull* published a cartoon showing a CO sitting comfortably by a hearth, in an easy chair, with the caption "This little pig stayed at home."

In this bleak spring, Bertrand Russell finally joined those Britons in prison. As their excuse, authorities seized on a few sentences in an article in the No-Conscription Fellowship's *Tribunal,* where Russell predicted that the American troops now starting to arrive in England and France might be used as strikebreakers, "an occupation to which the American Army is accustomed when at home." In court, the prosecutor claimed that this passage would have a "diabolical effect" and interfere with relations between Britain and a key ally. "A very despicable offence," thundered the judge, and sentenced Russell to six months. When he arrived to begin serving his time, Russell wrote, the warder taking down his particulars "asked my religion and I replied 'agnostic.'

He asked how to spell it, and remarked with a sigh: 'Well, there are many religions, but I suppose they all worship the same God.'"

Officials were so awed by Russell's intellectual stature and aristocratic lineage that, alone among British war resisters, he was allowed to be a "First Division" prisoner—an ancient, privileged status that permitted inmates to keep the tools of their trade, which for him were pen, books, and paper. He was allowed to receive the *Times* and to have books, flowers, and fruit sent in from outside, and was assigned an extra-large cell and a fellow convict to clean it for him at sixpence a day. Russell had a lively and unconventional love life, and, evading the limits on correspondence, was able to smuggle out letters to two women he was involved with, all the while still nominally married to a third. A set of letters to one lover, a young actress, were in French, which he knew his guards would not be able to read; Russell convinced them that these were historical documents copied from his research materials. A letter to another woman he slipped inside the uncut pages of the *Proceedings of the London Mathematical Society*, telling her the volume was more interesting than it appeared. The actress sent him love notes through the "Personals" column of the *Times*, until Scotland Yard caught on after a "many happy returns" message appeared on Russell's birthday. One of Thomson's sleuths showed up to question her. Always self-disciplined, Russell wrote four hours a day, producing, among other work, 70,000 words of his *Introduction to Mathematical Philosophy.*

Outside prison walls, mounted police broke up a rally in London's Finsbury Park in the midst of a speech by Charlotte Despard. And the authorities were particularly eager to shut down the NCF's *Tribunal,* which had long been an impertinent voice against the war's madness. Reluctant to tarnish Britain's free-speech image by banning the paper outright, they tried other methods.

At the National Labour Press, where the *Tribunal* was printed, the police arrived and dismantled the press machinery. The paper switched to a new printer, which was soon raided, and found its presses damaged too. Produced on a small hand press, the paper promptly reappeared as a one-page leaflet with the triumphant headline "Here We Are Again!!" When the two men who operated this press ran out of type for the large capital letters used for headlines, they borrowed them from friendly fellow printers on Lord Northcliffe's rabidly prowar *Daily Mail*. For months to come, moving once or twice because of suspicious neighbors, this secret press continued to print the paper, although distribution difficulties—the police were watching the mail—greatly reduced its circulation. Basil Thomson's men never found it.

Trying to figure out where the *Tribunal* was being printed, agents twice raided the NCF, and watched the office constantly. An impoverished-looking woman with a baby carriage who visited the building every few days, apparently hoping for a handout, never attracted their attention. She was smuggling proof sheets of the *Tribunal* beneath the blankets of her carriage. Indeed, as one after another of the NCF's male leaders had gone to prison for defying the draft, women had become the organization's backbone. Catherine Marshall, a talented organizer and suffrage movement veteran, was the group's central figure until she broke down from exhaustion in late 1917. Joan Beauchamp spent a month in prison for an article she published as the *Tribunal*'s editor, and Violet Tillard two months for refusing to reveal to police where the paper was being printed.

The COs in prison were getting more restive. In May 1918, following Stephen Hobhouse's example, some COs jailed in Liverpool announced that they would break all prison rules they considered "inhuman and immoral," including the rule of silence. For ten days the prison resounded with talk, laughter, and singing. Then the warders cracked down, moving the men they thought to be ringleaders to other prisons. Some COs went on hunger strikes, only to find themselves force-fed like the suffragettes. Many drew encouragement from knowing that they were not the only political prisoners in Britain. When Fenner Brockway was being punished for the Liverpool protest, he was placed in solitary on reduced rations. One day an older convict, a trusty who did odd jobs around the cellblock, slipped a note into his cell: "Dear Brockway—Just heard you are here. What can we do for you? . . . We are Irishmen and can do anything you want—except get you out. Have your reply ready for 'Trusty' when he calls to-morrow. Cheerio!"

Among these Irish prisoners was Eamon De Valera, who, a decade and a half later, would become his country's prime minister. With their help, Brockway smuggled a letter to his wife, and then got his hands on what he craved most: newspapers, including the *Labour Leader,* whose editor he had once been. He retrieved these by lowering a thread from his cell window to which his unseen Irish friends attached the precious cargo. In a corner of his cell out of sight of the spy hole, which now and then clicked open, Brockway devoured the papers. "Only those who have been cut off from family, friends and the world can understand what this meant to me."

Brockway's fellow prisoners were not the only Irish patriots in jail, for Ireland was in turmoil. The execution of the Easter Rising leaders two years earlier had inflamed long-simmering nationalist feeling, and the planned draft of Irishmen seemed like the final blow. Why be compelled to join a war supposedly fought for Belgium's national integrity when exactly that was denied to Ireland? The island's Catholic bishops, never known for their radicalism, issued a ringing manifesto against conscription; Irish trade unions called a 24-hour general strike, and everywhere (except in the Protestant north) factories, newspaper presses, trains, trolleys, and horse cabs came to a halt. Even the pubs closed.

With British troops on the Continent reeling, this new rebellion in Ireland posed a crisis. To contain it, the British cabinet felt it needed an experienced military man with a firm hand. On May 4, 1918, Milner, on behalf of Lloyd George, offered the position of Viceroy of Ireland to John French.

Five days later, the diminutive, bowlegged field marshal took the mail ship across the Irish Sea. Regarding his position as a war posting, he brought with him neither his wife nor Winifred Bennett (although she would later visit many times). Within days of being sworn in at Dublin Castle, he ordered the arrest of an array of independence leaders. Long convinced that his own Irish ancestry gave him special insight, he saw himself as more Irish than the nationalists, regarding them as "people steeped to the neck in the violent forms of crime and infamy and with the smallest possible proportion of Irish blood in their veins." Once this was widely understood, he believed, "The Irish would cast them out like the swine they are."

The Irish, he told Lloyd George, were "like nothing so much as a lot of frightened children who dread being thrashed." With proper discipline all would be well. Basil Thomson made his intelligence network indispensable to the new viceroy, and French was confident he could soon restore order.

The same month French set off for Ireland, Emmeline Pankhurst embarked on a speaking tour of the United States, aimed at encouraging war enthusiasm. Meanwhile, in *Britannia,* Christabel kept up a steady fusillade of support for her mother while calling for the burning of all socialist books "by the public hangman." On her return from her American trip, Emmeline told an audience at Queen's Hall in London: "Some talk about the Empire and Imperialism as if it were something to decry and something to be ashamed of. It seems to me that it is a great thing to be the inheritors of an Empire like ours."

To Sylvia, the transformation of both her mother and older sister still seemed incomprehensible. "I only look in wonder," she wrote to the banished Adela, in Australia, "and ask myself, 'Can those two really be sane?'"

Meanwhile, the war news grew worse. At the end of May the Germans launched yet another powerful surprise offensive northeast of Paris, preceded by two million artillery shells fired off in less than five hours. In three days, the Germans pushed panicked Allied troops back 20 miles, advancing with such speed that they captured a French military airfield with all its planes still on the ground. The jubilant Kaiser went back and forth from Berlin to the front, inspecting troops in the field, newly captured villages, and the great guns shelling Paris. However, it was not France that the Kaiser saw as the main enemy, but Britain and its empire, in "a conflict between the two approaches to the world. Either the Prussian-Germanic approach—Right, Freedom, Honor, Morality—is to remain respected or the Anglo-Saxon, which would mean enthroning the worship of gold."

With the enemy now only 37 miles from Paris, Clemenceau considered evacuating the city. Parisians fled south by the hundreds of thousands, and high stacks of baggage jammed the platforms of railroad stations. To the government in London, simultaneously dealing with a brewing upheaval in Ireland, the future looked bleak and terrifying. At one point the cabinet discussed evacuating all British troops from the Continent. Fierce backbiting between Haig and Lloyd George and their respective supporters over who was responsible for the British losses spilled over into parliamentary debate and the press. One high-ranking British general lost his job, but Haig once again survived.

"We must be prepared for France and Italy both being beaten to their knees," Milner wrote to Lloyd George in early June while on yet another emergency trip across the Channel. General Sir Henry Wilson, the friend who had been Milner's military counterpart on his 1917 mission to pre-revolution Russia, was now chief of the Imperial General Staff in London and shared Milner's fear of an Allied collapse before the seemingly unstoppable Germans. "What would this mean?" Wilson wrote in his diary. "The destruction of our army in France?"

21

THERE ARE MORE DEAD
THAN LIVING NOW

FROM DUBLIN CASTLE, with its round stone tower topped with ramparts, John French, officially Viscount of Ypres and now Lord Lieutenant of Ireland, set out to impose order on his rebellious realm. He established a secret budget to reward informers, ordered police to close meeting halls and seize printing presses, demanded additional troops from London, and sent out a stream of orders that in effect imposed different degrees of martial law on parts of the island. He dispatched special reports to the King, who, evidently unable to read his handwriting, asked French to send them typed. On July 4, 1918, he forbade all processions and meetings throughout Ireland held without permission. But he neglected to ban games of soccer and hurling, the Irish equivalent of field hockey, which quickly became gathering points for the most militant nationalists.

"Any hesitation or avoidable delay in carrying out the conscription policy," he wrote the King, "would be fatal to the future of the country." Drafting Irishmen, French believed, would solve two problems at once, providing the beleaguered British army with sorely needed troops and bringing about "the complete removal of useless and idle youths and men between 18 and 24 or 25" from Ireland. (Desperate for new troops at the front, Haig was also pressing for Irish conscription, one of the few things on which these two bitter rivals agreed.) But when French tried to begin calling up Irishmen, the British cabinet restrained him. Lloyd George and Milner, less ham-fisted than he, understood that decreeing a draft for Ireland had temporarily satisfied the English public. Actually imposing it, however, would give Irish nationalists an inflammatory rallying point. For months, French fumed impatiently, firing off messages of complaint to London.

And then, gradually, it appeared that Irish conscripts for the Western Front might not be so urgently needed after all.

Despite the expanse of newly captured French territory that now bulged ominously toward Paris on the map, all was not going well for the Germans. "The threat of an American Army gathers like a thunder-cloud in the rear of our other enemies," a German officer wrote in his diary, and every week brought that threat closer. The brief window of opportunity for a decisive German victory was starting to close.

Furthermore, the very speed of the German advance had caused a problem commanders had not anticipated. Short of food for months, consuming a diet heavy on turnips and horsemeat, exhausted German troops kept halting, against orders, to gorge on tempting supplies of French wine, British rum, canned beef, bread, jam, and biscuits left by the retreating Allies, and to slaughter cows and chickens taken from French farmers. It was a bad blow to German morale to see how well fed the Allies were—especially after soldiers had been repeatedly told that the U-boat campaign had left the enemy starving.

A new wave of German attacks in early June 1918 stalled when they reached the natural barrier of the Marne River and encountered fierce resistance from newly arrived American troops at Château-Thierry and in the wheat fields around Belleau Wood, names that would go down in U.S. military lore. When withdrawing French soldiers urged a U.S. Marine officer to do the same, he replied, "Retreat? Hell, we just got here." The several weeks of fighting at Belleau Wood were the largest American battle since the Civil War. By the time it was over, in late June, some three-quarters of a million U.S. troops were in Europe, with shiploads more arriving almost daily. The balance of forces on the Western Front was now changed for good.

In addition to confronting Americans eager for battle, the German high command found danger in another quarter. The impact of the

Russian Revolution was beginning to ripple through the German army. As its divisions of Eastern Front troops were transported to France and Belgium, the generals discovered that revolutionary ideas had come with them. Having read German-language newspapers distributed by the Bolsheviks or fraternized with soldiers from the fast-dissolving Russian army, many had lost all ardor for combat.

"Our victorious army on the Eastern Front became rotten with Bolshevism," a senior German general told an American newspaper after the war. "We got to the point where we did not dare transfer certain of our eastern divisions to the West." Soldiers shipped to the Western Front turned rowdy, firing shots from train windows, and from one troop train in May 1918 carrying 631 men, 83 deserted along the way. Cynical troops chalked "Cattle for Flanders" on the sides of the railway cars taking them west, and in half a dozen German cities underground networks sprang up to aid deserters. Leftist sympathizers—the Wheeldon family's German counterparts—provided men with shelter, money, forged papers and ration cards, and instructions on the best spots to slip across the border into neutral Holland.

Ludendorff, the German commander in the west, was not yet done, however; he ordered more attacks in July. His grasp on reality slipping, he also ordered his collapsing Turkish allies to undertake operations in Mesopotamia that would supposedly be a first step toward threatening British control of India. He was not the only German holding out hope for a last-minute miracle. Even as the tide was turning against his men, Kaiser Wilhelm II again came to the Western Front to watch a battle unfold from a tall wooden observation tower, "eyes glued to telescopes that show nothing but distant fumes and blurs and smudges," as Churchill put it later, "while his throne totters."

The Germans suffered half a million casualties in the five months following the launch of their 1918 offensive, with their highly trained storm troopers taking the brunt of the toll. There were few reinforcements left except the overage and the very young, and so the retreat began. Allied troop morale rose with the flood of Americans: every month more than 200,000 in their broad-brimmed hats poured into France. Although many required additional training, to war-weary British and French eyes they seemed astoundingly well fed, almost Olympian. "They looked larger than ordinary men," remembered the writer Vera Brittain, nursing British wounded in France. "Their tall, straight figures were in vivid contrast to the under-sized armies of pale recruits to which we had grown accustomed." The Americans were so impatient to fight that the U.S. Army's rear-area support units suffered an epidemic of men "deserting to the front." More than 3,000 of those combat-hungry "deserters" were killed.

The very speed of the German army's advances now left it vulnerable, for it had had no time to construct the concrete and steel machine-gun bunkers, wide fields of barbed wire, and other fortifications that had cost so many Allied lives in more than three years of trench warfare. In mid-July the French and Americans attacked together, pushing the Germans back in a series of battles. During one, Corporal Adolf Hitler got into a fistfight with a newly arrived soldier who insisted it was foolish to keep fighting. According to a man in his unit, Hitler "became furious and shouted in a terrible voice that pacifists and shirkers were losing the war."

On August 8, 1918, the British and French launched a powerful new offensive, which caught the Germans off guard because there was no preceding artillery bombardment. Equally surprised was Lloyd George: Haig, flaunting his control of all things military, did not bother to tell his prime minister in advance of the attack. This assault, the Battle of Amiens, offered a foretaste of twentieth-century wars to come: the Allies at last made effective use of tanks, deploying more than 500 of them, newer varieties less prone to break down. (Milner had just been to tank headquarters in France to ride in the latest models.) In the years ahead the speed and armor of the tank would allow it to supplant the cavalry in the age-old quest to transcend the limitations of the earthbound foot soldier. Tank regiments in some armies would outrage traditionalists by usurping the crossed-swords insignia of the cavalry.

The British had finally learned how to integrate the various new technologies of war: the tanks, to crush barbed wire so the infantry could get through; triangulation spotting of German artillery fire by recorded sound waves, so as to lay down counterfire and knock out enemy guns; manufactured radio traffic, to fool the Germans into thinking large numbers of troops were being moved elsewhere; camouflage, to mislead observation planes; flights by massive fleets of aircraft, to mask the noise of troops moving into position for an attack. Planes were even used to air-drop ammunition to advancing infantry, overcoming the vexing problem of transporting supplies forward across four years' worth of craters, rusted barbed wire, and old trenches. Haig and those around him had at last come to understand that war was now a complex industrial process. Grudgingly, without acknowledging it, he was leaving the era of the horseman behind; the five cavalry divisions once under his command had been quietly reduced to three.

More important than the territory gained in the new offensive was that suddenly the Germans, legendary fighters in this war, were surrendering, often throwing down their rifles and raising their hands when confronted by smaller numbers of Allied troops. It was this, and not lost ground, that began to convince a dismayed General Ludendorff that Germany had lost the war. The day the latest Allied offensive began, August 8, he wrote in his memoirs, "was the black day of the German Army." Two days later, he offered his resignation to the Kaiser, who rejected it. The war continued, but rumors of pessimism at the top began to seep out. Several hundred thousand soldiers well behind the lines either deserted or else remained in uniform but evaded orders to go to the front. In the minds of the German high command was a rising fear that, if army discipline and morale collapsed, something even worse than an Allied victory could occur: revolution at home.

The specter of revolution frightened rulers in Britain too. One hundred thousand workers protesting food shortages had marched to Manchester's town hall in January. British trade union membership was rising, and 1918 saw more than 5.8 million workdays lost to industrial disputes, by far the highest total during the war years. In July a rash of strikes by munitions workers were quelled by a combination of patriotic appeals, threats, and deception. Basil Thomson sent a Scotland Yard agent to an affected area, who would settle into a pub frequented by striking workers and, after a few drinks, in strict confidence, drop the information that he worked for the national conscription authorities and had come to town to arrange for call-up notices. How, men asked him, could they avoid being drafted? Simple, he said: immediately go back to work. Once this rumor was planted, it worked wonders—or so Thomson claimed.

Nonetheless, work stoppages spread. London's Paddington station briefly shut down, as did some rail lines. Military units were put on alert, and an entire brigade moved to Newport, a center of strike activity, while a company of Scots Guards was dispatched to East London as a show of force against picketing rail workers. The *Times* advocated a military takeover of the railways for the duration of the war.

Particularly unnerving for ruling circles was something Britain had never seen before, a police strike. As was true for most British workers, their pay had not kept up with the soaring cost of living. On August 30, 1918, 12,000 London bobbies, the majority of the force, walked off the job. Even some Scotland Yard detectives—who normally spied on would-be strikers—joined them. The government rushed in soldiers to guard public buildings, and then, after Lloyd George convened an emergency meeting, promised to raise police pay and pensions. The bobbies were back on the job in two days, but the prime minister later said he felt Britain had never come "nearer to Bolshevism."

Although there was a sometimes desperate demand for troops on the Western Front in the first half of 1918, Brock Millman, a careful scholar of Britain's internal security measures, makes a convincing case that the government held back men and arms for fear of revolution at home. Four Royal Navy battleships, for example, were stationed in the Thames estuary, to no visible military purpose. Still more revealing, at the beginning of 1918 there were roughly 1.5 million soldiers in Britain itself. After taking into account troops in Ireland, in training, recovering from wounds, underage for overseas service, or serving in antiaircraft units, Millman calculates that this still left 175,000 fully trained extra troops on army bases at home.

Contingency deployment plans showed them being sent, if need be, to districts adjacent to, but not actually within, areas of trade union militancy, such as Scotland's River Clyde. Millman suggests that this would have put soldiers close enough to be rushed in for strikebreaking duties, but not so close that, when off duty, they could mingle at local pubs or soccer fields with the very people whose strikes they were breaking, who might remind them of the old socialist saying that a bayonet was a weapon with a worker at each end. In July 1918, a month of many strikes, the boundaries of British military command districts were redrawn to coincide with those of national police districts. The authorities secretly drew up lists of people who, when the order was given, were to be jailed in preventive detention.

The French government also feared revolution. Unlike Haig, Clemenceau knew that cavalry was of little use at the front. Having had experience battling strikes as minister of the interior, however, he was well aware of how frightening armed men on horseback could be to a crowd. In March 1918, the very month the great German offensive started, he moved four cavalry divisions from the front to other parts of the country, to be on hand for use against strikers.

Few people worried more about revolution than Milner, but his thoughts on containing it were not bounded by Great Britain. Writing to Lloyd George in a letter marked "Very Confidential," he declared that the British sphere of influence "really extends from the Mediterranean shore of Palestine to the frontier of India. . . . We alone have got to keep Southern Asia." And he spoke in a similarly far-reaching way with others: "Much talk with Milner about our future action in Europe, in Russia, in Siberia," wrote General Wilson in his diary at a point when the Germans were safely in retreat. "From the left bank of the Don to India is our interest and our preserve." He agreed with Milner that "our real danger now is not the Boches but Bolshevism."

Russia was especially on the minds of men like Milner because a civil war had broken out there. The revolutionaries' Red Army was fighting on several fronts against various anti-Bolshevik forces. All sides shot prisoners and civilian hostages, as deaths, many from war-related famine, soared into the millions and bitter combat raged over the vast country. Among the early victims were the imprisoned Tsar Nicholas N and his family, all of them executed by the Bolsheviks—something that shocked the royalty-minded British public. As the war on the Western Front continued at full pitch, Milner became a key architect of the Allied campaign to support right-wing anti-Bolshevik forces in Russia with arms, training, supplies, and eventually troops, in an attempt to strangle the new ideology before it could spread to Western Europe.

Milner's love for Violet Cecil endured and they met often, although he always referred to her in his diary as "Lady Edward," as if someone might be looking over his shoulder. The new Allied successes made travel to France for civilians—at least well-connected ones—more possible, and on one occasion she was able to meet him in Paris. Clemenceau arranged permission for her to enter a military zone to visit the grave of her son, which the recent fighting had again washed over. "The cemetery has been shelled," she wrote, "though his grave was not touched. I stayed awhile both in the wood and at his grave side."

Her neighbors the Kiplings still did not know where their son's body lay, despite endless efforts. Kipling's output—poems, short stories, articles, pamphlets, speeches—remained prodigious, although his deep sorrow pulsed through it all. Working from official documents, countless interviews, and officers' diaries sometimes spotted with mud or blood from the trenches, he threw himself into a project of more than 600 pages that would take him five and a half years to complete, *The Irish Guards in the Great War,* a two-volume history of young John's regiment. Sober and restrained, quite unlike his other writing, the book painstakingly recounted battle upon battle, skirmish upon skirmish, losses, reinforcements, promotions, medals won, generals' messages of congratulation, and an endless list of officers and men killed, all written in the methodical manner of histories destined to be read mainly by those mentioned in them.

In explanation of his book's emotionally sparse style, Kipling wrote of the dead: "They . . . lived the span of a Second Lieutenant's life and were spent. Their intimates might preserve, perhaps, memories of a promise cut short, recollections of a phrase that stuck, a chance-seen act of bravery or of kindness. . . . In most instances, the compiler has let the mere fact suffice; since, to his mind, it did not seem fit to heap words on the doom." The book's detailed maps used the traditional emblem of little crossed swords to mark the sites of battles fought with more modern and deadly weapons, one such pair marking the engagement where John Kipling died. His father referred to him in just a few sentences, ending, "Here 2nd Lieutenant Clifford was shot and wounded or killed—the body was found later—and 2nd Lieutenant Kipling was wounded and missing."

Kipling's most striking comment about four years of bloodshed was this enigmatic couplet from his "Epitaphs of the War":

> If any question why we died,
> Tell them, because our fathers lied.

Did he mean, as he had often said, that prewar politicians lied in claiming that Britain was adequately prepared for a major conflict? Or was he speaking of a lie that went deeper? Perhaps the writer himself did not know.

Ludendorff was right: August 8, 1918, was indeed the black day of his army, and from then on, things only got worse. By September the combined Allied forces on the Western Front had grown to some six million men, nearly one-third of them American. On the home front, the war of attrition was taking its toll and German morale was crumbling. With nervous sweat visible on his face, the Kaiser spoke to sullen munitions workers at the giant Krupp factory in Essen, railing against rumormongers and antiwar agitators and urging a fight to the end. "To every single one of us his task is given," he said, "to you your hammer, to you at your lathe, to me upon my throne!" Embarrassingly, he was received with scattered laughs and silence.

In a matter of days, British and Belgian troops recaptured the ground that had taken Britain months and hundreds of thousands of casualties to win in the Battle of Passchendaele. With the front in motion, Haig began to spend more of his time in a railway car command post moving between his various advancing armies.

The headquarters of his German counterpart were in the thermal-springs resort town of Spa, in the hills of eastern Belgium. Although Field Marshal von Hindenburg was nominally the supreme commander and the Kaiser the head of state, the real decisions on the German side were made by General Ludendorff. And now, for the first time in the war that so many dissenters considered mad, one of the key players himself began to show symptoms of madness. By late September, Ludendorff was going through violent mood swings and panic attacks. He fell to the floor and, according to some witnesses, foamed at the mouth. A psychologist, hurriedly called in, urged him to calm himself by singing folk songs when he woke up in the morning. Instead, he exploded in fits of rage at his staff, defeatists in Germany, socialist agitators who were infecting his troops, weak-willed allies, even the Kaiser. Yet no one dared remove him from power.

At the beginning of October, Germany appealed for peace negotiations to President Woodrow Wilson, hoping to deal with him rather than the British and French and their four years' accumulation of anger. But Wilson rebuffed the offer. Tragically, though the outcome was by now clearly preordained, the combat would continue at a murderous intensity; both sides together suffered another half a million dead and wounded just during the war's final five weeks. The Allied forces rolled forward relentlessly, but to those who had already been fighting for years, the advances were without joy. "My senses are charred," Wilfred Owen wrote home. When it came to sorting mail for his men, the poet added, "I don't take the cigarette out of my mouth when I write Deceased over their letters."

Other members of the Central Powers began to plead for peace: Bulgaria asked for a ceasefire at the end of September; a month later, so did Ottoman Turkey and fast-dissolving Austria-Hungary. The latter's army, in any case, was draining away in mass desertions, and in a fever-ish explosion of centrifugal nationalism, one after another of the em-pire's ethnic groups proclaimed independence. The crest of the ruling Hapsburg dynasty bore some resemblance to that of its fallen relatives, the Romanovs of Russia, and so for the second time in two years crowds rampaged through an empire's streets, tearing down flags, signs, and plaques bearing a double-headed eagle.

The battered German army was eroding from its rear; the police chief of Berlin estimated that more than 40,000 deserters were hiding in his city. As exhausted soldiers were relieved from their front-line po-sitions, they sometimes shouted out "Strikebreakers!" at replacement troops heading forward. Ludendorff urgently ordered his commanders to "save us from the grave danger resulting from a *constantly increasing lack of discipline.*" Another crop failure had reduced the already meager Central Powers' food supply. Strikes and peace demonstrations broke out. When the high command of the navy ordered the fleet to sea for a last, suicidal battle to the death with the British, thousands of sailors defied orders, stokers putting out the fires in their ships' boilers. At the port of Kiel, 3,000 civilians demonstrated in their support. Mutinous sailors took over their ships and raised the red flag, broke into armories and seized rifles, several thousand of them traveling to Berlin and other cities to spread their demand for a revolution.

The Kaiser wanted to send army troops to retake Kiel, but his generals talked him out of it; his brother, the commander of the Bal-tic Fleet, had to flee the city disguised as a truck driver. In other Ger-man cities, dukes and princes fled their palaces, and workers and sol-diers formed soviets. One hundred thousand workers and other leftists filled a field in Munich and, joined by soldiers from a nearby barracks, cheered the proclamation of an independent revolutionary republic of Bavaria. Similar revolts seized factories and city halls elsewhere. This was a case — to use a more modern term — of blowback, and on a huge scale. The revolution the German high command had helped ignite by sending Lenin to Russia in the sealed train had spread to Germany itself.

Trying to stave off collapse, the Kaiser declared an amnesty for political prisoners, only to see 20,000 Berliners turn out to welcome the train that brought the socialist Karl Liebknecht back to the city. When Ludendorff and von Hindenburg telegraphed officers under them rejecting proposed peace terms and ordering a "fight to the finish," a socialist wireless operator in the army leaked the news to parliamentary deputies from his party and it was quickly published. The two commanders had, for several years, in effect run a military dictatorship. But knowing they had lost the war, they shrewdly maneuvered a new civilian government into power—headed by a chancellor responsible for the first time to the legislature, not to the Kaiser—so that the blame for what was certain to be a painful peace settlement would fall on civilians.

Desperate, the Kaiser now went to the German army's Western Front headquarters at Spa. Still believing that he could somehow retain his throne, he told his generals, "I shall remain at Spa until an armistice has been signed, and then lead my troops back to Germany." But he was shocked when, one after another, they told him that he could no longer count on his soldiers' loyalty. From the military commandant of Berlin a telegram arrived: "All troops deserted. Completely out of hand."

Worse followed: revolutionaries seized the Kaiser's own Berlin palace, and from the very corner window where the monarch had addressed crowds, Karl Liebknecht proclaimed a soviet republic. The city sprouted red flags and street barricades; young men pulled an elderly general out of a taxicab, broke his sword, and tore off his medals. Even here at Spa, enlisted men were organizing a soviet and had stopped saluting their officers, while reports came in that rear-area soldiers ordered to the front were cutting telegraph wires and sabotaging railway cars. Ludendorff resigned, and soon afterward donned a false beard and blue spectacles to flee to refuge in Denmark and then Sweden. The Kaiser was stunned by a phone call from Berlin that told him that his abdication had been announced there. "Treason, gentlemen!" the shocked monarch said to his entourage at Spa. "Barefaced, outrageous treason!" His world in tatters, he left for exile in Holland,

and a socialist government headed by a trade unionist and former sad-dlemaker took over in Berlin—just in time to sign a humiliating peace.

The negotiations had already begun. Spa headquarters arranged by radio with the Allies a local ceasefire at a point where a passable road crossed the front, and the German peace delegation traveled in three cars, with the lead vehicle flying a white flag and a young officer on the running board blowing blasts on a trumpet. When they crossed the front line, a French bugler replaced him. French soldiers they passed asked, "Is the war over?" Soon the delegates were in the midst of a crowd of Allied reporters and photographers. "To Paris!" someone called out, in a mocking reminder of the signs chalked on the sides of German troop trains in 1914. The delegates transferred to French autos for the remainder of the trip, to the headquarters of Marshal Ferdinand Foch of France in a railway car in the forest of Compiègne. British offi-cers were present, but yielded to their ally—some of its territory still occupied—the satisfaction of dictating the Allied terms to the Ger-man envoys.

Although the agreement signed several days later, over the protests of the shaken German delegates, was called the Armistice, in reality it was a German surrender. It was a most unprecedented one, however, for the surrendering army, despite being severely bloodied, remained well armed, several million strong—and almost entirely on the terri-tory of its enemies. But with a near-starving Germany in turmoil be-hind it, and rear-area troops deserting, it could not fight on, even though only a few months earlier, almost at the gates of Paris, it had seemed poised to win the war. Triumphal German government prop-aganda had continued to the last minute—newsreels never showed troops retreating or surrendering—leaving many civilians thinking that, whatever their sufferings, the country's soldiers were on the verge of victory.

That illusion persisted long after the fighting stopped, because front-line army units returned home to march in orderly columns into German cities full of cheering crowds and banners of welcome. Politi-cians gave speeches praising them as heroes undefeated on the bat-tlefield—which was, in a sense, true. All of this, of course, was the raw material out of which the Nazis within a few short years would build their deceptive but powerful legend of Germany's noble soldiers stabbed in the back and robbed of glorious victory by communists, pacifists, and Jews. And when, in 1940, they would overrun France in a new war to avenge this loss, Hitler would order that the French surrender be signed in the very same railway car.

In laying down the Armistice's terms on behalf of the Allies, Marshal Foch was representing a country that had suffered a staggering toll: 1,390,000 men killed. The marshal demanded that the German army withdraw from France, Belgium, the provinces of Alsace and Lorraine that had been captured from France in 1870, from Russia, and from parts of Germany itself, particularly all land on the west side of the Rhine. Germany was also to pay the cost of stationing Allied troops there, and more. And all this preceded a more detailed and far more onerous peace treaty that would be forced on the Germans at Versailles months later.

Many people, even at this early moment, foresaw the dangers of such harsh terms. The retired Admiral of the Fleet John Fisher, the former First Sea Lord, was asked how long it would be until the next war. "Twenty years time," he replied. Surprisingly, someone similarly worried was a man who, whatever his limitations, had always had a shrewd sense of politics, Douglas Haig. Shortly before the fighting stopped, but when the shape of the Allied demands had become clear, the field marshal wrote to his wife, "It is important that our Statesmen should . . . not attempt to so humiliate Germany as to produce the desire for revenge in years to come."

The Armistice was signed in Foch's railway car at 5 A.M. on November 11, 1918, to go into effect six hours later. Senselessly, to no military or political purpose, Allied infantry and artillery attacks continued full steam through the morning. On this final half day of the war, after the peace was signed, 2,738 men from both sides were killed and more than 8,000 wounded. The first and last British soldiers to die in the war—16-year-old John Parr of Finchley, North London, a golf caddy who lied about his age to get into the army, and George Ellison, a 40-year-old miner from Leeds who survived all but the last 90 minutes of fighting—were killed within a few miles of each other near Mons, Belgium. It was recently discovered that, by coincidence, they are buried beneath pine trees and rosebushes in the same cemetery, Saint-Symphorien, seven yards apart.

. . .

In the newspapers secretly supplied him by his Irish fellow inmates, Fenner Brockway read of socialists rising to power in Germany. He was in his prison cell, still on a punishment diet, when he heard the news that the Armistice was to take effect at 11 A.M. on November 11. Allowed no watch, he had learned to tell time by the position of a sunbeam on the wall.

> I remember sitting on the shelf-table in the denuded cell, my feet on the stool, watching the sun creep along the wall towards eleven o'clock. I cannot reproduce the chaos and intensity of my thoughts.
>
> Was the slaughter of four years to end? . . . Was I to see my family and children? . . . Was I to see the fields and woods and hills and sea?
>
> The line of the sun on the wall approached eleven.

When horns began to blare all over the city, Brockway wept.

In a prison at Ipswich, another resister, Corder Catchpool, recorded an event that afternoon when he and other COs were in the exercise yard: "An airman suddenly swooped down from 3,000 feet and skimmed over our heads, waving a black arm and oily rag. I was deeply touched by this little incident. I took it as peace overtures from the Army to us—a message of goodwill for the future, by-gones by-gones, all recrimination and misunderstanding, all heart-burnings over, wiped out by that kind, dirty bit of cloth."

Bertrand Russell, recently released from prison, walked up Tottenham Court Road and watched Londoners pour out of shops and offices into the street to cheer. The public jubilation made him think of the similar mood he had witnessed when war was declared more than four years earlier. "The crowd was frivolous still, and had learned nothing during the period of horror. . . . I felt strangely solitary amid the rejoicings, like a ghost dropped by accident from some other planet."

Alfred Milner was woken that morning by a message that the Armistice had been signed. At 11 A.M. fireworks were shot off, bugles sounded, church bells rang, and Big Ben began striking again after more than four years of silence. Later in the day, Milner and other War Office officials were received by the King and Queen. They emerged from Buckingham Palace to join a huge crowd wildly cheering the appearance of the royal family on the palace balcony while bands played. Another crowd started a celebratory bonfire in Trafalgar Square, ripping signs off the sides of London buses to feed the flames. That evening, "Lady Edward dined with me," Milner noted in his diary. Then, like the consummate bureaucrat he was, he recorded escorting her to her lodgings "through crowded streets of rejoicing people—very orderly. Walked home again and sat up working till 2 A.M."

As church bells rang triumphantly throughout Britain, Carrie Kipling wrote in her diary, "A world to be remade without a son."

John Buchan toured the Department of Information, shaking hands with members of his staff. Above all, he felt exhausted: "I never realised how tired I was till the war stopped." The war had cost the lives of his brother and half of his closest friends. At the end of the year he wrote, "There are far more dead than living now."

At only 25, Wilfred Owen had never published a book but had in his notebooks the finest body of poetry about the experience of war written in the twentieth century. At noon on November 11, an hour into the celebrations, Owen's mother received the black-bordered War Office telegram telling her that, a week earlier, her son had been killed in action.

In verses about this day, another poet, Thomas Hardy, wrote:

> Calm fell. From heaven distilled a clemency;
> There was peace on earth, and silence in the sky;
> Some could, some could not, shake off misery:
> The Sinister Spirit sneered: "It had to be!"
> And again the Spirit of Pity whispered, "Why?"

VII

Exeunt Omnes

22

THE DEVIL'S OWN HAND

THE WAR LEFT what Churchill called a "crippled, broken world." The full death toll cannot be known, because several of the governments keeping track of casualties had dissolved in chaos or revolution by the war's end. Even by the most conservative of the official tabulations—one made by the U.S. War Department six years later—more than 8.5 million soldiers were killed on all fronts. Most other counts are higher, usually by about a million. "Every day one meets saddened women, with haggard faces and lethargic movements," the writer Beatrice Webb noted in her diary a week after the Armistice, "and one dare not ask after husband or son." And the deaths did not end with the war: the *Times* continued to run its "Roll of Honour" each day for months afterward as men died of their wounds. Except in a handful of lucky neutral countries, on virtually every street in Europe could be found households in mourning where, in Wilfred Owen's words, "each slow dusk" was like "a drawing-down of blinds."

More than 21 million men were wounded; some carried pieces of shrapnel in their bodies, or were missing arms, legs, or genitals. So many veterans had mangled faces that those in France formed a national Union of Disfigured Men; in Britain, 41,000 men had one or more limbs amputated, another 10,000 were blinded, and 65,000 veterans were still receiving treatment for shell shock ten years after the war.

The toll was particularly appalling among the young. Of every 20 British men between 18 and 32 when the war broke out, three were dead and six wounded when it ended. One of the highest death rates was among those who, like the 18-year-old John Kipling, were born in the year of Queen Victoria's Diamond Jubilee. If the British dead alone were to rise up and march 24 hours a day past a given spot, four abreast, it would take them more than two and a half days. Although this book has concentrated on Britain, which lost more than 722,000 men killed (not to speak of more than 200,000 soldiers dead from the rest of the empire), the combat death toll was more than half again higher in Austria-Hungary, nearly double in France (which had a smaller population than Britain), more than double in Russia, and nearly triple in Germany. Of the many million pairs of grieving parents, we will never know how many felt that their sons had died for something noble, and how many felt what one British couple expressed in the epitaph they placed on their son's tombstone at Gallipoli: "What harm did he do Thee, O Lord?"

Parents of men declared missing sometimes could not bring themselves to accept that their sons would never return. "As a mother deprived of both her children through the war, one a naval officer," read a letter signed "Hope" that appeared in the *Times* two months after the Armistice, "may I plead with the Government to authorize a strict search being made throughout the North Coast of Egypt and in the islands in the Mediterranean . . . for missing English women and men? . . . There may be some who have lost their memories, and others who have been rescued by native fisherfolk."

Periodically some event would expose the continent's vast reservoir of grief. When Britain's Unknown Warrior was buried in Westminster Abbey on the second anniversary of the Armistice, across the country, at 11 A.M., crowds stopped in the street, and cars, buses, trains, assembly lines, and even mining machinery underground came to a halt for two minutes of silence. Heard everywhere, however, was the sound of women sobbing.

Higher than the military toll were the civilian war deaths, estimated at 12 to 13 million. Some of these lives were lost to shelling and air raids,

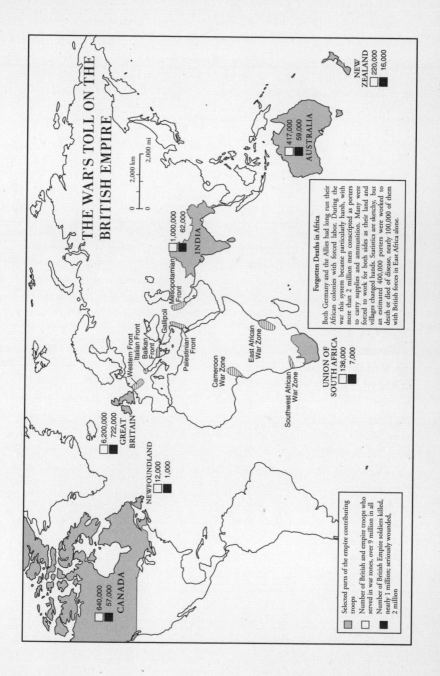

THE WAR'S TOLL ON THE BRITISH EMPIRE

NEW ZEALAND
□ 220,000
■ 16,000

AUSTRALIA
□ 417,000
■ 59,000

INDIA
□ 1,000,000
■ 62,000

2,000 mi

2,000 km

0

0

Mesopotamian Front

Western Front
Italian Front
Balkan Front
Gallipoli

Palestinian Front

Cameroon War Zone

East African War Zone

UNION OF SOUTH AFRICA
□ 136,000
■ 7,000

Southwest African War Zone

GREAT BRITAIN
□ 6,200,000
■ 722,000

NEWFOUNDLAND
□ 12,000
■ 1,000

CANADA
□ 640,000
■ 57,000

Forgotten Deaths in Africa

Both Germany and the Allies had long run their African colonies with forced labor. During the war this system became particularly harsh, with more than 2 million men conscripted as porters to carry supplies and ammunition. Many were forced to work for both sides as their land and villages changed hands. Statistics are sketchy, but an estimated 400,000 porters were worked to death or died of disease, nearly 100,000 of them with British forces in East Africa alone.

□ Selected parts of the empire contributing troops

□ Number of British and empire troops who served in war zones, over 9 million in all

■ Number of British Empire soldiers killed, nearly 1 million; seriously wounded, 2 million

a much greater number to massacres for which the war was an excuse, like the Turkish genocide of the Armenians, and even more than that to the near-famine conditions that spread through the Central Powers and the lands they had occupied. (Such deaths continued for many months after the war ended, for the Allies maintained the Royal Navy blockade to pressure Germany into signing the Versailles treaty.) And should we not add to the total the toll from other conflicts triggered by the war, like the Russian civil war, whose civilian and military deaths have been estimated at 7 to 10 million?

Should we not also include some of the deaths reflected in the elevated rates of suicide that followed the war? Many things, of course, can contribute to someone's decision to take his or her own life, but sometimes clues point to the war, even to a specific time and place. The Battle of Fromelles, for example, a forgotten sideshow to the Somme, saw more than 2,000 Australian and British soldiers die on July 19 and 20, 1916, in a foredoomed night attack against formidable German machine-gun nests in half-buried concrete bunkers. Brigadier General H. E. Elliott had protested beforehand to Haig—something few dared do—that his troops were being asked to do the impossible. After the battle Elliott stepped between the dead bodies, tried to comfort the wounded, then returned to his headquarters with tears streaming down his face. Fifteen years later, half a world away in Australia, he killed himself.

Some deaths governments barely bothered to count, such as those of underfed African porters, subjected to whippings as punishment, who for years carried wounded men or 60-pound loads of food and ammunition through rain forest, swampland, and savanna. As the fighting moved, some who had first been forced to work for one side found themselves carrying supplies for the other. Of more than two million of these forced laborers, an estimated 400,000 died, mostly of disease or exhaustion—a death rate far higher than that for British troops on the Western Front. With African farmers conscripted as porters and rival armies seizing villagers' grain and cattle, famine spread. Many African women and children were reduced to eating roots and grass before they starved. Their deaths went untabulated, but low estimates put them in the hundreds of thousands.

The war also left a ravaged landscape. The armies of the First World War faced each other on fronts hundreds of miles long, and when they retreated they usually destroyed everything the enemy could use, leaving wells poisoned, roads cratered, fruit trees sawed off at the base, mines flooded, and homes, farms, and factories dynamited into rubble. The Germans left territory twice the size of Massachusetts in northern France—the country's former industrial heartland—in smoking ruins. In tiny Belgium alone, more than 70,000 homes were completely destroyed. In Russia and Eastern Europe it was mostly retreating Russians who did the same to an immensely larger expanse of land.

Beginning in the last months of the war, an even more deadly cataclysm flamed across the world: the great influenza pandemic, whose total death toll is estimated at 50 million or more. Its spread was directly connected with the war, for the first outbreak to attract attention, in the spring of 1918, was at a large army base in Kansas. The following months saw hundreds of shiploads of American soldiers heading to Europe, bringing the disease with them. It spread rapidly from Brest, their main disembarkation port in France. With millions of soldiers sharing cramped quarters in troopships, trains, and huge army camps, the flu could jump from one person to another, with almost everyone in a packed ship's cabin, barracks, tent, or dugout sickening in a day.

The disease swept around the globe in several waves, speeded by the large numbers of troops on the move. In half-starving Germany, some 400,000 people died of influenza in 1918 alone. Most unusually for epidemic diseases, it took the worst toll on the fittest, those aged between 20 and 35, many of whom were soldiers feeling lucky to have survived combat. The human immune system fought the disease by filling the victim's lungs with frothy scarlet fluid, which contained antibodies but which in effect often drowned someone from the inside; healthy young bodies had the best immune systems and so suffered the highest death rate. Hundreds of thousands of young men in uniform on both sides succumbed in 1918 and 1919, as if in the aftermath of a gas attack, their faces quickly turning purple, their mouths, noses, and sometimes ears and eyes oozing blood, strangling to death.

Young men were also in close quarters in prison. The records are incomplete, but influenza was the likely killer of most of the 73 British conscientious objectors who died behind bars, in alternative-service work camps, or soon after their release.

Flu victims came from every level of society. Edward Cecil, who had remained at his post as a colonial bureaucrat in Egypt for most of the war, succumbed to the epidemic a month after the Armistice. His ashes were buried in the family graveyard near Hatfield House, next to those of his mother and father, prime minister in a sunnier time.

Some two months later, the disease claimed a victim from very different circumstances. When Lloyd George had released Alice Wheeldon from prison, she had returned to Derby, frail from her hunger strikes, needing help just to make her way along the railway station platform when she arrived. Although comrades on the left were loyal, neighbors ostracized her, and her secondhand clothes shop failed. Her daughter Hettie, who had managed to avoid jail, lost her job as a schoolteacher. When Sylvia Pankhurst paid the family a visit, she found mother and daughter supporting themselves by growing vegetables on a rented plot, and tomato plants in what had once been the shop window.

Alice Wheeldon died of the flu in February 1919. Winnie — just released from prison — and Hettie were both too ill themselves to come to their mother's burial. A reporter for a Derby newspaper managed to find the unannounced ceremony and wrote a story headlined, "Funeral of Mrs Wheeldon; Sensational Incidents at Graveside; Rhetorical Sneers at Prime Minister."

The disapproving journalist noted that Wheeldon's "severely plain oak coffin" was buried in a manner so "devoid of all Christian ceremony" that not a single one of the 20 mourners wore black. Indeed, Alice's son Willie, only recently released from prison for evading the draft, pulled a large red flag from his pocket and placed it, fluttering in the winter wind, over his mother's coffin. The only recorded speaker was John S. Clarke, whose appearance was all the more dramatic because he was still on the run from the police. Alice Wheeldon was the victim of "a judicial murder," he declared from atop the pile of dirt heaped up by the freshly dug grave. Lloyd George "in the midst of high affairs of State stepped out of his way to pursue a poor obscure family into the dungeon and into the grave."

To cries of "Hear, hear," Clarke continued: "Mrs. Wheeldon was a socialist. She was a prophet, not of the sweet and holy bye and bye but of the here and now. She saw the penury of the poor and the prodigality of the rich, and she registered her protest against it. . . . If Mrs.

Wheeldon could speak . . . she would tell us . . . to fight more fearlessly than before, so as to obtain that glorious time when peace and joyousness shall fill all life."

The mourners dispersed. The grave was not marked, for fear it would be defaced. Clarke slipped back underground. The following year, Hettie Wheeldon married a labor unionist comrade who had been part of the family's antiwar circle, gave birth to a premature baby who did not survive, and then herself died painfully from a burst appendix. Winnie and Alf Mason emigrated to Australia, to try to rebuild their lives. Willie Wheeldon, unable to regain his prewar job as a schoolteacher, worked in a dairy and then in the Rolls-Royce factory in Derby, but was fired after being active in the union during a strike.

With its economy drained and burdened with huge public debt by the war just ended, Britain was shaken by many more labor upheavals. Workers in Belfast and along the River Clyde went on strike, demanding that the wartime 54-hour work week be reduced to 40. On January 31, 1919, mounted police charged a crowd gathered in Glasgow's St. George's Square, injuring some 40 people. In the resulting uproar, the red flag was briefly raised over the town hall and the authorities panicked. At 10 Downing Street, Milner and his colleagues heard the secretary of state for Scotland say that "it was a misnomer to call the situation in Glasgow a strike—it was a Bolshevik rising." The cabinet swiftly dispatched six tanks and 8,000 troops, who set up machine-gun posts around the city.

Early 1919 saw sparks of rebellion even in the British armed services. Sailors on a Royal Navy patrol ship, the HMS *Kilbride,* mutinied and hoisted the red flag. Three thousand soldiers marched to the town hall in Folkestone, ripping down a "For Officers Only" sign on a railway station waiting room. Some 4,000 British troops manning the docks, trains, cranes, and warehouses at the French port of Calais went on strike. An enraged Haig demanded "the supreme penalty" for the rebels, but wiser heads restrained him. In other military protests there were more red flags and talk of solidarity with comrades in Russia, but the soldiers' greatest grievance was that they wanted to come home. As troops were demobilized, the demonstrations died away.

Another group of men were also impatient to come home: the more than 1,000 British war resisters still behind bars. Angry that their prison sentences were outlasting the war itself, some 130 went on a hunger strike. Among the voices calling for their release was an unexpected one, that of John Buchan. Unlike the pugnacious, short-fused heroes of his novels, he had a certain generosity of spirit, and once the war ended he drafted an appeal to the prime minister, which many other well-known figures signed, urging that COs be released. "A majority of these men," the petition said, "are sincerely convinced that they have acted under the demands of their conscience and in accordance with deep moral or religious convictions."

By mid-1919 the conscientious objectors were all free. Over the years, as the war's toll sank in, they and others who had gone to jail for their beliefs began to win considerable respect from a public that had once condemned them. Fenner Brockway and several others became members of Parliament. Five years after serving his hard-labor sentence in Pentonville Prison, the journalist E. D. Morel was the Labour Party's chief spokesperson on foreign affairs in the House of Commons. Bertrand Russell continued to write. Several decades after the war ended, his top-heavy thatch of hair now white but as thick as ever, Russell would appear in formal dress in Stockholm as one of the few writers of nonfiction ever to receive the Nobel Prize for Literature. A trade unionist named Arthur Creech Jones spent two and a half years in prison as a CO; 30 years later, he was in the cabinet. Ramsay MacDonald, an antiwar Labour MP, had not gone to prison during the war but had been under police surveillance and was repeatedly stoned when he spoke at peace meetings. Angry patriots had even voted to expel him from his golf club. In 1924, he became prime minister.

During 1919, militant labor revolts shook countries around the world, even including orderly little Switzerland, which had its own nationwide general strike. Germany, too, experienced great upheavals, but in the Armistice agreement the Allies had deliberately allowed the German army to keep thousands of machine guns for crowd control. In Berlin, after she took part in a failed general strike and uprising, her petite figure with its large hat and parasol still considered a threat by right-wingers, Rosa Luxemburg was beaten and shot by army officers and her body dumped in a canal. The hope that revolution would spread from Russia to other countries in Europe receded.

One of those who had felt that hope was Willie Wheeldon, who became an early member of the Communist Party of Great Britain.

Soon enough, however, like thousands of like-minded men and women in Western Europe, he began to think that if he wanted to live in a revolutionary society, he would have to go to Russia. In 1921, at age 29, he emigrated to the nation he was convinced had the best chance of achieving what John S. Clarke, at his mother's burial, had called "that glorious time when peace and joyousness shall fill all life." Learning Russian, Wheeldon became a Soviet citizen, settling in Samara, an old fortress city on the Volga River that the Bolsheviks were turning into a center of new industry, and marrying a local woman. For some years he wrote often to his sister Winnie and her husband Alf. Eventually he moved to Moscow, where he worked as a government translator. Then the letters stopped.

Another place where people hoped to bring a new and different society into being was Ireland, where nationalists were fighting to be free of British rule at last. The militant Irish Republican Army began attacking British troops and police barracks, and John French's forces fought back ruthlessly. In the guerrilla war of ambushes, assassinations, and torture that followed, well over 1,000 people on both sides were killed. With his own narrow vision reinforced by a lifetime in the army, French saw everything in military terms, dismissing officials he considered too soft and urging Boer War–style concentration camps. He also proposed removing all civilians from certain areas where the IRA was active, bringing in warplanes, and establishing what, half a century later in Vietnam, would be called free-fire zones. In December 1919, while he and his bodyguards were driving near Dublin's Phoenix Park, he narrowly escaped death when IRA guerrillas threw grenades at his car and opened fire from behind a hedge.

Adding to French's consternation, among the many supporters of the IRA was his sister. They appear to have broken off all contact at this time, and on her visits to Ireland he had her closely shadowed. "The pore lady was niver foive minutes widout somebody followin' her about, though she doesn't know ut," an Irishman in Cork told a visitor from England. At one point, Charlotte Despard and the Irish nationalist Maud Gonne were speaking to a crowd of sympathizers when French roared past in his motorcade without stopping. The two women traveled the country gathering testimony about violence by British forces.

"With her I was able to visit places I should never have been able to get to alone in the martial [law] areas," Gonne wrote to a friend. When they were stopped at roadblocks, "it was amusing to see the puzzled expressions on the faces of the officers . . . who continually held up our car, when Mrs. Despard said she was the Viceroy's sister."

Meanwhile, just as after the pancontinental war against Napoleon, the winners gathered in January 1919 to divide the spoils. The number of negotiators and their entourages of secretaries, cooks, valets, translators, messengers, chauffeurs, and guards soared into the thousands — the British Empire's mission alone totaled 524 — for many branches of every Allied government wanted a hand in reshaping the world. The Paris Peace Conference lasted, with a few breaks, for a full year, and out of it came a string of treaties and decisions that helped determine the course of the next 20 years and speed the way to a second, wider, more ruinous war. A noble-sounding but ineffectual League of Nations was created to settle international disputes. Everywhere the victors redrew boundaries and from Finland to Czechoslovakia recognized a bewildering array of new countries that emerged from the ruins of fragmented empires. Germany was partly demilitarized and its territory reduced by about 10 percent; it was also burdened with huge reparations payments and the humiliating requirement to formally acknowledge its guilt for starting the war.

The rearranged map was a global one. Germany's possessions in the Pacific and Africa, some of the latter with valuable deposits of gold, copper, and diamonds, were divided among the victors. The Ottoman Empire was partly dismembered and its various Arab lands parceled out, mostly to French and British control. In Paris, among the black top hats and morning coats of the triumphant prime ministers and the battle ribbons and epaulets of the generals, were representatives in more humble attire, coming to plead the cause of various colonized peoples. After all, hadn't the trigger for this war been the invasion and occupation of a small country, Belgium?

These visitors knocked on doors in vain. The Allied rhetoric about self-determination of peoples did not apply to African or Asian colonies, or to Arab territories known to have oil. With all these uppity colonials on hand, it was no wonder that the ubiquitous Basil Thomson was put in charge of security for the British delegation, adding two dozen intelligence agents in Paris to the several hundred already under his control in England and Ireland.

Violet Cecil was also in Paris for much of the conference, because Milner was part of the British delegation—in charge of it, in fact, whenever the prime minister was not in town. Day by day, his diary records how he and other delegates disposed of different parts of the globe, from the Cameroons and German Southwest Africa to the three former Ottoman provinces fatefully cobbled together into the British protectorate of Iraq.

After the bleak years of war, here was a chance for Violet to once again be in the glamorous center of great political events. She rented a house by the Bois de Boulogne, and together she and Milner walked in the park, visited with Lloyd George and Clemenceau, and took in the sights of the victorious city in spring: the captured German guns lining the Champs Élysées; the embassy receptions; the whirl of diplomats, generals, and French aristocrats at dinners and balls; the amateur theatricals—not considered fitting in wartime—that could now be staged by the younger British Foreign Office staff. Military bands were everywhere. Gone were the drab years of wartime restraint; long-stored jewels, pearls, and ostrich feathers adorned women once more. Famous restaurants were restored to their prewar glory, and the delegates from starving Germany—who had guards to protect them from jeering French patriots—were amazed by the array of food at their hotel.

There was, of course, an undertone that no victory celebration could wipe out. The war had been particularly devastating for the extended Cecil family. Of the ten grandsons of Lord Salisbury, the former prime minister, five, including George Cecil, had been killed at the front. Violet again made a pilgrimage to George's burial site, but now, in 1919, she was far from the only Englishwoman visiting a grave—or searching for one in vain. Thousands of British, French, American, and Canadian widows and mothers roamed the former war zone. Hotels were filled with the grieving, and former Red Cross hospital trains had to be pressed into service to house the overflow. Shattered tanks dotted meadows, and everything from cathedrals to farmhouses lay in ruins. Along hundreds of country roads, lined in European style with rows of plane or poplar trees, all that remained were bare trunks, the limbs victim to shrapnel. The mourning women mixed uneasily with French villagers trying to salvage their cratered fields, while police and soldiers tried to keep everyone away from unexploded shells. German POWs, still in custody, were at work clearing the rubble.

A Cecil cousin who survived the war wrote of visiting the Somme battlefield to try to find his brother-in-law's grave: "Everywhere lies the ordinary debris of occupied trenches—bully beef tins, biscuit tins, traces of half-executed meals. . . . A dented white basin with traces of soapy water stands on a box; shaving tackle all spattered with soil and mud spreads itself upon an improvised table. Something of a meal remains—a marmalade jar with tin plates and rusted knife and fork. A pair of muddy, hardened boots. . . . Will we find our friend, or do the dead lie too thick—are the crosses too many?"

An exhausted Milner returned to the peace talks seven times (on one such trip taking his first airplane ride), and on June 28, 1919—the fifth anniversary of the assassinations at Sarajevo—in the packed Hall of Mirrors at the palace of Versailles, he was one of the five men who, on behalf of Britain, placed their signatures next to the red ribbon and sealing wax on the final page of the main peace treaty. He and other skeptics had been unable to persuade Lloyd George to ease the harsh terms imposed on Germany. The prime minister had won an election the month after the Armistice by thundering about making Germany pay for the war, and Clemenceau of France was even more vehement. Having seen his country invaded twice in his lifetime, Clemenceau, it was rumored, had asked to be buried on his feet, facing Germany. Both leaders were also prisoners of four and a half years of the greatest political propaganda barrage history had seen: the xenophobic torrent to which Buchan, Kipling, and so many others, along with their counterparts in France, had contributed. All this had forged a public that demanded Germany be punished—and punished painfully. The resulting peace treaty, wrote the diplomat-historian George F. Kennan years later, had "the tragedies of the future written into it as by the devil's own hand."

That Germany and the now vanished Austria-Hungary really had started the war, that they had ruthlessly exploited the territory they conquered, that the Versailles treaty's provisions would be softened later, all made no difference whatever to Germans. The public ignominy of being dictated to by the Allies rankled deeply across the political spectrum, eroding support—just as Ludendorff and von Hindenburg had planned—for the moderate, civilian regime that was forced to accept the treaty, and providing essential grist for the rise of Hitler. As he wrote in *Mein Kampf* a few years later: "What a use could be made of the Treaty of Versailles. . . . How each one of the points of that Treaty could be branded in the minds and hearts of the German people until sixty million men and women find their souls aflame with a feeling of rage and shame; and a torrent of fire bursts forth as from a furnace, and a will of steel is forged from it, with the common cry: 'We will have arms again!'"

While Woodrow Wilson is said to have called the struggle just ended the war to end all wars, Milner, grimly realistic, called the Versailles treaty "a Peace to end Peace."

Just as Nazism was to spring directly from the ashes of the war, so was another of the twentieth century's great totalitarian systems. After several years of ruthless combat, the Russian civil war came to an end, and with it the attempt by Allied troops to prop up counterrevolutionary forces. The Bolsheviks began to refer to themselves as communists, and soon no other parties were allowed to exist in what in 1922 became the Union of Soviet Socialist Republics.

Although some British leftists of this era, like Willie Wheeldon, saw the Soviet Union as the world's best hope, one person who decided otherwise was Bertrand Russell. He traveled there in 1920 and was dismayed to find a police state where "our conversations were continually spied upon. In the middle of the night one would hear shots, and know that idealists were being killed in prison." Unswayed by the red-carpet treatment he received, he was chilled to hear Lenin laugh at a British socialist "for believing in Soviets without dictatorship."

Sylvia Pankhurst also traveled to Russia in 1920, and also met Lenin, whom she, by contrast, found "more vividly vital and energetic, more wholly alive than other people." She saw the country through totally optimistic eyes, managing to convince herself that in this glorious new society "the Russian people have mostly forgotten the very existence of alcohol." John S. Clarke, who was there at the same time, also fell under Lenin's spell and was able to use his knowledge of circus animals to cure the leader's dog of an unspecified illness.

Plenty of other Western leftists, in eager search for the embodiment, at last, of what Pankhurst once called a "Golden Age" of peace and plenty for all, also found paradise in the Soviet Union. Charlotte Despard was to visit in 1930, by which point Stalin's murderous dictatorship was completely entrenched. She found everything to be splendid: the diet was good, children privileged, education enlightened, orphanages first-rate, and the courts wise and generous. In Soviet prisons, she claimed, the worst punishment "inflicted by a court of the prisoners themselves was to be kept out of the club room for one month."

To give them some credit, John S. Clarke drifted away from his infatuation soon enough, and Pankhurst abandoned hers even more quickly and vocally, dissent getting her expelled from Britain's Communist Party in 1921. But the hunger among leftists to see the Soviet Union as a shining alternative to war-ravaged capitalist Europe remained deep. In the USSR's first decade and a half, tens of thousands of believers in that dream emigrated there from around the world.

Then in the mid-1930s, in what became known as the Great Purge, an increasingly paranoid Stalin ordered waves of arrests, gathering people by the millions into execution cellars or the far-flung prison camps of his expanding gulag. Tapping an ancient vein of xenophobia, the secret police always seized people on the pretext that they were spies or saboteurs for some foreign power, and so the many foreigners who had come to live in Russia were at particular risk. Thousands of them vanished. Government files on the fate of most were not opened until the early 1990s, with the collapse of the Soviet Union. Among the victims they revealed, arrested on October 5, 1937, and on Christmas Day of that year sentenced to be shot, was Willie Wheeldon.

23

AN IMAGINARY CEMETERY

THERE WAS NO ANNOUNCEMENT beforehand, and only a handful of guests were present for the ceremony at St. James's Church, Paddington. Although the bride was well into middle age, her wide-set dark eyes still evoked the renowned beauty of her youth. After lunch with a few friends, the couple slipped away from London by train. On their two-week honeymoon in Provence, they motored and strolled past the ruins of Roman amphitheaters and aqueducts, weathered stone relics of an empire past, while in Britain newspapers belatedly discovered the secret wedding of one of the great empire builders of the present. It was February 1921, and more than two decades after they first met, Alfred Milner and Violet Cecil were finally married.

He was 66, she 49. A respectable interval had passed since Edward Cecil's death, and so at last Lord and Lady Milner could be officially received by all, from the King and Queen on down, as the couple everyone had long known they were. But just as it was the twilight of the age when the appearance of conventional marriage mattered greatly, so it was the twilight of the empire in which Milner and his new wife had the deepest belief. "The man of no illusions," as Churchill had once called him, was facing the death of his greatest illusion.

Details of the empire's gradual unraveling crossed his desk daily, for the month after the war ended he had become colonial secretary. In India, where less than a decade earlier King George V and Queen Mary had been majestically installed as Emperor and Empress, Mohandas Gandhi was preaching civil disobedience as a weapon against British rule; and, in 1919, a hotheaded general ordered soldiers to open fire on a protest meeting in Amritsar, killing 379 people by the official—most likely understated—count and wounding at least 1,200 others. The massacre became a catalyst for Indian nationalists; although achieving independence would take nearly thirty years more, after Amritsar it was never in doubt. Later that year, trouble erupted in Egypt, and Milner was dispatched to Cairo to negotiate with restive nationalists. ("The difficulty," he reported back to Lloyd George, "is to find a way of making Egypt's relation to Great Britain *appear* a more independent and dignified one than it ever really can be.") The prospect of independence for Ireland—something he had furiously fought in 1914—now loomed as well, and bloodily so. In London, the year after he and Violet married, Irish militants assassinated Sir Henry Wilson, the friend with whom he had gone to Russia in 1917, on the field marshal's own doorstep. Milner rushed to the house to comfort his widow.

Paradoxically, the very war Milner had helped to win proved the death knell for another of his illusions, the dream of a "League of British Nations" with an overarching common parliament and cabinet. When he had put this idea before a meeting of dominion prime ministers during the war, it met with an embarrassing lack of enthusiasm. In his imagination, Canada and Australia had always been two major building blocks in such a federation, but neither government showed the slightest interest. The horrendous bloodshed of the war proved unexpectedly crucial in forming Canadian and Australian national identities sharply distinct from that of Britain. In both countries, the bitterest and most sacred war memories were of the tens of thousands of their men sacrificed at places like Passchendaele and Gallipoli by inept British generals. After the war, the various dominions went their separate ways politically more than ever, as the British Empire became the British Commonwealth of Nations in 1931, and finally, in 1949, merely the Commonwealth of Nations.

Imperialist true believers like Milner, Kipling, and Buchan had celebrated the way more than a million men from British colonies had fought for the empire in the war. But that experience had only raised expectations: these men often fought next to white soldiers who were far better paid, and in Europe they saw a continent of independent nations, not colonies. No one was more affected than the Indian troops. "Here the ladies tend us, who have been wounded, as a mother tends her child," a Sikh wrote to his father in the Punjab from England. ". . . They put us in motor cars and take us through the city. When, at four o'clock, we go out from the hospital, the ladies of the city give us fruit." He was astonished that British nurses emptied the hospital bedpans of wounded Indians. Another Indian soldier, quartered in a French home, was equally startled to find that Frenchwomen "attend to our wants and tidy our beds, and eat at the same table as we do." Such encounters nurtured something British colonial authorities had long tried to block: the idea of human equality.

Troops from other British colonies also found the war experience eye-opening. A month after the fighting ended, several thousand British West Indian soldiers at a base in Taranto, Italy, mutinied when they were ordered to clean white soldiers' latrines and failed to get a pay increase the whites had received. One man was killed in the fighting, 60 were sent to prison, and one was executed by a firing squad. Two weeks after the mutiny, in a sergeants' mess, 60 West Indian soldiers took part in the first political meeting ever held in which blacks from different British islands discussed how to work together for their rights. "Nothing we can do," a worried government official noted in a confidential memorandum the following year, "will alter the fact that the black man has begun to think and feel himself as good as the white."

In Belize, capital of British Honduras, returning veterans led a wave of rioting against their status as second-class citizens in their own homeland. The authorities declared martial law. "The participation of West Indian negroes in the war," the colony's governor wrote in a dispatch marked "Secret" to Milner, "has given rise to a strong and dangerous ill-feeling . . . against Europeans." His desk flooded with similar reports, Milner asked the Royal Navy for the loan of the armored cruiser HMS *Devonshire* "in connection with the preservation of order in Jamaica during the demobilisation of the British West India Regiment," and warned that a second warship might also be needed.

Milner retired from the cabinet in 1921. Three years later, he and his wife made a sea journey to South Africa, the scene of his imperial triumph and their falling in love. The trip was filled with nostalgic visits to Boer War battle sites, the government providing them a private train to Kimberley. While in South Africa, however, Milner was apparently bitten by a tsetse fly and infected with sleeping sickness. On his return to England, his health declined rapidly, and Violet asked that the church bells in the village next to their country home be silenced, so as not to disturb him. On May 12, 1925, he was elected to the honorary post of chancellor of Oxford University. He died the next day, at 71.

She survived him by 33 years, remaining a member of the Ladies Empire Club and continuing to befriend the powerful and influential of later generations, such as the CBS broadcaster Edward R. Murrow when he was a correspondent in London during the Second World War. After her brother, who had long edited the archconservative *National Review,* fell ill in 1929, it became, in the words of the bemused Kipling, a "she-edited magazine." Violet saw every issue into print and in editorials ferociously assailed such targets as the League of Nations, the possibility of Indian independence, and British military unpreparedness. "Never forget, Prime Minister," she said to Stanley Baldwin when he came to lunch one day, "our frontier is on the Rhine."

She and the Kiplings visited one another frequently, and Rudyard sometimes read his work aloud to her. Still grieving the loss of his son, he found solace in his work as a member of the Imperial War Graves Commission, writing inscriptions for monuments and visiting military cemeteries as far distant as Egypt and Jerusalem. He and his wife made a pilgrimage to Chalk Pit Wood near Loos at the time of day they estimated that John Kipling had been killed there. Fulminating against the fraying of the British Empire, he contributed to a fund for the general who had massacred the Indians at Amritsar. "I hate your generation," he once burst out to a much younger man, "because you are going to give it all away."

In this period of his life, however, Kipling wrote "The Gardener," a haunting story utterly bereft of his usual jingoism. In it, a heartbroken woman searches in France for the war grave of her "nephew," who is really her illegitimate son. At last a gentle cemetery gardener—who, unknown to her, is Christ resurrected—looks at her "with infinite compassion" and forgiveness.

"Come with me," he says, "and I will show you where your son lies."

But no one showed the Kiplings. Rudyard died in 1936 and his widow Carrie three years later, without finding out where John's body lay. British authorities continue to try to identify remains, and in 1992 thought they had finally found John's, erecting a headstone with his name. But several military historians argue convincingly that the identification is false and that John Kipling is still among the more than 400,000 British Empire dead from 1914–1918 whose resting place is not known.

One by one, other players left the stage. In John Buchan's postwar writing there were only one or two brief hints of doubt about the war; he revealed, for instance, that he could no longer bear to read Homer, because of the way the poet glorified battle. He never said more. Unlike his friend Kipling, however, at least a few of his ideas changed with the times: he placed great hope in the League of Nations as an alternative to war, and eventually accepted the concept of self-rule for India. Buchan died in 1940 while serving in the figurehead post of governor general of Canada, and a British destroyer carried his ashes home. Many of his novels remain in print today on both sides of the Atlantic, testimony to the lasting appeal of swashbuckling action, sinister conspiracies foiled by a bold hero, and an abiding, benevolent British Empire.

That empire slowly dissolved over the course of the century, starting with Ireland. As the bitter guerrilla warfare there grew more intense, the British cabinet came to understand that it could be ended only by some form of Irish independence, and that the mercurial John French was hardly the right person to carry on such talks. In April 1921 he was eased out of his job as viceroy, and others negotiated an agreement whereby Britain would retain naval bases and certain other privileges and the six predominantly Protestant counties of the north would remain part of the United Kingdom, while the rest of the island became the Irish Free State, in name part of the empire, but in effect a self-governing country.

Just as French's removal as commander in chief on the Western Front had been softened with a viscountcy, so now his dismissal was accompanied by an earldom. He slipped away to the south of France for a holiday with Winifred Bennett. Still believing that he was essentially a man of Ireland, where he already owned one country home, he extravagantly bought a second. But such purchases left him, as ever, short of cash, and French owed his sister money from a loan she had made while he was still speaking to her. For a few years, his mustache now turned white, he kept busy giving speeches to veterans' associations and unveiling war memorials. Cancer ended his days in 1925, not long after he sat up in his sickbed near a window to return the salutes of some veterans who had gathered outside. He would have been furious had he known that one of the pallbearers at his funeral would be Haig.

During her brother's final months, Charlotte Despard hoped for a reconciliation. Several times she wrote affectionately to "My dearest Jack," and once went to the hospital where he was being treated, but was not allowed to see him—whether on his orders or the doctor's we do not know. She remained on good terms with French's long-neglected wife, but neither Eleanora French nor her children could comprehend Despard's politics, nor why, when she arrived for visits, she called her chauffeur "Comrade Tom." To the end of her life, no cause was too radical for her. A friend once said, "I've only got to send a telegram to Mrs. Despard to say, 'Tomorrow noon I'm going to attack Battersea Town Hall,' and she'd be there, she won't ask me why."

Despite their differences, she shared one improbable faith with her brother: Despard, too, was convinced that at heart she was Irish. "I have to go to Ireland," she told a group of supporters who had gathered to celebrate her birthday. "It is the call of the blood." She settled there for good in 1921.

The following year, a fierce civil war broke out in the Irish Free State over whether in the independence negotiations its leaders had given away too much to Britain. The fratricidal fighting ended only after several thousand deaths, but many of the most radical nationalists continued to belong to an uncompromising underground faction of the Irish Republican Army, determined to unite Northern Ireland with the south and create a socialist revolution. Despard, of course, was among them. She bought a large Victorian mansion north of Dublin where IRA men on the run sometimes found shelter or stashed their arms. The police raided the building from time to time, but always took care to leave the venerable Despard alone. Black mantilla fluttering in the breeze, she still spoke at large political rallies in Ireland, England, and on the Continent. She died in 1939, at the age of 95.

. . .

Few of the COs sent to British jails during the war had ever been behind bars before, and they were shocked by what they saw. Soon after the war's end, Stephen Hobhouse took a job coordinating a comprehensive study of the nation's prisons. When his health broke down, Fenner Brockway joined him and helped complete *English Prisons Today*. Published in 1922, the 735-page book was an acknowledged landmark in prison reform and, among other accomplishments, helped end the infamous rule of silence. Hobhouse, living frugally but guiltily on his inherited wealth, spent the rest of his life writing on mysticism and Quaker history, and died in 1961 at 79. After the Armistice, his cousin Emily, whose convictions had helped shape his own, worked on getting relief supplies to the hungry in Germany and Austria. She died in 1926.

As the government's wartime paranoia about radicals receded, John S. Clarke was able to emerge from underground. In 1929 he began serving several years as an Independent Labour Party member of Parliament, where he successfully argued against a bill that would have imposed strict regulations on circuses. When colleagues protested that the training of circus animals required cruelty, Clarke assured them that it did not — and invited them to join him in a lion-and-tiger cage so he could demonstrate. No one took him up on this. Late in life, while serving as a member of the Glasgow City Council, he would periodically perform again. Once he had been the country's youngest lion tamer; now he was the oldest.

Of all the careers that were built on defending the British government against threats from antiwar radicals like Clarke, Brockway, and Hobhouse, and from imaginary conspirators like the Wheeldon family, none involved a more dramatic fall than that of Basil Thomson, who had become Sir Basil in 1919. Two years later, he and the home secretary had a falling-out and he left government service, but remained in the public eye, embarking on a successful lecture tour of the United States, and in rapid succession writing *My Experiences at Scotland Yard* and other books in the same vein. In 1925, however, he suffered an embarrassing blow when arrested one night in Hyde Park for committing "an act in violation of public decency" with a woman who gave her name as Thelma de Lava. In court, Thomson indignantly protested that he was "writing a book dealing with vice conditions in the West End, and had gone to Hyde Park to gather data. . . . As I entered the park I was accosted by a young woman. . . . When she said she was hard up, I unbuttoned my coat for the purpose of getting out a few shillings and giving them to her." Thomson's lawyer tried a different tack, claiming that his client had gone to the park "to follow up certain information about an alleged Communist, who was to be found there." Although his punishment was only a fine of £5, according to one news account, "the crowds of spectators who jammed the court room throughout the trial whooped gleefully and had to be quelled." We do not know if the audience included any of those Thomson had so assiduously spied on during the war.

The person most identified in the public mind with that war was, of course, Field Marshal Sir Douglas Haig. After the Armistice, he led his army, in somber triumph, into Germany, to occupy the west bank of the Rhine. Invited to London for a ceremony in which Lloyd George was honoring Marshal Foch of France, he was miffed to discover "that I was to be in the fifth carriage. . . . I felt that this was more of an insult than I could put up with." He refused to attend. Before long, though, honors began to flood in: an earldom, medals, a £100,000 gift from Parliament, and a successful public fund-raising campaign to buy him the ancestral seat of the Haig family, Bemersyde House, on Scotland's River Tweed.

Even though by the war's end his mind had opened up enough to embrace new advances in military technology, when he soon afterward retired from the army it seemed to close down again. "Some enthusiasts to-day . . . prophesy that the aeroplane, the tank, and the motor-car will supersede the horse in future wars," he wrote a half-dozen years after the war ended. "I believe that the value of the horse and the opportunity for the horse in the future are likely to be as great as ever. . . . Aeroplanes and tanks . . . are only accessories to the man and the horse."

Haig deployed his skills as a political infighter better than he had ever deployed his forces, to ensure that he would be remembered for winning the war and not for the disastrous offensives of 1916 and 1917. While he disingenuously claimed to be "very lazy on the question of the history of the war," he was anything but. The new battlefield, which he dominated with considerable success, was the preparation of the multivolume *Official History* of the war, as well as other histories and memoirs; his weapons were the texts of his self-serving diary, letters, dispatches, and other documents that he gave to trusted loyalists, including the *Official History*'s main author. Knowing that his reputation would probably be under assault after his death, Haig even orchestrated a posthumous counterattack on his future critics by mobilizing two generals to write a long memorandum in his defense, which was deposited with the British Museum for release in 1940.

The unruly world of postwar Britain, filled with vocal labor unionists who staged a general strike in 1926, dismayed Haig, but on a visit to Italy he was impressed with the fascist dictator Benito Mussolini: "I found him most pleasant. There is no doubt that he has already done much good in this country. His view is, that everyone is a servant of the State and must honestly do his best to serve the State. If anyone fails he is punished. We want someone like that at home at the present time." Curiously, the field marshal who had formerly commanded millions now did not even use a secretary, and answered all letters by hand. Haig died suddenly of a heart attack in 1928 and was mourned at an elaborate state funeral in Westminster Abbey. Only that same year was the cavalry lance officially retired as a combat weapon of the British army.

Another funeral also took place in London in 1928. Its procession also marched in orderly ranks, but instead of guardsmen and army bagpipers, the marchers were almost all women. And instead of scarlet and khaki, they wore purple, white, and green; some displayed, as badges of honor, the arrow insignia of prison garb. When they followed the coffin to the cemetery there was some tension in the air, for one of the mourners stood, solitary and defiant, apart from the others.

In the casket was the body of Emmeline Pankhurst. More than a thousand followers gathered at the graveside, where they surrounded her daughter Christabel, whose eyes were red from weeping. The solitary mourner, of course, was Sylvia, estranged from her mother for the past 15 years. Also at the cemetery was someone whose arrival had deepened the estrangement, causing Mrs. Pankhurst, supporters said, a shock that hastened her death: a six-month-old baby boy to whom Sylvia had given birth out of wedlock. Emmeline had nothing but contempt for the baby's father, Silvio Corio, with whom Sylvia now lived. An Italian radical and convert to Islam, he already had two earlier illegitimate children.

Emmeline Pankhurst's life had been a wild journey between extremes, from socialist to rock-throwing suffragette to staunch prowar patriot to enthusiast for Russia's Women's Battalion of Death. But one strand of her character remained constant: her strict Victorian sense of sexual morality. When she read in the newspaper that Sylvia, who advocated "marriage without a legal union," had had a baby, she wept all day and kept saying, "I shall never be able to speak in public again." She never did.

Although loyal to her mother to the end, Christabel took another of the abrupt turns so common to this family. The strident voice that had once urged suffragettes to smash the windows of government offices and then harshly denounced Britain's enemies would be devoted with no less fervor for the remainder of her life to proclaiming the second coming of Christ. She eventually settled in that home of so many messianic movements, Southern California. After their mother's funeral, she and Sylvia never saw each other again, and she died in Santa Monica in 1958.

Adela Pankhurst, banished to Australia in 1914, never returned to England. Emmeline had cut off contact with her when she took a strong stance against the war, and urged the Australian prime minister to denounce her. Adela's politics, too, began to take a strangely twisting course. She was a founder of the Australian Communist Party, then veered rightward to start a branch of the Women's Guild of Empire, and eventually was interned as a Japanese sympathizer during the Second World War. She and her husband named their dogs Adolf and Benito, after the leaders of Japan's two European allies. Her final conversion, a year before her death, was to Roman Catholicism.

Of all the Pankhurst women, Sylvia best escaped — at least for a time — the family's attraction to rigid, all-encompassing belief systems. After the war she continued to edit the *Workers' Dreadnought,* which employed Britain's first black correspondent and also published Indian writers; hers was a rare voice against the tightening of racial discrimination in South Africa, the foundations of what would become apartheid. In a foresighted 1922 pamphlet she predicted that in the later part of the twentieth century the major nations of the world would be fighting over oil. On a postwar trip to Italy, she saw some of Mussolini's thugs in action and began speaking out against fascism, something few people in Britain yet took seriously.

In 1935, fascist Italy invaded Ethiopia, whose ruler, Emperor Haile Selassie, appealed in vain to the League of Nations for help. Sylvia now had the cause that would occupy her for the rest of her life. She and her lover Corio began publishing *New Times and Ethiopia News,* which reported on Italian atrocities in Ethiopia and denounced the rise of the Nazis. When his country was a victim of Mussolini, Haile Selassie was widely supported by many other progressives and intellectuals. Once restored to his throne by the Allies in the Second World War, however, he again became a ruler whose absolute power was underlined by his official titles: Conquering Lion of the Tribe of Judah, King of Kings, and Elect of God. None of this deterred Sylvia from once again becoming a quintessential Pankhurst true believer. "In those irresistible eyes," she wrote, "burns the quenchless fire of the hero who never fails his cause." At the age of 74, she moved to Ethiopia and continued to sing the Emperor's praises in print. He awarded her various medals, and she was one of the few people given the privilege of not having to bow and walk backward on leaving his presence. She died in Addis Ababa in 1960.

When Adela suffered a fatal heart attack in Australia the following year, the last of the Pankhurst sisters was gone. It was as if the mother and three daughters had been split apart by centrifugal force: each of the four ended her life on a different continent.

Among the millions of veterans released from the British army in the months after the Armistice was Albert Rochester. Returning to his job in Wiltshire as a signalman for the Great Western Railway, he resumed writing for labor newspapers. Now bitterly disillusioned with the war, he praised those who had gone to jail as COs. In print and on the lecture platform, he returned repeatedly to his most searing wartime memory, witnessing three British soldiers executed one freezing January dawn in 1917. In the early 1920s, he joined forces with a founder of the No-Conscription Fellowship, who had spent most of the war in prison, to press for an official inquiry into the executions. The War Office rebuffed them. Rochester's anger at the generals who had ordered these three working-class lives snuffed out was of a piece with his position as an untamed labor militant. In speeches he gave as he traveled the country by train and motorcycle, he offered to show anyone who doubted his story the location of the three unmarked graves. In 1926, he died suddenly at the age of 41, of septicemia following minor surgery.

In recent decades, argument over the army's death sentences revived, and became a curious proxy battle for how the entire conflict should be remembered. Were the First World War's 346 known British military executions—minus a few dozen for murder, rape, or other noncombat-related crimes—merely measures essential to maintaining military discipline in an age that took capital punishment for granted? Or were they the work of bullheaded generals who refused to acknowledge that trench warfare could drive men mad? And was the whole war itself a matter of such madness that soldiers executed for cowardice, desertion, or casting away arms were tragic victims, if not heroes, for refusing their parts in it?

In 1990, a citizens' group called Shot at Dawn began demanding posthumous pardons for the executed; among its members were relatives of Lance Sergeant Joseph Stones and Lance Corporal Peter Goggins, both of whom Rochester had seen shot. The war's executions became the subject of a half-dozen books, several TV documentaries, at least two plays, a children's book, a memorial in sculpture, and a song, "Deserter," by a Bristol rock band. Local newspapers in England and Ireland took up the cases of executed soldiers from their communities, and bishops, city councils, labor unions, and the Irish government added their voices to the demand for pardons. Each year, Shot at Dawn members joined the November remembrance ceremony at the Cenotaph, the London war memorial, wearing white badges to symbolize the white handkerchiefs or envelopes pinned over the hearts of condemned men to provide targets for firing squads. Finally, in 2006, the British government granted a blanket pardon to more than 300 executed First World War soldiers, including the three men Rochester had watched die.

The pardon may have ended the public argument over the executions, but a larger dispute over how to judge the war goes on. Was its horrendous death toll heart-rending but necessary to prevent the German conquest of all of Europe? Or was it senseless, a spasm of brutal carnage that in every conceivable way remade the world for the worse? Nowhere has the argument been more heated than in Britain, which, because it had not been attacked in 1914, had a clearer choice than France or Belgium about whether to join the fighting.

Within a decade after its end, the war had already come to be seen by many as a needless tragedy that, at least where Britain was concerned, should have been avoided. In films, novels, and onstage the conflict today is usually portrayed as an unmitigated catastrophe, where both sides wasted men's lives and cynically coveted territory and colonies in the manner of empires immemorial. In 1998, the *Daily Express,* which was unsurpassed in its drum-beating chauvinism during the war years, published a call to remove the equestrian statue of Haig from its prominent place on Whitehall in London.

In recent decades, however, a number of British military historians have, surprisingly but unconvincingly, come to Haig's defense. The field marshal's admirers have even formed the Douglas Haig Fellowship, which presents a lecture in his honor each year, and in Britain theirs has become the new academic orthodoxy. In an onslaught of books and articles they have argued that, whatever his flaws, Haig did more than anyone else to contain the German assault of early 1918, turn the tables, and win the war. More important, these historians insist, the war had to be won: Germany had violated Belgian neutrality and, without resistance, an aggressive, militaristic Germany and its allies would have overrun Europe.

To this, it is easy to respond: the Second World War, which grew so inevitably out of the First, *did* result in Germany's overrunning almost all of Europe—and the Nazis carried out an immeasurably more murderous agenda than Kaiser Wilhelm II ever would have. The war that prevented a German conquest of Europe in 1914 virtually guaranteed the one that would begin in 1939.

Although this argument over the war's worth has often been one between the political right and left, one powerful contemporary voice arguing that Britain should have stayed out comes from the Scottish-born conservative historian Niall Ferguson, who has called the war's toll "the worst thing the people of my country have ever had to endure." He points out that one of the Kaiser's principal war aims was to establish a pan-European customs union, a "United States of Europe," which Germany, by its size, would dominate. How different is that, he asks provocatively, from today's European Union? Germany was indeed the aggressor in 1914, but would a German conquest of France then—

something that had already happened once, in 1870–71—have been so disastrous? Whatever brutalities or shifts in the balance of power this would have caused, Ferguson argues, seem paltry compared to the war's death toll and catastrophic aftereffects, above all the rise of Nazism.

To this we can add that the war of 1914–1918 left a wider legacy as well. For example, the unprecedented, massive government propaganda operations on both sides, filled with false claims of glorious battlefield victories and wild exaggerations of the other side's atrocities, engendered a deep postwar cynicism—a cynicism that years later made many people first dismiss as propaganda the early reports of Nazi death camps. More important yet, the war smashed many barriers in the realm of what most Europeans considered morally permissible. In the frenzy for military advantage, international agreements and the long-standing distinction between soldiers and civilians went up in smoke: chemical warfare by both sides, German torpedoing of neutral ships, the British attempt to blockade Germany into starvation—the list could go on. And these barriers, once broken, were gone forever. The barbed-wire-ringed camps in Germany for laborers conscripted from France, Belgium, and Russia would be duplicated in far larger and crueler dimensions by the Nazis and the Soviets. The Turkish genocide of the Armenians would be repeated, on a vaster scale, against Europe's Jews. The poison gas attacks foreshadowed the gruesome toll in birth defects from the American spraying of defoliants across South Vietnam. The indiscriminate German bombings of British and French cities would be replicated by both sides, with an immensely greater death toll, in the Second World War, reaching a climax in the atomic leveling of Hiroshima and Nagasaki. The unexpected aristocratic dissenter of 1917, Lord Lansdowne, was entirely right to see that the war had irrevocably unleashed "the prostitution of science for purposes of pure destruction."

Would we have devised such means of inflicting pain, terror, and death without the First World War? Probably yes, for human beings have been inventing new ways to kill each other for thousands of years. But the scale of the conflict and the way the belligerents mobilized their economies for total war accelerated such developments greatly, and left a bloodied Germany determined to seek revenge. The most toxic legacy of the conflict and its misbegotten peace settlement lies in the hardly imaginable horrors that followed. If we were allowed to magically roll back history to the start of the twentieth century and undo one—and only one—event, is there any doubt that it would be the war that broke out in 1914?

On a warm, sunny day in Ypres, the land seems at peace. Just outside of town, a farmer on his tractor says, yes, a visitor can certainly step inside one of the seven half-buried British bunkers on his property, their rounded concrete roofs bearing the ribbed imprint of corrugated iron. They now house a flock of bleating baby goats, who rush out, frightened by the sound of approaching footsteps. A few miles away, a German trench has been carefully reconstructed, with wattle holding the sides firm, duckboards on the bottom, a rim of sandbags along the parapet. The nearby small villages like Passchendaele, whose very names were once synonymous with mass death, are now filled with old men chatting in sidewalk cafés, leafy town squares with bandstands, schoolchildren heading home with leather bookbags, shops selling Belgian chocolates. The air smells of fresh-cut grass. Every road is so well paved, every street so clean, every red-roofed home with its window boxes of bright flowers so well kept, that it is difficult to imagine this same countryside engulfed in blood and flame, this same blue sky filled with deadly shards of metal and the screams of the wounded, this same breeze carrying the pervasive stink of rotting bodies.

In the reconstructed German trench, metal grates block off the entrances to two shafts. These lead to parts of what was an underground battlefield: the hundreds of miles of tunnels that the British and Germans constructed, sometimes digging down through decaying corpses, to plant mines under each other's trenches and to post underground sentries with stethoscopes to listen for tunneling by the other side. Sometimes miners accidentally hacked through the wall of an enemy tunnel, and then they fought in the claustrophobic passageways, with pistols, knives, picks, and shovels. In one tunnel, under Mount Sorrel near Ypres, researchers today have found in the support timbers scars from bullets fired during an underground fight that appears in the records of the 2nd Canadian Tunneling Company. In another, beneath Vimy Ridge in France, they found 8,000 pounds of explosives in rubberized bags that failed to go off in 1917. A huge, previously unexploded British mine beneath a Belgian ridge was ignited by a lightning strike in 1955. Tunnels are so common around Ypres that periodically a heavy tractor or harvester crossing a field or farmyard will suddenly drop five or ten feet when, somewhere below ground, a rotting support timber gives way at last.

Beneath these placid farms lies a layer of soil densely sprinkled with rusted metal: cartridge clips, belt buckles, helmets, canteens, tobacco tins, bells used to sound the alarm for a gas attack, barbed wire, the screw-in metal stakes to which the wire was fastened, shell fragments and shells, rifles with their stocks rotted away, plus the occasional artillery piece, swallowed whole by mud. Plows unearth it all; some half-million pounds of First World War scrap is still collected from French and Belgian fields each year. And everywhere along the old Western Front the soil continues to yield up bones: the remains of 250 British and Australian soldiers were found beneath a French field in 2009.

The thin band of territory stretching through northern France and this corner of Belgium has the greatest concentration of young men's graves in the world. Mile after mile of orderly thickets of white tombstones or crosses climb low hills and spread through gentle valleys, dotted here and there with the spires, columns, and rotundas of larger shrines. From the New Zealand Monument in Messines, Belgium, to the South African National Memorial at the Somme battlefield in France to the less grand cemeteries holding the bones of Senegalese troops or Chinese laborers, the land is dotted with reminders of how far men traveled to die. Even those lucky enough to be in a marked grave were sometimes buried twice over, after cemeteries from the first year or two of the war were blown up by shells in later battles. Today there are more than 2,000 British cemeteries alone in France and Belgium, cared for by almost 500 gardeners.

An entire week of travel along the old Western Front, however, reveals only a single memorial celebrating anyone for doing something other than fighting or dying. A few miles outside of Ypres, across a one-lane country road from a brick barn, is a chest-high cross of sturdy wooden beams, stained dark. Next to it is a small fir tree in a pot, blown over by the summer wind; three silver balls are still attached to it, for it is a Christmas tree, and this homemade cross, not erected or maintained by any country's official graves agency, stands in memory of the soldiers from both sides who took part in the Christmas Truce of 1914. One of the soccer games in no man's land that day is said to have taken place near this spot. Stuck into the ground around the cross are more than a dozen smaller wooden crosses, a foot or so long, which you can buy in Ypres shops that cater to battlefield visitors. "In Remembrance" is stamped on each in English, and you can write a soldier's name beneath it. But on one of the little crosses, in the space for the name, someone has written "All of You," and, above that, "Imagine."

And so, if we could imagine another cemetery, of all those who understood the war's madness enough not to take part, whether just on that Christmas Day or for longer, whose graves might it contain? It would certainly be an international cemetery, for in it would be Eugene V. Debs, whose opposition to the war won him a prison term in the United States, along with other ex-prisoners like Rosa Luxemburg and Karl Liebknecht from Germany and E. D. Morel from England. There would be many soldiers too, from the French troops who mutinied in 1917 and the million or more Russians who, that same year, simply left the front and made the long walk home to their villages, to the German sailors who in the war's final days put out the fires in their ships' boilers and refused orders to go to sea.

Like Sylvia Pankhurst, few in this imaginary cemetery would be saints or paragons of good judgment, but when it came to the war, even someone as indiscriminate in her enthusiasms as Charlotte Despard made a better choice than her brother and those who dutifully marched off to be slaughtered under his command. Emily Hobhouse might have been wildly impractical in thinking that she could single-handedly start peace negotiations in Berlin, but no one else so much as tried. Keir Hardie would be in this cemetery with them, as would his friend Jean Jaurès, though he was murdered just before the war began, and Bertrand Russell, who foresaw with such clarity the shattered world the war would leave. Stephen Hobhouse and the more than 6,000 other British conscientious objectors who went to prison would be here too, with a special place of honor reserved for those taken to France in handcuffs who did not abandon their principles even when threatened with death.

This would be a cemetery not of those who were confident they would win their struggle, but of those who often knew in advance that they were going to lose yet felt the fight was worth it anyway, because of the example it set for those who might someday win. "I knew that it was my business to protest, however futile protest might be," wrote Russell decades later. "I felt that for the honour of human nature those who were not swept off their feet should show that they stood firm." And stand firm and honor the best of human nature they did. Their battle could not be won in 1914–1918, but it remained, and still remains, to be fought again — and again. For even a century's worth of bloodshed after the war that was supposed to end all wars, we are painfully far from the day when most people on earth will have the wisdom to feel, as did Alice Wheeldon in her prison cell, "The world is my country."

SOURCE NOTES

With the primary sources quoted here, I have, when possible, indicated the ultimate origin of every quotation. Official documents in the British National Archives I have listed by their file numbers. A full list of departmental letter codes can be found on the National Archives website; the ones that most commonly appear in the notes that follow are HO, the Home Office; WO, the War Office; FO, the Foreign Office; CAB, cabinet papers; and AIR, the Air Ministry, where, for unknown bureaucratic reasons, records of surveillance of British civilians by military intelligence in the latter part of the war came to rest. When I've not been able to look at a document myself and have relied on a secondary source, I have so indicated. However, even the most reliable scholars sometimes give incomplete source data. Where I've not been able to track down the quotation elsewhere, rather than using cumbersome locutions like "Smith to ?, n.d., n.s., quoted in Jones, p. 38," I've simply put "Jones, p. 38."

The edition of Douglas Haig's wartime diaries and letters edited by Gary Sheffield and John Bourne, the most extensive in print, contains slightly more than a quarter of Haig's diaries for this period. When a diary quotation is not to be found here, I've quoted authors, usually Haig's biographer Gerard De Groot, citing the full text of the diary, whose original is in the National Library of Scotland.

For statistics, I have relied on books with an overview of the war that I found most helpful, such as those by Trevor Wilson, Hew Strachan, John Keegan, David Stevenson, and Anthony Livesey listed in the Bibliography. However, these experts and the British *Official History* sometimes differ about the casualty toll of a particular battle or the number of miles or yards troops advanced. Precision in war is elusive: there is no arbitrary moment when one battle ended and the next began, and sometimes it was unclear which army held a particular patch of ground. The British and Germans calculated their casualties slightly differently, having to do with how soon wounded soldiers were returned to active duty, and for some German and many Russian operations there are only estimates available. Historians are still arguing about how many casualties the Germans suffered in the Battle of the Somme, for example. And, for British casualties at Passchendaele, although we know the rough numbers, the *Official History* notes that "the clerk-power to investigate the exact losses was not available." (This may or may not be true; eager to vindicate Haig, the *Official History's* authors dramatically inflate German casualty figures.) For death figures in 1918 it is not always clear when these include victims of the great influenza pandemic. When reliable sources give conflicting figures, I've generally used the most cautious, and so when I've said that there were at least 20,000 casualties in a particular battle, it usually means some sources cite higher numbers.

Within quotations, I have on a few occasions silently adjusted a comma or dash, but no words have been changed and all ellipses are indicated.

page INTRODUCTION: CLASH OF DREAMS

xi   *My father's sister married:* See pp. 21–101 of his lively autobiography: Boris Sergievsky, *Airplanes, Women, and Song: Memoirs of a Fighter Ace, Test Pilot, and Adventurer* (Syracuse, NY: Syracuse University Press, 1999).
       The magnitude of slaughter: Whalen, p. 41.

xii   *"The Great War of 1914–18":* Tuchman 1, p. xiii.
       "This is not war": David Omissi, *The Sepoy and the Raj: The Indian Army, 1860–1940* (London: Macmillan, 1994), pp. 117–118, quoted in Keegan 1, p. 197.
       "Supply me with socks": Gilbert, p. 82.

xiii *"had won, nor could win":* Mind's Eye: Essays* (Manchester, NH: Ayer, 1977), p. 38.
       "Humanity? Can anyone": Alexander Nemser, "Low Truths," *New Republic*, 30 July 2008.

"It cannot be that": Alan Bullock, *Hitler: A Study in Tyranny* (New York: Harper & Row, 1962), p. 88.

xiv *more than 20,000 British:* Pearce, p. 169. For some years scholars used a smaller figure, but Pearce's careful calculations are convincing as to why the earlier estimates were too low. A more precise number is impossible to determine.

xvi *"They advanced in line"*: Travers, p. 158. Travers, like other writers, attributes this account to Brigadier General Hubert C. Rees. But Rees, in his papers at the Imperial War Museum (IWM 77/179/1), as more recent scholars have pointed out, complains that his corps commander, Lieutenant General Sir Aylmer Hunter-Weston, "put my remarks in his own language." It is likely that Rees was less responsible for the tone of this passage than Hunter-Weston, who is on record (see CAB 45/188, quoted in Middlebrook, p. 80) as being wildly unrealistic in believing that the troops would meet no obstacles to their advance on July 1, 1916.

1. BROTHER AND SISTER

4 *"How many millions"*: Morris 2, p. 31.
"I contend that we": Marlowe, p. 5.

5 *"We are a part"*: *New York Times*, 24 June 1897.
"From my heart": *Times,* 23 June 1897.
"a small select aristocracy": A. G. Gardiner, *Prophets, Priests and Kings* (London: Alston Rivers, 1908), p. 229.
"Only heaven left": Chauncey Depew to Lord Rosebery, 1894, quoted in Tuchman 1, p. 23.

6 *"I didn't know"*: Morris 2, p. 408.

7 *"You have the heartfelt"*: French to Buller, 15 July 1902, John French, p. 95.

8 *more than £70,000:* Farwell 1, p. 27.
"An army tries to": n.p., quoted in Ellis 1, p. 105.

9 *"Play the game"*: Farwell 1, p. 134.

10 *"I took a ticket"*: "In the Days of My Youth," Charlotte Despard Papers, Public Record Office of Northern Ireland, Belfast, p. 4.

11 *"That hymn was"*: Linklater, p. 23.
"How bitterly ashamed": "In the Days of My Youth," pp. 11–12.

12 *"She does not find them"*: Charles Booth, *Life and Labour of the People of London,* vol. 5 (London: Macmillan, 1902), p. 153.

13 *"I determined to study"*: Mulvihill, p. 58.

14 *"those who slave"*: Linklater, p. 89.

15 *"It certainly was amusing"*: Gerald French, pp. 44–45.
"Only nervous people": Despard 2, p. 17.

2. A MAN OF NO ILLUSIONS

17 *"The whole side of the hill"*: Churchill 2, p. 87.
"standing at a table": Churchill 2, p. 98.

"jams, tinned fruits": Haig to Henrietta Jameson, 17 February 1898, quoted in De Groot 1, p. 56.

"I am not one": Haig 2, p. 4.

18 *"The enemy went down"*: Ellis 1, p. 86.

19 *"the rapture-giving delight"*: Farwell 1, p. 117.

"It is a weapon": Ellis 1, p. 102.

20 *"It is the British race"*: Farwell 2, p. 27.

21 *"the man of no illusions"*: Winston Churchill, *London to Ladysmith and Ian Hamilton's March* (London: Eyre & Spottiswoode, 1962), p. 123. Churchill first used the phrase in writing of Milner in the *Morning Post* during the Boer War.

"as lucid as a page of print": Buchan 3, p. 98.

"a civilian soldier": Marlowe, pp. 38–39.

"to Brixton . . . to see C": 23 January 1898, quoted in Pakenham 1, p. 34.

22 *"a frock-coated Neanderthal"*: Gilmour, p. 140.

"great day of reckoning": Gollin, p. 33.

"great game between ourselves": Johannes S. Marais, *The Fall of Kruger's Republic* (Oxford: Clarendon Press, 1961), p. 330.

"Will not the arrival": Milner to Selborne, 24 May 1899, quoted in Marlowe, p. 68.

"no civilizing experiment": Gilmour, p. 78.

23 *"that an empire is"*: "Rudyard Kipling," in George Orwell, *A Collection of Essays* (New York: Doubleday, 1954), p. 126.

"Accept my felicitations": Lansdowne to Chamberlain, 10 October 1899, quoted in Pakenham 2, p. 567.

24 *"just like a good fox hunt"*: James 1, p. 434.

"Strain everything": Judd and Surridge, p. 147.

borrowed a hefty £2,000: Haig claimed it was £2,500. See De Groot 4, p. 50n12. Biographers disagree over whether the loan was ever repaid.

25 *"The feeling was"*: Anonymous officer, quoted in German General Staff, p. 147.

"An epoch in the history": L. S. Amery, ed., *The Times History of the War in South Africa, 1899–1902*, vol. 3 (London: St. Dunstan's House, 1905), pp. 394–395.

"The Cavalry—the despised *Cavalry"*: Haig to Lonsdale Hale, 2 March 1900, quoted in De Groot 1, p. 80.

26 *"The charge of French's"*: German General Staff, p. 147.

"who has taught the British": Rice, p. xvi.

"a first-class dress-parade": "The Captive," in *Traffics and Discoveries* (New York: Scribner's, 1904), p. 30.

3. A CLERGYMAN'S DAUGHTER

28 *"without evening dress"*: Cecil, pp. 152–153.

"to have a clever wife": Georgina, Marchioness of Salisbury, to Eleanor, Viscountess Cecil, quoted in Cecil, p. 69.

29 *"one, so to speak"*: Cecil, p. 80.

"I wish Milner had": Cecil, p. 116.

"One day I know": Cecil, p. 126.

"the solidarity of the British": Violet Milner, p. 138.

30 *"Sir Alfred is very"*: Annie Hanbury-Williams to Violet Cecil, in Cecil, p. 160.

"Was it a declaration": Cecil, p. 159.

31 *"the wicked war of this"*: Linklater, p. 96.

"three a penny": Farwell 2, p. 315.

32 *"very low indeed"*: Cecil, p. 175.

33 *"the mad men at home"*: Milner to Bagot, 21 November 1900, quoted in Jacqueline Beaumont, "The *Times* at War, 1899–1902," in Lowry, p. 83n39.

34 *as a "screamer"*: Milner to Haldane, 1 July 1901, quoted in Kaminski, p. 99.

"He struck me as": Emily Hobhouse to Mary Hobhouse, 8 January 1901, Van Reenen, p. 37.

35 *"My heart wept"*: Emily Hobhouse, *The Brunt of the War and Where It Fell* (London: Methuen, 1902), p. 72.

27,927 Boers: Figures compiled by Transvaal government archivist P.L.A. Goldman, cited in Roberts, p. 252, and Morgan, p. 68.

"a little six months' baby": Emily Hobhouse to Mary Hobhouse, 31 January 1901, Van Reenen, pp. 54–55.

"I rub as much salt": Emily Hobhouse to Mary Hobhouse, 26 January 1901, Van Reenen, p. 49.

"If we can get over": Milner to Chamberlain, 7 December 1901, quoted in Krebs, p. 52.

36 *"What an army"*: Balme, p. 183.

"pro-Boer ravings": Milner to Kitchener, 7 June 1901, quoted in Pakenham 1, p. 511.

37 *"Sir, the lunacy"*: Hobhouse to the Committee of the Distress Fund, n.d., Van Reenen, p. 148.

"I had thought of that": Roberts, p. 224.

"Your brutal orders": Hobhouse to Milner, 1 November 1901, Van Reenen, p. 151.

"restarting the new": Farwell 2, p. 444.

"The white man": Cecil Headlam, ed., *The Milner Papers*, vol. 2 (London: Cassell, 1933), p. 467, quoted in Adam Smith, pp. 123–124.

38 *"play the game like gentlemen"*: *Blackwood's Magazine,* 1902, quoted in Adam Smith, p. 122.

"fascinating and most hopeful work": Adam Smith, p. 117.

"I must say I am": Adam Smith, p. 118.

39 *"A very small memento"*: Cassar, p. 32.

"I daresay that he": Esher to Knollys, 16 January 1904, in "French, John Denton Pinkstone," *Oxford Dictionary of National Biography* (online), accessed 9 March 2010.

"This is certainly": French to Sir Charles Boxall, 20 October 1901, quoted in Holmes, p. 117.

4. HOLY WARRIORS

41 *"In the campaigns"*: French to Winifred Bennett, 19 March 1915, quoted in De Groot 1, p. 138.
"I am thoroughly satisfied": Haig 3, pp. 223–224.
"moral factor of an": Ellis 1, p. 56.

42 *"I have often made up"*: Denis Winter, p. 33.
"the rôle of Cavalry": Douglas Haig, *Cavalry Studies: Strategical and Tactical* (London: Hugh Rees, 1907), pp. 8–9.

44 *"I asked myself"*: Women's Franchise, 11 July 1907.
"I'm quite safe": Mulvihill, p. 73.
"The women began to": Daily Mirror, quoted in Linklater, pp. 113–114.

45 *21 days in solitary*: HO 144/847/149245.
"If she insists on": Linklater, p. 114.
She called for equality: Despard 1, p. 6.
"I had sought and found": Women's Franchise, 11 July 1907.

46 *"I began to think"*: Emmeline Pankhurst, p. 28.
"like a stringed instrument": Ethel Smyth, *Female Pipings in Eden* (Edinburgh: Peter Davies, 1933), pp. 194–195, quoted in Purvis 1, p. 100.

47 *"She was slender, young"*: E. Sylvia Pankhurst 4, p. 221.
"She was one of those": Helen Crawford, quoted in Winslow, p. 13.

48 *"We are soldiers"*: Standard, 27 May 1913, quoted in Purvis 1, p. 221.
"We leave that to": Emmeline Pankhurst, pp. 264–265.
"I wish that a sensible": Kipling to Mrs. Humphry Ward, 2 February 1912, Kipling Collection, Dalhousie University.

49 *"a short, wiry"*: Rupert Grayson, *Voyage Not Completed* (London: Macmillan, 1969), quoted in Holt, p. 104.
"Howe wood yu": Kipling to John Kipling, 6 October 1908, Kipling 2, p. 73.
"Don't you bother": Kipling to John Kipling, 18 May 1908, Kipling 2, p. 59.
the poet declared he admired: Gilmour, p. 198.

50 *but what would they do*: Cecil, p. 180.
"It is a spirit": John Buchan, *A Lodge in the Wilderness* (Edinburgh: Blackwood, 1906), p. 28.
"Do ye wait for": "The Islanders," 1902.

51 *"withholding from others"*: Roberts, p. 252.
"a fatal mistake": Cecil, pp. 181–182.

52 *"looks well, a bit thinner"*: Cecil, p. 220.

53 *"I shall tear up"*: Purvis 2, p. 159.

5. BOY MINER

55 *"That night the baby"*: Hardie, pp. 1–2.
"We were great friends": Hardie, p. 2.

56 *"The rich and comfortable classes"*: Benn, p. 259.

"We'll hae nae damned": Benn, p. 22.

"a longing, profound": Countess of Oxford and Asquith, ed., *Myself When Young: By Famous Women of To-Day* (London: Frederick Muller, 1938), p. 262.

57 *"walk and sing and meditate"*: Tuchman 1, p. 421.

"Abandon hope all ye": Hope Hay Hewison, *Hedge of Wild Almonds: South Africa, the Pro-Boers and the Quaker Conscience, 1890–1910* (London: Currey, 1989), p. 340, quoted in Lowry, p. 17.

"Are you working here, mate?": *Labour Leader*, February 1906, quoted in Benn, pp. 211–212.

58 *"Can I do anything?"*: Benn, p. 203.

59 *"worth having lived"*: John Bruce Glasier, *James Keir Hardie: A Memorial* (Manchester, UK: National Labour Press, 1915), p. 24, quoted in Benn, p. 189.

"militarism": Benn, p. 161.

"I sat among my boxes": E. Sylvia Pankhurst 4, p. 217.

60 *"what a terribly important"*: Keir Hardie to John Bruce Glasier, 22 October 1903, quoted in Benn, p. 182.

"strange behaviour to him": Glasier to his sister, Lizzie, 29 September 1903, quoted in Benn, p. 181.

"We are for free": Notebook entry, 1918, quoted in Romero, p. 118.

"Last night when all was quiet": E. Sylvia Pankhurst Papers, Reel 1.

"All the night I have been": Hardie to Pankhurst, n.d., Pankhurst Papers, Reel 1.

"I like to think of you": Hardie to Pankhurst, 10 March[?] 1911, Pankhurst Papers, Reel 1.

61 *"They did not hide"*: Interview with Fenner Brockway, quoted in Benn, p. 238.

"He told me": E. Sylvia Pankhurst 4, p. 320.

"I am fighting, fighting": Sylvia Pankhurst to Emmeline Pankhurst, 18 March 1913, quoted in Winslow, p. 44.

62 *total arms expenses:* Fromkin, p. 94.

64 *"Look at those fellows"*: Valentine Chirol, *Fifty Years in a Changing World* (New York: Harcourt, 1928), p. 274, quoted in Tuchman 1, pp. 417–418.

6. ON THE EVE

66 *"When he came up"*: *Times*, 2 January 1912.

67 *"His fellow-rulers had"*: *Times*, 6 January 1912.

"A perfect parade . . . I have never seen": 11, 14 December 1911, Haig 3, pp. 303, 304.

"Schools are like": Marguerite Poland, *The Boy in You: A Biography of St Andrew's College, 1855–2005* (Simon's Town, South Africa: Fernwood Press, 2008), p. 165. I am indebted to Prof. Francis Wilson for pointing out this striking quotation.

68 *"pluck up the courage"*: Fischer, p. 25.

"We will never fire on you": Joll, p. 151.

"a victory of the proletariat": *L'Humanité*, quoted in Haupt, pp. 113–114.

69 *"Jaurès thinks with"*: Remy de Gourmont, quoted in Tuchman 1, p. 421.

"we all knew": Interview with Fenner Brockway, quoted in Benn, p. 315.

"All sides are preparing": Fromkin, p. 31.

"let the French commanders": Esher to Huguet, General A. Huguet, *Britain and the War: A French Indictment* (London: Cassell, 1928), p. 18, quoted in Tuchman 1, p. 54.

"Peace may and has": "Linesman," 24 October 1912. Quoted in Glenn R. Wilkinson, "'The Blessings of War': The Depiction of Military Force in Edwardian Newspapers," *Journal of Contemporary History* 33:1 (January 1998), p. 103.

70 *"Good morning, one day"*: Stephen E. Koss, *Lord Haldane: Scapegoat for Liberalism* (New York: Columbia University Press, 1969), p. 66, quoted in Gilmour, p. 205.

"camping comfortably on": Kipling to Dunsterville, c. 1911, quoted in Gilmour, p. 207.

"And because there was need": "The City of Brass," 1909.

"unless there were": Thomson 2, p. 298.

71 *"A good big war"*: Sitwell, p. 137.

inflicted £500,000 worth: *Standard*, 25 February 1913, cited in Purvis 1, p. 210.

"the horrid woman": James Pope-Hennessy, *Queen Mary, 1867–1953* (New York: Knopf, 1960), p. 465.

"one of our bravest soldiers": *Daily Herald*, 10 June 1913, quoted in Purvis 1, p. 222.

73 *"were armed with"*: Report of William Hestet [?], 15 October 1913, HO 144/1558/234191.

"The arms were raised": Despard 2, pp. 12–13.

"I was older at twenty": Linklater, p. 126.

"I was thrilled to see": Emmeline Pethick-Lawrence, quoted in Mulvihill, p. 74.

74 *"I have never heard"*: Lytton and Wharton, chap. 6.

"News in the Paper": Despard Diary, 25 March 1914, Public Record Office of Northern Ireland.

75 *"Friends in past"*: Gilbert, p. 18.

"falling short of violence": Memorandum to committee of the British League for the Support of Ulster, 16 January 1914, quoted in Marlowe, p. 224.

"For the last 3 or 4 months": 11 March 1914, quoted in Gollin, p. 186.

76 *"the Orientals of the West"*: Kipling to Mrs. Guthrie, 16 November 1901, quoted in Gilmour, p. 242.

raised funds to buy arms: Marlowe, p. 235n19.

"Today the cry of": Fromkin, p. 184.

7 · A STRANGE LIGHT

81 *"the issue will be"*: Gilbert, p. 9.

"Slavs and Gallics": Fischer, p. 33.

"This unorganised Asiatic": Gilbert, p. 40.

talked privately of annexing: Fischer, p. 103f.

"difficult to discuss": Sir Mark Sykes, quoted in Fromkin, p. 140.

82 *"to lead the march on Paris":* Tuchman 2, p. 106.

"this war which I": von Moltke to von der Goltz, June 1915, quoted in Fromkin, p. 305.

83 *"We are ready":* Baron von Eckhardstein, *Lebenserinnerungen, Vol. 3, Die Isolierung Deutschlands* (Liepzig, 1921), p. 184, quoted in Tuchman 2, p. 27.

"the omission of the customary": Fromkin, p. 166.

84 *"The quiet grave tones":* Churchill 1, pp. 94–95.

"We are in measurable": Michael and Eleanor Brock, eds., *H. H. Asquith: Letters to Venetia Stanley* (Oxford: Oxford University Press, 1985), pp. 122–123, quoted in Fromkin, p. 188.

85 *"This country has gone":* War 1914: Punishing the Serbs (London: His Majesty's Stationery Office, 1919), p. 74, quoted in Fromkin, p. 216.

"We shall never hit": Fromkin, p. 218.

"likewise obliged to mobilize": Serge Sverbeev to St. Petersburg, 29 July 1914, quoted in Albertini, vol. 2, p. 499.

86 *"I will . . . smash":* Fromkin, p. 231.

87 *"men's wars":* Suffragette, 19 June 1914.

"The walls of the room": Tuchman 1, p. 421.

88 *"It is impossible":* Tuchman 1, p. 460.

"I have done all": Telegram, Nicholas II to George V, *Times,* 5 August 1914.

89 *"In spite of all my":* Stefan Zweig, *The World of Yesterday* (Alcester, UK: Read Books, 2006), p. 173.

"The victory of Germany": "Reflections of a Nonpolitical Man" (1917), quoted in Tuchman 2, p. 311.

90 *"Every German friend of peace":* Carsten, p. 18.

"The government has managed": R.J.W. Evans and Hartmut Pogge von Strandmann, eds. *The Coming of the First World War* (Oxford: Clarendon Press, 2001), p. 120.

"Few English people": Manchester Guardian, 3 August 1914.

91 *largest demonstration there:* Manchester Guardian, 3 August 1914.

"You have no quarrel": Benn, p. 324.

"we are fighting against": Times, 20 September 1914.

92 *"that the fatherland's poorest":* Carsten, p. 17.

"Henceforth I know no parties": Tuchman 1, p. 462.

"There are no more": Paul Deschanel, quoted in Tuchman 1, p. 462.

"holy war of civilization": 4 August 1914, quoted in Kramer, p. 183.

"wants to crush": Rheinische Zeitung, 5 August 1914, quoted in Kramer, p. 244.

93 *"The working class went":* Tuchman 1, p. 462.

94 *"A single worry":* Weintraub, p. 70.

"joined with our elders": Waugh, p. 93.

"Semi-barbarians": Hobhouse to Smuts, 8 August 1914, quoted in Kaminski, p. 287.

95 *"look of surprise"*: A. Mor-O'Brien, ed. *The Autobiography of Edmund Stonel-ake* (Mid-Glamorgan Education Committee, 1981), p. 157, quoted in Benn, p. 326.

"I would rather see my two": E. Sylvia Pankhurst 1, p. 34.

"He looked neither left": Emrys Hughes, quoted in Benn, p. 326.

96 *"It is better to have"*: Cecil, p. 236.

"flushed, excited face": Cecil, p. 239.

8. AS SWIMMERS INTO CLEANNESS LEAPING

99 *"God's vengeance upon"*: *Suffragette*, 7 August 1914 (postdated; this issue actually appeared some days earlier), quoted in Mitchell, p. 247.

"this criminal war": Mulvihill, p. 110.

100 *"crumpled in body"*: Fenner Brockway, quoted in Benn, p. 329.

"Across the roar of guns": *Labour Leader*, 13 August 1914, quoted in Boulton, pp. 44–45.

"to go up to him": John Bruce Glasier, *James Keir Hardie: A Memorial* (Manchester, UK: National Labour Press, 1915), p. 66, quoted in Benn, p. 332.

101 *"Now, God be thanked"*: "Peace," *1914 and Other Poems* (London: Sidgwick and Jackson, 1918), p. 11.

102 *"purification, liberation"*: Kramer, p. 163.

"You will be home": Tuchman 2, p. 119.

103 *"Never!"*: Tuchman 2, p. 38.

"easy to see": Kenneth Godsell Diary, quoted in Richard Holmes, "The Last Hurrah: Cavalry on the Western Front, August–September 1914," in Cecil and Liddle, p. 280.

"Keep constantly on your guard": Macdonald 1, p. 62.

104 *"They are a low lot"*: French to Kitchener, 15 November 1914, quoted in Holmes, pp. 202–203.

"In my own heart": Haig 1, 11 August 1914, p. 56.

105 *"well and cheery"*: John French, p. 144, 14 August 1914.

"I think I know": French to Kitchener, 21 August 1914, quoted in Cassar, p. 104.

"The usual silly reports": John French, p. 145, 15 August 1914.

"I saw the 4th Brigade": French Diary, 20 August 1914, quoted in Holmes, p. 211.

"than I am of the bullets": Cecil, p. 241.

106 *"He said that up to date"*: Cecil, p. 243.

"The empty stage": E. Sylvia Pankhurst 1, p. 66.

"We cannot discuss": E. Sylvia Pankhurst 1, p. 66; see also *Times*, 9 September 1914.

"I listened to her": E. Sylvia Pankhurst 1, p. 66.

"an impenetrable barrier": E. Sylvia Pankhurst 1, p. 66.

107 *"Do not let us"*: Published in *Jus Suffragii*, 1 January 1915, quoted in Purvis 1, p. 272.

"I want men to go": Linklater, p. 177.

"If you go to this war": Purvis 1, p. 272.

108 *"I am ashamed to know":* E. Sylvia Pankhurst 1, p. 67.

"tea and conversation": Despard Diary, 8 August 1914, Public Record Office of Northern Ireland, Belfast.

109 *"Sir John as usual":* Sir Henry Wilson Diary, 3 September 1914, quoted in Trevor Wilson, p. 44.

"I met the men": French Diary, 28 August 1914, quoted in Holmes, pp. 226–227.

110 *"Perhaps the charm of war":* John French, p. 148, 29 August 1914.

"Louder and louder": Lt. E. L. Spears, quoted in Macdonald 1, p. 90. Spears was liaison officer to the nearby French forces.

"The Germans just fell": Trumpeter J. Naylor, 3rd Division, Royal Field Artillery, quoted in Macdonald 1, p. 116.

"It is with keen admiration": Despard Diary, 10 September 1914.

112 *"your heathery hair":* Collette Malleson to Russell, 2 October 1916, quoted in Ronald W. Clark, p. 308.

"seemed almost to give": Malleson in Ralph Schoenman, ed., *Bertrand Russell: Philosopher of the Century* (Boston: Little, Brown, 1967), p. 20, quoted in Ronald W. Clark, p. 329.

"tortured by patriotism": Russell 1, pp. 6–7.

"this war is trivial": Russell 2, pp. 13–14.

113 *"swept away in a red blast":* Russell to Lucy Donnelly, 22 August 1914, quoted in Vellacott, p. 10.

"One by one": Bertrand Russell, "Some Psychological Difficulties of Pacifism in Wartime," in Julian Bell, p. 329.

9. THE GOD OF RIGHT WILL WATCH THE FIGHT

115 *"He and his officers":* The businessman was my father, an executive of the American Metal Company. Harold K. Hochschild to George F. Kennan, 2 January 1964.

"A French businessman": Alan Clark, p. 22.

"Gentlemen, no stealing": A. G. Gardiner, *The War Lords* (London: Dent, 1915), p. 133.

116 *"cases of light wounds":* Stone, p. 169.

"The enemy has luck": Alfred Knox, *With the Russian Army, 1914–1917: Being Chiefly Extracts from the Diary of a Military Attaché,* vol. 1 (London: Hutchinson, 1921), p. 74.

117 *the Russians lost:* Rutherford, p. 59.

118 *"The Russian Steam-Roller":* Ernest Shackleton, *South: The Story of Shackleton's Last Expedition, 1914–1917* (New York: Macmillan, 1920), p. xv.

"I would not be out": Trevor Wilson, p. 111.

"Come, leave the lure": Times, 24 November 1914.

119 *"he's rather like":* Kipling to Dunsterville, 24 February 1915, Pinney, vol. 4, p. 287.

120 *"Charge lads"*: Cecil, p. 254.

left dozens of Grenadier Guardsmen": Macdonald 1, p. 266.

"terribly distressed": Cecil, p. 245.

"I have every reliance": Cecil, p. 245.

121 *"It is* only a rumour": Violet Cecil to Col. R. G. Gordon Gilmour, 1 October 1914, quoted in Craster, p. 63.

"Mr. Roosevelt is asking": Holt, p. 63.

"She dying daily": Kipling to Andrew Macphail, 5 October 1914, quoted in Cecil, p. 246.

122 *"I don't feel as if"*: Cecil, p. 248.

123 *"the spade will be"*: French to George V, 2 October 1914, quoted in Holmes, p. 241.

"In my opinion": French to Kitchener, 21 October 1914, quoted in Holmes, p. 246.

"The little fool": Sir Henry Wilson Diary, 10 December 1914, quoted in Cassar, p. 187.

124 *"When immediately in front"*: M. Kranzberg and C. W. Pursell, eds., *Technology in Western Civilisation* (New York: Oxford University Press, 1967), p. 499, quoted in Ellis 1, p. 54.

"I saw trees as large": E. Alexander Powell, quoted in Gilbert, p. 67.

126 *"It is all* the *best fun"*: "Grenfell, Julian Henry Francis," in *Oxford Dictionary of National Biography* (online), accessed 9 March 2010.

127 *"enraptured by being"*: French to Winifred Bennett, 5 March 1915, quoted in Holmes, p. 277.

"in an entirely private": French to Kitchener, 14 May 1915, quoted in Holmes, p. 289.

"Too many whores": General Sir Horace Smith-Dorrien, quoted in Holmes, p. 380n51.

"Grave opened George": Cecil, p. 251.

"thrown like carrion": Cecil, p. 251.

"You and I can't talk": Cecil, p. 252.

128 *"every troop or regiment"*: George Lansbury, *Sixty-four, Ninety-four,* quoted in Caroline Playne, *Society at War, 1914–1916* (Boston: Houghton Mifflin, 1931), p. 58.

130 *"Suddenly from the enemy"*: *Vorwärts,* January 1915, quoted in Brown and Seaton, p. 90.

"The Germans came out": Anonymous, *Times,* 2 January 1915.

131 *played games of soccer:* Although there are no photographs of these games among those of the truce, Brown and Seaton, pp. 142–147, consider the various pieces of evidence and conclude that some kicking about of soccer balls, both real and makeshift, did take place.

"We marked the goals": Brown and Seaton, p. 145.

"Have you no German": Weintraub, p. 71.

"Soldiers should have": Field-Marshal Viscount French of Ypres, *1914* (Boston: Houghton Mifflin, 1919), quoted in Brown and Seaton, p. 166.

"Why are men who can": *Merthyr Pioneer,* 9 January 1915.

10. THIS ISN'T *WAR*

135 *"county men of position"*: Field-Marshal Viscount French of Ypres, *1914* (Boston: Houghton Mifflin, 1919), p. 301.

136 *"at some points in the trench"*: Blunden, pp. 11, 49.

"Spent the morning": Macdonald 2, p. 19.

137 *"I've a little wet home"*: Macdonald 2, p. 29.

"This afternoon we went": *Times,* 23 January 1915.

138 *"thinks he may be"*: French Diary, 8 March 1915, quoted in Holmes, p. 274.

"The Germans were shooting": Macdonald 2, p. 102.

139 *"the defeat of the enemy"*: John French, *The Despatches of Lord French* (London: Chapman & Hall, 1917), p. 23, quoted in Holmes, p. 272.

"If these two had": Haig 1, 11 April 1915, pp. 114–115.

140 *"the peace-at-any-price crowd"*: *Minneapolis Daily News,* 30 March 1915, quoted in Purvis 1, p. 274.

"It is unthinkable": *Sunday Pictorial,* 11 April 1915, quoted in Purvis 1, p. 274.

141 *"The chaps were all"*: Sgt. Bill Hay, 9th Battalion, Royal Scots, quoted in Livesey, p. 66.

"Germany has stooped": Gilbert, p. 145.

142 *"were not at present normal"*: 15 May 1915, WO 106/1519; R.H.K. Butler to GOC First Army, November 1915; Robertson to Haig, 14 January 1916; all quoted in Travers, p. 98n7.

"I don't know what": Viscount Grey of Fallodon, *Twenty-five Years, 1892–1916,* vol. 2 (New York: Frederick A. Stokes, 1925), p. 72.

143 *"Come on, Jocks"*: Trevor Wilson, p. 144.

"Precious documents": Wigram to Lady Haig, 28 September 1916, quoted in Denis Winter, p. 234.

"Take and shoot two": Haig to Lady Haig, 10 April 1915, quoted in De Groot 1, p. 184.

144 *"break thro' this"*: French to Winifred Bennett, 24 May 1915, quoted in Holmes, p. 294.

"shipwrecked souls": 18 February 1915, quoted in Holmes, p. 278.

"you can't trust them": 28 April 1915, quoted in Cassar, p. 225.

"I devoutly wish," "While they are": 21 May 1915, quoted in Holmes, p. 279.

145 *"They've been married"*: 15 September 1915, quoted in Holmes, p. 281.

"He is so hot tempered": Haig to Rothschild, 9 December 1915, Haig 1, p. 172.

"French seems to have": Haig to Rothschild, 20 May 1915, quoted in De Groot 1, pp. 193–194.

"had lost confidence": Haig 1, 14 July 1915, p. 130.

146 *"The enemy . . . can't go on"*: Haig to Lady Haig, 10 August 1915, quoted in De Groot 1, p. 202.

11. IN THE THICK OF IT

148 *"all the English-speaking race"*: *Times*, 18 September 1914.
"is the sovereign disinfectant": Edmund Gosse, *Inter Arma: Being Essays Written in Time of War* (New York: Scribner's, 1916), p. 3.
149 *"this war may rank"*: John Buchan, *The Future of the War* (London: Hodder and Stoughton, 1916), pp. 13–14, quoted in Buitenhuis, p. 93.
"it is a war": Rudyard Kipling, *The New Army* (New York: Doubleday and Page, 1914), "Indian Troops," p. 7, quoted in Buitenhuis, p. 25.
150 *"What will be"*: Kipling, *The New Army*, "A Territorial Battalion and a Conclusion," p. 9, quoted in Buitenhuis, p. 26.
"very straight and smart": Gilmour, p. 257.
"This is the life": John Kipling to his family, 17 August 1915, Kipling 2, p. 195.
"Bread, sardines, jam": John Kipling to his family, 18 August 1915, Kipling 2, p. 197.
"Neither of them look": Morton Cohen, ed., *Rudyard Kipling to Rider Haggard* (Rutherford, NJ: Fairleigh Dickinson University Press, 1965), p. 81, quoted in Kipling 2, p. 14.
"in a splendid little": John Kipling to his family, 20 August 1915, Kipling 2, pp. 198–199.
"The cigarettes, tobacco": John Kipling to his family, 22 August 1915, Kipling 2, p. 201.
"What he doesn't know": John Kipling to his family, 29 August 1915, Kipling 2, p. 213.
151 *"I tried to stop"*: Robb, p. 125.
"Kill Germans!": Eksteins, p. 236.
"The little hall was crowded": Brockway, p. 64.
152 *"Ten million Socialist"*: Robb, p. 69.
"They are well worth": Hardie to Sylvia Pankhurst, 27 May 1915, E. Sylvia Pankhurst Papers, Reel 1.
"You have been very brave": E. Sylvia Pankhurst 1, p. 227.
"His Majesty feels": Buckingham Palace to Lloyd George, 28 June 1915, quoted in Purvis 1, p. 276.
153 *"The Ablest Woman"*: *New York Journal*, 12 November 1915, quoted in Purvis 1, p. 278.
154 *"It's no business"*: Dorothy Peel, *How We Lived Then: 1914–1918: A Sketch of Social and Domestic Life in England During the War* (London: John Lane, 1929), p. 152, quoted in Trevor Wilson, p. 511.
"shout of bestial triumph": Russell 1, p. 19.
"The air was filled": E. Sylvia Pankhurst 1, p. 196.
155 *"with no more mind"*: E. Sylvia Pankhurst Papers, Reel 1.

"He is dying": E. Sylvia Pankhurst 1, p. 228.

"un-English," "the weapon of cowards," "an underhanded method": Massie, p. 123.

157 *"Whole families with all"*: Alfred Knox, *With the Russian Army, 1914–1917*, vol. 1 (London: Hutchinson, 1921), p. 305.

well over three million: Gatrell, pp. 3, 212.

"diversionary themes not": Lincoln, p. 48.

"afflicted with the misfortune": George Buchanan, *My Mission to Russia and Other Diplomatic Memories,* vol. 2 (London: Cassell, 1923), p. 77, quoted in Clay, p. 172.

"My brain is resting": Lincoln, p. 152.

158 *"were never in better"*: Haig 1, 12 September 1915, p. 146.

"It is against wild": Rudyard Kipling, *France at War: On the Frontier of Civilization* (Garden City, NY: Doubleday, Page, 1916), pp. 48, 86–87, 90.

"wouldn't like to have": Rudyard Kipling to Carrie Kipling, 21 August 1915, Kipling 2, p. 13.

159 *"I don't think I have"*: John Kipling to his family, 26 August 1915, Kipling 2, p. 208.

"my visage is the colour": John Kipling to his family, 29 August 1915, Kipling 2, p. 212.

"older and fatter": Haig 1, 22 September 1915, p. 151.

"Whatever may happen": 18 September 1915, quoted in Cassar, p. 261.

"a really good pair": John Kipling to his family, 23 September 1915, Kipling 2, p. 221.

"Just a hurried line": John Kipling to his family, 25 September 1915, Kipling 2, p. 222.

12. NOT THIS TIDE

161 *"For the future"*: Ministry of Munitions, *History of the Ministry of Munitions,* vol. 11 (London: His Majesty's Stationery Office, 1918–1922), sec. 3, p. 42. The wording of an earlier draft of the history, in BT 66/6/46, is almost identical and adds no more information. See also MacLeod and MacLeod, pp. 171–175.

some 32,000 pairs: Hartcup, p. 182. The official *History of the Ministry of Munitions* implies — apparently falsely — that the British-German trade was not consummated, because alternative sources of optical glass were found in Britain and the United States. Hartcup's source for the number of binoculars actually delivered in 1915 is a memorandum he found in BT 66/6/46, "Negotiations with Germany and America for optical instruments, Aug. 1915." Sometime after he did the research for his well-documented 1988 book, the memo was removed from this file in the National Archives, and I was unable to find it in a number of other files. My thanks to Guy Hartcup for taking the time to correspond with me about this.

162 *"each about a thousand"*: F. Forstner, *Das Reserve Infanterie Regiment 15* (Berlin, 1929), pp. 226–232, quoted in Keegan 1, pp. 201–202.

"My machine gunners": Cherry, pp. 198–199.

163   *"The communication trench"*: Philip Warner, *The Battle of Loos* (Ware, Hertfordshire: Wordsworth, 2000), p. 54.

164   *"The C.O. wishes"*: Macdonald 2, p. 536.
"The whole slope in front": Cherry, pp. 198–199.

166   *"They advanced as if"*: Vansittart to Secretary for War, 7 October 1917, CAB
45/121.
"bring out more": Vansittart to Brigadier-General Sir James Edmonds, 30 January 1926, CAB 45/121.
"Dead, dying and badly": 27 September and 2 October 1915, quoted in Holmes,
p. 305.
"It was impossible to bury": Macdonald 2, p. 572.

167   *"The introduction of"*: "The Question of Training Men for Employment with
the Machine Guns now under Supply," General Staff, GHQ, 23 November
1915, quoted in Travers, p. 85.
only one machine gun: Paul Clark to Pershing, 15 May 1918, quoted in Denis
Winter, p. 148.
"My attack, as has been": Haig to Kitchener, 29 September 1915, Haig 1, p. 160.
"Douglas Haig came": n.d., Cherry, p. 329.

168   *"I was not faint"*: E. Sylvia Pankhurst 1, p. 230.

169   *"He was built for"*: *Woman's Dreadnought*, 2 October 1915.
"How can you expect": E. Sylvia Pankhurst 1, p. 239.
"corrupted . . . by Germanism": 8 December 1916, quoted in Millman, p. 120.
"I absolutely agree": 7 December 1915, Milner Papers, Bodleian Library, Oxford,
dep. 351.
"through little old": Buchan 1, p. 31.

171   *"DH never shines"*: Charteris, regarding a New Year's Eve party at headquarters,
Cherry, p. 336.

172   *"How deep is it"*: Gibbs, pp. 207–208.
"we suddenly confronted": Herbert Read, *Annals of Innocence and Experience*
(London: Faber & Faber, 1946), pp. 142–143, quoted in Ashworth, p. 104.

173   *"They tell me John"*: Rupert Grayson to the Kiplings, quoted in Holt, p. 106.
"We can but trust": Edward to Rupert Grayson, 15 October 1915, quoted in Holt,
p. 106.
"He is dark with": Kipling to Page, 5 October 1915, Pinney, vol. 4, p. 337.

174   *"We fear he is killed"*: 4 October 1915, quoted in Thompson, p. 321.
"No news": Holt, p. 105.

13. WE REGRET NOTHING

177   *"the greatest expression"*: Roland N. Stromberg, quoted in William Pfaff, *The
Bullet's Song: Romantic Violence and Utopia* (New York: Simon and Schuster,
2004), p. 29.
volunteering for the army: Robb, p. 72; Winter 1, p. 118.
"national control of": *Clarion*, 17 March 1916, quoted in Stubbs, p. 729.

"All-British from the core": C. B. Stanton, MP, in the *Times*, 18 March 1918.

178   *"beyond all question"*: *Times*, 28 May 1917.

"I am trying, very hard": Marlowe, p. 245.

"It would be difficult": Marlowe, p. 245.

"Shall we call": Astor to Milner and Milner to Astor, 12 January 1916, quoted in Lockwood, p. 124.

179   *"all seem to expect"*: Haig to Lady Haig, 27 December 1915, quoted in De Groot 1, p. 217.

180   *"preach . . . about the objects"*: Haig Diary, 4 June 1916, quoted in De Groot 1, p. 241.

"We lament too much": Haig Diary, 23 April 1916, quoted in De Groot 1, p. 241.

"The nation must be": Haig, "Memorandum on Policy for the Press," 26 May 1916, quoted in De Groot 1, p. 242.

"The Germans might bargain": Haig Diary, 7 June 1916, quoted in De Groot 1, p. 245.

"some officers who think": Haig Diary, 9 April 1916, quoted in De Groot 1, p. 234.

"lately a certain number": Gilbert, p. 212.

"take the same sort": John Jolliffe, ed. *Raymond Asquith: Life and Letters* (London: Collins, 1980), p. 217, quoted in "Asquith, Raymond," *Oxford Dictionary of National Biography* (online), accessed 15 March 2010.

181   *"It was a storied antique"*: Montague, p. 32.

"slackness . . . in the matter": Haig 1, 4 September 1916, p. 226.

182   *"All the troops here"*: Haig to Rothschild, 14 May 1916, quoted in De Groot 1, p. 235.

"The briefing lasted": Morton to Liddell Hart, 17 July 1961, quoted in Denis Winter, p. 13.

"If by any chance": Cuthbert Headlam to Georgina Headlam, 21 July 1916, quoted in Denis Winter, p. 137.

"The so called sharp": Haig to Henrietta Jameson, 1 September 1904, quoted in De Groot 1, pp. 105–106.

185   *"The hopeless bravery"*: E. Sylvia Pankhurst 1, p. 321.

"I shall never be": Wilson to Milner, 25 August 1915, quoted in Gollin, p. 281.

186   *"This place is polluted"*: Cecil, p. 275.

"I knew the dear London": E. Sylvia Pankhurst 1, p. 304.

187   *"Strongly repudiate and condemn"*: Purvis 1, p. 285.

"Freedom's battle has not": Rowbotham, p. 34.

A burly man of: Morel is a principal figure in my *King Leopold's Ghost: A Story of Greed, Terror, and Heroism in Colonial Africa* (Boston: Houghton Mifflin, 1998).

188   *"a war which enables"*: E. D. Morel, *Truth and the War* (London: National Labour Press, 1916), p. 302.

more than 20,000 men: Pearce, p. 169.

"we women . . . will tolerate": Trevor Wilson, p. 402.

189   *"The conscientious objector"*: Martin, pp. 53–54.

"I did not think": W. S. Adams, *Edwardian Portraits* (London: Secker & Warburg, 1957), p. 212.

"did not wish to incite": Brockway, p. 70.

"Six men have been condemned": *Times*, 17 May 1916.

190 *"in various secret places"*: Chamberlain, p. 68.

"The singers can have": *Tribunal*, 4 January 1917.

191 *"Are you doing work"*: *Socialist*, October 1916.

"war will become impossible": *Tribunal*, 1 June 1916.

"Once you are across": Boulton, p. 165.

192 *"if they disobey orders"*: Boulton, p. 166.

"As we were leaving": Russell 1, p. 17.

"In France a court-martial": *Herald*, 6 May 1916, Russell 3, p. 357.

193 *"We have been warned"*: Boulton, p. 171.

"We regret nothing": *Tribunal*, 8 June 1916.

"Tell me, when was": Ernest Shackleton, *South: The Story of Shackleton's Last Expedition, 1914–1917* (New York: Macmillan, 1920), p. 208.

194 *"Had we used the Navy's"*: Rudyard Kipling, *The Fringes of the Fleet* (Garden City, NY: Doubleday, Page, 1916), p. 118.

195 *"the lash and the chain"*: Kruse, p. 102.

196 *"When a German holds"*: John G. Gray, *Prophet in Plimsoles: An Account of the Life of Colonel Ronald Campbell* (Edinburgh: Edina, 1977), p. 27.

"fighting the Enemy": Haig 1, 5 April 1916, p. 184.

197 *"Nothing could exist"*: Sir John Edmonds, *Military Operations: France and Belgium, 1916* (London: Macmillan, 1932), p. 288, quoted in Trevor Wilson, p. 318.

"Carmen Etonense": *Eton College Chronicle*, 15 June 1916. My thanks to Mark Goodman for referring me to this source.

198 *"The situation is becoming"*: Haig to Lady Haig, 20 June 1916, quoted in De Groot 1, p. 251.

"I feel that every": Haig to Lady Haig, 22 June 1916, quoted in De Groot 1, p. 251.

"The men are in splendid": Haig 1, 30 June 1916, p. 195.

14. GOD, GOD, WHERE'S THE REST OF THE BOYS?

200 *"We were placed"*: Boulton, p. 168.

201 *"Rats were not infrequent"*: Boulton, p. 171.

202 *"I cast many a glance"*: Anonymous CO, quoted in Boulton, pp. 172–173.

Bertrand Russell and others: Without which, concludes Ellsworth-Jones, p. 203, "at least some of the conscientious objectors shipped to France would almost certainly have been executed."

"As I stood listening": Anonymous CO, quoted in Boulton, p. 173.

203 *"The hospital received"*: Brittain, p. 274.

"one could see ripples": Lieutenant G. Chetwynd-Staplyton, quoted in Keegan 2, p. 238.

204 *"I did not come across"*: G. M. Sturgess, in John Hammerton, ed., *The Great*

War—"I Was There!": Undying Memories of 1914–1918, vol. 2 (London: Amalgamated Press, 1938), quoted in Trevor Wilson, p. 323.

205 *"It was an amazing":* M. Gerster, *Die Schwaben an der Ancre* (Heilbronn, Germany: Eugen Salzer, [1918]), quoted in Churchill 1, pp. 658–659.

"When we got to": Private Tomlinson of the Sherwood Foresters, quoted in Keegan 2, p. 258.

206 *"Only three out of":* Middlebrook, p. 132.

207 *"I have never had":* Middlebrook, p. 261.

"This cannot be": Haig 1, 2 July 1916, p. 197.

"In another fortnight": Haig to Lady Haig, 8 July 1916, Haig 1, p. 201.

"If we don't succeed": Haig to Lady Haig, 13 July 1916, quoted in De Groot 1, p. 253.

208 *"a squadron of Indian":* Hutchison, pp. 126–132. Men from two cavalry regiments charged the Germans that day; the Indians were from the 20th Royal Deccan Horse, with the higher-ranking officers all British. The Deccan Horse regimental history records 9 dead and 41 wounded for this engagement, with, surprisingly, half a dozen German prisoners taken. Much of the time, however, the cavalrymen fought dismounted.

209 *"The tide of wounded":* Philip Gibbs, *Ten Years After: A Reminder* (London: Hutchinson, 1925), pp. 32–33.

"cannot have been less": Haig to Robertson, 23 August 1916, quoted in De Groot 1, p. 262.

"the total losses": Haig I, 4 September 1916, p. 226.

"Lawford dined": Travers, p. xix.

"The expectation of mankind": Anonymous to Haig, 30 July 1916, quoted in De Groot 1, p. 255.

210 *"felt that it was":* Alistair Horne, *The Price of Glory: Verdun 1916* (London: Penguin, 1993), p. 22.

"Stretchers blocked the cellar": Lawrence Gameson Papers, pp. 52–53, Imperial War Museum, quoted in Peter Barham, *Forgotten Lunatics of the Great War* (New Haven: Yale University Press, 2004), p. 148.

"the spirit of the wounded": Haig Diary, 25 July 1916, quoted in De Groot 1, p. 255.

"a hale and hearty": J.F.C. Fuller, in Wolff, p. x.

211 *"'The powers that be'":* Haig 1, 1 August 1916, p. 213.

"the maintenance of a steady": Haig to Robertson, 1 August 1916, Haig 1, p. 214.

"Have another glass": Lord Birkenhead, *Life of F. E. Smith* (London: Eyre & Spottiswoode, 1960), p. 287.

212 *"For God's sake":* Gilbert, p. 285.

"esprit de corps": Arthur Surfleet, "Blue Chevrons: An Infantry Private's Great War Diary," Imperial War Museum, quoted in Trevor Wilson, pp. 355–361.

"There is something": Bickersteth, p. 178.

"Once you have lain": Guy Chapman, *A Passionate Prodigality: Fragments of Autobiography* (London: MacGibbon and Kee, 1965), p. 226.

214 *in 2005 alone:* Mark Bostridge, "'We Go Tomorrow,'" *Guardian*, 1 July 2006.

"a very large number": Haig to Robertson, 7 October 1916, quoted in De Groot 1, p. 269.

almost 500,000 casualties: Both lower and higher figures are sometimes used; this one comes from a generally pro-Haig book, John Hussey, *Portrait of a Commander in Chief,* quoted in Bond and Cave, p. 35n35.

"advanced toward our men": Gibbs, p. 422.

15. CASTING AWAY ARMS

216 *"Women rushed towards"*: The Danish actress Asta Nielsen, in Dieter Glatzer and Ruth Glatzer, *Berliner Leben,* vol. 1 (Berlin: Rütten & Loening, 1986), pp. 265–266, quoted in Thomas Levenson, *Einstein in Berlin* (New York: Bantam Books, 2003), pp. 143–144.

Germans lined the border: Kramer, pp. 42–43.

217 *"It makes my blood boil"*: Russell to Ottoline Morrell, 1 September 1916, quoted in Vellacott, p. 93.

218 *"a woman known"*: Cecil to Simon, 8 November 1915, quoted in Kaminski, p. 300.

was the sole Briton: Nation, p. 273n10. This meeting was a follow-up to the better-known one at Zimmerwald the previous year, at which no Britons were present.

219 *"Arrive London about midday"*: 29 June 1916, FO 372/894/125014.

"A bridge is needed": Hobhouse to Smuts, 25 March 1917, quoted in Balme, p. 558.

"After a good deal": 2 November 1916, CAB 41/37/38.

220 *"the sort of conclusions"*: Thomson to Dormer, 1 July 1916, FO 372/894/128477.

"patriotic ardor for": Hobhouse 1, p. 53.

221 *"I cannot make up"*: Hobhouse to Courtney, Wills, p. 15.

"the look of eager": Hobhouse 1, p. 148.

222 *"Few things moved me"*: Wills, pp. 46–47.

"A danger which the country": Douglas Haig, "Memorandum on Policy for the Press," 26 May 1916, quoted in De Groot 1, p. 242.

"So far as Britain is": Ferguson 1, p. 213.

"which should not be": INF 4/1B, quoted in Millman, p. 182.

223 *"Even as he lies"*: Gilbert, p. 298.

"I was thoroughly and": William Beach Thomas, *A Traveller in News* (London: Chapman and Hall, 1925), p. 109.

"Gentlemen, you have played": Gibbs, p. 30.

"in a certain jauntiness": Montague, pp. 97–98, 94.

drafting the weekly communiqués: Some of these are in FO 395/53.

224 *"most anxious to help"*: Haig Diary, 30 September 1916, quoted in De Groot 1, p. 272.

"send him a line": Haig Diary, 23 July 1917, quoted in De Groot 1, p. 259.

"It was his last attempt": Buchan 3, p. 175n.

"When eminent and cultivated": Buchan 3, p. 177.

225 *"clerks and shopboys"*: Buchan 2, pp. 34–35.
"strange machines": Buchan 2, pp. 115, 121–122.
"a shattering blow": Buchan 2, p. 167.
"our major purpose": Buchan 2, p. 171.
"the strain of duplicity": Buitenhuis, p. 98.
"Whenever the German man": *Daily Express*, 24 May 1916, quoted in Angus Wilson, p. 300.

226 *"human beings and Germans"*: *Morning Post*, 22 June 1915, quoted in Gilmour, p. 250.
"My son was killed": "Epitaphs of the War," 1919.
"Down on your knees": Angus Wilson, p. 304.

228 *"have stirred London"*: James Douglas, "The Somme Pictures. Are They Too Painful for Public Exhibition?" *Star*, 25 August 1916, quoted in Reeves, p. 17.
"I have lost a son": "Orbatus" to the editor, *Times*, 2 September 1916.

230 *"Haig took me into"*: "Diary of Lord Milner's Visit to France, Nov. 11–19, 1916," Milner Papers, Bodleian Library, Oxford, dep. 353, pp. 77–98.

231 *"We are the Bantam sodgers"*: Allinson, p. 142.

232 *"seemed to have lost"*: Private Pinkney, testifying at Stones's court-martial, WO 71/535, quoted in Corns and Hughes-Wilson, p. 163, and Putkowski 3, p. 44.
"in a very exhausted": Sergeant Foster, testifying at Stones's court-martial, WO 71/535, quoted in Corns and Hughes-Wilson, p. 164, and Putkowski 3, pp. 44–45.

233 *89 percent of the death sentences*: Corns and Hughes-Wilson, p. 450.
"I have personally been": Corns and Hughes-Wilson, p. 167; Putkowski 3, p. 50.
confirmed the sentences: The record of Stones's court-martial is in WO 71/535, and that of Goggins and McDonald in WO 71/534. See also Putkowski and Sykes, pp. 156–159; Corns and Hughes-Wilson, pp. 157–175; and Putkowski 3, p. 36f, the most extensive account.

236 *"until we reached"*: "A reminiscence of the Great War—for Liberty. How Some Durham Lads were 'Shot at Dawn.' British Militarism in Operation," *Forward* (Glasgow), 15 April 1922. Reprint of article from *Railway Review*, 3 February 1922.
"To-night here on the Somme": Russell 1, pp. 97–98.

237 *"My own disposition"*: Cecil, p. 270.

16. BETWEEN THE LION'S JAWS

241 *"I am sending out"*: Joseph Stones to Isobel Stones, 12 December 1916, quoted in Putkowski 3, p. 67.
"The court recommend": WO 71/485, quoted in Corns and Hughes-Wilson, pp. 141–144.

242 *"noted" under Haig's comments*: WO 71/485, quoted in Corns and Hughes-Wilson, pp. 141–144.
"Reports of large numbers": E. Sylvia Pankhurst 1, p. 311.
military executions: John Peaty, "Haig and Military Discipline," in Bond and

Cave, pp. 205, 209; Oram 2, p. 13. Oram 1, p. 186n5, offers an estimate of total British executions of more than 400, but this appears to include some after the Armistice. It is possible that additional German executions may not have been recorded in the last weeks of the war.

"Apart from the number": Lt. G. V. Carey, Gilbert, p. 178.

243 *"I confirmed the proceedings"*: Haig 1, 11 January 1917, p. 267.

"As a military prisoner": "A reminiscence of the Great War—for Liberty. How Some Durham Lads were 'Shot at Dawn.' British Militarism in Operation," *Forward* (Glasgow), 15 April 1922. Reprint of article from *Railway Review,* 3 February 1922.

244 *"Dear Rochester"*: Tom Hickey and Bryan Maddocks, "Debts of Honour," Rochester Papers.

"Bath-rooms, smoke-rooms": [Albert Rochester,] "With the R.O.D. in France," *Railway Review,* 23 July 1922. I am grateful to Julian Putkowski for sending me this series of articles by Rochester.

246 *"fully alive to his"*: Haig Diary, 5 January 1917, quoted in De Groot 1, p. 286.

"It gives me great": George V to Haig, 27 December 1916, quoted in De Groot 1, p. 283.

247 *"endured cold and hunger"*: Stevenson, p. 282.

selling food and medicine: Frank G. Weber, *Eagles on the Crescent: Germany, Austria and the Diplomacy of the Turkish Alliance* (Ithaca, NY: Cornell University Press, 1970), pp. 119–121.

248 *the Germans sank:* Trevor Wilson, pp. 428–429.

"In five months at this": Churchill 1, p. 742.

249 *"the bullying and unscrupulousness"*: Milner to Ian Colvin, n.d., quoted in Marlowe, p. 275.

alarmist reports: Most of these are in dep. 377 of the Milner Papers, Bodleian Library, Oxford. Copies of some also appear in the Addison Papers at the same library and in two of the National Archives files on the Wheeldon case, DPP 1/150 and HO 144/13338.

"It is impossible": William Melville Lee, "Notes on the Strike Movement Now Developing in the North and West of England," pp. 3–4, 15 December 1916, Milner Papers, dep. 377.

the agents who penned: Rowbotham, pp. 44–46.

250 *"a quadruple line"*: Lee, "Notes on the Strike Movement," p. 11, 15 December 1916.

"We are undoubtedly": Lee, "Notes on the Strike Movement," Appendix 1, p. 7, 12 December 1916.

"What the working classes": Lee, "Notes on the Strike Movement," Appendix 11, document D, 2 December 1916.

251 *"I never moved"*: Clarke 1, p. 100.

"The landlord calls it rent": Challinor 1, p. 23.

"You gave us war": Challinor 1, p. 38.

put under surveillance: Challinor 1, p. 43; Rowbotham, p. 11.

252 *"Many comrades kept"*: Thomas Bell, p. 126.

"is terrified": Hettie to Winnie, January 1917, quoted in Rowbotham, p. 39.

253 *"all the working-men"*: Russell to Ottoline Morrell, 15 July 1916, quoted in Vellacott, p. 91.

255 *"although very pleasant"*: Sir Henry Wilson Diary, 3 February 1917, Callwell, p. 315.

"kept throwing himself": Robert D. Warth, *The Allies and the Russian Revolution: From the Fall of the Monarchy to the Peace of Brest-Litovsk* (Durham, NC: Duke University Press, 1954), p. 20.

enjoyed themselves: Sir Henry Wilson Diary, 30 January and 7 February 1917, Callwell, pp. 314, 316.

256 *"If an upheaval"*: Wrench, p. 325, and Marlowe pp. 263–264, quoting Milner Papers, Bodleian Library, Oxford, dep. 222.

17. THE WORLD IS MY COUNTRY

257 *"Now I write the truth"*: Bhagail Singh to Chain Singh, 22 January 1917, Omissi, pp. 271–272.

"We are like goats": Abdul Rahim Khan to Mir Hassan Khan, 7 February 1917, Omissi, p. 275.

258 *"Down the corridor"*: Campbell, p. 258.

"The persons in this case": *Times,* 5 February 1917.

"I think this is": Hettie Wheeldon to Lydia Robinson, 16 February 1917. My thanks to Julian Hendy for sharing these letters to Lydia Robinson with me.

"Yes, we will keep": Alice Wheeldon to Lydia Robinson, 26 February 1917.

259 *"haggard and pale"*: *Manchester Guardian,* 7 March 1917.

"that for reasons which seem": *Times,* 4 February 1917.

260 *"bad and wicked influence"*: Trial transcript, DPP 1/50, p. 324.

"language which would be": *Daily Mail,* 12 March 1917.

"My Lord": Trial transcript, DPP 1/50, p. 325. See also correspondence in CRIM 1/166 between Pankhurst's lawyer and the Wheeldon prosecutors.

261 *"We have tried"*: HO 45/10695/231366/27. WSPU meeting, Cardiff, 19 February 1913, quoted in Purvis 1, p. 210.

262 *"a thin, cunning-looking"*: Thomson 1, pp. 238–239.

"Gordon went to Leicester": Anonymous informant, 10 March 1917, Milner Papers, Bodleian Library, Oxford, dep. 377, p. 148.

263 *"Stop! stranger, thou art"*: *Socialist,* August 1918.

"During the afternoon": Winston S. Churchill, *The Unknown War: The Eastern Front* (New York: Scribner's, 1932), pp. 374–375.

265 *"The old order was dead"*: Benn, p. 377.

"a stupendous event": Vellacott, p. 153.

"I longed to shout": Russell to Ottoline Morrell, 1 April 1917, quoted in Vellacott, pp. 156–157.

"I remember the miners": Labour Party Annual Conference Report, 1951, p. 194, quoted in Coates, p.8.

"Revolutions like charity": Clinton and Myers, p. 73.

"the first ray of dawn": "In the Red Twilight" (unpublished), p. 65, quoted in Winslow, p. 137.

266   *"a veritable cemetery"*: Churchill 1, p. 744.
  "were imbued with a proud": Trevor Wilson, p. 435.

269   *"Across the central space"*: Stephen Hobhouse 1, p. 163.
  "through which at times": Stephen Hobhouse 1, p. 162.
  "while I was singing": Stephen Hobhouse 1, p. 164.
  "Every soldier realises": Wills, p. 48.

270   *"Stephen had a very"*: Wilfred E. Littleboy, Wills, p. 49.
  "The spirit of love requires": Stephen Hobhouse 1, p. 165.
  "Tell Stephen not to": Stephen Hobhouse 1, p. 166.
  "The warder bluntly refused": Stephen Hobhouse 2, p. 26.
  "Sorry to see you": Stephen Hobhouse 1, p. 159.

271   *typed excerpts copied from a letter*: HO 144/22259.
  "If it were possible": 12 February 1917, HO 144/22259.
  "the majority of them": Derby to Milner, 27 March 1917, HO 144/22259.
  "Though she thought": Stephen Hobhouse 1, p. 179.

272   *"They maintain, paradoxical"*: Margaret Hobhouse, *I Appeal unto Caesar* (London: Allen & Unwin, 1917), p. 6, quoted in Vellacott, pp. 211–212.
  "As a result largely of": *Tribunal*, 15 November 1917.

273   *"I am with you"*: Linklater, p. 193.
  "of this and all the other": Philip Snowden, *Labour Leader*, 31 May 1917, quoted in Gollin, p. 548.
  "My dear Prime Minister": Milner to Lloyd George, 1 June 1917, Lloyd George Papers, F38/2/8, Parliamentary Archives, London.

274   *"There can be no"*: B.E.B., "Report on the Russian Revolution Conference at Leeds," CAB 24/16, G. T. 1049.
  "the thousand men now": Russell 3, p. 182.
  "The control of events": *Tribunal*, 7 June 1917.

18. DROWNING ON LAND

277   *"Revolution is never"*: Haig to Derby, June 1917, quoted in Reid, p. 391.
  "breaking point may be": Gilbert, p. 336.

278   *"The argument seems to be"*: Marlowe, p. 282.
  "Their brains were cluttered": Ferguson 1, p. 303.
  "He spread on a table": David Lloyd George, *War Memoirs*, vol. 4 (Boston: Little, Brown, 1934), p. 359.
  "Everybody in my hotel": Robertson to Kiggell, 27 July 1917.
  "How proud you must feel": Haig to Lady Haig, 24 July 1917, quoted in De Groot 1, p. 328.

279   *"I should like the words"*: Linklater, p. 195.
  "I consider the Pacifists": *Britannia*, 3 August 1917, quoted in Angela K. Smith, p. 109.
  "Could you listen to": *Britannia*, 7 December 1917.

"*turn into a pacifist*": Milner to Cave, 31 August 1917, quoted in Millman, p. 212.

280 "*did the government prohibit*": Millman, p. 305.

"*Shaw will make the most*": Samuel to Asquith, 5 October 1916, quoted in Millman, p. 78.

Several hundred hostile: Times, 30 July 1917.

"*The mob is a terrible*": Russell to Ottoline Morrell, 28 July 1917, quoted in Vellacott, p. 170.

281 "*explain to the Russian*": Times, 2 June 1917.

"*I came to Petrograd*": Britannia, 13 July 1917, quoted in Purvis 1, p. 295.

282 "*a big peasant woman*": Rheta Childe Dorr, *A Woman of Fifty* (New York: Funk & Wagnalls, 1924), p. 360, quoted in Purvis 1, p. 409n17.

Its recruits shaved: See Stoff, p. 69f, and Joshua S. Goldstein, *War and Gender: How Gender Shapes the War System and Vice Versa* (Cambridge: Cambridge University Press, 2001), pp. 72–75.

"*The creation of the Women's*": Stoff, p. 88.

283 "*Down with capitalism!*": Purvis 1, p. 297.

"*I am making this statement*": Workers' Dreadnought, 28 July 1917.

284 "*I was driven out*": French to Esher, 7 September 1918, quoted in John French, p. 300.

285 "*I do so want to*": French to Bennett, 1 and 6 January 1916, quoted in Holmes, p. 314.

"*Haig's plans required*": De Groot 1, p. 336.

286 "*I cannot attempt*": Sphere, 24 November 1917, quoted in Denis Winter, p. 109.

"*The moment you set off*": Trevor Wilson, p. 473.

"*From the darkness*": Edwin Campion Vaughan, *Some Desperate Glory: The Diary of a Young Officer, 1917* ([London:] Warne, 1981), pp. 228–229 (27 August 1917).

287 "*A party of 'A' Company*": Trevor Wilson, p. 473.

19. PLEASE DON'T DIE

291 "*There's an east wind*": Sir Arthur Conan Doyle, *His Last Bow: A Reminiscence of Sherlock Holmes* (New York: Review of Reviews, 1917), pp. 307–308.

The total of British dead: Sheffield, p. 180, citing Richard Holmes. See Denis Winter, p. 110, for comments on this bitterly debated figure.

"*When I look at*": In Paris, 12 November 1917. Trevor Wilson, p. 547.

292 "*For the first time*": Gibbs, p. 485.

"*Reinforcements . . . shambled up*": Aubrey Wade, *The War of the Guns* (London: Batsford, 1936), pp. 57–58, quoted in Trevor Wilson, p. 482.

"*Col. Rawlins, leave the room*": Travers, p. 105.

294 "*Glorious News from Russia!*": Socialist, December 1917.

"*May they open the door*": Workers' Dreadnought, 17 November 1917.

"*our prison doors*": Brockway, p. 98.

"*A breach of discipline*": Times, 31 July 1917.

295 *"I am only here"*: Samuel Hynes, *A War Imagined: The First World War and English Culture* (London: Bodley Head, 1990), p. 186.

296 *"The probabilities are"*: G 173, 13 November 1917, CAB 24/4, quoted in Andrew, p. 201.

"I feel certain that": Thomson 3, p. 392, 22 October 1917.

"safely lodged in gaol": FO 371/2828/202398, quoted in Catherine Cline, *E. D. Morel, 1873–1924: The Strategies of Protest* (Belfast: Blackstaff Press, 1980), p. 111.

"In no country but this": Milner to Lloyd George, 26 May 1917, quoted in Williams thesis, p. 14.

"a piece of bread": E. D. Morel, *Thoughts on the War: The Peace—and Prison* (London, 1920), pp. 60–62.

297 *"I saw E. D. Morel"*: Russell to Murray, 27 March 1918, quoted in Vellacott, p. 231.

"My first experience of": Brockway, p. 92.

"The place was deadly silent": Brockway, p. 103.

298 *"Christmas morning"*: HO 144/13338.

"Oh Mam I don't know": Winnie Mason to Alice Wheeldon, 30 December 1917, HO 144/13338.

299 *"Sometimes advanced socialistic"*: Haig 1, 23 December 1917, pp. 362–363.

"Look smart": J. G. Fuller, *Troop Morale and Popular Culture in British and Dominion Armies, 1914–1918* (Oxford: Oxford University Press, 1990), p. 51, quoted in James 1, p. 473.

"They were giving so much": Englander and Osborne, p. 601.

300 *"during the war"*: Stephen Badsey, "Plumer, Herbert Charles Onslow," *Oxford Dictionary of National Biography* (online), accessed 25 March 2010.

"All the time the big guns": Robert Saunders, quoted in Trevor Wilson, p. 508.

301 *"We're telling lies"*: Lucy Masterman, *C.F.G. Masterman* (London: Nicholson and Watson, 1939), p. 296, quoted in Messinger, p. 45.

302 *"We are slowly but surely"*: Lansdowne to Asquith, 13 November 1916, "Fitzmaurice, Henry Charles Keith Petty-," *Oxford Dictionary of National Biography* (online), accessed 25 March 2010.

"Before long, it will": *Tribunal*, 6 December 1917.

"old imbecile": Gilmour, p. 270.

303 *"Lansdownism"*: See, for example, AIR 1/560/16/15/60, "Pacifist Propaganda—Position as at 26th March 1918," London District Intelligence Summary.

With Milner pulling strings: See, for example, references to several War Cabinet meetings in the fall of 1917 in WO 32/5474.

"differences of outlook": Stephen Hobhouse 1, p. 172.

"I thought P. changed": Kathleen Courtney, *Extracts from a Diary During the War* (London[?], privately printed, 1927), p. 144.

304 *Adolph Joffe*: For an interview with Joffe's daughter, Nadezhda, see Hochschild, pp. 143–149. For an interview with the son of Lev Kamenev, the other lead Bolshevik envoy, see Hochschild, pp. 84–92.

305 *"All that is taking place"*: Czernin, pp. 244–245.

"I hope we may be": Czernin, p. 246.

20. BACKS TO THE WALL

310 *"Lads of eighteen and nineteen"*: Churchill 1, p. 754.

311 *"to decide where"*: John Barnes and David Nicholson, eds., *The Leo Amery Diaries*, vol. 1 (London: Hutchinson, 1980), p. 188.

"The P.M. and Milner": *Diaries, 1912–1924* (London: Longmans, Green, 1952), pp. 111–116 (1 March 1918), quoted in A.J.P. Taylor, *English History, 1914–1945* (Oxford: Clarendon Press, 1976), p. 95.

312 *"The cargo was piled"*: Winter and Baggett, p. 249.

313 *"an offensive on a big"*: Haig Diary, 2 March 1918, quoted in De Groot 1, p. 367.
"thought she should": HO 144/13338.

314 *"a rather sudden growth"*: GT 3424, 22 January 1918, CAB 24/40, quoted in Andrew, p. 225.
"Repent?": Caroline Moorehead 1, p. 71.
"What the hell are we": AIR 1/558/16/15/55.
"There is scarcely": AIR 1/560/16/15/59.

315 *"The whole tone of"*: AIR 1/561/16/15/61.
"Mrs. Pankhurst and Miss Christabel": AIR 1/560/16/15/59.
"rule by terror": *Die Russische Revolution* (Berlin, 1922), p. 67f, quoted in Elżbieta Ettinger, *Rosa Luxemburg: A Life* (Boston: Beacon, 1986), p. 225.

316 *"Exactly as a pianist"*: Churchill 1, p. 768.

317 *"At half-past four"*: Aubrey Wade, *The War of the Guns* (London: Batsford, 1936), p. 89, quoted in Trevor Wilson, p. 558.
"The first to be affected": Martin Middlebrook, *The Kaiser's Battle* (London: Allen Lane, 1978), p. 161, quoted in Trevor Wilson, p. 559.

318 *"Germany must go under"*: Stevenson, p. 327.

319 *"I thought we had"*: Middlebrook, *The Kaiser's Battle*, p. 192, quoted in Keegan 1, p. 399.
"Old women in black": Lieutenant H.E.L. Mellersh, Imperial War Museum personal accounts, quoted in Toland, p. 54.
"The battle is won": George Alexander von Müller, *The Kaiser and His Court* (London: Macdonald, 1961), p. 344, quoted in Toland, p. 58.
"The force of the blow": 24 March 1918, quoted in Thompson, p. 348.

321 *"Many amongst us are"*: 11 April 1918, quoted in De Groot 1, p. 378.

322 *"I was very glad"*: Stephen Hobhouse 1, p. 173.

323 *"The recent severe fighting"*: AIR 1/560/16/15/60.
"at Liverpool recent events": AIR 1/560/16/15/60.
"has a great respect": MUN 5/48/267/3. Many of Kipling's memos, like this one, were to Lord Beaverbrook.
"This little pig stayed at home": 4 May 1918.
"an occupation to which": *Tribunal*, 3 January 1918.
"asked my religion": Russell 1, p. 30.

325 *"Dear Brockway—"*: Brockway, p. 113.

326 *"Only those who have"*: Brockway, p. 113.
"people steeped to the neck": French to Esher, 26 May 1918, John French, p. 296.

"like nothing so much": French to Lloyd George, 5 March 1918, quoted in Dangerfield, p. 272.

327 *"by the public hangman":* Britannia, 30 August 1918, quoted in Bullock and Pankhurst, p. 85n91.

"Some talk about": Britannia, 8 November 1918, quoted in Purvis 1, p. 312.

"I only look in wonder": Sylvia Pankhurst to Adela Pankhurst Walsh, 11 July 1918, quoted in Purvis 1, p. 311.

"a conflict between the two": Toland, p. 317.

"We must be prepared": Milner to Lloyd George, 9 June 1918, quoted in Gollin, p. 565.

328 *"What would this mean?":* Sir Henry Wilson Diary, 1 June 1918, quoted in Trevor Wilson, p. 579.

21. THERE ARE MORE DEAD THAN LIVING NOW

329 *"Any hesitation or":* French to King George V, 10 September 1918, quoted in Holmes, p. 343.

"the complete removal": French to King George V, 12 July 1918, quoted in Holmes, p. 343.

330 *"The threat of an American":* Rudolf Georg Binding, A Fatalist at War (London: George Allen & Unwin, 1929), p. 220, quoted in Sheffield, p. 219.

"Retreat? Hell, we": Captain Lloyd Williams. Keegan 1, p. 407.

331 *"Our victorious army":* Major General Max Hoffmann, Chicago Daily News, 13 March 1919, quoted in Wheeler-Bennett, p. 352.

"eyes glued to telescopes": Churchill 1, p. 802.

"They looked larger": Brittain, p. 420.

332 *"became furious and shouted":* Toland, p. 381.

333 *"was the black day":* Livesey, p. 166.

Several hundred thousand: The number of these men is commonly cited as a million or more, but Alexander Watson, in Enduring the Great War: Combat, Morale and Collapse in the German and British Armies, 1914–1918 (Cambridge: Cambridge University Press, 2008), pp. 207–208, 212, convincingly shows why the actual number is probably far lower.

334 *"nearer to Bolshevism":* Porter 3, p. 143.

Millman suggests that: Millman, pp. 4, 170. See Chapter 11 for most of his description of British plans for containing revolution at home.

335 *"really extends from":* Milner to Lloyd George, 20 March 1918, quoted in Gollin, p. 563.

"Much talk with Milner": Sir Henry Wilson Diary, 4 November 1918, quoted in Marlowe, p. 318.

"The cemetery has been shelled": Cecil, p. 280.

336 *"They . . . lived the span":* Kipling 1, vol. 1, introduction.

"Here 2nd Lieutenant Clifford": Kipling 1, vol. 2, chap. 1.

337 *"To every single one of us":* Toland, pp. 412–413.

"My senses are charred": Gilbert, p. 476.

338 *"save us from the grave danger"*: Toland, p. 372.

339 *"I shall remain at Spa"*: Toland, p. 558.

   "Treason, gentlemen!": Toland, p. 565.

341 *"Twenty years time"*: James 1, p. 557.

   "It is important that": Haig to Lady Haig, 31 October 1918, quoted in De Groot 1, p. 394.

342 *"I remember sitting on"*: Brockway, p. 116.

   "An airman suddenly swooped": Corder Catchpool, *Letters of a Prisoner: For Conscience Sake* (London: George Allen & Unwin, 1941), p. 123.

   "The crowd was frivolous": Russell 1, p. 35.

343 *"Lady Edward dined"*: Milner Papers, Bodleian Library, Oxford, dep. 89.

   "A world to be remade": Holt, p. 166.

   "I never realised how tired": Adam Smith, p. 214.

   "There are far more dead": Adam Smith, p. 217.

22. THE DEVIL'S OWN HAND

347 *Most other counts are higher:* For a breakdown by country of one such estimate—at least 9.4 million total military deaths—see Spencer C. Tucker, ed., *World War I Encyclopedia,* vol. 1 (Santa Barbara, CA: ABC-CLIO, 2005), pp. 272–274.

   "Every day one meets": Margaret Cole, ed., *Beatrice Webb's Diaries* (London: Longmans, Green, 1952), p. 137 (17 November 1918), quoted in Hew Strachan, *The First World War* (London: Penguin, 2005), p. 337.

348 *"As a mother deprived"*: Times, 3 January 1919.

   civilian war deaths: 12 million: Hanson, p. 284; 13 million: "World War I," in *Encyclopedia Britannica* (online), accessed 28 March 2010.

349 *400,000 died:* Ferguson 1, p. 301. See also Paice, pp. 392–398, whose various death figures add up to a higher total, although they include civilian deaths other than those of porters.

   in the hundreds of thousands: Paice, p. 288.

350 *50 million:* Barry, p. 397; Jeffery K. Taubenberger and David M. Morens, "1918 Influenza: The Mother of All Pandemics," *Emerging Infectious Diseases* 12:1 (January 2006), p. 15.

351 *"Mrs. Wheeldon was"*: Derby Daily Express, 26 February 1919.

352 *"it was a misnomer"*: CAB 23 WC 523.

353 *"A majority of these men"*: Adam Smith, p. 215.

354 *He also proposed:* French to Long, 1 July 1920, quoted in Holmes, p. 352.

   "The pore lady": Mrs. Philip Snowden, *A Political Pilgrim in Europe* (London: Cassell, 1921), p. 263.

355 *"With her I was able"*: Gonne to Quinn, 21 February 1921, quoted in Nancy Cardozo, *Lucky Eyes and a High Heart: The Life of Maud Gonne* (New York: Bobbs-Merrill, 1978), p. 343.

357 *"Everywhere lies the ordinary"*: Wilfrid Ewart, *Scots Guard,* quoted in Cecil, pp. 294–295.

"the tragedies of the future": American Diplomacy (Chicago: University of Chicago Press, 1985), p. 69.

358 *"'We will have arms again!'":* Quoted in Winter and Baggett, p. 341.

war to end all wars: Several of Wilson's biographers contend that he never actually said the phrase. John Milton Cooper Jr. ascribes it to Lloyd George, J. W. Schulte Nordholt to H. G. Wells.

"a Peace to end Peace": O'Brien, p. 335. The phrase has also been attributed to several other people.

"our conversations were": Russell 1, pp. 141–142.

"for believing in Soviets": Diary, 19 May 1920, quoted in Ronald W. Clark, pp. 378–379.

"more vividly vital": E. Sylvia Pankhurst 2, p. 109.

"the Russian people": E. Sylvia Pankhurst 3, p. 184.

359 *"inflicted by a court":* Russia Diary, Despard Papers 7/CFD, Women's Library, London.

Thousands of them vanished: See Hochschild, pp. 153–185, for accounts of some American-born victims.

Willie Wheeldon: My thanks to Julian Hendy for sharing with me Willie Wheeldon's Comintern personnel file, from which some of these details come.

23. AN IMAGINARY CEMETERY

361 *"The difficulty is":* Milner to Lloyd George, 28 December 1919, quoted in Gollin, p. 591.

362 *"Here the ladies tend us":* Omissi, p. 38.

"attend to our wants": Anjamuddin Khan to Muhammad Suraj-ud-Din Khan, 20 December 1915, Omissi, pp. 126–127.

"Nothing we can do": Morrow, p. 312.

"The participation of West Indian": 22 October 1919, CO 123/296/65767.

"in connection with the preservation": CO 318/350/8426.

363 *"she-edited magazine":* Kipling to Crewe, 27 September 1932, Pinney, vol. 6, p. 131.

"I hate your generation": Gilmour, p. 310.

364 *military historians argue:* The Holts argue this at length, backed by several other historians.

365 *not allowed to see him:* Despard to French, 19 May 1925, French Papers, Imperial War Museum.

"I've only got to send": Cicely Hamilton, as quoted by Harold Frederick Bing, interview, Imperial War Museum #000358/11, p. 46.

"I have to go to Ireland": Linklater, p. 220.

366 *"an act in violation":* Time, 18 January 1926.

367 *"to follow up certain information":* Times, 6 January 1926.

"the crowds of spectators": Time, 18 January 1926.

"that I was to be": Haig 1, 30 November 1918, p. 489.

"Some enthusiasts to-day": B. H. Liddell Hart, The Tanks: The History of the Royal

Tank Regiment and Its Predecessors, Heavy Branch Machine-Gun Corps, Tank Corps and Royal Tank Corps, 1914–1945, vol. 1 (New York: Praeger, 1959), p. 234.
"*very lazy on the question*": Ian F. W. Beckett, "Haig and French," in Bond and Cave, p. 60.

368 "*I found him most pleasant*": Haig to J. P. Allison, 27 February 1926, quoted in De Groot 1, p. 405.

369 "*I shall never be able*": Purvis 1, p. 350.

370 "*In those irresistible*": Anthony Mockler, *Haile Selassie's War: The Italian-Ethiopian Campaign, 1935–1941* (New York: Random House, 1984), p. 150.

372 *a number of British military:* See, for example, the books in the Bibliography by Bond and Cave, Sheffield, Terraine, and Todman.
"*the worst thing the people*": Ferguson 1, p. xxi.

375 *only a single memorial:* On November 11, 2008, some time after my own travels on the Western Front, a small plaque about the Christmas Truce was dedicated at Frelinghien, France. It is the only other such memorial I know of.

376 "*I knew that it was my business*": Russell 1, p. 7.

BIBLIOGRAPHY

BOOKS AND ARTICLES

Adam Smith, Janet. *John Buchan: A Biography.* Oxford: Oxford University Press, 1985.

Albertini, Luigi. *The Origins of the War of 1914.* 3 vols. Oxford: Oxford University Press, 1952.

Allinson, Sidney. *The Bantams: The Untold Story of World War I.* Oakville, Ontario: Mosaic Press, 1981.

Andrew, Christopher. *Secret Service: The Making of the British Intelligence Community.* London: Heinemann, 1985.

Ashworth, Tony. *Trench Warfare, 1914–1918: The Live and Let Live System.* London: Macmillan, 1980.

Badsey, Stephen, and Philip Taylor. "Images of Battle: The Press, Propaganda and Passchendaele," in Peter Liddle, ed., *Passchendaele in Perspective: The Third Battle of Ypres.* London: Leo Cooper, 1997.

Balme, Jennifer Hobhouse. *To Love One's Enemies: The Work and Life of Emily Hobhouse Compiled from Letters and Writings, Newspaper Cuttings and Official Documents.* Cobble Hill, British Columbia: Hobhouse Trust, 1994.

Barry, John M. *The Great Influenza: The Epic Story of the Deadliest Plague in History.* New York: Viking, 2004.

Bartley, Paula. *Emmeline Pankhurst.* London: Routledge, 2002.

Barton, Peter, Peter Doyle, and Johan Vandewalle. *Beneath Flanders Fields: The Tunnellers' War, 1914–1918.* Montreal: McGill–Queen's University Press, 2004.

Bell, Julian, ed. *We Did Not Fight: 1914–18 Experiences of War Resisters.* London: Cobden-Sanderson, 1935.

Bell, Thomas. *Pioneering Days.* London: Lawrence & Wishart, 1941.

Benn, Caroline. *Keir Hardie.* London: Hutchinson, 1992.

Bickersteth, John, ed. *The Bickersteth Diaries: 1914–1918.* London: Leo Cooper, 1995.

Birkenhead, Earl of. *Famous Trials of History.* New York: George H. Doran, 1926.

Blunden, Edmund. *Undertones of War.* London: Penguin, 2000.

Bond, Brian, ed. *The First World War and British Military History.* Oxford: Clarendon Press, 1991.

Bond, Brian, and Nigel Cave. *Haig: A Reappraisal 70 Years On.* Barnsley, South Yorkshire: Leo Cooper, 1999.

Boulton, David. *Objection Overruled.* London: MacGibbon & Kee, 1967.

Brittain, Vera. *Testament of Youth: An Autobiographical Study of the Years 1900–1925.* New York: Penguin, 1994.

Brockway, Fenner. *Inside the Left: Thirty Years of Platform, Press, Prison and Parliament.* London: George Allen & Unwin, 1942.

Brown, Malcolm. *The Imperial War Museum Book of the Somme.* London: Sidgwick & Jackson, 1996.

Brown, Malcolm, and Shirley Seaton. *Christmas Truce.* London: Leo Cooper / Secker & Warburg, 1984.

Buchan, John.
  1. *The Four Adventures of Richard Hannay: The Thirty-Nine Steps, Greenmantle, Mr. Standfast, The Three Hostages.* Boston: David R. Godine, 1988.
  2. *The Battle of the Somme.* New York: George H. Doran, 1917.
  3. *Pilgrim's Way: An Essay in Recollection.* Boston: Houghton Mifflin, 1940.
  4. *A Lodge in the Wilderness.* Edinburgh: Blackwood, 1906.

Buitenhuis, Peter. *The Great War of Words: British, American, and Canadian Propaganda and Fiction, 1914–1933.* Vancouver: University of British Columbia Press, 1987.

Bullock, Ian, and Richard Pankhurst. *Sylvia Pankhurst: From Artist to Anti-Fascist.* New York: St. Martin's, 1992.

Burg, David F., and L. Edward Purcell. *Almanac of World War I.* Lexington: University Press of Kentucky, 1998.

Callwell, C. E. *Field-Marshal Sir Henry Wilson, Bart., G.C.B., D.S.O.: His Life and Diaries,* vol. 1. London: Cassell, 1927.

Campbell, John. *F. E. Smith, First Earl of Birkenhead.* London: Jonathan Cape, 1983.

Carsten, F. L. *War Against War: British and German Radical Movements in the First World War.* Berkeley: University of California Press, 1982.

Cassar, George H. *The Tragedy of Sir John French.* Newark: University of Delaware Press, 1985.

Cecil, Hugh and Mirabel. *Imperial Marriage: An Edwardian War and Peace.* London: John Murray, 2002.

Cecil, Hugh, and Peter Liddle. *Facing Armageddon: The First World War Experienced.* London: Leo Cooper, 1996.

Challinor, Ray.
  1. *John S. Clarke: Parliamentarian, Poet, Lion-Tamer.* London: Pluto, 1977.
  2. *The Origins of British Bolshevism.* London: Croom Helm, 1977.

Chamberlain, W. J. *Fighting for Peace: The Story of the War Resistance Movement.* London: No More War Movement, 1928.

Cherry, Niall. *Most Unfavourable Ground: The Battle of Loos, 1915.* Solihull, West Midlands: Helion, 2005.

Churchill, Winston.

    1. *The World Crisis, 1911–1918.* Abridged and revised edition. New York: Free Press, 2005.

    2. *The River War: An Historical Account of the Reconquest of the Soudan,* vol. 2. London: Longmans, Green, 1900.

Clark, Alan. *Suicide of the Empires: The Battles on the Eastern Front, 1914–1918.* New York: American Heritage Press, 1971.

Clark, Ronald W. *The Life of Bertrand Russell.* New York: Knopf, 1976.

Clarke, John S.

    1. *Circus Parade.* London: B. T. Batsford, 1936.

    2. *Pen Pictures of Russia Under the "Red Terror."* Glasgow: National Workers' Committees, 1921.

Clay, Catrine. *King, Kaiser, Tsar: Three Royal Cousins Who Led the World to War.* New York: Walker, 2006.

Clinton, Alan, and George Meyers. "The Russian Revolution and the British Working Class—Two Episodes," *Fourth International,* November 1967.

Coates, Ken, ed. *British Labour and the Russian Revolution: The Leeds Convention: A Report from the Daily Herald.* Nottingham: Bertrand Russell Peace Foundation, 1974.

Coleman, Verna. *Adela Pankhurst: The Wayward Suffragette, 1885–1961.* Carleton South, Australia: Melbourne University Press, 1996.

Constantine, Stephen, Maurice W. Kirby, and Mary B. Rose. *The First World War in British History.* London: Edward Arnold, 1995.

Corns, Cathryn, and John Hughes-Wilson. *Blindfold and Alone: British Military Executions in the Great War.* London: Cassell, 2001.

Craster, J. M. *"Fifteen Rounds a Minute": The Grenadiers at War, August to December 1914.* London: Macmillan, 1976.

Czernin, Ottokar. *In the World War.* New York: Harper, 1920.

Dangerfield, George. *The Damnable Question: A Study in Anglo-Irish Relations.* Boston: Little, Brown / Atlantic Monthly, 1976.

Davey, Arthur. *The British Pro-Boers, 1877–1902.* Cape Town: Tafelberg, 1978.

De Bloch, Jean. "The Wars of the Future," *Contemporary Review* 80:429 (September 1901).

De Groot, Gerard J.

    1. *Douglas Haig, 1861–1928.* London: Unwin Hyman, 1988.

    2. *Blighty: British Society in the Era of the Great War.* London: Longman, 1996.

    3. *The First World War.* Houndsmills, Hampshire: Palgrave, 2001.

    4. "Ambition, Duty and Doctrine: Douglas Haig's Rise to High Command," in Bond and Cave.

Despard, Charlotte.

    1. *Women's Franchise and Industry.* London: Women's Freedom League, 1912[?].

2. *Woman in the New Era. With an Appreciation by Christopher St. John.* London: The Suffrage Shop, 1910.

3. *Theosophy and the Woman's Movement.* London: Theosophical Publishing Society, 1913.

Eksteins, Modris. *Rites of Spring: The Great War and the Birth of the Modern Age.* Toronto: Key Porter Books, 1989.

Ellis, John.

1. *The Social History of the Machine Gun.* New York: Pantheon, 1975.

2. *Eye-Deep in Hell: Trench Warfare in World War I.* New York: Pantheon, 1976.

Ellsworth-Jones, Will. *We Will Not Fight: The Untold Story of World War One's Conscientious Objectors.* London: Aurum, 2007.

Engen, Rob. "Steel Against Fire: The Bayonet in the First World War," *Journal of Military and Strategic Studies* 8:3 (Spring 2006).

Englander, David, and James Osborne. "Jack, Tommy, and Henry Dubb: The Armed Forces and the Working Class," *Historical Journal* 21:3 (1978).

Farwell, Byron.

1. *Mr. Kipling's Army.* New York: Norton, 1981.

2. *The Great Anglo-Boer War.* New York: Harper & Row, 1976.

3. *The Great War in Africa, 1914–1918.* New York: W. W. Norton, 1986.

Ferguson, Niall.

1. *The Pity of War.* New York: Basic Books, 1999.

2. "The Kaiser's European Union: What If Britain Had 'Stood Aside' in August 1914?," in Niall Ferguson, ed., *Virtual History: Alternatives and Counterfactuals.* New York: Basic Books, 1997.

Fischer, Fritz. *Germany's Aims in the First World War.* London: Chatto & Windus, 1967.

Fisher, John. *That Miss Hobhouse.* London: Secker & Warburg, 1971.

FitzGibbon, Constantine. *Out of the Lion's Paw: Ireland Wins Her Freedom.* London: Macdonald, 1969.

Fortescue, John. *Narrative of the Visit to India of Their Majesties, King George V. and Queen Mary, and of the Coronation Durbar Held at Delhi, 12th December, 1911.* London: Macmillan, 1912.

Frances, Hilary. "'Dare to Be Free!': The Women's Freedom League and Its Legacy," in Purvis, June, and Sandra Stanley Holton, eds., *Votes for Women.* London: Routledge, 2000.

French, Gerald. *The Life of Field-Marshal Sir John French, First Earl of Ypres, K.P., G.C.B., O.M., G.C.V.O., K.C.M.G.* London: Cassell and Company, 1931.

French, John (Earl of Ypres). *Some War Diaries, Addresses and Correspondence.* Ed. Gerald French. London: Herbert Jenkins, 1937.

Fromkin, David. *Europe's Last Summer: Who Started the Great War in 1914?* New York: Knopf, 2004.

Fry, A. Ruth. *Emily Hobhouse: A Memoir.* London: Jonathan Cape, 1929.

Fussell, Paul. *The Great War and Modern Memory.* New York: Oxford University Press, 1975.

Garner, Les. *Stepping Stones to Women's Liberty: Feminist Ideas in the Women's Suffrage Movement, 1900–1918*. Cranbury, NJ: Associated University Presses, 1984.

Gatrell, Peter. *A Whole Empire Walking: Refugees in Russia During World War I*. Bloomington: Indiana University Press, 1999.

German General Staff. *The War in South Africa: Prepared in the Historical Section of the Great General Staff, Berlin*. Trans. W.H.H. Waters. London: John Murray, 1904.

Gibbs, Philip. *Now It Can Be Told*. New York: Harper, 1920.

Gilbert, Martin. *The First World War: A Complete History*. New York: Holt, 1994.

Gilmour, David. *The Long Recessional: The Imperial Life of Rudyard Kipling*. New York: Farrar, Straus and Giroux, 2002.

Gollin, A. M. *Proconsul in Politics: A Study of Lord Milner in Opposition and in Power*. New York: Macmillan, 1964.

Gregory, Adrian. *The Last Great War: British Society and the First World War*. Cambridge, UK: Cambridge University Press, 2008.

Groom, Winston. *A Storm in Flanders: The Ypres Salient, 1914–1918: Tragedy and Triumph on the Western Front*. New York: Atlantic Monthly Press, 2002.

Haig, Douglas.
   1. *War Diaries and Letters, 1914–1918*. Ed. Gary Sheffield and John Bourne. London: Weidenfeld & Nicolson, 2005.
   2. *Rectorial Address Delivered to the Students in the University of St. Andrews, 14th May 1919*. St. Andrews, Scotland: W. C. Henderson, [1919].
   3. *The Preparatory Prologue, 1861–1914: Diaries and Letters*. Ed. Douglas Scott. Barnsley, South Yorkshire: Pen & Sword Military, 2006.

Hanson, Neil. *The Unknown Soldier: The Story of the Missing of the Great War*. London: Doubleday, 2005.

Hardie, James Keir. *Keir Hardie's Speeches and Writings: From 1888 to 1915*. Ed. Emrys Hughes. Glasgow: Forward, [1927?].

Hartcup, Guy. *The War of Invention: Scientific Developments, 1914–18*. London: Brassey's, 1988.

Haste, Cate. *Keep the Home Fires Burning: Propaganda in the First World War*. London: Allen Lane, 1977.

Haupt, Georges. *Socialism and the Great War: The Collapse of the Second International*. Oxford: Clarendon Press, 1972.

Hiley, Nicholas.
   1. "Internal Security in Wartime: The Rise and Fall of P.M.S.2, 1915–1917," *Intelligence and National Security* 1:3 (1986).
   2. "Counter-Espionage and Security in Great Britain During the First World War," *English Historical Review* 101:400 (July 1986).

Hiley, Nicholas, and Julian Putkowski. "A Postscript on P.M.S.2," *Intelligence and National Security* 3:2 (1988).

Hobhouse, Stephen.
   1. *Forty Years and an Epilogue: An Autobiography, 1881–1951*. London: James Clarke, 1951.

2. *An English Prison from Within.* London: George Allen & Unwin, 1919.

Hochschild, Adam. *The Unquiet Ghost: Russians Remember Stalin.* Boston: Houghton Mifflin, 2003.

Holmes, Richard. *The Little Field-Marshal: Sir John French.* London: Jonathan Cape, 1981.

Holt, Tonie and Valmai. *"My Boy Jack?": The Search for Kipling's Only Son.* London: Leo Cooper, 1998.

Howard, Michael. *A Part of History: Aspects of the British Experience of the First World War.* London: Continuum, 2008.

Howe, Glenford Deroy. *Race, War and Nationalism: A Social History of West Indians in the First World War.* Kingston, Jamaica: Ian Randle, 2002.

Hutchison, Graham Seton. *Warrior.* London: Hutchinson, 1932.

Jackson, John. "Losing the Plot: Lloyd George, F. E. Smith and the Trial of Alice Wheeldon," *History Today* 57:5 (May 2007).

James, Lawrence.
 1. *Warrior Race: A History of the British at War.* New York: St. Martin's, 2001.
 2. *Mutiny: In the British and Commonwealth Forces, 1797–1956.* London: Buchan & Enright, 1987.

Joll, James. *The Second International, 1889–1914.* New York: Harper & Row, 1966.

Judd, Denis, and Keith Surridge. *The Boer War.* New York: Palgrave Macmillan, 2003.

Keegan, John.
 1. *The First World War.* New York: Knopf, 1999.
 2. *The Face of Battle: A Study of Agincourt, Waterloo and the Somme.* New York: Vintage, 1977.

Kennedy, Thomas C. *The Hound of Conscience: A History of the No-Conscription Fellowship, 1914–1919.* Fayetteville: University of Arkansas Press, 1981.

Kipling, Rudyard.
 1. *The Irish Guards in the Great War: Edited and Compiled from Their Diaries and Papers.* Garden City, NY: Doubleday, 1923.
 2. *"O Beloved Kids": Rudyard Kipling's Letters to his Children.* Ed. Elliot L. Gilbert. New York: Harcourt Brace Jovanovich, 1983.

Kramer, Alan. *Dynamic of Destruction: Culture and Mass Killing in the First World War.* New York: Oxford University Press, 2007.

Krebs, Paula M. "'The Last of the Gentlemen's Wars': Women in the Boer War Concentration Camp Controversy," *History Workshop* 33 (Spring 1992).

Kruse, Juanita. *John Buchan (1875–1940) and the Idea of Empire: Popular Literature and Political Ideology.* Lewiston, NY: Edwin Mellen, 1989.

Lincoln, W. Bruce. *Passage Through Armageddon: The Russians in War and Revolution, 1914–1918.* New York: Simon and Schuster, 1986.

Linklater, Andro. *An Unhusbanded Life: Charlotte Despard—Suffragette, Socialist and Sinn Feiner.* London: Hutchinson, 1980.

Livesey, Anthony. *The Historical Atlas of World War I.* New York: Henry Holt, 1994.

Lockwood, P. A. "Milner's Entry into the War Cabinet, December 1916," *Historical Journal* 7:1 (1964).

Longford, Elizabeth. *Queen Victoria: Born to Succeed.* New York: Harper & Row, 1964.

Lownie, Andrew. *John Buchan: The Presbyterian Cavalier.* London: Constable, 1995.

Lowry, Donal, ed. *The South African War Reappraised.* Manchester, UK: Manchester University Press, 2000.

Lytton, Constance, and Jane Wharton. *Prisons & Prisoners: Some Personal Experiences.* London: William Heinemann, 1914.

Macdonald, Lyn.

   1. *1914.* London: Michael Joseph, 1987.

   2. *1915: The Death of Innocence.* New York: Henry Holt, 1995.

   3. *The Roses of No Man's Land.* London: Macmillan, 1980.

MacDonald, Robert H. *The Language of Empire: Myths and Metaphors of Popular Imperialism, 1880–1918.* Manchester, UK: Manchester University Press, 1994.

MacLeod, Roy, and Kay MacLeod. "War and Economic Development: Government and the Optical Industry in Britain, 1914–18," in J. M. Winter, ed., *War and Economic Development: Essays in Memory of David Joslin* (Cambridge: Cambridge University Press, 1975).

Marlowe, John. *Milner: Apostle of Empire. A Life of Alfred George the Right Honourable Viscount Milner of St. James's and Cape Town, KG, GCB, GCMG (1854–1925).* London: Hamish Hamilton, 1976.

Marshall-Corwall, James. *Haig as Military Commander.* New York: Crane, Russak, 1973.

Martin, Christopher. *English Life in the First World War.* London: Wayland, 1974.

Massie, Robert K. *Castles of Steel: Britain, Germany, and the Winning of the Great War at Sea.* New York: Random House, 2003.

Mayhall, Laura E. *The Militant Suffrage Movement: Citizenship and Resistance in Britain, 1860–1930.* Oxford: Oxford University Press, 2003.

McCracken, Donal P. *Forgotten Protest: Ireland and the Anglo-Boer War.* Belfast: Ulster Historical Foundation, 2003.

Messinger, Gary S. *British Propaganda and the State in the First World War.* Manchester, UK: Manchester University Press, 1992.

Middlebrook, Martin. *The First Day on the Somme.* London: Pen & Sword, 2006.

Millman, Brock. *Managing Domestic Dissent in First World War Britain.* London: Frank Cass, 2000.

Milner, Violet. *My Picture Gallery, 1886–1901.* London: John Murray, 1951.

Mitchell, David. *Queen Christabel: A Biography of Christabel Pankhurst.* London: Macdonald and Jane's, 1977.

Montague, C. E. *Disenchantment.* London: Chatto & Windus, 1922.

Moorehead, Alan. *The White Nile.* London: Hamish Hamilton, 1960.

Moorehead, Caroline.

   1. *Troublesome People: The Warriors of Pacifism.* Bethesda, MD: Adler & Adler, 1987.

   2. *Bertrand Russell: A Life.* New York: Viking, 1992.

Moorhouse, Geoffrey. *Hell's Foundations: A Social History of the Town of Bury in the Aftermath of the Gallipoli Campaign.* New York: Henry Holt, 1992.

Morgan, Kenneth O. "Britain's Vietnam? Lloyd George, Keir Hardie, and the Importance of the 'Pro-Boers,'" in William Roger Louis, ed., *Still More Adventures with Britannia: Personalities, Politics and Culture in Britain* (London: I. B. Taurus, 2003).

Morris, James.
1. *Heaven's Command: An Imperial Progress.* New York: Harvest/HBJ, 1973.
2. *Pax Britannica: The Climax of an Empire.* New York: Harvest/HBJ, 1968.
3. *Farewell the Trumpets: An Imperial Retreat.* New York: Harvest/HBJ, 1978.

Morrow, John H., Jr. *The Great War: An Imperial History.* London: Routledge, 2004.

Mulvihill, Margaret. *Charlotte Despard: A Biography.* London: Pandora, 1989.

Nash, David. "The Boer War and Its Humanitarian Critics," *History Today* 49:6 (June 1999).

Nation, R. Craig. *War on War: Lenin, the Zimmerwald Left, and the Origins of Communist Internationalism.* Durham, NC: Duke University Press, 1989.

Newton, Douglas. "The Lansdowne 'Peace Letter' of 1917 and the Prospect of Peace by Negotiation with Germany," *Australian Journal of Politics and History* 48:1 (2002).

O'Brien, Terence H. *Milner: Viscount Milner of St. James's and Cape Town.* London: Constable, 1979.

Omissi, David, ed. *Indian Voices of the Great War: Soldiers' Letters, 1914–18.* London: Macmillan, 1999.

Oram, Gerard.
1. *Military Executions During World War I.* Houndsmills, Hampshire: Palgrave Macmillan, 2003.
2. *Death Sentences Passed by Military Courts of the British Army, 1914–1924.* Revised edition. Ed. Julian Putkowski. London: Francis Boutle, 2005.

Paice, Edward. *Tip and Run: The Untold Tragedy of the Great War in Africa.* London: Weidenfeld & Nicolson, 2007.

Pakenham, Thomas.
1. *The Boer War.* London: Weidenfeld and Nicolson, 1979.
2. *The Scramble for Africa: The White Man's Conquest of the Dark Continent from 1876 to 1912.* New York: Random House, 1991.

Pankhurst, Christabel. *Unshackled: The Story of How We Won the Vote.* London: Cresset, 1987.

Pankhurst, Emmeline. *My Own Story.* London: Eveleigh Nash, 1914.

Pankhurst, E. Sylvia.
1. *The Home Front: A Mirror to Life in England During the World War.* London: Hutchinson & Co., 1932.
2. *A Sylvia Pankhurst Reader.* Ed. Kathryn Dodd. Manchester, UK: Manchester University Press, 1993.
3. *Soviet Russia as I Saw It.* London: Workers' Dreadnought, 1921.
4. *The Suffragette Movement: An Intimate Account of Persons and Ideals.* London: Longmans, Green, 1931.

Pearce, Cyril. *Comrades in Conscience: The Story of an English Community's Opposition to the Great War.* London: Francis Boutle, 2001.

Pearsall, Ronald. *Edwardian Life and Leisure.* Newton Abbot, UK: David & Charles, 1973.

Pearson, Michael. *The Sealed Train.* New York: Putnam's, 1975.

Pinney, Thomas, ed. *The Letters of Rudyard Kipling.* 6 vols. Iowa City: University of Iowa Press, 1990–2004.

Porter, Bernard.

1. *The Lion's Share: A Short History of British Imperialism, 1850–2004.* Harlow, Essex: Pearson, 2004.
2. *The Origins of the Vigilant State: The London Metropolitan Police Special Branch Before the First World War.* London: Weidenfeld & Nicolson, 1987.
3. *Plots and Paranoia: A History of Political Espionage in Britain, 1790–1988.* London: Unwin Hyman, 1989.

Purvis, June.

1. *Emmeline Pankhurst: A Biography.* London: Routledge, 2002.
2. "Christabel Pankhurst and the Women's Social and Political Union," in Joannou, Maroula, and June Purvis, eds., *The Women's Suffrage Movement: New Feminist Perspectives.* Manchester, UK: Manchester University Press, 1998.

Putkowski, Julian.

1. *The Kinmel Park Camp Riots, 1919.* Hawarden, Wales: Flintshire Historical Society, 1989.
2. *British Army Mutineers, 1914–1922.* London: Francis Boutle, 1998.
3. "Incident at King Crater," mss. subsequently published as *Les Fusillés de King Crater.* Louviers, France: Ysec, 2002.

Putkowski, Julian, and Julian Sykes. *Shot at Dawn: Executions in World War One by Authority of the British Army Act.* London: Leo Cooper, 1989.

Rae, John. *Conscience and Politics: The British Government and the Conscientious Objector to Military Service, 1916–1919.* London: Oxford University Press, 1970.

Raeburn, Antonia. *The Militant Suffragettes.* London: Michael Joseph, 1973.

Reeves, Nicholas. "Cinema, Spectatorship and Propaganda: 'Battle of the Somme' (1916) and Its Contemporary Audience," *Historical Journal of Film, Radio and Television* 17:1 (March 1997).

Reid, Walter. *Architect of Victory: Douglas Haig.* Edinburgh: Berlinn, 2006.

Rice, Michael. *From Dolly Gray to Sarie Marais: The Boer War in Popular Memory.* Noordhoek, South Africa: Fischer Press, 2004.

Rippon, Nicola. *The Plot to Kill Lloyd George: The Story of Alice Wheeldon and the Pear Tree Conspiracy.* Barnsley, UK: Wharncliffe, 2009.

Robb, George. *British Culture and the First World War.* Houndsmills, Hampshire: Palgrave, 2002.

Robbins, Keith. *The Abolition of War: The "Peace Movement" in Britain, 1914–1919.* Cardiff: University of Wales Press, 1976.

Roberts, Brian. *Those Bloody Women: Three Heroines of the Boer War.* London: John Murray, 1991.

Romero, Patricia W. *E. Sylvia Pankhurst: Portrait of a Radical.* New Haven: Yale University Press, 1987.

Rosen, Andrew. *Rise Up, Women!: The Militant Campaign of the Women's Social and Political Union, 1903–1914.* London: Routledge & Kegan Paul, 1974.

Rothstein, Andrew. *The Soldiers' Strikes of 1919.* London: Macmillan, 1980.

Rowbotham, Sheila. *Friends of Alice Wheeldon.* London: Pluto, 1986.

Russell, Bertrand.
   1. *The Autobiography of Bertrand Russell, 1914–1944.* Boston: Little, Brown, 1968.
   2. *Justice in War-Time.* Chicago: Open Court, 1916.
   3. *The Collected Papers of Bertrand Russell:* Vol. 13, *Prophecy and Dissent, 1914–16.* London: Unwin Hyman, 1988.
   4. *The Collected Papers of Bertrand Russell:* Vol. 14, *Pacifism and Revolution, 1916–18.* London: Routledge, 1995.

Rutherford, Ward. *The Russian Army in World War I.* London: Gordon Cremonesi, 1975.

Sheffield, Gary. *Forgotten Victory: The First World War, Myths and Realities.* London: Headline, 2001.

Silbey, David. *The British Working Class and Enthusiasm for War, 1914–1918.* London: Frank Cass, 2005.

Sitwell, Osbert. *Great Morning!* Boston: Little, Brown, 1947.

Smith, Angela K. *Suffrage Discourse in Britain During the First World War.* Aldershot, UK: Ashgate, 2005.

Smith, Richard. *Jamaican Volunteers in the First World War: Race, Masculinity and the Development of National Consciousness.* Manchester, UK: Manchester University Press, 2004.

Stevenson, David. *Cataclysm: The First World War as Political Tragedy.* New York: Basic Books, 2004.

Stoff, Laurie S. *They Fought for the Motherland: Russia's Women Soldiers in World War I and the Revolution.* Lawrence, KS: University Press of Kansas, 2006.

Stone, Norman. *The Eastern Front, 1914–1917.* London: Hodder and Stoughton, 1975.

Strachan, Hew. *The First World War, Vol. 1: To Arms.* Oxford: Oxford University Press, 2001.

Stubbs, J. O. "Lord Milner and Patriotic Labour, 1914–1918," *English Historical Review* 87:345 (October 1972).

Swartz, Marvin. *The Union of Democratic Control in British Politics During the First World War.* Oxford: Clarendon Press, 1971.

Terraine, John.
   1. *Ordeal of Victory.* Philadelphia: J. B. Lippincott, 1963.
   2. *The Smoke and the Fire: Myths and Anti-Myths of War, 1861–1945.* London: Sidgwick & Jackson, 1980.

Thompson, J. Lee. *Forgotten Patriot: A Life of Alfred, Viscount Milner of St James's and Cape Town.* Madison, NJ: Fairleigh Dickinson University Press, 2007.

Thomson, Basil.
   1. *The Story of Scotland Yard.* London: Grayson & Grayson, 1935.

2. *My Experiences at Scotland Yard.* Garden City, NY: Doubleday, Page, 1923.

3. *The Scene Changes.* Garden City, NY: Doubleday, Doran, 1937.

Thurlow, Richard. *The Secret State: British Internal Security in the Twentieth Century.* Oxford: Blackwell, 1994.

Todman, Dan. *The Great War: Myth and Memory.* London: Hambledon and London, 2005.

Toland, John. *No Man's Land: 1918, the Last Year of the Great War.* Garden City, NY: Doubleday, 1980.

Travers, Tim. *The Killing Ground: The British Army, the Western Front and the Emergence of Modern Warfare, 1900–1918.* London: Allen & Unwin, 1987.

Tuchman, Barbara.

1. *The Proud Tower: A Portrait of the World Before the War, 1890–1914.* New York: Macmillan, 1966.

2. *The Guns of August.* New York: Macmillan, 1962.

Tucker, Spencer C., ed. *World War I Encyclopedia.* 5 vols. Santa Barbara, CA: ABC-CLIO, 2005.

Van Reenen, Rykie, ed. *Emily Hobhouse: Boer War Letters.* Cape Town: Human & Rousseau, 1984.

Vellacott, Jo. *Bertrand Russell and the Pacifists in the First World War.* New York: St. Martin's, 1980.

Watt, Richard M. *The Kings Depart: The Tragedy of Germany: Versailles and the German Revolution.* New York: Simon and Schuster, 1968.

Waugh, Alec. *The Early Years of Alec Waugh.* New York: Farrar, Straus and Giroux, 1963.

Webster, Donovan. *Aftermath: The Remnants of War.* New York: Vintage, 1998.

Weintraub, Stanley. *Silent Night: The Story of the World War I Christmas Truce.* New York: Free Press, 2001.

Weller, Ken. *"Don't Be a Soldier!": The Radical Anti-War Movement in North London, 1914–1918.* London: London History Workshop Centre, 1985.

Whalen, Robert Weldon. *Bitter Wounds: German Victims of the Great War, 1914–1939.* Ithaca, NY: Cornell University Press, 1984.

Wheeler-Bennett, John. *Brest-Litovsk: The Forgotten Peace, March 1918.* New York: Norton, 1971.

Wills, W. David. *Stephen Henry Hobhouse: A Twentieth-Century Quaker Saint.* London: Friends Home Service Committee, 1972.

Wilson, Angus. *The Strange Ride of Rudyard Kipling: His Life and Works.* New York: Viking, 1978.

Wilson, Trevor. *The Myriad Faces of War: Britain and the Great War, 1914–1918.* Cambridge, UK: Polity Press, 1986.

Winslow, Barbara. *Sylvia Pankhurst: Sexual Politics and Political Activism.* New York: St. Martin's, 1996.

Winter, Denis. *Haig's Command: A Reassessment.* London: Viking, 1991.

Winter, J[ay] M.

1. *The Experience of World War I.* New York: Oxford University Press, 1989.

2. *The Great War and the British People*. Cambridge: Harvard University Press, 1986.

Winter, Jay, and Blaine Baggett. *The Great War and the Shaping of the 20th Century*. New York: Penguin Studio, 1996.

Winter, Jay, Geoffrey Parker, and Mary R. Habeck, eds. *The Great War and the Twentieth Century*. New Haven: Yale University Press, 2000.

Wolff, Leon. *In Flanders Fields: The 1917 Campaign*. New York: Viking, 1958.

Wrench, John Evelyn. *Alfred Lord Milner: The Man of No Illusions, 1854–1925*. London: Eyre & Spottiswoode, 1958.

Wright, Patrick. *Tank: The Progress of a Monstrous War Machine*. New York: Viking, 2002.

Zuckerman, Larry. *The Rape of Belgium: The Untold Story of World War I*. New York: New York University Press, 2004.

THESES

Kaminski, Diane Clements. *The Radicalization of a Ministering Angel: A Biography of Emily Hobhouse, 1860–1926*. University of Connecticut, Ph.D., 1977.

Mayhall, Laura E. Nym. *"Dare to Be Free": The Women's Freedom League, 1907–1928*. Stanford University, Ph.D., 1993.

Williams, Carl R. *The Control of Civilian Populations in War: The Policing of Political Beliefs in Great Britain, 1914–1918*. London School of Economics, M.Sc., 1999.

ARCHIVAL MATERIAL

National Archives, Kew

Charlotte Despard Papers, Public Record Office of Northern Ireland, Belfast

Charlotte Despard Papers, Women's Library, London

John French Papers, Imperial War Museum, London

David Lloyd George Papers, Parliamentary Archives, London

Alfred Milner Papers, Bodleian Library, Oxford

E. Sylvia Pankhurst Papers, Internationaal Instituut voor Sociale Geschiedenis, Amsterdam (microfilm copies in many libraries)

Albert Edward Rochester Papers, in private hands
— transcript of Rochester's court-martial, 12 January 1917
— Rochester's unpublished letter to the *Daily Mail*, 31 December 1916
— "Albert Edward Rochester, 1884–1926," unpublished mss. by Tom Hickey and Brian Maddocks
— "Debts of Honour," unpublished mss. by Tom Hickey and Brian Maddocks

Imperial War Museum Sound Archive interviews
— Fenner Brockway 000476/04
— Wilfrid Ernest Littleboy 000485/06
— Howard Cruttenden Marten 000383/06
— Harold Frederick Bing 000358/11

Comintern personnel files, Moscow
— William Wheeldon file: 495/198/537

ACKNOWLEDGMENTS

Sometimes, over the six years I worked on this book, I almost felt as if its subject matter were pursuing me, even when I thought I was far away from it. Crossing South Africa by car with a friend, we arrived after dark at the house of some people he knew who put us up for the night at a small town in the interior; only when driving away in the morning did I see they lived on Milner Street. After a day of work in London not connected with the book, I went to relax on the grass at Tavistock Square, happened to glance up — and there was a small monument to conscientious objectors. And the week I finished reading the proofs, we buried my wife's 98-year-old aunt in the small town in Maine where she lived; only at the cemetery did we learn for the first time, from a relative of his, that her long-dead husband had been gassed on the Western Front in 1918. "None of them liked to talk about it," he said.

Many people were willing to talk, however, not about their war experiences, but about my struggles to get that era onto paper. An array of friends, which over time began to seem as large as one of the First World War's smaller armies, provided essential help. To begin with, a low bow to all who read the manuscript and gave me their feedback: Harriet Barlow, Vincent Carretta, Vivian Dent, Elizabeth Farnsworth, Mary Felstiner, Peter Goldmark, Hermann Hatzfeldt, Tracy Kidder, Jeffrey Klein, Mark Kramer, Elinor Langer, Meghan Laslocky, Mike Meyer, Michael Rice, Rebecca Solnit, Francis Wilson, and Monty

Worth. Some of them deserve an extra medal of valor for wading through an early draft that was some 60 percent longer than the book is now—a form of war against readers that ought to be outlawed by the Geneva Conventions.

For more pairs of eyes on the manuscript I'm deeply indebted to four historians of the war who generously helped this newcomer to terrain they know so well. The first of them I met next to the information desk at the British National Archives when he overheard a question I asked, and it soon became clear he knew far more than the man behind the counter. He turned out to be Julian Putkowski, and subsequently sent me a transatlantic torrent of useful references. Vigilant to the last, he gently pointed out that the lancers on the cover of this book's American edition are not British. (They're French.) Careful readings of this book by him and by Cyril Pearce in England, Peter Stansky in the United States, and Jo Vellacott in Canada—each of whom has studied this period far longer than I have—saved me from many errors. They are not responsible for any mistakes that have nonetheless subsequently crept in, or for my point of view.

As always, my wife, Arlie, was my dearest comrade-in-arms, in this book as she has been in life itself. She was with me through ups and downs, getting to know these characters as if they were members of our family, gently critiquing that endless early draft, tramping through trenches, museums, and an underground tunnel when we visited the battlefields in France, all the while writing a wise and trenchant new book of her own.

Great editors are rarer than great writers, and Tom Engelhardt, who has worked on four of my books now, is the best of them all. He has the uncanny ability to climb inside a writer's skull and see what you're trying to do better than you can, and to know exactly which notes you should strike to make the chord you've been imagining. It is all the more amazing to me that he manages to do this while simultaneously writing much of, and running, a remarkable one-man website, which keeps a close eye on the imperial dreams and delusions of our own time, www.tomdispatch.com.

At Houghton Mifflin Harcourt, Bruce Nichols and Andrea Schulz read the manuscript and gave me useful comments, as did my longtime editor Georgina Morley at Pan Macmillan in London and my literary agent Georges Borchardt. My gratitude goes as well to Larry Cooper at

Houghton Mifflin Harcourt for catching literally hundreds of extraneous words, awkward repetitions, and other infelicities of language in his careful manuscript editing of the third book we have worked on together. I hope there will be many more. Melanie Haselden did superb detective work in British photo archives, tracking down portraits of the characters in this book as well as striking photographs of a war that all too often is presented to us in certain familiar stock images.

Others helped in many ways, among them Julian Hendy, who shared with me his copies of letters and other material about the Wheeldon family; Carl Williams, who sent me his dissertation; Nicholas Hiley, who steered me to some useful sources and thoughtfully provided several illustrations; and Guy Hartcup and Mark Goodman, who answered questions I had. My thanks also to the Lannan Foundation, from whom an extraordinarily generous grant arrived unexpectedly just as I was starting work on this book. Years ago, it was the chance to read a superb filmscript — a project still needing a bold producer — by Brian Maddocks and Tom Hickey that first made me aware of Alfred Rochester. Don Coleman, Rochester's grandson, sent me more information and a photograph.

Although it will be clear from the endnotes which authors I am most indebted to, I want to acknowledge several here in particular. Barbara Tuchman has long been a model for me as a writer; it was a pleasure to be working on a period where I could draw heavily on two of her splendid books — even though historians today tend to take a slightly different perspective on the outbreak of the war than she did. Trevor Wilson's magisterial history of Britain's experience in the war was a constant companion. Hugh and Mirabel Cecil's *Imperial Marriage* is a graceful, moving volume from which I drew a great deal; I hope the writers will forgive me for having a more critical view of the politics of their characters than they might. And finally, like anyone writing on British history in recent years, I was grateful I could rely on the new, comprehensively revised edition of one of the great reference tools in our language, the *Oxford Dictionary of National Biography*.

Many libraries and archives sent me photocopies on request, sometimes without charge, including the National Library of Scotland, the Bodleian Library at Oxford, the University of Warwick, the Imperial War Museum, Dalhousie University, and the Swarthmore College Peace Collection. My thanks to the Reverend Gabriel O'Prey and the

Public Record Office of Northern Ireland for permission to quote from Charlotte Despard's papers deposited there. I visited some of these institutions and many more, in both Britain and the United States, in researching this book, but a special word of gratitude goes to those libraries where I spent the most time, at the University of California at Berkeley and at Bates College in the summer months. And, even after several visits, I never ceased to marvel at the National Archives at Kew and its wondrous overhead conveyor belt that, from a millennium of British history and 187 kilometers of shelving, so magically fetches you almost any conceivable document in a matter of minutes. It's enough to give you the illusion that we really can understand the past.

INDEX

ABOUT THE AUTHOR

Adam Hochschild's first book, *Half the Way Home: A Memoir of Father and Son,* was published in 1986. Michiko Kakutani of the *New York Times* called it "an extraordinarily moving portrait of the complexities and confusions of familial love . . . firmly grounded in the specifics of a particular time and place, conjuring them up with Proustian detail and affection." It was followed by *The Mirror at Midnight: A South African Journey, The Unquiet Ghost: Russians Remember Stalin,* and *Finding the Trapdoor: Essays, Portraits, Travels. King Leopold's Ghost: A Story of Greed, Terror, and Heroism in Colonial Africa* was a finalist for the 1998 National Book Critics Circle Award. His *Bury the Chains: Prophets and Rebels in the Fight to Free an Empire's Slaves* was a finalist for the 2005 National Book Award and won the *Los Angeles Times* Book Prize and the PEN USA Literary Award. For the body of his work he has received a Lannan Literary Award and the Theodore Roosevelt–Woodrow Wilson Award of the American Historical Association. His books have been translated into thirteen languages.

In addition to his books, Hochschild has written for *The New Yorker, Harper's,* the *New York Review of Books, Granta,* the *New York Times Magazine,* the *Atlantic,* and many other newspapers and magazines. He was a cofounder of *Mother Jones* magazine and is a teacher of narrative writing at the Graduate School of Journalism at the University of California at Berkeley. He and his wife, sociologist and author Arlie Russell Hochschild, have two sons and two granddaughters.

PHOTO CREDITS